URBAN POLICY AND POLITICS

URBAN POLICY AND POLITICS

in a Bureaucratic Age

SECOND EDITION

CLARENCE N. STONE
University of Maryland

ROBERT K. WHELAN
University of New Orleans

WILLIAM J. MURIN
University of Wisconsin, Parkside

Prentice-Hall, Inc., Upper Saddle River, New Jersey 07458

Library of Congress Cataloging in Publication Data

Stone, Clarence N. (Clarence Nathan), (date)
Urban policy and politics in a bureaucratic age.

Includes bibliographies and index.

1. Municipal government—United States.
2. Municipal officials and employees—United States.
3. Municipal services—United States. 4. Political participation—United States. I. Whelan, Robert K.
II. Murin, William J. III. Title.
JS331.S76 1986 320.8'0973 85-6481
ISBN 0-13-939562-8

Editorial/production supervision: Alice Erdman
Manufacturing buyer: Barbara Kelly Kittle
Cover design: Lundgren Graphics
Cover photo courtesy of Massachusetts Department of Commerce and Development, Division of Tourism, 100 Cambridge St., Boston, Mass. 02202.

Printed in the United States of America

10 9 8 7 6 5

ISBN 0-13-939562-8 01

Prentice-Hall International (UK) Limited, London
Prentice-Hall of Australia Pty. Limited, Sydney
Prentice-Hall Canada Inc., Toronto
Prentice-Hall Hispanoamericana, S.A., Mexico
Prentice-Hall of India Private Limited, New Delhi
Prentice-Hall of Japan, Inc., Tokyo
Pearson Education Asia Pte. Ltd., Singapore
Editoria Prentice-Hall do Brasil, Ltda., Rio De Janeiro

To Mary Murin, Albert and Bea Stone,
and Juliana Whelan

in memory of
William Murin and Robert E. Whelan

Contents

Preface

Revising a textbook for a second edition is a much different exercise from writing the first edition. In some ways, of course, revising is easier. Much is unchanged. In the instance of an urban politics text, the evolution from village politics through the era of machines and the later period of reform into the present day of postreform politics is a pattern that holds constant. Many of the issues and policy questions of the 1970s remain for the 1980s. Bureaucratic practice is largely the same from one decade to another. Yet, new events do occur and perspectives change. And these changes make the task of revision difficult. Reconciling the old and the new is no simple matter. In the case of contemporary urban politics, the task assumes large proportions. Not only are cities themselves undergoing change, but national politics, which sets many of the terms that guide and constrain local politics, is also altering in fundamental ways.

This second edition acknowledges change through the addition of new material: expanded discussion and a separate chapter on local finances; a new chapter on Latinos in urban politics to illustrate the importance and diversity of the "new minorities;" an updated discussion of black politics with particular attention to the growing black electorate in cities and the increased number of black elected officials; a new chapter on the politics of education and its implications for practice in post-industrial

America; new chapters on the impacts of bureaucratic decision rules and on contracting out to the private sector; and substantial revised discussions of power, group influence and executive leadership. To make way for the new, some old material has been dropped.

Revision, however, is not merely a matter of adding and subtracting. New perspectives must be blended with old concerns. In the mid-1980s, the overridingly important new perspective is one that highlights the constraints on local politics. Cities seem to have lost control of their own economic destinies. The investment decisions of multinational corporations, the pressures of international economic competition, tax incentives and depreciation allowances accorded businesses by the national government, state and national transportation policies, national decisions about the amount and location of defense expenditures, water and power subsidies, a shifting national budget priorities are just a few of the forces shaping city economic life. Most are beyond the control of local officials.

In some ways the most fundamental change affecting city politics lies outside any particular policy action or corporate investment decision. It has to with the scale of modern life. Ours is a time of social complexity and large-scale organizations. Present-day urban policy and politics must be understood against that background. The powerful players in the contemporary urban drama are those who command big organizations and the substantial resources these organizations control. This, of course, is not a new development of the 1980s; but the 1980s have brought a new awareness of just how important formal organization is in urban life. Those who operate outside the bounds of organizational life have little leverage with which to reshape the urban environment. Significant influence is channeled through large, formal organizations. Ours, indeed, is a bureaucratic age. The politics and administrative practices of local communities reflect that fact.

C.N.S.
R.K.W.
W.J.M.

Acknowledgments

Authors of textbooks are especially dependent upon a supporting community of scholars, and we gratefully acknowledge our indebtedness to the community or urban scholars. The number of individuals who have given us written and oral comments somewhere along the way, from first draft of the first edition to final draft of the second edition, is too great to list here. However, in the spirit of the "last shall be first," we want to mention Martin Shefter, Adolph Reed, Jr., and Steve Mazurana, readers of the final draft of this second edition. Their comments were indeed helpful, and we hope that the published volume reflects that helpfulness. The careful thought they put into their manuscript reviews in no way implicates them in the shortcomings of this book. They can be comforted to know that had they gotten to us sooner, we would have been less entrenched in our waywardness.

Authors owe debts not only to the scholarly community but also to their families—those who remain the primary support group for individuals even in, or perhaps especially in, a bureaucratic age. Since a second edition is heavily indebted to a first edition, it seems fitting that the three authors take this occasion to acknowledge how much they owe to their respective "first editions," their parents. We have dedicated this book to them.

chapter 1

Urbanization in the United States

The United States is an urban nation but not a nation of cities—certainly not a nation that loves its cities. The great majority of Americans live in metropolitan areas, but within these metropolitan areas more Americans live in suburbs around large cities than in the large cities themselves. Population density, even in the cities, is decreasing. While some people prefer big-city life, most Americans prefer suburbs, other smaller communities, or the more open spaces beyond the metropolitan fringe.

In the chapters ahead we will talk often of large central cities. They are important in the political, cultural, and economic life of the nation. Although they may be becoming less important in some ways, more often than not they are the places where significant change first surfaces. We will not confine our attention to big cities, however. We will also consider other urban places—suburbs (big and little), smaller cities, and even towns and villages not in the metropolitan orbit. Thus, while large cities will get special attention, our concern is with urban communities of all types—their policies, their politics, and the governmental and administrative processes they use.

In the next few chapters, we will explore the urban context. The present chapter deals with definitions and trends. What is urbanization? What is a city? Are cities and urban places different names for the same thing? How has urbanization changed? What population and economic trends are now in evi-

dence, and what do they mean for urban life generally? Those are questions we will address. We also consider some important regional shifts in jobs and population. Increasingly, analysts talk about our country in terms of the sunbelt and the frostbelt. What are the trends associated with these terms and what bearing do they have on urban life in the United States?—those, too, are important questions.

In Chapter 2 we look at three sociocultural influences. There are others, of course, but we wish to concentrate on three of extraordinary importance:

1. *An anticity bias in American culture*
2. *A tradition of privatism and individualism involving (a) a heavy reliance on the private sector that has left most urban development decisions in the hands of investors, speculators, businessmen, and other private owners of property, and (b) an antipoor strain in the American belief system, a strain that has regarded the poor as responsible for their own lot in life*
3. *The factors of race and ethnicity*

These three influences, we argue, help account for the absence of a national policy of urban growth and development.

In Chapter 3, we examine a particularly significant development on the urban scene—the growth and increased salience of the nation's Hispanic population. This is a diverse population and one whose political experience is quite varied.

Intergovernmental relations provide the focus for the fourth chapter. Local government is only one layer in a complex federal system. What local governments can do and sometimes what they must do are influenced by their relationships to other units of government. Federal and state officials write many of the ground rules by which local government must play the game. Local governments are literally the legal creatures of the states that empower them. Their authority to exist, to operate, and to tax—and varying amounts of financial help, too—all come from the state. The governments of urban communities thus operate in the tall shadows of their respective state capitol buildings. Local governments are also legally subordinate to the United States Constitution, as it is interpreted by the various branches of the national government.

Legal relationships are supplemented in important ways by financial relationships. Chapter 5 takes up the vital topic of fiscal influences. It treats financial aspects of local-state and local-national relations as part of the revenue picture for urban communities. It also looks closely at the local politics of taxation and considers the impact of recent tax-limitation moves, such as Proposition 13 in California.

The United States officially became an urban nation in 1920 when, for the first time, more people reported living in urban places than in rural ones. Today nearly three out of four Americans live in urban areas, and more than 90 percent of us live within the zone of influence of one of the nation's 318 metropolitan areas. But urban area does not necessarily mean big city; more Americans live in the suburbs than in the central cities of metropolitan areas. Over the last few decades, the pattern has been for fewer and fewer people to live on farms, but at the same time, population in large cities has decreased. It's the suburbs that have grown—as the urbanized fringe around cities has expanded, farms and small towns have changed status and become part of suburbia.

Urbanization is not an easy process to define and describe, but with modern transportation and communication, we are all part of the urban society, whether we live in a central city, a suburb, or an outlying small town. Let us look at what urbanization means. We will sketch some historical distinctions between nineteenth-century and twentieth-century urbanization and conclude with a discussion of some significant recent trends affecting cities and their surrounding metropolitan areas.

URBANIZATION AND THE CITY

What is urbanization and how does it shape the lives of most Americans? An obvious point is to associate urbanization with population concentration. It can proceed as the multiplication of points of concentration or as an increase in the size of a particular concentration. Some writers look beyond population statistics to conclude that urban areas have a distinctive way of life. They point to the growth of industry and the development of new technologies.[1] With those come changes in family and neighborhood, politics, and other patterns of living. The most obvious change is in occupational structure. Today less than 3 percent of the American work force is in agriculture, a massive shift from an earlier day.

An oddity of studying urbanization is that it is sometimes hard to define what is a city. Certainly there would be near unanimous agreement that New York, Boston, Chicago, San Francisco, Houston, and New Orleans are cities. But what about Kenosha, Wisconsin, and Lubbock, Texas, or Golden, Colorado? What is the essence of the city? Does a city imply more than sheer numbers? Must it have skyscrapers? What about the arts, theater, a symphony, professional sports, fine restaurants? Can we

[1] Richard T. Geruson and Dennis McGrath, *Cities and Urbanization* (New York: Praeger Publishers, 1977), p. 3.

have a city without any or all of these characteristics? The U.S. Census Bureau, though it does not define a city, offers a good beginning:

> An *urban place* is an identifiable geographic area with a population of 2,500 or more.
>
> An *urbanized-area* includes a central city (or twin central cities) of at least 50,000 population plus adjacent closely settled areas. Some 60 percent of all Americans live in such areas.
>
> A *Standard Metropolitan Statistical Area* (SMSA) consists of a central city (or twin central cities) of at least 50,000 population along with the surrounding counties that are economically and socially dependent upon the city.[2]

A community of 2,500 fails to meet most people's idea of a city. The SMSA concept is quite useful in explaining metropolitanization, but since it makes counties its basic building block, it generally includes some areas that are rural. If numbers are important in defining a city, we might agree on a population base of at least 50,000 persons.

A major effort to define the city and explain urbanization was made by sociologist Louis Wirth in the 1930s.[3] He emphasized three components of community life: a physical structure, a social structure and organization, and the attitudes and personalities of the inhabitants. Defining a city as ". . . a point of population concentration of large size, high density, and heterogeneity of inhabitants," he argued that urbanization changes every aspect of human life and most aspects of human consciousness. It is both physical phenomenon and state of mind, characterized by formality and impersonality, rationality, secularization, tolerance, specialization, standardization, and perhaps above all else, the decline of the dominance of the family.

Thus a city is a network of human relationships. Many observers underline this social structure as making cities unique in the annals of human history. Heterogeneous and constantly changing, the city is a mosaic of social worlds arranged in often confusing and seemingly incompatible patterns. Yet along with this social heterogeneity is a high degree of economic interdependence. Finally, there is a political dimension: cities exercise a significant amount of self-government.

We think that a city, therefore, must meet three criteria: (1) It is "a settled aggregation of people who by their density tend toward heterogeneity and impersonality."[4] (2) It is large enough (the Census Bureau's 50,000 is not a bad figure) to have a high degree of specialization of labor

[2] U.S. Department of Commerce, Bureau of the Census, Census of Population: 1980, Vol. 1, *Characteristics of the Population*, Washington, D.C.: U.S. Government Printing Office, 1982.

[3] Louis Wirth, "Urbanism as a Way of Life," *American Journal of Sociology* 44, July (1938), 1-24.

[4] E. Gordon Erickson, *Urban Behavior* (New York: Macmillan Co., 1954), p. 22.

and other activity. (3) It has relative political independence in terms of home rule or possesses some type of municipal charter.

However we define them, cities, in the United States and throughout the world, are now developing along patterns that differ significantly from the trends of the past. It should be useful, then, to contrast nineteenth- and twentieth-century urbanization.

THE NINETEENTH-CENTURY AMERICAN CITY

In about 1820 the urbanization process began, and by 1920 the United States was an urban society with seventy-eight cities having populations larger than 50,000. Three cities (New York, Chicago, and Philadelphia) had more than one million residents. Perhaps the most important urban-growth decades of the nineteenth century were the years from 1840 to 1870, when "people poured into cities in unprecedented proportions. At no other time in the history of the United States has such a large percentage of Americans voted with their feet for urban life."[5]

What brought these large numbers of people from the family farm to the cities? Principally the search for better opportunities—the chance to make more money and live a more exciting life. These opportunities were linked to the industrial expansion that had begun in England in the mid-eighteenth century and that transformed America in the nineteenth century. As America industrialized, it became an economic mecca for successive waves of immigrants, most of whom headed for the city.

The nineteenth-century industrial cities were densely populated and geographically compact, primarily because of primitive transportation and communication facilities. Most workers lived within a short walk of their place of employment. The more fortunate, or wealthy, could live a little farther away from their job and depend upon horse-drawn streetcars to get them to work on time. The central business district (CBD) was the dominant economic focus of the entire area.

Urban compactness was symbolized by the development, in the late nineteenth century, of the skyscraper, which allowed many people to work in close proximity, facilitating face-to-face contact in businesses dependent upon the speedy and accurate exchange of information and goods. Earlier development of the telephone and electric elevators made downtown land extremely valuable, driving the costs of land ever upward, and requiring the construction of even taller buildings to pay for the land. These forces literally shaped most major cities, their skylines dominated by steel, iron, and more recently, glass towers.

[5] Adrienne Siegel, "When Cities Were Fun: The Image of the American City in Popular Books, 1840-1870," *Journal of Popular Culture* 9 (Winter 1975), 574.

The dark side of nineteenth-century city life was described by historian Sam Bass Warner, Jr.:

> This sudden reorganization of American life, the forcing of a rural society into an urban mold, exacted a terrible toll in everyday life. Nineteenth-century urbanization and industrialization inflicted punishment and suffering on city dwellers and tore at the fabric of society. . . . Never were conditions more exploitative and dangerous to human life. . . .[6]

The American city of the last century was therefore complex, dynamic, a place of almost unlimited opportunity, but also a place of death, disease, filth, poverty, illiteracy, crime, and social and political disorganization.

THE TWENTIETH-CENTURY AMERICAN CITY

As the twentieth century arrived, conditions of urbanization were changing even further, establishing or hinting at new patterns. Electrically-powered streetcars brought increased speeds that allowed employees to continue to live in the city and shorten their commuting time or to move farther out and still be able to get to work. Of even greater impact was the private automobile.

Changes in transportation and communication made possible *metropolitanization*, a term that sums up the major physical, social, and economic changes the twentieth-century city has undergone. Metropolitanization means more people living in urbanized areas, but in increasingly dispersed patterns

For the city dweller, metropolitanization has simply added new problems to those that were left over from the nineteenth century. European ethnics were replaced by southern blacks, and Appalachian whites, immigrants from various parts of Asia, Chicanos, Puerto Ricans, and other Hispanics; but the accustomed processes whereby newcomers moved up the economic ladder were ruptured. White-collar *workers* and blue-collar *jobs* were moving out to the suburbs, leaving behind high unemployment among those newest to urban life. The wholesale replacement of the tax-paying middle class with a new constituency that was more service demanding has put many cities under heavy fiscal pressure. Furthermore, the job market was radically different by mid-twentieth century. Another problem of metropolitanization has been that of cities' inability to control economic development throughout the metropolitan area. And, on top of other

[6] Sam B. Warner, Jr., *The Urban Wilderness* (New York: Harper & Row, 1972), pp. 64-65.

changes, manufacturing has declined in importance in the overall economy of the nation.

Propelled by changes in transportation and communication technology, the twin phenomena of suburbanization and metropolitanization have characterized twentieth-century urbanization. Population and employment densities have lessened, and this dispersion of people and jobs has allowed contemporary urbanites to practice a large amount of "social segregation," sorting themselves out into one-class neighborhoods. Gone is the densely populated geographically compact city of the nineteenth century, which literally threw people from different backgrounds together.

Yet modern urban and metropolitan America is a highly interdependent place. Our occupations, avocations, and social activities are becoming increasingly specialized so that we literally cannot survive or prosper in today's metropolis without the cooperation and good will of our fellow citizens. A garbage strike, transit strike, power failure, or other natural or man-made calamity shows just how fragile the web of metropolitan interdependency really is.

RECENT POPULATION AND LAND-USE TRENDS

Two great population migrations have reshaped the nation's cities in the twentieth century. Racial and language minorities, from within this country and from other nations, have moved into America's urban areas; black migration has been especially important. And second, central cities have lost population, especially white population, to the suburbs.

In 1910, 91 percent of the nation's black population lived in the South, predominantly in the rural South. Blacks first began moving northward during World War I when the industrial demands of the war created a need for unskilled labor in northern industrial cities. After the war and through the Great Depression, this movement slowed, only to resume during World War II. Then and in the years that followed, the movement of rural blacks to the cities progressed rapidly. Jobs in defense industries attracted black workers, while the mechanization of agriculture decreased the need for farm labor and eliminated the small, marginal farmer. In 1940, only half of all blacks lived in urban areas; this figure reached 85 percent by 1980.

While blacks have migrated into cities, many whites have migrated out to the suburbs, where population has surged both absolutely and relatively. At the end of World War II, the suburban proportion of SMSA population was about 40 percent. In 1960, suburbs and cities each accounted for 50 percent of SMSA population. Since that time, the suburbs have increased their share of the metropolitan population. In the decade from 1970 to

1980, the suburbs added nearly twenty million people while the expanded universe of central cities only added three million.

While the suburbs have grown, many older cities have experienced large losses in population. Several cities that ranked in the top ten in population in 1950 have tumbled to lower rankings as their populations decreased by large proportions. St Louis, for example, had a 1980 population scarcely half its 1950 size and dropped in rank from eighth to twenty-sixth. Cleveland and Detroit have declined by more than a third since 1950. Of the top ten cities in 1950, only Los Angeles had a larger population in 1980 than in 1950. The other nine had lost, on the average, a quarter of their 1950 population. Newer cities, notably those in the sunbelt, have grown, and the number of central cities has increased as the nation's population continues to disperse. However, by 1980, just 30 percent of the nation's population was located in central cities, whereas the suburban proportion had risen to 45 percent. The remainder of the national population is divided among those who live in small cities and towns, their suburbs, and the countryside.

With the move to the suburbs becoming such a dominant trend, it is important to ask who is doing the moving. The answer, overwhelmingly, is whites. From 1950 to 1970, over twelve million whites left central cities. During the 1970-80 period there were some changes in this historical pattern, but it is too early to determine their full magnitude. While whites continued to move out of cities and into suburbs, they did so at a slower rate than earlier. At the same time, blacks and other minorities began moving into suburbs, especially close-in and older suburbs, in small but appreciable numbers.

Given the combination of white flight, black population growth, and declining size of the central city, it is obvious that the proportion of blacks in central cities is greater than ever. Blacks now make up 23 percent of central city population. Nine large cities have black majorities: Atlanta, Baltimore, Birmingham, Detroit, Gary, New Orleans, Newark, Richmond, and Washington, DC. In thirty-four others, blacks make up more than 30 percent of the population.

Along with the two migrations have come significant disparities between central cities and suburban areas in such matters as age of population, education, income, and type of labor force. One has to be cautious about generalizing, however. Metropolitan areas differ greatly from one another. In many of the smaller and newer metropolitan areas, the city—not the suburban—population has a higher income, greater education, and more workers engaged in white-collar employment.[7] And, as we shall see in more detail later, suburbs themselves—even in a given metropolitan area—may be quite diverse. Thus, while there is much truth to the standard view that the central city is hard pressed financially by the exodus of the white

[7]John C. Bollens and Henry J. Schmandt, *The Metropolis*, 4th ed. (New York: Harper & Row, 1981), pp. 68-69.

middle class, it is well to remember that this diagnosis applies readily only to larger and older central cities. And it is also well to remember that some suburbs have sizeable and even growing lower-socioeconomic-status populations.

Not only are there city and suburban differences to consider, but there are regional differences as well. The sunbelt phenomenon is in full swing as people and jobs move from the cold and snow of the East, North, and Midwest to the sunshine of the Southeast and Southwest. The fact that the boom towns of the 1970s were places like Houston and Phoenix is no mere happenstance. The American people seem to be undertaking another great migration. Initially it was from the farm to the cities and then from the cities to the suburbs. Now we are seeing great movements from the cities and suburbs of the North and Midwest to the cities and suburbs of the South and Southwest.

What factors explain the sunbelt growth phenomenon? Favorable climate is the most obvious explanation. Another is the abundance of energy and other natural resources. A third is an attractive tax and business atmosphere. It is not uncommon for southern metropolitan areas looking for new industry to give manufacturers new structures designed to their specifications and a moratorium on real estate taxes for up to ten years, or even longer. Some would add one more factor: the development of new industries and technologies that came into being because of increased defense and public works spending and the friendliness of congressional committees chaired by durable sunbelt legislators.[8] And, of course, many sunbelt areas are heavily dependent upon a federally subsidized water supply.

We are not talking about small swings in population by region. While many older cities of the frostbelt have lost population, sunbelt cities have been growing at incredible rates. In the years 1945 to 1980 Fort Lauderdale, Florida, went from 18,000 to 153,000; Huntsville, Alabama, from 13,000 to 143,000; Houston from 385,000 to 1,595,000; Phoenix from 65,000 to 790,000; San Jose, California, from 68,000 to 630,000.[9] While economies of sunbelt cities boomed, older northern industrial cities were racked by high unemployment rates. As with other trends, there are policy implications in these regional patterns. The fact that many federal programs base payments upon population produces an ironic situation in which areas with already booming economies will get more and more benefits as their populations continue to increase, while other communities that are gradually losing residents will get fewer and fewer benefits even though their population mix means that their needs have intensified.

[8] Geruson and McGrath, *Cities and Urbanization*, p. 132.

[9] Cf. Kirkpatrick Sale, *Power Shift: The Rise of the Southern Rim and Its Challenge to the Eastern Establishment* (New York: Random House, 1975), p. 18.

JOBS AND THE FUTURE

Conventional wisdom holds that snowbelt cities have lost jobs as well as population to southern and southwestern cities. However, not all observers of the current urban scene agree that there has been a mass exodus to the sunbelt by corporate America. Several studies suggest that shifts in employment are more complicated than a simple relocation of factories from north to south.

What seems to be taking place, according to these reports, is that when relocation does occur it usually does not result in inter-regional or interstate shifts but merely in a move to a relatively nearby location. For example, in a study done for the Joint Center for Urban Studies at Harvard/M.I.T., Professor Roger Schmenner looked at the industrial relocation decisions of 410 corporations during the 1970s. His data covered 17,759 plants with 7,354,000 jobs, about one-third of the nation's total manufacturing jobs. The basic conclusion of the Schmenner study and others is that plant closings and the subsequent job loss that accompanies them is not a northern or eastern phenomenon; they occur as frequently in the South and West. Specifically, the Schmenner study found that almost twice as many jobs were lost through plant closings in California, Oregon, and Washington as in the six New England states. If measured as a percentage of the total work force, the three western states suffered a 5.7 percent loss of jobs while the New England area's loss was 4.3 percent. In the Southeast sunbelt area, plant closings caused a 3.2 percent loss in manufacturing jobs. The states included in this region were Florida, Georgia, North and South Carolina, Maryland, Virginia, and West Virginia. In the Midwest industrial belt of Wisconsin, Michigan, Illinois, Indiana, and Ohio, there was a 3.1 percent loss of manufacturing jobs. So there does not appear to be much difference between snow and sun states in terms of manufacturing job losses through plant closings.

There is, however, considerable difference when *new job creation* is looked at either via expanding existing plants or by opening new branches. Again, relying on the Schmenner study, 121,224 jobs were created in the southeastern states while only 25,026 jobs were lost due to plant closings. Thus, these states experienced a net increase of almost 100,000 jobs. Of importance to northern states is the fact that 16,426 of those new jobs could be traced to plants that closed somewhere else and re-opened in the southeast region. By contrast, in the Midwest some 57,746 jobs were lost due to plant closings while only 59,608 were created, with 18,627 of the new jobs coming from other parts of the country. New jobs barely matched losses.[10]

Several factors seem to be at work simultaneously. The snowbelt has lost an historic advantage. America's first urban centers were in the eastern

[10] *Chicago Tribune*, October 19, 1980.

and north-central parts of the country (Boston to Chicago), and manufacturing facilities tended to cluster in those regions to take advantage of nearby markets and transportation systems. However, population is more dispersed now and has shifted westward. Further, because of advances in transportation and communications, firms have found that they can locate virtually anywhere and still have access to their markets. As a result, there has been a redistribution of jobs with the sunbelt growing at a rapid rate. Yet, while the sunbelt areas are increasing their share of manufacturing jobs, the Northeast still contains most of the nation's manufacturing capacity. But further declines in northern manufacturing jobs can be expected as the historical locational advantages of the Northeast, now lost, fail to draw new industries in to replace aging ones. Moreover, the location of new production activities overseas signals the declining importance of manufacturing employment to the nation's work force.

When all is said and done, the data indicate that northern cities are losing jobs, especially manufacturing jobs as plants age, and that the growth in service industry jobs has been concentrated more in the South and West. The regional shift in employment is thus not primarily a matter of plant location by stable industries. Rather, it has to do with changes in the nature of the national economy and an altered position of the United States in the world economy.

CONCLUSION

The suburbanization phenomenon has been in full swing for over half a century, and its origins can be traced back at least a hundred years. Suburbs are not new, they are not going to go away, and the days when the central city dominated the social, economic, and political life of a metropolitan area are gone. In its stead is a new kind of metropolitan place whose components are arranged in more or less mutually supportive interdependencies and networks.

Reverse commuting and intra- and inter-suburban commuting are the growing patterns of travel in most metropolitan areas. A poll conducted by *The New York Times* found that only 20 percent of the main wage earners in area families lived in the suburbs and commuted to New York City, while 60 percent worked in their own or other suburbs.[11]

Population movement in and out of cities continues at a high level. Sunbelt cities are adding people and land at phenomenal rates, and even some of the older northern cities are showing signs of life. Yet there is little we can say with assurance at this point except that the city in the next decade will not be a replica of the city we have known.

[11] July 5, 1979, p. B5.

SUGGESTED READINGS

ABBOTT, CARL. *The New Urban America: Growth and Politics in Sunbelt Cities.* Chapel Hill: University of North Carolina Press, 1981.

BERNARD, RICHARD M., and BRADLEY R. RICE. *Sunbelt Cities: Politics and Growth Since World War II.* Austin: University of Texas Press, 1983.

BERRY, BRIAN J. L. *Comparative Urbanization: Divergent Paths in the Twentieth Century.* New York: St. Martin's Press, 1982.

BRADBURY, KATHARINE L., ANTHONY DOWNS, and KENNETH A. SMALL. *Urban Decline and the Future of American Cities.* Washington, D.C.: The Brookings Institution, 1982.

GERUSON, RICHARD T., and DENNIS MCGRATH. *Cities and Urbanization.* New York: Praeger Publishers, 1977.

JACKSON, KENNETH T., and STANLEY K. SCHULTZ, eds. *Cities in American History.* New York: Alfred A. Knopf, 1972.

JAMES, FRANKLIN. *Minorities in the Sunbelt.* Piscataway, NJ: Center for Urban Policy Research, 1984.

MILLER, ZANE L. *The Urbanization of Modern America.* New York: Harcourt Brace Jovanovich, 1973.

PERRY, DAVID and ALVIN WATKINS, eds. *The Rise of the Sunbelt Cities.* Beverly Hills, CA: Sage, 1977.

SAWERS, LARRY, and WILLIAM K. TABB. *Sunbelt/Snowbelt: Urban Development and Regional Restructuring.* New York: Oxford University Press, 1984.

WARNER, SAM BASS, JR. *Street Car Suburbs: The Process of Growth in Boston, 1870-1900.* Cambridge, Mass.: Harvard University Press, 1962.

______. *The Urban Wilderness.* New York: Harper & Row, 1972.

chapter 2

Sociocultural Influences

We turn now to some of the sociocultural forces that make Americans somewhat indifferent to the problems of cities. We will be asking why it is that most people have so little sense of urgency about enabling urban governments (city or noncity) to solve the problems and provide the services required of a nation that aspires to treat its people well.

Why do we have no explicit national policy of urban growth and development? Three factors may help account for our national disinterest in the urban condition: a deeprooted anticity bias, an equally strong tilt toward private over public responsibility for most economic activities, and a bias against the poor—especially the poor who are in a racial or ethnic minority.

AN ANTICITY BIAS

Thomas Jeferson was, among other things, a severe critic of city life, viewing it as "a pestilence to the morals, the health and the liberties of man."[1]

[1] Quoted in Charles N. Glaab and A. Theodore Brown, *A History of Urban America* (New York: Macmillan Co., 1967), p. 55.

Such anticity feelings have persisted to the present. They are recognized by a former mayor of New York City, John Lindsay, who has bluntly observed that "Americans don't like our cities very much."[2] The notion of the superiority of agrarian society is a very old theme in Western thought and philosophy and can be traced back to ancient, even biblical, times.

To this legacy can be added the strong frontier belief in the democracy of the common man—ideas we associate with Andrew Jackson. Threaded throughout Jeffersonian-Jacksonian philosophy is the belief that democracy and all its virtues could not survive in the cities because of the evils and distractions lurking there.

While procity sentiments have appeared from time to time and the agrarian mythology has gradually been adjusted to the reality of urban life, old ways die hard. The disorders and crises of the 1960s stimulated yet a new wave of desire to return to the good old days when life was less harried and complex. Even though surveys continually show that most Americans want to enjoy urban amenities, they also show that Americans want to have those amenities in places other than the city. A sequence of surveys done by the George Gallup polling organization offer the best reading of trends. In 1966, 1970, 1972, and 1976 Gallup asked Americans where they preferred to live. Overwhelmingly, the response was for places other than the city. In 1966, 22 percent of the respondents considered the city the ideal place to live; in 1970 only 18 percent stated that preference, and by 1972 the figure had fallen to 13 percent, where it remained in 1976. Figures from a 1976 poll, though not exactly comparable to the earlier surveys, suggest a continuing trend toward smaller communities and a definite upsurge in preferences for rural life.

Because the questions posed are hypothetical, surveys of this type should be read with caution. Still, there are indications that people are translating wishes into reality. During the period 1970-1975, nonmetropolitan areas grew faster (6.6 percent) than metropolitan areas (4.1 percent). Some of the nonmetropolitan growth was on the fringes of existing metropolitan areas, a fact that gives some support to the view that while many people say they prefer rural or small town life, they also want to be within thirty miles or so of a large city.[3] Some of the growth led to the emergence of new metropolitan areas. However, some growth was in counties not bordering a city area, indicating a significant rise in truly non-metropolitan population.

Whether or not our society will continue to enjoy the best of the urban and rural is open to question. Highway congestion and the maintenance of highways are rising problems. What is certain, however, is that many

[2] John V. Lindsay, "Why Americans Don't Like Cities," *New York*, March 23, 1970, p. 31.

[3] William Alonso, "Urban Disamenities," *Society* 13, no. 4 (May/June 1976), 52.

TABLE 2-1 Community Preference 1966, 1970, 1972, 1976

PREFERENCE	1966	1970	1972	1976*
City	22%	18%	13%	13%
Suburban area	28	26	31	29
Small town	31	31	32	20
Farm	18	24	23	38
No opinion	1	1	1	n/a

Source: Gallup Poll data.

*1976 community-size categories are: large city—over 100,000; small city—10,000 to 100,000; town or village—up to 10,000; and rural area.

Americans will continue to escape urban conditions so long as it is socially, politically, and economically possible to do so. If the future requires more compact and dense living patterns, most citizens will probably grudgingly accept it. But that is not a future we are willing to face and plan for.

THE TRADITION OF PRIVATISM AND INDIVIDUALISM

A second strong current in American life has also shaped our urban society. Americans have always prided themselves on being individualistic. Indeed, one reason cities are viewed with some distrust is that urban living imposes constraints on individual behavior. Out of our tradition of the frontier and the wilderness, we have as a nation resisted legal restrictions on freedom of economic action, as our behavior about land attests.

The battles going on all over the country about government imposition of environmental land-use controls reveal how jealously Americans guard the right to do as they please with their property. Abetting this individualistic attitude is an ethos of privatism—whereby decisions in the private sector are presumed to be superior to and immune from government actions. The private ethos has also meant that the nation's cities have depended for their prosperity, wages, and employment upon the individual and collective decisions of hundreds and thousands of individual corporations and businesses, whose decisions to locate in a given community or relocate to a new community are dictated primarily on the basis of profits and not on community well-being or even a generalized sense of responsibility. Privatism has gone largely unchecked as technical and economic changes made it possible for large numbers of central-city businesses and industries to flee the city for suburban, rural, or overseas locations. As conglomerates grew and companies sought to maximize short-term investment gains, many American cities were virtually helpless to prevent the movement of jobs and industry out of the city, and equally powerless to do much to offset the resulting decreased property taxes and payroll taxes and other economic liabilities.

An ethos of privatism has shaped the development of America from the beginning. According to urban historian Sam Bass Warner, Jr., a first goal of American citizens is the private search for wealth, and the goal of the city is to be a community of private money makers.[4] Thus, individual successes and failures, not city planning, have defined a city's successes and failures. This process is not, of course, uniquely applicable to urban development; it is but a microcosm of our national development.

Not until the great dislocations caused by the depression of the 1930s did the idea of an active government role in economic planning and development even begin to be legitimized. Even today, a half century later, Warner and other historians can call privatism "the most important element of American culture for understanding the development of cities."[5]

Individualism and Antipoor Attitudes.

The twin preferences for individualism and privatism have shaped many aspects of urban life, affecting not only our choice about urban development but also our attitudes toward the poor. We can trace antipoor attitudes as far back into history as we care to and the results are almost always the same; only the dates and places change. Author John Alexander has analyzed Philadelphia's long tradition of tolerating poverty but fearing the poor. In late eighteenth-century Philadelphia, ". . . established and respectable Philadelphians apparently believed that the actions of the poor endangered civilized society. . . . "[6] This fear manifested itself in several ways, not the least of which was the establishment of an educational system designed primarily to teach the poor the "habits of industry" but also to keep them under control.

In our time, also, we can see the attempt to separate the deserving from the undeserving poor. Welfare programs and welfare recipients are examined, supervised, reported on, and investigated to assure the majority of taxpayers that their tax dollars are not being spent frivolously. Every attempt to reform the welfare system is linked closely with job opportunities and the preservation of the work ethic. The vast majority of people appear firmly convinced that the poor could work if they wanted to. This is a thinly veiled way of saying that if the poor worked they would not be poor—even though most of the poor do, in fact, live in working households.

[4] Sam Bass Warner, Jr., *The Private City* (Philadelphia: University of Pennslyvania Press, 1968), p. xi.

[5] Ibid., p. 4.

[6] John K. Alexander, "The City of Brotherly Fear," in *Cities in American History*, ed. Kenneth T. Jackson and Stanley K. Schultz (New York: Alfred A. Knopf, 1972), p. 79.

Most people believe that status is determined by individual effort, not by luck or impersonal forces. They think poverty is caused by defects of character, success by attributes like hard work.

Beliefs about the causes of poverty carry over to attitudes toward welfare recipients. On these issues, hostility becomes overt. In one national survey two-thirds of the people agreed that "the relief rolls are loaded with chiselers and people who just don't want to work."[7] And 84 percent said, "There are too many people receiving welfare money who should be working."[8] Nearly two-thirds (64 percent) favored guaranteed jobs, but less than one-third (30 percent) favored a guaranteed annual income.

Antipoor attitudes were apparently a factor in the 1978 tax revolt in California. One poll taken after voters approved tax-limiting Proposition 13 revealed that two-thirds of the voters for the measure believed that welfare payments to the poor should be cut.

RACE AND ETHNICITY

Few factors are more important in the American city today than the factor of race. Housing patterns, educational policy, attitudes on social policy issues and employment opportunities are all intertwined with the factor of race. Some may argue that race is not *really* the problem, but that poverty is, or the presence of a lower class is. Certainly racial problems and poverty problems are related. But there are racial antagonisms that transcend class differences. Racial attitudes have sources other than beliefs about the poor.

Race, of course, is not unique as a friction point in the American experience. Friction between religious and nationality groups runs throughout our history. Yet Americans have, by and large, taken an optimistic view of intergroup relations. We tend to assume that previous immigrants to the nation's cities were thoroughly and painlessly assimilated into a generally accepted American way of life and that blacks and other new minorities will likewise make their way. However, our recent difficulties in achieving public school integration combined with the sobering experience of urban violence in the 1960s have led to some serious rethinking and to a closer look at our immigration experience.

Despite a vast amount of research and writing on ethnic and racial attitudes in the past decade or so, there are no clear-cut answers as to whether the society as a whole is becoming more tolerant or less so. Is ethnic assimilation increasing, or does the reawakening of white ethnic

[7] Survey data from Lloyd A. Free and Hadley Cantril, *The Political Beliefs of Americans* (New York: Simon and Schuster, Clarion Books, 1968), p. 27.

[8] Joe R. Feagin, "Poverty: We Still Believe that God Helps Those Who Help Themselves," *Psychology Today*, November 1972, p. 107.

consciousness reflect a new pattern in social development? Frankly, we do not know. There are persuasive arguments and counterarguments but no authoritative evidence.

The idea of America as the great melting pot is a myth long cherished in our social history. It comes from a perception of America's cities as magnificent ". . . cauldrons in which old bloods, cultures, and rivalries would be simmered into an invigorated and uniquely American blend."[9] Sociologist Andrew Greeley, who questions this romantic perspective, argues that what really happened is something he calls anglo-conformity—the gradual movement of the immigrant into the larger society until the host and the immigrant were part of one culture, the host culture.

In *Beyond the Melting Pot,* the idea of cultural pluralism is presented as "a patchwork of ethnic enclaves." With time, ethnic uniqueness and consciousness tend to fade, but a residual of unassimilated or unmelted identity exists. Immigrants become like their hosts to some degree; they become citizens and adopt the political values of the host community.

From a political perspective, it is important to determine which, if any, of these approaches more accurately mirrors reality. Unfortunately, the answer is not easily arrived at. Many studies show that ethnic identification is a powerful determinant of voting patterns and policy preferences, and the fact that politicians continue to make ethnic appeals argues that ethnic identities are still important in the political arena. At the other end of the spectrum, American sociology, which exhibits strong assimilationist biases, generally concludes that ethnicity is not especially important in either a sociological or political perspective.[10]

What, then, does all this discussion mean? Even with a recent upsurge in ethnic consciousness, the presence of diverse white ethnics is no longer a major source of social tension. Moreover, many white ethnics have made breakthroughs to get a greater share of the benefits of American life. White ethnic consciousness may reflect more a desire to hold onto what has already been achieved than a wish for new levels of acceptance and accomplishment.

With race, the matter is more complicated, and more volatile. As we saw in the first chapter, blacks continue to be concentrated in the central cities of large metropolitan areas, but there is some movement to the suburbs. While public school integration remains as elusive as ever, black educational achievements continue to increase. Most important, although blacks are gaining entry to the mainstream of the nation's political, economic, and professional life, there is still resistance at many points, with the result that gains lag far behind aspirations.

[9] See Nathan Glazer and Daniel P. Moynihan, *Beyond the Melting Pot* (Cambridge, Mass.: Harvard University Press and MIT Press, 1963).

[10] Andrew Greeley, *Ethnicity in the United States* (New York: John Wiley and Sons, 1974), pp. 14-16.

Twenty years after the urban disorders of the 1960s, and thirty years after the *Brown* v. *Board of Education* school desegregation case, we are no more certain as to the future of racial justice in America than observers were at those times. It is much too simplistic to resurrect the warnings of the Kerner Commission in 1968 that we are becoming two nations, one black and one white; separate and unequal. There are data to support virtually any point one wishes to push. We can present numbers to show that American society is becoming more racially segregated in terms of housing and schooling; we can also present numbers to show the opposite. We can demonstrate that blacks are becoming more suburbanized; but in some suburbs, realtors are practicing ghettoization—showing homes to blacks only where blacks are already living.

Of course, the racial issue is no longer just black and white. Hispanics are becoming an increasingly powerful force in American and urban politics. Mexicans, Puerto Ricans, and Cubans are becoming more organized and powerful politically and economically. Hispanic awareness might well become a cause of increased tension between Hispanic and black groups in the years ahead. In Miami, middle-class, upper-middle-class, and professional-class Cuban immigrants have succeeded to the point that after the June 1980 Liberty City riots, one black spokesman noted that, in Miami, blacks were not even second-class citizens; they were third class. In Miami, Cubans have an economic and political power base; blacks do not. In Los Angeles, however, an opposite situation exists. Hispanics, primarily Mexican-Americans, are the largest single minority within the city, but they have no elected representatives on the city council. Although blacks are a smaller percentage of the population, they nevertheless are sufficiently organized to have three black council members. The mayor, Thomas Bradley, is also black.

Melting-pot ideas probably need to be discarded and cultural pluralism might also be on the way to oblivion as another explanation of racial reality or desirability. No ready symbol or phrase comes to mind to describe the immigration of the 1980s. In Los Angeles, New York City, and other metropolitan areas, immigrants are arriving in large numbers and placing great demands upon the city's service-delivery structure. In Los Angeles, for example, many of the new immigrants are Asians, coming from Vietnam, Cambodia, Korea, Japan, the Philipines, and other countries. Currently, some eighty-three languages are spoken in Los Angeles County with sixty being spoken by students in Hollywood High School alone. Blacks who have finally gained a power base in Los Angeles city government may find that base eroding as their presence in the population becomes statistically smaller. Out of Los Angeles' almost three million people, some 40 percent are anglo, 30 percent Latino; 20 percent black; 10 percent Asian. Within the last five years, Koreans, Vietnamese, and Mexicans have provided most of the increase in immigrant population. With so many cultures and languages, tension and hostility are commonplace. In the schools, teachers and students sometimes cannot communicate with one another. Asian immigrants complain of police brutality; blacks and new immigrants sometimes clash, while Asian groups do not necessarily get along with one another. The Asian immigrants, who represent dozens of cultural and regional groups, have long histories that often include mutual animosities originating in their home countries. These hostilities are occasionally renewed on the streets of Los Angeles as rival Asian youth gangs fight each other as well as engage in combat with black and Latino youth gangs.

Not all of the signs point to discord, however. Black leaders, such as Jesse Jackson, have called for uniting minorities in a "rainbow coalition." And in cities such as Boston and Chicago, Latino voters have provided crucially important support to black candidates. Reciprocally, black support was important in Denver in electing the city's first Latino mayor, though Mayor Pena's core support came through a well-organized mobilization of Latino voters.

Further easing of racial tension will depend on a number of things. Will we accommodate cultural pluralism? If so, how? Will blacks continue to experience political and economic gains? What about the new minorities? What role will they play? The outcome of these issues may be determined more by the policies of the national government than by the actions and inactions of local governments, though local governments are still very significant actors on the intergroup-relations scene.

CONCLUSION

As background for the study of urban governance, we have now surveyed three sociocultural influences: an anticity bias, a tradition of individualism and privatism, and an uncertain and uneven process of acculturation and assimilation for the ethnic and racial groups that make up this nation. Each of these factors has a bearing on how people look at the urban community and how, in particular, the national government reacts to the urban condition.

Unlike many other countries, we have had no enunciated, consciously formulated policy of urban growth and development. As we saw in the first chapter, enormously significant population and economic shifts are occurring. But the nation, so far, has not enacted a policy to control or guide these trends. Perhaps, when all things are considered, it would have been unwise to set a national urban policy. But even if that is the case, we should have reached that conclusion only after due deliberation. Instead, up to now debate has been foreclosed because a national policy of urban growth and development has not even crossed the minds of most decision makers.

The factors discussed in this chapter help explain why such a policy has never been adopted. We have had no heritage of valuing city life, and we continue to spend much of our personal energy escaping from the city and all that it represents. We have had a tradition of urban development guided by private profit making. And to top off our attitudes toward the city, there has been much fear of and antagonism toward two of its most visible subgroups—minorities and the poor.

Of course, our indifference has not been total. Anti-urban bias notwithstanding, the nation could hardly ignore its units of local government. Since they are engaged first hand in providing vital services, city and other local governments are too important to neglect totally. So, while steering clear of the issue of a national policy of urban growth and development, the federal government has evolved an important relationship with urban communities. Some of these are direct, as in providing financial aid. Others are indirect, as in guaranteeing the rights of citizens under the Constitution.

Three themes in the urban experience have recurring importance. One is the effort to build a sense of community and common destiny in the presence of social diversity. Another is the struggle between central authority and varied local conditions. The third theme is the attempt to promote the public interest under circumstances in which private interests control most of society's resources. The next three chapters illustrate those three themes by taking up (1) the rising importance of the Latino population, (2) an overview of intergovernmental relations, and (3) a brief examination of local government fiscal policy.

SUGGESTED READINGS

BROWNELL, BLAINE A. "The Agrarian and Urban Ideals: Environmental Images in Urban America." *Journal of Popular Culture* 5 (Winter 1971), 576-87.

ELAZAR, DANIEL J. "Are We a Nation of Cities?" *The Public Interest*, No. 4 (Summer 1966), pp. 42-58.

FEAGIN, JOE R. "Poverty: We Still Believe That God Helps Those Who Help Themselves." *Psychology Today*, November 1972, pp. 102ff.

GLAZER, NATHAN, and DANIEL P. MOYNIHAN. *Beyond the Melting Pot*, 2nd rev. ed. Cambridge, Mass.: MIT Press, 1970.

GORDON, MILTON M. *Assimilation in American Life*. New York: Oxford University Press, 1964.

GREELEY, ANDREW. *Ethnicity in the United States*. New York: John Wiley & Sons, 1974.

HANDLIN, OSCAR. *Boston's Immigrants*. Cambridge, Mass.: Harvard University Press, Belknap Press, 1941.

LIEBERSON, STANLEY. *A Piece of the Pie: Black and White Immigrants since 1880*. Berkeley: University of California Press, 1980.

PETTIGREW, THOMAS F. *Racially Separate or Together?* New York: McGraw-Hill Book Co., 1971.

SMITH, MICHAEL P. *The City and Social Theory*. New York: St. Martin's Press, 1979.

SOWELL, THOMAS. *Ethnic America*. New York: Basic Books, 1981.

TAEUBER, KARL, and ALMA TAEUBER. *Negroes in the City*. Chicago: Aldine Publishing Co., 1965.

WARNER, SAM BASS, JR. *The Private City: Philadelphia in Three Periods of Growth*. Philadelphia: University of Pennsylvania Press, 1968.

chapter 3

Latinos in Urban America

In the middle of the twentieth century, the major migration into the nation's cities was by blacks, mainly from the rural South. As the twentieth century draws to a close, new patterns of migration have begun to emerge. Immigrants from Latin America, and in smaller numbers from Asia, are adding to the diversity of urban life. Long known for its ethnic diversity, Chicago reflects the changing composition of city population. At 40 percent, blacks are the most numerous group. Orientals constitute only 2 percent, but that small proportion represents a near doubling in size over the past decade. Perhaps the most spectacular growth has been in Chicago's Latino population,[1] now officially numbering nearly a half million and composing 14 percent of the population. Mexican-Americans especially have increased their numbers at a rapid rate, tripling in size between the 1970 and 1980 census. At more than 250,000, Mexican-Americans have come to outnumber the various European ethnic groups. Puerto Ricans have grown less rapidly, but at 112,000 they are larger than most European

[1] There is considerable disagreement over the correct designation for people from Spanish-language countries. The term *Hispanic*, is often used, but it is rejected by some on the grounds that many people from Latin America are not of Spanish origin and that the term is one originated by Anglos. In this chapter we use the term *Latino*, to refer collectively to people from Latin American countries. We use Cuban, Puerto Rican, and Mexican to refer to people whose origins are in these three Latin American places.

ethnic groups. Only the Poles at 200,000 and the Germans at 134,000 are larger.[2]

In surveying the urban scene, it is appropriate to give special attention to Latinos as a rapidly growing minority. Although numbering only slightly more than half the size of the black population nationwide, Latinos are nevertheless an increasing presence in the political and social life of cities. Already Denver, Tampa, Miami, San Antonio, and Santa Fe have Latino mayors. The 1980 census puts the number of Spanish-origin people in the United States at just over 14.6 million. As shown in Figure 3-1, three-fifths of this population is Mexican-American, but other nationalities, especially Puerto Ricans and Cubans, are also substantially represented.

Even though Latinos make up only about 6.5 percent of the total U.S. population, they merit our close attention for several reasons. With a birth rate twice that of whites and 60 percent higher than blacks, Latinos are the fastest growing population group in the country and, according to some estimates, will surpass blacks in total numbers by the year 2020. As shown in Table 3-1, Latinos are the youngest population group in the country.

More than 60 percent of all Latinos in the United States live in California, Texas, and New York, and they are 37 percent of New Mexico's population, 21 percent of Texas', 19 percent of California's, 16 percent of Arizona's and 12 percent of Colorado's. Ohio and Minnesota have as many Mexicans as Colorado and Nevada, and the Latino population in

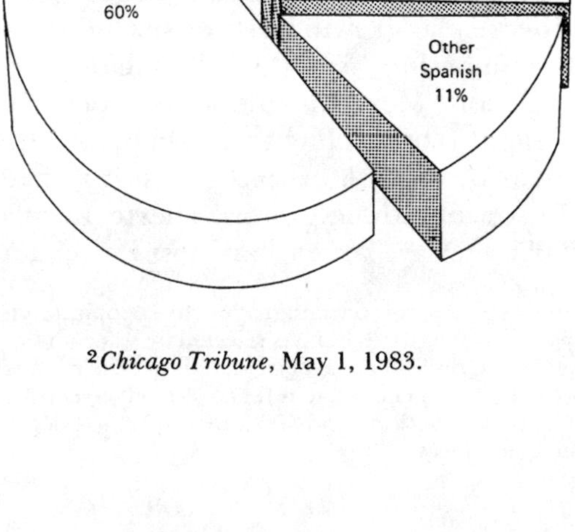

FIGURE 3-1.
Percent distribution of persons of Spanish origin by type of Spanish origin, March 1979. Source: U.S. Bureau of the Census, *Current Population Reports,* Series P-20, No. 347, "Persons of Spanish Origins in the U.S.P March 1979" (Advance Report) (Washington D.C.: Government Printing Office.)

[2] *Chicago Tribune,* May 1, 1983.

TABLE 3-1 Age of Major Racial Groups in the United States, 1980

	PROPORTION OF GROUP 15 AND UNDER	PROPORTION OF GROUP 65 AND OVER	MEDIAN AGE
White	21.3%	12.2%	31.3
Black	28.7%	7.9%	24.9
Spanish Origin	32.0%	4.9%	23.2

Source: 1980 Census

the United States is expanding by about 1 million people each year, mostly Mexican, and many through illegal entry.[3] Put another way, the United States is the fifth largest Latino nation in the world having more Latino people than every country except Mexico, Spain, Argentina, and Colombia.

While census and other population figures can give us a feeling for the numbers of Latinos in the United States, they should not be relied upon too heavily.

The oft-cited census undercount of blacks is also true for Latinos. The undercount problem is seen as so serious that, in 1980, the city of Detroit and several Latino groups went to court challenging the accuracy of census figures. At stake were federal aids, subsidies, and political power.

In addition, there are somewhere between 3 million and 12 million illegal Spanish-origin aliens in the country, most probably in urban areas; thus potentially doubling the size of the Hispanic population. The census data are not beyond question. For example, the 1980 report reveals that about 635,000 Spanish-origin people reside in Illinois and 1,659,000 in New York. Yet a marketing study done in 1980 shows that the Chicago area alone had approximately 660,000 Latinos and the New York City area had 2.3 million Latino residents.

Our focus in this section will be on the growth and influence of Latinos in the urban United States. We will pay particular attention to the Cuban influence in Miami, Puerto Ricans in the New York area, and Mexican-Americans in the Southwest and in Chicago. We will be quite cautious in drawing conclusions about Latino influence in urban politics simply because there are few reliable data to draw upon. Population and other demographic evidence are sketchy and known to be faulty. In addition, the reasons why Cubans, Mexicans, and Puerto Ricans came to the United States are different, and despite a nominally common background and culture, we cannot assume that the politics, sociology, and economics

[3] *Christian Science Monitor*, April 28, 1981, p. 13.

of Mexicans in San Antonio are similar to the experiences of Cubans in Miami or Puerto Ricans in Newark or New York. Thus we caution against placing all Latinos in one group and then drawing conclusions. We also caution against assuming that blacks and Latinos, being "minorities," will naturally form alliances to better their fate. While electoral coalitions have been brought together in various contests, in cities such as Miami and Los Angeles there is substantial tension between Latino and black populations.

Gary Orfield, a political scientist at the University of Chicago, has concluded that there are some important differences between the black and Latino experiences in Chicago. One conclusion is that Chicago Latinos may simply be the latest wave of immigrants, temporarily located in the inner city, and will in time move on to the suburbs and be assimilated. Orfield points out that unlike race, a permanent identifying trait, the conditions that cause Chicago Latinos to locate in urban ghettos are transitory conditions such as Spanish language dependency, cultural identification, and possibly illegal status. While there are important behavioral conditioners for first generation people, they are less important for American-born, second-generation Latinos and might well be insignificant for third-generation Latinos. Orfield suggests that Latino suburbanization is proceeding more quickly than black suburbanization and seems to be resulting in suburban Latinos being more evenly distributed throughout an SMSA's population and not concentrated in a few suburbs. Thus, at least in Chicago, Latinos who are primarily Mexicans are edging into the mainstream. In Miami, Cubans *are* the mainstream. By comparison, the Puerto Rican experience in the United States is less promising.

MEXICANS

The country's second-largest and fastest-growing minority group are Mexican-Americans. For many years, issues involving Mexicans in the United States were seen as local, state, or regional ones simply because most Mexicans lived in Texas, California, Arizona, Colorado, or New Mexico. Even though the Mexican population is still concentrated in the Southwest, recent dispersal has given national attention to the size of the Mexican population and to its problems as well.

Mexicans are some of the newest and oldest residents of the United States. The southwestern part of the United States had Mexican settlements long before those areas were states, or even territories, of the United States. The history of Mexicans and the Southwest has been intertwined for so long that many Mexicans simply view it as an extended neighborhood, certainly not a "foreign" country.[4] However, most Mexicans in the United

[4] Alan Riding, "The U.S. and Mexico: An Uneasy Truce," *The New York Times*, February 12, 1979, p. B.10.

States arrived here during and after World War II. There are at least six distinct categories of people of Mexican ancestry living in the United States: (1) decendants of the original Mexican settlers in the Southwest, before it was part of the United States; (2) illegal aliens from Mexico; (3) emigrants from Mexico who are here legally but are not citizens; (4) transients from Mexico staying in the United States for varying periods of time (from days to decades) on various kinds of official documents (visas, work permits, and so on); (5) naturalized American citizens from Mexico; and (6) American-born citizens descended from immigrants or transients.

In addition, there is some disagreement over the proper use of the terms Mexican, Mexican-American, Latino, Hispanic, and Chicano. Older Mexicans have preferred the use of Latin and Spanish identifiers while younger Mexican-Americans, notably activist, student groups reject those names and prefer the more militant Chicano. One writer notes that the intensity of feeling about names and titles has resulted in Mexican-American political groups refusing to form coalitions or merger because they could not agree on what the new group would be called.[5]

Data presented elsewhere in this chapter show that Mexican-Americans are younger than other population groups in the United States, are geographically concentrated in a few states (primarily in the Southwest but with a major population base in Chicago), have income levels less than the median family income for the United States but higher than that for blacks, and experience an unemployment rate that is less than for blacks but higher than the national average.

There are several other demographic factors that must be understood about Mexicans in the United States. When measured against contemporary U.S. standards, Mexican families are larger than average. In 1977, the average size of non-Hispanic families in the United States was 3.3 people, while for Mexican families it was 4.3 people. Taking various factors into account, one can reasonably anticipate that Mexicans will be the largest minority in the country in some future census.

The other Mexican-American phenomenon that must be considered is the large number of Mexicans who are in this country as illegal aliens. As we indicated in the introduction to this section, the number of such illegal aliens is placed anywhere between 3 million and 12 million. While they are not all of Mexican origin, many are. With about two thousand miles of common border between the United States and Mexico there is no easy way that the flow of illegals can be significantly reduced. In some circles, using terms like "illegal aliens" is rejected with a preference for euphemisms like "undocumented alien." According to some observers, illegals take jobs away from citizens, especially blacks. Because they are illegal, they will work

[5] Leo Grebler, Joan W. Moore, and Ralph C. Guzman, *The Mexican-American People*, (New York: The Free Press, 1970), pp. 385-87.

for less money, avoid unions, and tolerate poorer working conditions. They cannot report working-conditions violations without revealing their illegal status (*Washington Post*, August 7, 1983). Other observers argue that illegals simply perform the unskilled, temporary jobs that blacks and other citizens reject. So rather than displacing other workers, illegal aliens provide a valuable service at less cost.

Mexicans share some characteristics with other Latin groups and with blacks, but they also differ from those other groups in some significant ways. In many areas of the country, Mexicans are typecast as illegal aliens who cross the border to work for substandard wages as migratory farm workers. The image of Mexicans as farm workers and rural residents is simply no longer true.[6] A 1978 Census Bureau report shows that 81 percent of the Chicanos living in the United States were in the central city areas of metropolitan areas.[7]

MEXICAN IMMIGRATION TO THE UNITED STATES

The history of Mexican immigration to the United States can best be summarized as consisting of three periods of massive immigration with two periods of equally large deportation between them. These inconsistent policies of first encouraging immigration and then forcibly removing Mexicans from the United States reflects the changing priorities of the Southwest from concern for a supply of plentiful, cheap labor to one of concern about the social problems associated with large numbers of rural immigrants.

While the first exchanges between Mexicans and Americans occurred when the American Southwest was still part of Mexico, the first great migration of Mexicans to the United States took place in the three decades between 1900 and 1930. The Mexican Revolution that began in 1909 brought the first permanent and substantial migration to the United States. Unlike later immigrants who were primarily rural, peasant, farm workers, the immigrants at the turn of the century included many middle-and upper-class people who wished to escape the conflict. Thus many of these people might better be understood as refugees than immigrants. About 250,000 Mexicans came to the United States in the 1900-1930 period, but there are no comparable figures on the number of return migrants. Most of these immigrants were employed in agriculture, mining, or railroad construction.

[6] Ibid., pp. 113-114 and U.S. Bureau of the Census, *1970 Census of Population*, Subject Reports, PC(2)-LD, p. 1.

[7] U.S. Bureau of the Census, *Current Population Report*, Series B-20, No. 328. "Persons of Spanish Origin in the United States: March 1978 (Advance Report)," Table 4 (Washington, D.C.: Government Printing Office).

The Reclamation Act of 1902, which authorizes a series of reservoirs for parts of the Southwest, changed agricultural technology in that part of the country. It was during this period that the image of Mexicans as farm laborers gained support. Children often worked with their parents performing the "stoop labor" in the fields. The story of migrant Mexican farm laborers is one of low earnings, abysmal health and housing conditions, virtually no education for the children, child labor, and isolation in a migrant labor camp away from the Anglo population. Still despite these conditions, Mexican farm workers in the southwestern United States made two or three times what they would have made in Mexico in 1900 and the disparities increased over the next two decades. In 1930, the pay difference had reached a factor of six, and away from the border where there was a smaller supply of laborers, the pay rates were even greater.

Those who returned home to Mexico after working in agriculture, mining, or on the railroads were able to buy farm animals and implements, radios, and sometimes even automobiles.[8]

Immigration ended and the first of the large-scale deportation of Mexicans occurred in the 1930s with the Great Depression. As Anglos lost their jobs and farmers and the urban unemployed sought work, they formed the nucleus of a new pool of low-cost farm workers. Americans desired to be rid of Mexicans both because they took jobs that could be filled by U.S. citizens and because an agricultural depression in the Southwest in the 1920s put many Mexican agricultural workers on welfare and relief roles. The result was that between 1929 and 1934 some 400,000 Mexicans were deported. Sharply reduced immigration to the United States (a little less than 28,000 Mexicans entered the United States on permanent visas in the 1930s) and deportation reduced the Mexican-born population in the United States from 639,000 in 1930 to 377,000 in 1940.[9]

An account of the Los Angeles repatriation process is illustrative of the feelings of the times:

> It was discovered that, in wholesale lots, they could be shipped to Mexico City for $14.70 per capita. The sum represented less than the cost of a week's board and lodging. And so, about February 1931, the first trainload was dispatched, and shipments at the rate of about one a month have continued ever since. A shipment consisting of three special trains left Los Angeles on December 8. The loading commenced at about six o'clock in the morning and continued for hours. More than twenty-five such special trains had left the Southern Pacific Station before last April.
>
> The repatriation programme is regarded locally as a piece of consummate statecraft. The average per family cost of executing it is $71.14, including

[8] Arthur F. Corwin, "Causes of Mexican Emigration to the United States: A Summary View," in *Perspectives in American History*, Vol. III (1973) pp. 565-66.

[9] Joan W. Moore, *Mexican Americans* (Englewood Cliffs, New Jersey: Prentice Hall, 1971), p. 42.

> food and transportation. It cost one Los Angeles County $77,249.29 to repatriate one shipment of 6,024. It would have cost $424,933.70 to provide this number with such charitable assistance as they would have been entitled to had they remained—a savings of $347,468.40.[10]

During the deportation period, anyone who "looked Mexican" ran the risk of being stopped and questioned. As a result, it is estimated that as many as one-half of the repatriates were American-born citizens who were sent "home" to a country they had never seen before and whose language they could not speak.

During World War II, the labor shortage made Mexicans welcome again in the United States. However, legal immigrants were slow to respond because Mexico was enjoying economic prosperity and needed workers for her own industries. In addition, immigrants to the United States faced conscription into the U.S. armed forces. The need for agricultural labor resulted, in 1942, in the creation of the famous *bracero* program whereby thousands of Mexicans came into the United States as contract laborers. A *bracero* is a person who works with his arms (brazos) and has become the Spanish equivalent for farm worker. Under the agreement, the United States paid for the travel costs of *braceros*, guaranteed a fair wage, and assured them they would be treated equitably. Although intended only as a war-time measure to provide a solution to shortages of agricultural labor, the agreement lasted for twenty-two years, ending in December 1964. At its peak in the late 1950s, over 400,000 laborers a year came to the United States. At the same time the *bracero* program was in operation, a steady flow of illegal workers entered the country. For employers, these illegals were an advantage because they could be hired for less than workers under the *bracero* program because no bonds had to be posted, and because the other regulations of the *bracero* program could be avoided.

The second wave of immigration, like the first, ended in a massive deportation of Mexicans. By 1954, after a stable supply of farm laborers had been guaranteed for agribusiness in the Southwest, the Immigration and Naturalization Service began "Operation Wetback." By 1960, almost 4 million Mexicans had been deported, with only 2 percent of that number undergoing formal deportation procedures.[11]

A third immigration wave began in about 1960 and is still continuing. In the 1960s about 440,000 people emigrated from Mexico to the United States.[12] This last migration coincides with the urbanization of the Mexican population in the United States. Mexicans migrated to U.S. cities for the

[10] Leo Bardo F. Estrada, et al., "Chicanos in the United States: A History of Exploitation and Resistance," Daedalus, V. 110, No. 2 (Spring, 1981), p. 118.

[11] Ibid., p. 120.

[12] Corwin, *Causes*, p. 632.

same reasons that southern blacks and whites came to the cities—for the hope of better jobs, housing, a good education for their children, and a better life in general. As in the case of blacks from the South, the Mexican urban migration was also an effort to get away from the social exclusion and discrimination of the Southwest. For example, in 1945 it was revealed at a U.S. Senate subcommittee hearing that Mexicans from McCarney, Texas had to travel forty-five miles to get a haircut because Anglo barbers would not cut Mexican hair and Mexicans could not legally become barbers in McCarney. In another Texas city, Mexicans could not use a public street to celebrate the Fourth of July because that holiday was for white people only.[13]

THE CHICANO MOVEMENT

The social unrest that America experienced in the 1960s involved Mexican-Americans. A number of militant organizations appeared that can be collectively identified as a Chicano movement. Like any movement, many of its goals and objectives were heterogeneous. As Estrada, et al. have observed:

> Often very critical of certain of the basic assumptions of U.S. society, they sought fundamental transformation in the distribution of power in the United States. Many promoted radical alternatives, preferring socialism, for example, to the prevailing economic and political system. Others hoped to create various kinds of alternative or separatist institutions, with alternative schools, community control of law enforcement, health, educational, and political institutions, and the like. They were looking, in short, for a radical and equitable transformation of a racist society. Almost all such groups emphasized the distinctiveness of Mexican culture. They actively promoted Chicano cultural norms and values. Chicano culture represented the common ground that bound together all the members of the group. Political terms such as "Chicano" and *LaRaza Nueva* were used to symbolize unity, and were intended to increase the cohesiveness of otherwise diverse elements.[14]

In the decade between 1965 and 1975, the Chicano movement gained momentum in the United States. Charismatic leaders appeared. Although not as well known to the larger society as their black counterparts, several Chicano leaders popularized the cause. Reies Lopez Tijerina hoped to restore lost Spanish and Mexican land grants in New Mexico. Rodolfo "Corky" Gonzales, organized the Crusade for Justice and established alter-

[13] Statement of Alonzo S. Perales, Chairman, Committee of One Hundred, Director General, League of Loyal Americans, San Antonio, Texas, U.S. Congress Senate, Subcommittee of the Committee on Education and Labor, Hearings, Fair Employment Practice Act on S. 101, S. 459, 79th Congress, 1945, 150.

[14] Estrada, et al., "Chicanos," pp. 122-123.

native community institutions in the Denver area; and working conditions of Mexican agricultural laborers became the special concern of Cesar Chavez and the United Farm Workers Organizing Committee.

In the Southwest and Midwest, political and educational issues sparked organizing activity. In Texas, Jose Angel Gutierrez, and others, replaced the Anglo-dominated governments of several South Texas cities and counties, primarily through *El Partido de La Raza Unida*.

From the perspective of the 1980s it is hard to gauge the success of the Chicano movement. The movement has changed and the society has changed. Certainly there have been Mexican political and economic successes. Whether they can be attributed to the Chicano movement, or whether they simply evolved is open to debate. In San Antonio, Texas, for example, the end of at-large voting and the election of the city council from wards resulted in the council's composition changing from eleven Anglos to six Anglos and five Chicanos. While this is a major success, it should be noted that San Antonio's population is 54 percent Mexican-American. Politically the current status of Mexican-Americans in the Southwest might be understood a little better by a look at San Antonio. It is the tenth largest city in the United States, the majority of the population is Mexican-American, and the city's ethnic tensions drew national media attention in the 1970s. In 1981, Henry Cisneros was elected mayor of the city. He became the first Mexican-American elected to the mayoralty of a major American city. The fact that he won should not be too surprising given the majority population in the city, but the narrowness of the victory was a surprise.

Cisneros' opponent in the election was an Anglo named John Steen. The campaign avoided divisive Anglo-versus-Chicano issues, and on the substantive issues the two men held very similar attitudes. Both are pro-business with economic development, the creation of jobs, reduced government spending, and the like being supported by both candidates. What caused Cisneros' some particular concern was that the Hispanic vote was not automatically his. A third candidate, Dr. Jose San Martin III, also a Mexican-American, had the potential to take some of the Hispanic vote away from Cisneros. Pre-election estimates saw San Martin running a distant third, but in a low turnout, he might attract enough Hispanic votes to keep Cisneros from winning. Despite these fears, Cisneros did win an absolute majority in the April election thus avoiding a run-off election. But as *The Wall Street Journal* speculated in a pre-election story: "If Mr. Cisneros prevails, he will indeed be launching the 'Hispanic Decade,' in San Antonio but it will look a lot more like the neo-conservative 1980s than the 1960s."[15] In office, Cisneros emphasized economic development and easily won re-election in 1983 against token opposition.

[15] *The Wall Street Journal*, April 2, 1981, p. 12.

LATINOS IN CHICAGO

As we have indicated, the primary experience of Mexicans in the United States has been in the Southwest. But the city of Chicago has a large Latino population, many of whom are second generation Chicagoans.[16] In 1981, Hispanics made up about 15 percent of Chicago's population. Superficially, Latinos in Chicago face the same problems and have the same hopes and dreams as Latinos throughout the United States. So why then look at Chicago Latinos separately from Latin experiences in New York, Miami, and cities of the Southwest? For one reason, Chicago is the only major city in the United States in which the three major Latino groups in the United States live in substantial numbers. Thus we have an opportunity to examine the interactions and tensions between and among Mexicans, Puerto Ricans, and Cubans. Further, Chicago Latinos deserve a special look because Chicago is not in the Southwest. The southwestern Anglo-Latino model simply does not exist in Chicago. And to the extent that Latinos in the United States, especially Mexicans, become more evenly distributed throughout metropolitan areas, the more likely it is that the lessons of Chicago and its Latinos will be more useful than those learned from the Southwest with its several century old traditions and expectations.

Chicago Hispanics have yet to make their presence truly felt in either Illinois, Cook County, or Chicago politics. Illinois has the fifth largest Latino population in the country with most in the Chicago metropolitan area. Yet there are few Latinos in public office. In the 1970s the West Town Puerto Rican community was gerrymandered into several wards. Currently, Latinos are a majority of the population in four Chicago wards, the twenty-sixth and the thirty-first on the near northwest side, and the twenty-second and twenty-fifth on the near southwest side. Thus, if Latinos can organize politically and support a candidate, they stand a chance of electing up to four Latino aldermen. Even when the first Latino alderman is elected, and observers in the Latino community feel that it will come from the predominatly Puerto Rican parts of the city, there is no guarantee that the individual will be anyone but a machine loyalist. Benjamin Reyes, a political activist from the Puerto Rican West Town area has said: "If the machine takes that ward, then the only thing that changes is the alderman's color and the name. Everything else stays the same."[17]

If Chicago city politics has not yet experienced the full weight of the Latino presence in the city, Chicago school politics has. In 1981, three Latinos served on the school board and attorney Raul Villalobos was board president. The presence of these individuals on the school board is said to

[16] *Chicago Tribune*, "Hispanic Chicago: A Special Issue," 11/1/81.

[17] Ibid., p. 16.

give the Latino community hope that their time is coming.[18] As we pointed out earlier, Chicago is the only major city in the country with substantial numbers of Mexicans, Cubans, and Puerto Ricans. Of the three Latino school board members, one is Mexican, one Puerto Rican, and one Cuban. But even in education, Latinos are under-represented in policy-level positions. While almost 20 percent of Chicago public school students are Latino, there were only five Latino principals out of 515 in 1980-81, none of the thirty-five district superintendents was Latino, and out of 23,190 teachers, only 4 percent or 992 were Latino.[19]

On a more positive note, there are signs that the city is providing a level of acceptance for its Hispanics. In the 1950s, a Mexican opened a store in a place called Little Village on Twenty-sixth Street. Within three months he was out of business because no one wanted to buy from a Mexican. Today, Twenty-sixth Street is a thriving neighborhood business area. There are no vacant stores on the street, and almost all the storeowners are Mexican.

The current generation of Chicago Latinos are more aggressive, better educated, and more "city smart" than their parents. Unlike many New York Puerto Ricans who desire to go back to the island and buy a home, and unlike many southwest Mexicans who emigrate, return to Mexico, and then emigrate once again to the United States, many younger Chicago Latinos were born and raised in the city. There is no "back home" to go to other than the streets and neighborhoods of West Town, Pilsen, and South Chicago. One young Puerto Rican leader said: "Chicago can serve as a role model for all Latino communities in the nation. This is the only place where it all comes together for all Latino groups. We can demonstrate to the country that we are capable of working together, and quite capable of defending our rights and dealing with society in an effective manner."[20]

PUERTO RICANS

Like other Latino groups in the United States, Puerto Ricans might be viewed as among the latest ethnic immigrants to America and its cities. This view holds that while first generation Puerto Ricans will live in urban ghettos and will eke out a marginal survival, second and third generation Puerto Ricans will be assimilated into the larger society as so many millions of immigrants before them.

An opposing view, held by many Puerto Ricans, suggests that because the island is a possession (some say "colony") of the United States, because

[18] Ibid., p. 18.
[19] Ibid., p. 22.
[20] Ibid., p. 24.

of its geographic nearness, because Puerto Ricans are U.S. citizens, and because of an activist pro-statehood movement for the island, Puerto Rican immigrants cannot be viewed simply as the newest arrivals whose problems will simply disappear over time. Lack of certainty over the place of Puerto Ricans in American urban society even involves the proper name for the group. Unlike earlier generations of white immigrants, black migrants, and Mexican immigrants, there is almost no use of the hyphenated term Puerto Rican-American to differentiate island Puerto Ricans from those living in the United States. Other ethnic identities are customarily hyphenated to distinguish between people living in the homeland from those in the United States, to reflect a degree of assimilation and acculturation, and so on. Thus, while German-American, Polish-American, Italian-American, and Afro-American are common terms, Puerto Rican-American is not. A word that is acceptable and differentiates between island and mainland Puerto Ricans is "Rican." The name "New Yorican" is also used in many instances. While they do not appear to carry the connotations of ethnic pride that Chicano does and black did in the 1960s, the search for a name for Puerto Ricans living in the United States does lend support to the belief that the categorizations used to describe other immigrant groups are not necessarily applicable to Puerto Ricans.[21]

The history of Ricans in the United States involves mainly New York City. By 1930, for example, 84 percent of all Puerto Ricans living in the United States resided in New York City, settling into such areas as the Chelsea district in west Manhattan, the Brooklyn Navy Yard, and upper Manhattan near 116th Street.[22] An interesting racial pattern is revealed in these early settlements. Puerto Ricans who were "white" moved into the first two areas while those with darker-skin wound up in the 116th Street areas forming a buffer zone between black Harlem and Italian Harlem.[23] In 1970, there were almost 1,500,000 Puerto Ricans in the United States and 69 percent lived in the greater New York area with 58.8 percent living in New York City.

As the economy of the Northeast changed, Puerto Ricans moved out of New York City and into New Jersey, Pennsylvania, Connecticut, Rhode Island, and Massachusetts. As a result, Puerto Ricans currently make up more than 50 percent of the population of Union City and West New York, New Jersey, and there are sizable Puerto Rican populations in such New Jersey cities as Elizabeth, Newark, Jersey City, Hoboken, Paterson, Passaic, Weehawken, and Kearney.

[21] Antonio M. Stevens Arroyo and Ana Maria Diaz-Ramerez, "Puerto Ricans in the States: A Struggle for Identity," in *The Minority Reports* (New York: Holt, Rinehart & Winston, 1982), p. 197.

[22] Ibid., p. 200.

[23] Ibid., p. 200.

It is also appropriate to point out, in view of the United States' historical treatment of racial minorities, that there are more successful white than black Puerto Ricans. Herman Badillo, a former congressman from New York, Robert Garcia, his successor in Congress, and Maurice Ferre mayor of Miami, Florida are all white Puerto Ricans.

As we saw in looking at Mexicans, the depression of the 1930s meant a severe reduction in the number of Puerto Rican migrants. But after World War II, the number of Puerto Rican migrants was so large that it is simply known as "The Great Migration." One writer concludes that so many people left the island between 1946 and 1964 that "it is the greatest migration in the history of the modern world. Never has such a large proportion of one nation migrated to another nation in so short a time."[24] Today, some 40 percent of all Puerto Ricans live in the United States with the other 60 percent on the island. It is estimated that by the year two thousand there will be more Puerto Ricans in the United States than in Puerto Rico. No doubt the end of the war and the freedom from travel restrictions had a great deal to do with the beginning of the great migration. But of even greater significance was the fact that, in 1946, regular commercial air service was begun between San Juan and New York City. Thus, like Mexicans who could immigrate to the United States by simply crossing a border, Puerto Ricans could be in the United States after a relatively inexpensive, short airplane flight. The ease of movement also makes it possible to return to Puerto Rico if life in New York City becomes unacceptable. Migration to the United States for Puerto Ricans might, over a period of fifteen or twenty years, become a number of distinct series of events. In other words, an individual or family can leave the island, try to make it in New York, return to the island in several years, return again, and so on. The possibility of this type of *va y ven* (back and forth) migration reinforces links to the island.

A 1980 *New York Times* survey of Latinos, primarily Puerto Ricans, in New York City showed that four out of five did not consider themselves to be "Americans" despite being U.S. citizens and many spoke of returning to the island.[25] An in-depth series of stories by the *Christian Science Monitor* in 1980 confirmed Vidal's findings as Puerto Ricans in the United States most wanted a home of their own in Puerto Rico.[26]

There is an interesting sidelight to the Puerto Rican migration figures. Since the figures represent total net migration, they grossly understate the actual movement of people. For example, in 1955, 343,720 Puerto Ricans came to the United States and 297,706 returned to the island. While the net migration figure was only a little more than 45,000,

[24] Ibid., p. 202.

[25] David Vidal, "Living in Two Cultures: Hispanic New Yorkers," *The New York Times*, May 11, 1980, p. 1.

[26] Geoffrey Godsell, "The Puerto Ricans," *Christian Science Monitor*, May 1, 1980, p. 12.

more than 600,000 people moved to or from the island. In 1961 and 1963, more Puerto Ricans left the United States than arrived from the island. While migration figures for those years show no net migration, more than 1,500,000 people moved between the United States and Puerto Rico in each of those years. In 1967, the total movement was in excess of 3,500,000 people with a net migration figure of only 26,000.[27]

These figures must also be taken cautiously since they do not clearly show the numbers of *new* people arriving in the United States. If 50,000 new Puerto Ricans migrate to the United States for the first time, and 45,000 return to the island, while the net migration figure is only 5000, there are 50,000 *new* Puerto Rican immigrants in the country. These are people who need to become socialized, learn the ways of an urban lifestyle in the United States, learn a new language, educate their children, get a job, and so on. The service demands placed on a city's infrastructure thus far exceed what might be expected by looking at immigration figures alone.

While it is risky to make cross-group comparisons, it does appear that Puerto Ricans as a minority, immigrant group are probably worse off than Cubans, Mexicans, or blacks. In 1976, the U.S. Commission on Civil Rights published *An Uncertain Future: Puerto Ricans in the Continental United States.*

The Commission concluded that Puerto Ricans constantly placed below all other minority groups regardless of how success or achievement was measured. Puerto Ricans were as far below Chicanos and blacks in terms of median family income as those other groups were below the national average. A 1976 Census Bureau Survey of Income and Education showed that almost 40 percent of Puerto Rican families were below the poverty level, and 30 percent were barely above it, compared to 23 percent of all Spanish-origin families and just under 9 percent of non-Spanish families. The 1978 and 1979 data reveal a similar pattern of poverty as Table 3-2 shows.

As one might expect, the income and unemployment position of Puerto Ricans results in large numbers of people being on welfare. Again, using 1976 data, almost 23 percent of Puerto Rican households in the United States were receiving Aid to Families with Dependent Children (AFDC), 32 percent were receiving food stamps while 60 percent were eligible for food stamps. Educationally, in 1976, 34 percent of the white males, 22 percent of the white females, and 11 percent of black males and females in the United States attended college. Only 6 percent of the Puerto Rican males and 4 percent of the females were in college in the same year.

These demographics show that the employment picture and employment patterns for Puerto Ricans in the United States are less than encouraging. The largest category of employment for Puerto Ricans is as factory

[27] Thomas Sowell, *Ethnic America* (New York; Basic Books, 1981), p. 231.

TABLE 3-2 Selected Income, Poverty, and Unemployment Data for Puerto Ricans in the United States, 1978 and 1979.

MEDIAN FAMILY INCOME (1978)

United States	Cubans	Mexicans	Blacks	Puerto Ricans
$17,640	$15,326	$12,835	$10,879	$8,282

PERCENTAGE OF FAMILIES BELOW POVERTY LEVEL (1978)

United States	All Latinos	Cubans	Mexicans	Puerto Ricans
9.3%	21.4%	15%	18.9%	38.9%

UNEMPLOYMENT RATE (3rd QUARTER, 1979)

United States	Blacks	All Latinos	Cubans	Mexicans	Puerto Ricans
5.8%	10.8%	8.2%	7.6%	7.9%	11.5%

Source: Geoffrey Godsell, "The Puerto Ricans," *Christian Science Monitor*, May 1, 1980, p. 12.

operatives. Nationally, these types of jobs are growing barely, if at all, and are declining rapidly in the Northeast, where most Puerto Ricans live. The 1976 *Survey* revealed no Puerto Ricans in the United States holding positions as scientists, lawyers, physicians, dentists, architects, planners, or other well-paid, high-status occupations. Now obviously, there are Puerto Ricans in these occupations, but their numbers are so small that they do not appear in nationally-based sample surveys. The dismal situation regarding Puerto Rican workers led one observer to conclude ". . . the white collar alternative is limited and unlikely to become typical in the near future."[28]

In the face of this overwhelming poverty, is there any hope for Puerto Ricans in the United States? There is some sketchy evidence that Puerto Ricans are beginning to organize to improve their position socially, politically, and economically. In the Willamsburg section of Brooklyn, a neighborhood group known as "Los Sures" has rehabilitated several buildings and has taken over the management and operation of at least eight others. They control at least $5 million in money and property. Also in New York City the Puerto Rican Forum provides skills, training, and job placement efforts to more than 20,000 Puerto Ricans a year. As of 1980, five training centers were outside the barrios in New York City. The locations were chosen to get Puerto Ricans into the mainstream of society, thereby increasing their ability to interact with the larger society. This is, of course, only one very small step.

[28] Stevens-Arroyo, *Puerto Ricans*, p. 209.

THE CUBANS

There are two significant migrations of Cubans to the United States that we need to be concerned with. The first brought almost 200,000 Cubans to south Florida between 1963 and 1973. The second saw an additional 120,000 come to the United States in the Spring of 1980. In many ways, the story of Cubans in the United States is closely tied to their presence in Miami. Thus our analysis will concentrate on Cuban influence in Miami and the resulting *latinization* of a major American city.

The first group of refugees contained many middle-class professionals. Castro's turn toward the Soviet Union resulted in many doctors, lawyers, engineers, publishers, accountants, business people, and other highly skilled professionals leaving Cuba for the United States. Many of these immigrants had been educated in U.S. schools, were fluent in English, and had established business connections in the United States before their immigration to the United States.

If we once again review Table 3-2 in this chapter, it begins to become clear why Cuban immigrants appear to be more economically successful than other Latin migrants to the U.S. mainland. Most Mexicans and Puerto Ricans who come to the United States are economically motivated. They come to the United States to find jobs and to be able to earn more money than was possible back home. Cuban immigrants, especially the first group, were economically successful at home. They left Cuba to escape political repression and Marxism. Once in the United States, it was only a matter of time before the economic success they had realized in Cuba was reestablished here.

These refugees were also eligible for AFDC, job training, and language training in English. The combination of professional skills and federal money has resulted in almost 10,000 Cuban-owned businesses in Miami. It has also made Miami "The Capital of Latin America," a title given the city by President Jaime Roldos of Ecuador in 1979. Miami Mayor Maurice Ferre (a Puerto Rican) has concluded that without the Cuban influence, Miami would just be another sunbelt resort city past its prime. But the Cuban economic influence has established Miami as the center of Latin America's 342 million people. The economic success of the earlier Cubans attracted business interests from other Latin countries impressed by the relative ease with which Cuban immigrants became successful. As the Latin economic base in Miami grew, the city also became a favorite vacation place for Latin business people and their families. Thus Miami entered the 1980s as a bilingual and bicultural community where Spanish is not simply a handy second language to have, it is a requirement for successful business enterprises.

The 1980 Cuban immigrants are more similar to other Latino immigrants than they are to the earlier group of Cuban immigrants. For example, the current group is composed largely of single, unskilled, or blue-collar workers rather than the married, middle-class professionals of the 1960s. One set of estimates shows that about half of the current Cuban immigrant population is made up of single men between the ages of eighteen and thirty.[29] With most of the new immigrants eager to find work there is a surplus of ready, cheap labor available. There already is evidence that many jobs in the low skilled, low-paid personal-services industry (dishwashers, bell boys, waiters, laundry workers, and so on) are seeing the salary rate cut as non-unionized Cubans compete with high-paid union workers.[30]

Thus, the new Cuban immigrant poses a peculiar dilemma for Miami and for that city's earlier Cuban immigrants. Can the successful Cuban business community find or make enough jobs to keep the new Cubans from becoming a public problem? And if enough jobs can be found, what will the impact be on the black and Anglo communities who are increasingly unsettled over the latinization of Miami?

With about 41 percent of the greater Miami area population now Latino, the seemingly inevitable backlash has begun. Miami's Anglo and black communities are beginning to resist the increased latinization of Miami. Fifteen percent of Miami's population is black, and by and large, it has been left out of the economic boom brought on by Cuban and other Latin dollars. After the Liberty City riots of May 1980, that killed eighteen people and caused $100 million in damage, one black resident noted that while blacks were second-class citizens in most U.S. cities, in Miami they were third class behind Latinos and whites. Anglos in Miami are not especially sanguine about the growing Latin influence either. Since 1973, the Dade County, Florida government has been officially bilingual. Most government business is conducted in, translated into, or has reports available in English and Spanish. In 1979, Dade County spent about $800,000 for various Spanish language services. An English-only campaign began in 1980 that would make it illegal for any language other than English to be used in conducting the county's official business. The resolution that appeared on the November 1980 ballot read as follows:

> The expenditure of county funds for the purpose of utilizing any language other than English, or promoting any culture other than that of the United States, is prohibited. All county governmental meetings, hearings, and publications shall be in the English language only.[31]

[29] *Business Week*, August 25, 1980, p. 87.

[30] Ibid., p. 88.

[31] Robert M. Press, "English-only Drive Mirrors Deeper Miami Unrest." *Christian Science Monitor*, October 20, 1980, p. 12.

Supporters of the proposal claimed that they merely wanted ". . . to keep Dade County as part of the United States."[32] They saw Spanish as an irritant in daily life and the English-only drive as a response to situations such as encountering sales clerks who could not speak English. Others allege that there are hotels, restaurants, and other such establishments where no one can speak English.

The proposal passed by a three to two margin. Almost 71 percent of the non-Latins who voted, voted for the measure, but a majority of blacks who voted, voted against it.[33] Some saw the black vote against the measure as a hopeful sign that a more cooperative atmosphere was being created between the two groups and the practical reality that if such a measure affecting over 40 percent of the area's population could pass, what would prevent similar retributive measures from being proposed against the 15 percent of the population which is black.

If Miami has become the financial center for Latin America and has also brought stunning economic success for Cubans, then it must be noted that the rebirth of Miami also has its darker side. Some of the wealth in Miami comes from illegal drugs. The popular press reports stories of home sales in the $250,000-to-$400,000-and-higher range being transacted in cash. *The Wall Street Journal* estimates that 90 percent of all the wholesale marijuana and cocaine brought into the United States in a year, worth about $4 billion, involves Miami.[34] As much as 15 percent of the $2.7 billion deposited at the Federal Reserve branch in Miami may have come in cash from Colombian drug deals. Again, the popular press suggests, perhaps with a touch of irony and sarcasm, that Miami area bankers ask no questions and only ask that they be given sufficient advance notice of a major cash deposit so that they can have enough tellers on hand to count the money.

From the surface, Miami appears to be a city that has undergone a significant rebuilding process. New office complexes, apartment buildings, and condominium projects are sprouting up everywhere. More than ninety multi-national corporations have their Latin American headquarters in Miami, and more than forty foreign banks are located there. The city gives every impression of a cultural mix having taken place successfully. Yet the high unemployment rate among Miami's blacks, the Liberty City riots of 1980, a dramatic rise in the city's crime, the rates attributed to the new immigrants, the successful English only campaign, and the ever-present reality that much of the area's successful economic boom is linked to drug money, must cause us to wonder about the city's ability to deal with these challenges.

[32] Ibid.

[33] *The New York Times,* November 9, 1980, Sec. 1, p. 24.

[34] *The Wall Street Journal,* November 28, 1979, p. 1.

CONCLUSION

Latinos are part of the "new immigration" to America. As illustrated in this chapter, they are a varied group. They bring differences in background and tradition into the country, and they settle into diverse urban situations. Much the same could be said of other immigrant groups. The term, "minority," perhaps hides as much as it reveals. Each language and racial group not only differs from the others, but each also contains considerable diversity in education and class background. Political coalescence and mobilization thus will follow no predetermined pattern. Alignments among minorities and between majority and minority groups will depend upon political leadership, the particular features of given communities, and structural constraints of the larger system.

SUGGESTED READINGS

Anders, Evan. *Boss Rule in South Texas.* Austin: University of Texas Press, 1982.

Boswell, Thomas D. and James R. Curtis, *The Cuban-American Experience.* Totowa, New Jersey: Rowman and Allanheld, 1983.

Estrada, Leo Bardo F., et al. "Chicanos in the United States: A History of Exploitation and Resistance." *Daedalus* 110 (Spring 1981), 103-31.

Garcia, F. Chris, ed. *La Causa Politica: A Chicano Politics Reader.* Notre Dame, IN: University of Notre Dame Press, 1974.

Garcia F. Chris and Rudolph O. De La Garza. *The Chicano Experience: Three Perspectives.* North Scituate, MA: Duxbury Press, 1977.

Garcia, John A. "Self-Identity Among the Mexican-American Population." *Social Science Quarterly* 62 (March 1981), 88-98.

Grebler, Leo, Joan, W. Moore, and Ralph C. Guzman, *The Mexican-American People: The Nation's Second Largest Minority.* New York: Free Press, 1970.

Gutiérrez, Armando. "Hispanics and the Sunbelt." *Dissent* 27 (Fall 1980), 492-9.

Gutiérrez, Armando and Herbert Hirsch. "The Militant Challenge to the American Ethos: Chicanos and Mexican Americans." *Social Science Quarterly* 53 (March 1973), 830-45.

Jennings, James. *Puerto Rican Politics in New York City.* Washington: University Press of America, 1977.

Jennings, James and Monte Rivera, eds. *Puerto Rican Politics in Urban America.* Westport, CN: Greenwood Press, 1984.

Johnson, David R. et al. *The Politics of San Antonio.* Lincoln, Nebraska, University of Nebraska Press, 1983.

"The Mexican Origins Experience in the United States." Special issue of *Social Science Quarterly* (June 1984).

Romo, Ricardo. *East Los Angeles.* Austin: University of Texas Press, 1983.

San Miguel, Guadalupe, Jr. "Mexican American Organizations and the Changing Politics of School Desegregation in Texas, 1945 to 1980." *Social Science Quarterly* 63 (December 1982), 701-15.

Sekul, Joseph D. "Grass Roots Power in a Businessman's Town: An Analysis of the Political Methods of Communities Organized for Public Service." Prepared for presentation at the Annual Meeting of the Southwestern Political Science Association, San Antonio, Texas, March 18, 1982.

Sexton, Patricia Cayo. *Spanish Harlem.* New York: Harper & Row, 1965.

West, Stanley A. and June Macklin, eds. *The Chicano Experience.* Boulder, CO: Westview Press, 1979.

chapter 4

Intergovernmental Influences

Local governments in the United States enjoy a great deal of autonomy, but they are, in some ways, weak units of government. Because local governments are legal creations of the states, they are dependent on the states for taxing and other powers. Partly because of this dependency, many local governments are in a perpetual financial squeeze. Struggling to make do with their limited powers to raise revenue, they have a strong incentive to compete with one another for revenue sources and other economic advantages. This reality helps to explain another important fact: metropolitan areas are fragmented governmentally—that is, metropolitan areas are governed by no single entity but by many entities legally independent of one another.

What is the fit among the layers of government? The national government can give financial help to the states and local governments. And the national government uses this power of the purse to induce both state and local governments to act in some ways and not act in other ways. These federal carrots are a significant part of the intergovernmental system in the United States.

In an earlier chapter, we argued that a number of forces work against the formulation of an explicit national policy of urban growth and development. But the leverage of the national government is great in carrying out other federal policies—tax, transportation, and energy policies, to name but a few that have an enormous impact on urban growth and development.

The question of whether the national government should give financial aid has long been answered affirmatively. Ever since the New Deal, the issues have been how much aid and with what conditions. However, the future is uncertain. After a long period of increasing financial assistance, the Reagan administration has reversed that trend. The Reagan record on federal requirements is mixed. Some have been eased, but others—especially regulations and requirements relating to the social agenda of the New Right—have been increased. The intergovernmental relations picture is thus an extraordinarily complicated one.

This chapter explores three interlocking relationships:

1. Metropolitan fragmentation, including the problem of fiscal disparities
2. State and local relationships
3. Federal-local relations: governmental aspects

METROPOLITAN FRAGMENTATION

The metropolitan problem is often presented as a problem of "too many governments," and it is easy to wheel in the figures to support that thesis. There are over 25,000 local governments in our Standard Metropolitan Statistical Areas (SMSAs). The crux of the metropolitan problem is not, however, simply the number of governments. Rather it is that some policy problems cannot be worked out within the confines of local jurisdictions and could not be, even if these jurisdictions were reduced in number. There are four dimensions to the metropolitan problem, according to political scientist Robert L. Lineberry: externalities, political non-responsibility, a lack of coordination, and fiscal and service inequalities.[1]

Externalities. Policy that one municipality undertakes often affects other parts of the metropolitan region that have no say in setting that policy. Economists call these consequences *externalities* or *spillover effects.* Policies on land use and zoning or air and water pollution are pertinent examples.

Political nonresponsibility. In many metropolitan areas, there are multiple lines of political responsibility. The citizen is confronted with an array of local governments. In some cases, the citizen does not know which government is responsible for what. Some of the distinctions are quite technical. For example, one study in Oakland, California, showed that even in a

[1] Robert L. Lineberry, "Reforming Metropolitan Governance: Requiem or Reality?" *Georgetown Law Journal* 58 (March-May 1970), 675-718.

group of citizen leaders there was widespread confusion about Oakland's sewer service charge and how it differed from that of the East Bay Municipal Utility District.[2] If these citizen leaders, who were generally well-informed on tax matters, fail to understand tax policy because of the multiplicity of local jurisdictions, where does this leave the average citizen?

Closely related is the question of administrative accountability. Many of the special authorities created to handle problems of various scale are not administered by elected officials who must face citizen review at the polls. Thus, the appointed administrators of these public authorities are sometimes beyond public control. The classic example is New York's Robert Moses, who controlled highways, parks, bridges and tunnels, and housing and urban renewal. Although his administrtive empire was eventually dismantled, for many years he was beyond effective citizen control.

Lack of coordination. The coordination between different jurisdictions that is needed for high quality service is often hard to come by. Law enforcement is an example of an activity that may require coordination. Criminals can work freely and easily throughout a metropolitan area unless there is inter-jurisdictional cooperation and coordination. Smaller police departments may have no crime labs, perhaps even no investigative forces. To be effective, they must undertake joint efforts or they must work with larger departments.

Fiscal and service inequalities. While central cities have been losing both middle-class residents and revenue-producing business and industry, they have been getting and keeping a heavy proportion of the poor and elderly population. Since these are the very people who are most in need of government services, the two-way money squeeze has been devastating. Similar problems confront some of the older suburbs. But many newer suburbs are on the receiving end of the outflow of affluent taxpayers and businesses, and they are not experiencing a severe revenue shortage. As a result, the per capita expenditures on service vary strongly from jurisdiction to jurisdiction. The public school tax picture illustrates the disparities best. In a given metropolitan area, the property tax value behind each school-age child may be six times greater in the wealthiest school district than in the poorest.

Metropolitan Reform

Not everyone believes that metropolitan fragmentation is a serious problem. Public choice theorists argue that multiple, overlapping jurisdictions are more responsive and efficient than metropolitan area-wide gov-

[2] Arnold J. Meltsner, *The Politics of City Revenue* (Berkeley: University of California Press, 1971), pp. 193-94.

ernment would be. Multiple jurisdictions are "closer to the people," and the citizens like their small-scale police departments, schools, and the like. According to the public choice theorists, consumers of urban public services can "vote with their feet," as they select jurisdictions with service packages most agreeable to their preferences.

The traditional view in public administration is that metropolitan reform is necessary to deal with the problem of fragmentation. As stated above, fragmentation brings externalities. Business groups, such as the Committee for Economic Development (CED), are often strong supporters of metropolitan reform.

There is no shortage of proposals for reform, and some have been put to the test of actual use. *Annexation*, the extension of a city's limits to bring more area into the municipality, is one of the oldest approaches. In recent decades, many cities in the South and West—where state law has been less rigid on this score—have augmented their tax bases through annexation. In contrast, many of the large, older northern cities are completely surrounded by incorporated municipalities. Thus this option is no longer available to them.

Another common way of dealing with the metropolitan problem is through the *contracting of services*. Smaller communities buy basic, minimal services from a larger community (city or county). These services include such major urban services as police, fire, and water. Sometimes, we make reference to the "Lakewood Plan," because Lakewood, California, was one of the first cities to adopt this approach. Lakewood, a community in Los Angeles County, contracted with Los Angeles County for a package of services.[3]

Special districts are the most numerous of the many governmental types found in SMSAs. Most special districts were established to perform a single-function or provide a single service, such as fire protection. Special districts have increased greatly in recent decades. Probably the main reason for their proliferation is that they raise money for needed services, with low visibility.

Some special districts operate at the metropolitan area level. The Port Authority of New York and New Jersey is the most famous example. The Port Authority runs airports, bridges, transportation facilities, the World Trade Center, and has its own police force. The authority was established by interstate compact in 1921 to deal with commercial and transportation facilities in the New York Metropolitan area.[4]

[3] The best discussion of the Lakewood Plan is Gary Miller, *Cities by Contract: The Politics of Municipal Incorporation* (Cambridge, Mass: MIT Press, 1981).

[4] On the Port Authority, see Annmarie Hauck Walsh, *The Public's Business: The Politics and Practices of Government Corporations* (Cambridge, Mass: MIT Press, 1978), pp. 89-103, 172-183, 224-227.

Many metropolitan areas have organizations called *councils of government.* Briefly, a council of governments is a voluntary association of cities and counties in a metropolitan area that gets together to coordinate activity on regional problems. Councils of government grew greatly during the 1960's, because of the availability of federal-planning monies. These organizations have been useful in getting people together and in reviewing grants. However, the lack of power and the overrepresentation of suburban jurisdictions prevents COGs from being a really effective force on social access questions. The Twin Cities Metropolitan Council, in the Minneapolis-St. Paul metropolitan area, is a metropolitan planning and policymaking agency, which was created by the Minnesota legislature in 1967. It has substantial power in metropolitan planning. With members representing council districts in the Metropolitan area, the Twin Cities body avoids the "one-government, one-vote" problem which plagues COG's.

City-county consolidation, a more comprehensive approach, usually involves the merger of a county government with the principal city (or all cities) within its borders. Nashville-Davidson County (Tennessee), Jacksonville-Duval County (Florida), and Indianapolis-Marion County (Indiana) with its "Unigov" are examples of city-county consolidations that have been effected in the last twenty five years.

Other broader approaches are found in the structures for metropolitan service provision in Portland, Oregon and Miami, Florida. Portland established a metropolitan service district in 1978. This was the most significant metropolitan government reform voted during the decade of the 1970s. Portland's multi-service district possesses metropolitan planning powers, and also provides such services as sewage treatment, liquid and solid waste disposal, public transit, the zoo, drainage and flood control. Miami-Dade county's comprehensive urban county plan started in 1957. The county government provides such areawide services as mass transit and public health. Local municipalities control such traditional "grassroots" functions as education and zoning. Whatever the problems of the Miami area, most observers feel that the highly professionalized county government has been an asset as the metropolitan area grew in the last twenty five years.[5]

The most wide-reaching metropolitan governments are found outside the United States. Toronto, Canada has a federated plan, which is widely admired by would-be American reformers. Toronto has a Metro council, which includes representatives of suburban jurisdictions, and the City of Toronto. Only public transportation is administered wholly by Metro. Many government programs have shared administrative respon-

[5] Raymond A. Mohl, "Miami" in *Sunbelt Cities: Politics and Growth Since World War II* (University of Texas Press, 1983).

sibilities, while such basic functions as police and fire remain at the municipal level.[6] The London system of government, created in 1965, is also admired by American metropolitan reformers. It is a two-tier system with the Greater London Council (GLC) as an area wide body with elected councillors, and strong powers in fire, in planning and transportation. At the same time, London has thirty-two boroughs which are in charge of such basic functions as refuse collection, sewers, and education (in twenty boroughs in the outer city).[7]

Despite the strong interest in metropolitan reorganization, there is no hard evidence to demonstrate that city-county consolidations and more comprehensive arrangements are more efficient than the usual fragmented metropolis. Are externalities *really* less of a problem with metropolitan governments? Are consolidated governments *really* more responsible? Are services *really* better coordinated with comprehensive arrangement? There is no firm evidence to answer each question.

In recent years, a strong decentralizing trend has been manifest in theory and practice. Many of the powers of the Greater London Council have been ceded to the boroughs, or taken away. The powers of the higher tier have been so eroded that knowledgeable observers ask, "Who, today, would mourn its [the GLC's] passing?"[8] At present, the Thatcher government is attempting to abolish GLC, and place all London administration in the hands of the boroughs. In the United States, empirical investigations of service delivery by public-choice theorists find higher citizen satisfaction and lower (or no higher) costs in a decentralized system. Decentralization, in many ways, seems to be the current policy in Washington. President Reagan speaks of "the right of the citizen to vote with his feet . . . If the state is badly managed the people will either do one of two things: they will either use their power at the polls to redress that or they'll go someplace else."[9] The weakness of the president's and public-choice theorists' argument is the equity issue. Not all citizens have the money to live where they would choose.

In all fairness, however, it is even possible that fiscal and service inequities might be worsened and magnified in a metropolitan-government arrangement. A metropolitan government has a bigger tax base, but still it may respond more to the majority (the middle-class citizens) and their concerns than to the minority (the poor, central-city citizens). Indeed, stud-

[6] Harold Kaplan, *Urban Political Systems: A Functional Analysis of Metro Toronto* (New York: Columbia University Press, 1967), pp. 50-53.

[7] Donald Foley, *Governing the London Region: Reorganization and Planning in the 1960's* (Berkeley: University of California Press, 1972), pp. 28-43. For additional information, see Joseph Zimmerman, "Substate Regional Government: Devising a New Procedure," *National Civic Review*, 61 (June 1972), 290.

[8] Max Hastings, "Fire alarm for the GLC: But Who Will Listen?" *The Standard* (London), February 18, 1982, p. 7.

[9] Interview, *New York Times*, November 22, 1981, p. 14.

ies of metropolitan governments indicate that they are very good at building public works, but they are not nearly so successful in dealing with social problems. Many black leaders oppose efforts to expand central city boundaries on just such grounds. They fear that blacks might lose the access they have so recently attained in city halls. The combination of central-city blacks (who fear a loss of political power) and white suburban officials (who fear higher taxes, as well as a loss of political power) has been enough to defeat most attempts to expand central-city boundaries in recent years. Yet, because many older localities face a declining economic base, black political gains in the cities could turn into a hollow prize.

Finally, it is noteworthy that citizens tend to move beyond the boundaries of consolidated areas into outlying exurban jurisdictions. In the 1970s merged Indianapolis-Marion County lost 28,000 people, while surrounding counties gained 83,000. Jacksonville-Duval County grew only slightly (8 percent or approximately 42,000 people) in the 1970-1980 decade. The county actually *lost* population in the last years of the decade—hardly a typical pattern for a reasonably prosperous sunbelt community. In the meantime, the four small outlying counties in the metropolitan area (Baker, Clay, Nassau and St. John's) had growth rates of 60-109 percent from 1970 to 1980. People want to avoid the problems and the taxes of metropolitan areas. It is fair to say that we are not likely to see many adoptions of comprehensive metropolitan arrangements in the years ahead.

State-Local Governmental Relations

In a governmental sense, American cities are greatly constrained in their ability to act by the fact that they are legal creatures of their state governments. This relationship is called "Dillon's Rule," after Judge Dillon, an Iowa judge who handed down the classic decision setting the limited legal powers of municipalities in 1858. In brief, in the United States, cities may not act except in areas where they have been expressly authorized to act by their state governments. Dillon asserted that municipalities were created by state legislatures, and owed their powers and existence to the legislatures. His decision stands as valid law today. Indeed, the powers of states over city governments are so great, that unless some specific state constitutional provision forbids it, states could abolish all the municipalities within their boundaries.

In the next chapter, we will discuss the complicated issue of state-local fiscal relations. For our purposes here, we need to emphasize that cities are limited in their geographic area, and governmental activities by state law. A state may force a city to provide a service. State law sets out, for example, what percentage of educational and welfare expenditure cities must provide. Varying amounts from state to state create greater or lesser burdens for city governments. New York State, for example, has mandated large welfare expenditures in New York City, thus aggravating greatly the fiscal stress of the city.

Often, cities must petition their state governments when they want to do something. In addition to the state legislature, city governments must often win the approval of the electorate in a statewide referendum. One of the authors has voted, in three different states (in different statewide elections) *on* whether a city could raise its level of bonded indebtedness, on whether a city could undertake an urban renewal project, and on whether a city could build a high school football stadium. In a similar vein, the cities are greatly limited by state law in changing metropolitan boundaries. We saw in an earlier section, that some states (Indiana, Minnesota) facilitated metropolitan reform. It is more usual for state law to make metropolitan reform difficult by requiring a positive vote of all affected legislative delegations, or even by requiring a statewide referendum.

For many years, there has been a movement toward increasing the powers of city governments, and away from Dillon's rule. The *home rule movement*, in many states, gives cities the ability to draw their own charters and to organize their governmental structure without obtaining the permission of the state legislature.

Federal-Local Relations

Federal grant-in-aid programs expanded tremendously in the years 1960-1980. In the next chapter, we will discuss the financial growth of federal programs and the impact on city governments. Here, we are concerned with the governmental impacts of federal grants.

Much controversy in federal-local relations centers around the issue of federal regulations and federal mandates. There is much more regulation in the intergovernmental system than occurred in earlier periods of American history. Federal programs frequently impose cross-cutting or generally applicable requirements on all grants. These general requirements further national-social-and-economic policies. They include nondiscrimination provisions on the basis of race, physical handicap, age, and sex (in the case of education programs). Cross-cutting requirements also include environmental regulations, such as the need to provide environmental impact statements in federal grant programs. In some instances, federal programs directly order local governments to undertake activities, with the threat of civil or criminal penalties. For example, job discrimination in state and local governments on the basis of race, sex, color, religion, and natural origin is expressly prohibited by national legislation, and in order to correct past discrimination, jurisdictions may be ordered to undertake programs of affirmative action. Usually, the federal government does not expressly order things. It is more typical for the federal government to withhold money. For example, it can withhold 10 percent of a state's highway construction funds if it does not comply with federal billboard control requirements. Finally, the federal government lets states and localities administer certain programs, provided that they meet certain nationally determined standards. This is the case in environmental areas, such as water and air pollution.[10]

Mayors and other local officials have been highly critical of federal and state mandates. Mayor Ed Koch of New York City estimated that federal and state mandates would cost the city $6.25 billion in expense-budget dollars, $711 milllion in capital expenditures, and $1.66 billion in lost revenue in the years 1980-1984. Koch spoke of "the mandate millstone" hung around the neck of the nation's cities.[11] In addition to cost, mayors are often unhappy about the inflexibility of federal mandates. Federal mandates have also been criticized for their inconsistency. Finally local officials resent the intrusiveness of federal grants. Local officials are told not just *what* to do, but *how* they have to do it. Donald Kettl cites the example of the local official in Richmond, Virginia, who changed his filing system three times to satisfy the obscure and petty requirements of federal monitors.[12] Many issues, however, are not petty. The issue of how to balance the urban governments' desire for autonomy with national standards in civil rights is a major policy question.

In addition to increased regulation, city governments have created new bureaucracies to reflect federal program changes. Kettl speaks of the "fourth face of Federalism,"[13] a phrase he coined to describe city agencies which supervise the activities of non-city agencies (neighborhood groups, non-profit organizations) who deliver services with federal funds. In this situation, urban governments act as a conduit and as a monitor. Such administrative developments were frequent with programs like Community Development Block Grants (CDBG) and Comprehensive Employment and Training Act (CETA). Whether these bureaucracies will remain permanently on the urban scene is an interesting question, because CETA, CDBG, and other programs of this type have been cut back heavily in the Reagan administration's budgets.

As grants to urban areas increased, sentiment developed within the federal government for a metropolitan area wide review process to examine the implications of federal grants throughout a metropolitan area.

[10] This discussion is based on David R. Beam, "Washington's Regulation of States and Localities: Origins and Issues," *Intergovernmental Perspective* 7 (Summer 1981), 8-18. For a more detailed discussion, see the U.S. Advisory Commission on Intergovernmental Relations report, *The Federal Role in the Federal System: The Dynamics of Growth*, publication A-77, 1980.

[11] Edward I. Koch, "The Mandate Millstone," *The Public Interest*, No. 61 (Fall 1980), 42.

[12] Donald F. Kettl, "The Fourth Face of Federalism," *Public Administration Review* 41 (May-June 1981), 368.

[13] Ibid, 366-371.

Since the procedures were set forth in Office of Management and Budget Circular A-95, this process was called A-95 review. Most commonly, A-95 reviews were conducted by councils of governments. Councils of government had serious limitations as review agencies. They had no power to enforce their decisions. If a COG, for example, rejected a proposal to build a new hospital in a metropolitan area, the relevant federal agency could simply go ahead and fund the proposal, anyway. Much review comment was at best, uneven, and at worst, sketchy, trivial, and ill-informed.[14] Significantly, the Reagan administration ordered the elimination of A-95 review, with the states now having the responsibility for developing review procedures. Most states, however, adopted new processes which closely resembled the old A-95 review process.

It is obvious that there is a great deal of uncertainty for urban governments in their relations with the national government. One implication of this uncertainty is that urban governments must be skilled in bargaining and negotiating with the national government. Obviously, the federal government has the power of the purse, and other coercive powers at its command. Federal bureaucrats will typically use coercive powers only as a last resort. On the other side, urban governments can mobilize their representatives in Congress, and can generate other group pressures from the local level.[15]

CONCLUSION

The question of the relationship between levels of government is more than a theoretical issue of centralization versus decentralization. As we shall see in the next chapter, the economic competition among states and localities encourages them to rely on more regressive forms of taxation. To shift program responsibilities to those levels is thus to rely on less progressive forms of raising revenue. There are other considerations as well. Some states and localities have long histories of inattention to (or even hostility toward) minority rights. Constraining the national role in civil rights means a contraction in civil rights efforts.

There are partisan and ideological differences over the roles of various levels of government. Since the New Deal, conservatives have generally opposed a more active national government. But much depends on who controls the White House and whose interests are affected. The Reagan administration, for example, came into office with a promise to shrink the

[14] See the paper by Irene Fraser Rothenberg, "Regional Planning Commissions, A-95, and the Changing Intergovernmental Grant System." (presented to the 1982 Annual Meeting of the American Political Science Association, Denver, Colorado, Sept. 2-5, 1982).

[15] See Donald B. Rosenthal, "Bargaining Analysis in Intergovernmental Relations," *Publius* (Summer 1980), 5-44.

role of the national government and decrease regulation. Yet, in pursuit of a New Right social agenda, the Reagan administration has promulgated extensive federal regulations to make birth control assistance less available to unmarried teenagers ("the squeal rule"), to curtail abortions, and to monitor the medical care of severely handicapped infants ("the Baby Doe rule").

Liberals, on the other hand, generally oppose such regulations but support strong and comprehensive environmental controls to combat air and water pollution. Yet, even within the environmental area, there are inconsistencies on the matter of centralization versus decentralization. For example, on the issue of locating atomic power plants, liberals tend to favor a strong local voice. Clearly much of the debate is not over the abstract principle of centralization/decentralization, but over who will be regulated and for what purpose. Conservatives and liberals differ issue by issue. Generally liberals favor extensive regulation of business interests for purposes such as environmental and consumer protection; conservatives oppose such regulations. On the other hand, conservatives are more inclined to favor government regulations in such areas as personal and sexual morality. There are other differences as well. The Reagan administration, for example, has increased restrictions within the policy area of social welfare, but has moved to free community development from targeting requirements that block grant funds be spent largely on low and moderate income areas. Liberal Democrats in Congress have taken the opposite position on both sets of issues. Willingness to employ federal regulatory power in local communities is thus very much a partisan matter, with positions shifting in accordance with the purpose and target of the regulatory effort.

SUGGESTED READINGS

ANTON, THOMAS J., *Federal Aid to Detroit*. Washington, D.C.: Brookings Institution, 1983.

ASHFORD, DOUGLAS J., ed. *National Resources and Urban Policy*. New York: Methuen, 1980.

BULLOCK, CHARLES III and CHARLES M. LAMB, *Implementation of Civil Rights Policy*. Monterey, Ca: Brooks/Cole, 1984.

DANIELSON, MICHAEL N. and JAMESON W. DOIG, *New York: The Politics of Urban Regional Development*. Berkeley: University of California Press, 1982.

DAVID, STEPHEN and PAUL KANTER, "Urban Policy in the Federal System: A Reconceptualizaton of Federalism," *Polity*, 16 (Winter 1983), 284-303.

FENSTERMAN, JERRY. "Antitrust and Local Governments." *Intergovernmental Perspective* 9 (Fall 1983), 7-16.

GLASSBERG, ANDREW D. *Representation and Urban Community*. London: Macmillan, 1981.

GLENDENING, PARIS N. and MAVIS MANN REEVES, *Pragmatic Federalism*, 2nd ed. Pacific Palisades, Ca: Palisades, 1984.

HAWKINS, ROBERT B. ed. *American Federalism: A New Partnership for the Republic*. San Francisco, Institute for Contemporary Studies, 1982.

HOWITT, ARNOLD M. *Managing Federalism: Studies in Intergovernmental Relations*. Washington, D.C.: Congressional Quarterly Press, 1984.

LOVELL, CATHERINE. "Evolving Local Government Dependency." *Public Administration Review*, 41 (January 1981), 189-202.

MCKAY, DAVID H. "Theory and Practice in Public Policy: The Case of the New Federalism." *Political Studies* (forthcoming June 1985).

MACMANUS, SUSAN A. *Federal Aid to Houston*. Washington, D.C.: Brookings Institution, 1983.

MOLLENKOPF, JOHN H. *The Contested City*. Princeton, N.J.: Princeton University Press, 1983.

PETERSON, PAUL E. *City Limits*. Chicago: University of Chicago Press, 1981.

SHAPEK, RAYMOND A. *Managing Federalism: Evolution and Development of the Grant-in-Aid System*. Charlottesville, Va: Community Collaborators Prcss, 1981.

U.S. ADVISORY COMMISSION ON INTERGOVERNMENTAL RELATIONS. *The Federal Role in the Federal System: The Dynamics of Growth*, 11 vols. Washington, D.C.: Government Printing Office, 1980.

WALKER, DAVID B. *Toward A Functioning Federalism*. Cambridge, Mass: Winthrop, 1981.

WRIGHT, DEIL S. *Understanding Intergovernmental Relations: Public Policy and Participants' Perspectives in Local, State and National Governments*, 2nd ed. North Scituate, Mass: Duxbury Press, 1982.

ZIMMERMAN, JOSEPH F. *State-Local Relations: A Partnership Approach*. New York: Praeger, 1983.

chapter 5

Fiscal Influences

THE FINANCIAL SQUEEZE ON LOCAL GOVERNMENTS

The fiscal crisis at the local level is not new. Everyone is familiar with the financial plight of New York and other older large industrial cities. Various other localities, including small and medium-sized communities have struggled for years to meet their budgets. Oakland, California, is a good example. The Oakland study of local revenue politics, mentioned earlier, is one of the most thorough ever done. Oakland falls in the 250,000-500,000 population range, and is reasonably typical of this size category. Its monetary resources have grown slowly, while the city's social and economic problems have grown rapidly: high unemployment, high median age of population, loss of population, high density, low education level, and a large poverty population.

Oakland, which has been quite conservative fiscally, has maintained an excellent bond rating because of its pay-as-you-go policy. In contrast, New York City has serious financial problems that stem in part from its attempts to respond to the needs of a wide segment of its population. Oakland's budget keeps expanding not because of expanded services to the poverty population but because of rising operating costs. Indeed, the Oakland study indicates that it would take an 8 percent growth in expenditures every year just to hold the line on services.[1] At the same time, cities, like Oakland, with older populations and older dwelling units have trouble keeping up with rising costs. Property taxes are especially vulnerable to taxpayer resistance. Property taxes are highly visible and affect something very central to family security and status—home ownership.

A study by the Advisory Commission on Intergovernmental Relations (ACIR) found that financial pressures generated by economic conditions in the nation at large have the most acute effect in big cities.[2] The ACIR analysis noted the following:

1. Pressure for expansion of city services—the public expects more and better traditional services as well as services in new areas of governmental activity such as the environment.
2. Pressure of inflation—as noted in the Oakland experience, it takes more money to maintain the same level of services in an inflationary period. City services are labor intensive, with labor-related costs making up 70 to 80 percent of most city budgets.
3. Pressure of external forces—especially in labor relations. If private and federal employees get wage increases, city employees also expect a raise.
4. Pressures of metropolitan socioeconomic disparities—population and economic movements that have given many central cities the greatest share of the problems and given their suburbs a better tax base.

Twenty of the twenty-nine large cities studied by the ACIR had an annual percentage increase in general-fund expenditures that exceeded 10 percent, in the two most recent years compared.

Meanwhile, city governments have become more dependent on money from higher levels of government, while the property tax—the backbone of local revenue—has declined relatively as a source of money. There are three reasons for this relative decline: growth in the property-tax base does not keep pace with growth in expenditures; the public, which does not like the property tax, resists higher levies; and higher levels of government have increased their aid (though federal assistance is now being diminished).

The fiscal troubles of American cities are evidenced by the extent of city dependency on the federal government. This dependency grew substantially during the decade of the 1970s. One computation, made by the Advisory Commission on Intergovernmental Relations (ACIR), shows that the average of direct federal aid as a percent of own-source general revenue in fifteen large cities rose from 1.1 percent in 1957 to 5.2 percent in

[1] Arnold Meltsner, *The Politics of City Revenue* (Berkley: University of California Press, 1971), pp. 13-21.

[2] The discussion following is based on U.S. Advisory Commission on Intergovernmental Relations, *City Financial Emergencies* (Washington, D.C.: Government Printing Office, 1973).

1967, to 28.1 percent in 1976, and was estimated at 47.5 percent for 1978. By 1978, the figure was over 50 percent in St. Louis, Newark, Buffalo, Cleveland, Philadelphia, Detroit and Phoenix. Per capita federal aid rose from $95 in 1976 to $179 in 1978 (estimated).[3] The Reagan budgets have, however, brought about substantial cuts, particularly in funds targeted on older and larger cities.

The current local fiscal situation is bleak. One study for the congressional Joint Economic Committee found that more than 50 percent of the cities in its survey reported operating deficits in both 1979 and 1980. The committee saw three major trends concerning changes in revenue: "less federal aid, little growth in state aid and large increases in fees for such purposes as driving licenses, car registration, building permits and the like."[4] The Joint Economic Committee found municipalities increasingly turning to user fees for services previously provided for free. Coproduction or the use of volunteers has also grown.

In the 1970s, local governments turned to higher levels of government—federal and state—for financial assistance. Intergovernmental revenues, primarily from the federal and state governments, rose to about a fourth of municipal revenues. In a similar fashion, federal and state governments pay a greater part of public school expenditures than they did in the past. Today, more than half of public school revenue comes from nonlocal sources.

STATE GOVERNMENTS AND URBAN FISCAL PROBLEMS

The tax revolt and broader fiscal limitations movement have added a new dimension to the financial squeeze on local government. This movement was highlighted by California's approval of Proposition 13 in a statewide referendum in 1978, although other measures (such as Massachusetts' passage of Proposition 2½ in 1980) may be as important in their impacts.

Proposition 13 did four things. First, it limited property taxes to 1 percent of the market value of real property. Second, it established assessed values at the 1975-76 level, and limited increases to no more than 2 percent a year, with the exception of new construction or traded structures. Third, it allowed local governments to increase other taxes only with the approval of a two-thirds vote of the qualified electorate. Last, it required

[3] This information is taken from "Federal Initiatives and Impacts," *Intergovernmental Perspective* 4 (Winter 1978) p. 9.

[4] Joint Economic Committee, Congress of the United States, *Trends in the Fiscal Condition of Cities: 1979-81*, 97th Congress, 1st Session (Washington: U.S. Government Printing office, 1981), pp. 3-4.

that state tax increases be approved by a two-thirds vote of both houses of the state legislature.[5]

Massachusetts' proposition 2½ was even more broad-ranging, as it contained numerous changes in state and local finance. Among its important limitations were: (1) a reduction in the level of effective local tax rates to 2.5 percent of full market value; (2) a reduction in the state's annual automobile excise tax (a tax which generates much revenue for local governments) from $66 to $25 per thousand dollars value; (3) a repeal of local school committees fiscal autonomy, which previously included the ability to tax and spend independent of municipal governments; (4) elimination of binding arbitration in municipal collective bargaining; and (5) capping local budget increases at 2.5 percent per year.[6]

After tax revolts in California and Massachusetts, many states and even more localities have enacted some form of taxation or spending limitation since 1978. At the national level, there is a proposed constitutional amendment which would require a balanced national budget. According to one study, during the 1978 and 1979 legislature sessions, thirty-seven states reduced property taxes, twenty-eight states cut income taxes, and thirteen states restricted sales tax collections. Income and sales tax cuts exceeded $4 billion.[7] These limits drastically changed the fiscal situation of the states and localities. In 1978, these governments enjoyed a large ($7.9 billion) surplus of revenue over expenditures. By 1981, not only were cities hard-pressed, but the fiscal condition of the states also deteriorated. A 1981 study by the National Governors Association found that thirty states expected to spend more money on operations than they would take in as revenue.[8]

Scholars and journalists have advanced a number of explanations for the recent tax revolt. Morgan's study of the vote on Proposition 2½ in Massachusetts found that the only measures which consistently correlated with support for the proposition (in every case) were local tax effort, and 1981 equalized school tax rate. In short, the vote for 2½ was significantly higher when local school tax rates and tax efforts were higher, and when the local population tended to be made up of homeowners.[9] Kuttner suggests that support for Proposition 13 stemmed from conditions unique to

[5] William K. Tabb, *The Long Default: New York City and the Urban Fiscal Crisis* (New York: Monthly Review Press, 1982), p. 114.

[6] Edward P. Morgan, "Public Preferences and Policy Realities: Proposition 2½ in Massachusetts," (paper presented to the Northeastern Political Science Association Meeting, Newark, New Jersey, November, 1981), p. 3-4.

[7] Alvin Rabushka and Pauline Ryan, *The Tax Revolt* (Stanford, California: Hoover Institution, 1982), p. 1.

[8] Robert Pear, "Study Finds Fiscal Conditions of States is Deteriorating," *The New York Times* (October 11, 1981), p. 18.

[9] Morgan, "Public Preferences and Policy Realities," p. 20.

California at the time, especially the rapid escalation of residential property values and taxes, and the existence of a large state surplus which permitted local tax reductions without a loss in service quality in the short run.[10] Indeed, one of the consistent findings about taxpayer sentiment is the great extent to which people believe that taxes can be cut without a serious reduction in services. A national poll by Gallup, taken at the time that Proposition 13 passed in California, found that 42 percent of those surveyed believed that taxes could be cut at least 20 percent without a serious reduction in services. Only 9 percent believed that taxes could be cut "none or hardly any" without such service reductions.[11]

While various studies of taxpayer sentiment yield no conclusive results, some findings do recur. Higher-income, property-owning, and nonminority respondents tend to oppose taxes most strenuously. Similarly, those who espouse a conservative ideology and who are unsympathetic toward racial and language minorities score high on anti-tax sentiment.

Attitudes toward taxation seem to be quite volatile. There is a wide base of anti-tax, anti-government sentiment that can be mobilized, especially if people can be convinced of government waste and inefficiency. Sentiment also varies according to the purpose for which tax monies will be spent. In every survey, welfare is the overwhelming favorite as a target for program cuts. By contrast, majorities never favor cuts in police and fire protection, and they look kindly on expenditures for such tangible facilities as highways and road repair. For example, in California at the time of Proposition 13, only 4 percent favored cuts in police service, if service cuts were to be required. The figure rose to 12 percent for street repair, 13 percent for schools, and 31 percent for parks and recreation. For welfare, the figure reached 59 percent. Differences in income groups also vary by program area. Affluent and nonaffluent differ sharply over willingness to spend for welfare services, but in areas such as education and environmental services, income differences disappear.[12]

Attitudes also vary with the type of tax. Sales taxes are generally regarded as most fair, even though in reality the incidence of a sales tax falls most heavily on those with less income. The sales tax is a low visibility tax, paid in small increments incidental to purchasing goods. The tax has an appearance of fairness because everyone pays at the same rate. But, of course, those who must spend all that they have pay a larger portion of their income than do those who can afford to save and invest. The sales tax is thus regressive with regard to the ability to pay. Higher income people are especially likely to favor the sales tax, which is regressive, over the

[10] Robert Kuttner, *The Revolt of the Haves* (New York: Simon and Schuster, 1980).

[11] *Newsweek*, June 19, 1978.

[12] Terry N. Clark and Lorna C. Ferguson, *City Money* (New York: Columbia University Press, 1983), p. 179.

income tax, which is generally progressive with regard to the ability to pay. There is some dispute about the incidence of the property tax, but two-thirds of the cut from California's Proposition 13 went to business. Similar findings have come out of the experience of Prince George's County, Maryland, with its referendum-adopted measure to limit the property tax.[13] Whatever the incidence, the main weakness of the property tax as a revenue source is its high visibility. It is paid in a lump sum rather than being spread over a myriad of consumer transactions.

The vote on Proposition 13 in California is now political history, but its consequences are still being felt. Its impacts were substantial: property taxes were cut, future revenue-raising was constrained, and local governments were made more dependent on the state.[14] Of course, the state of California has by no means covered all of the local revenue lost from Proposition 13. While the evidence is less than systematic, findings point toward substantial service cuts. In 1983, five years after the adoption of Proposition 13, the *Los Angeles Times* did a survey of its impact and found widespread cuts in expenditures and services as well as a turn toward increased reliance on user fees.[15] Reporters found that 70 percent of California's cities and counties have reduced or eliminated public works services, such as street cleaning; 60 percent have deferred street repair or maintenance. The Oakland public service department, for example, has shrunk its work force from 600 to 380. Its budget has gone down by 46 percent, and the city estimates that it can afford to resurface its streets only once every two hundred years. The Los Angeles Flood Control District, to take a sporadically salient service area, has cut its capital expenditures in half and its work force by a third.

Libraries have also experienced service reductions. Staffing is down 10 percent, and hours open to the public have decreased, on the average, by 20 percent. All indicators of patron service are down. Circulation has decreased, as have reference questions answered. Book acquisitions continue, but at a declining level. The Riverside library, for example, went from 47,000 acquisitions in 1978 to 32,000 in 1982—a drop of nearly a third.

Not all expenditures have decreased. Police expenditures are up, but this is partly to cope with the increased number of street people brought about by the deinstitutionalization of the mentally ill.

Some service budgets have come to rely increasingly on user fees. The *Los Angeles Times* survey found that 63 percent of California's cities and counties had imposed new fees, and 74 percent had raised previous fees. In

[13] *Washington Post*, August 16, 1983.

[14] John J. Kirlin, *The Political Economy of Fiscal Limits*, (Lexington, MA: Lexington Books, 1982), p. 53.

[15] *Los Angeles Times*, June 17 and 18, 1983.

recreation, for example, over half of the local governments had imposed new fees, and most of them had increased existing fees. In the city of Hayward, for example, in 1978 user fees were 9 percent of the park and recreation budget. By 1983, fees had risen to 20 percent of the budget.

Even with increased reliance on user fees, park and recreation services have declined. Per capita expenditures on urban parks shrank by 17 percent between 1978 and 1983. Maintenance service has been reduced in over half the parks, and in Los Angeles twenty-four small recreation centers have been closed. At the large centers, hours have been cut by nearly 40 percent.

While fees add to budgets, they make programs less available. Indirectly, cuts have a class character. For example, Northbridge—a middle class community—has raised $100,000 in private funds to restore programs; but at the Harvard recreation center in a poor South Central District, only a quarter of that amount was raised through private donations. In one city, swimming-class fees have tripled, making lessons less available to the nonaffluent.

A *Washington Post* special on San Jose, California, reported cuts in almost every service area.[16] The mayor said, "We fought the guns-and-butter issue . . . and the guns won." The number of police has increased, but parole supervision and institutionalization of the mentally ill have decreased. When expected state funds for education were not forthcoming, the school district declared bankruptcy and rolled back teachers' salaries to the level of two years earlier. The school day was shortened, supplies and bus transportation were cut, and school nurses and guidance counselors were eliminated. Elementary schools, in particular, experienced curriculum cutbacks as many music, science, and physical education teachers were let go. When asked how Proposition 13 was working out for the people of San Jose, 53 percent said unfavorably and only 34 percent said favorably.

Although increased state aid has cushioned some of the impact of Proposition 13, that circumstance changes the state-local relationship. Increased financial assistance from the state comes with strings attached. State controls appear to be on the increase, and with declining federal money local governments find themselves increasingly dependent on the state. The federal role, of course, continues to be important, and it is to that matter we now turn.

GRANT-IN-AID PROGRAMS

The federal government provides financial assistance to local governments through grant-in-aid programs. Grants-in-aid can be defined as payments of federal funds to a lower level of government for specified purposes,

[16] September 18, 1983.

usually with some supervision or review by the federal government. (State governments also give grants-in-aid.) Grants are of two types, categorical and block. Categorical grants are given for specific purposes—early childhood education, vocational education, or adult literacy classes, for example. Block grants are given for broadly defined purposes such as public school education.

Federal controls tend to be much more extensive with categorical grants than with block grants. Local governments might, for example, have to provide a local share of money to match a federal share; or they might have to submit detailed plans for federal approval. By contrast, block grants provide more flexibility of purpose and approach, and usually have no matching requirement. The local jurisdiction develops its own programs, sets its own priorities, and allocates money for various activities accordingly. In the case of a block grant for education, for instance, the school system would be the local jurisdiction.

In general, federal programs emphasized categorical grants from the New Deal years through the 1960s. The "New Federalism" of recent years has shifted the emphasis to block grants. Federal-city relations were institutionalized in those New Deal programs of the 1930s, and the notion of some federal responsibility for the plight of the cities also dates from this period. The United States Conference of Mayors (USCM), the major lobbying organization for big cities, was formed in 1932 because of the acute fiscal crisis in American cities.

The Kennedy and Johnson administrations of the 1960s greatly expanded the categorical-grant programs available to cities, and both administrations fought for the creation of a cabinet-level Department of Housing and Urban Development through which such categorical programs as urban renewal and water-and-sewer grants could be administered. (HUD was established in 1965.) An especially significant development, from the perspective of intergovernmental relations, was that many of the categorical-grant programs involved direct, federal-local relations, by-passing the states.

Role of the urban lobby. The federal-local approach was, in part, a response to the efforts of the "urban lobby" in Washington. This lobby was spearheaded by the USCM, an organization for cities with over 50,000 population, and the National League of Cities (NLC), which represents the interests of smaller cities. These organizations maintain a full-time staff in Washington, which interacts with federal agencies dealing with urban problems. The "urban lobby" operates a Man-in-Washington Service. A city can contract with this service for a full-time person to monitor federal action and to assist it in obtaining grants. The USCM and the NLC mobilize public opinion, and mayors testify before congressional committees on behalf of the "urban lobby." Meetings of the organizations serve as rallying points in the ongoing efforts by cities to get more federal funds.

Criticisms and problems. Criticisms of the federal grant-in-aid programs have been widespread, commonly citing fragmented administration, both federal and local, and duplication of effort. One example may suffice. In Albuquerque, New Mexico, the U.S. Department of Transportation (DOT) funded a computer routine for the metropolitan area's Council of Governments (COG) to do transportation surveys, which included a license check on outstanding motor vehicle violations. At the same time, the U.S. Law Enforcement Assistance Administration (LEAA) gave a grant to the local courts to develop a computerized system of warrants on outstanding traffic violations. Finally, LEAA also funded a computerized system for the Correction and Detention Department that reported the status of each outstanding police warrant. There was effort triplicated! Nor could the systems be coordinated, because different computer languages, formats, and consultants were used.[17]

FEDERAL REVENUE SHARING: A NEW CONCEPT

Modern federal revenue sharing was developed but never enacted in the Kennedy-Johnson years. The original plans were based on the assumption that federal income tax revenues would grow, and called for resulting budgetary surpluses to be returned to the states. Later revisions included cities as recipients of funds. To distinguish it from other forms of federal aid, this program is called *general* revenue sharing.

After years of public discussion, federal revenue sharing did become law as the Fiscal Assistance Act of 1972. The Nixon administration changed the pass-through provisions from cities to all local governments. The obvious political reasons for this change were that big-city mayors were mostly Democrats while suburban governments and counties were often controlled by Republicans. There were also Republican governors in thirty-one states when Nixon, a Republican, took office. Thus the Republicans favored formulas that benefited suburbs, counties, and states more than central cities. Even though they did not get the formula they wanted, Democrats in Congress went along because they wanted some aid for cities.

The 1972 revenue-sharing act included these features:

[17] Peter A. Lupsha, "New Freedom: Centralization and Local Control in Perspective," in *The New Urban Politics*, Masotti and Lineberry, p. 231.

1. The dollar amount for distribution was determined by a specific dollar appropriation instead of a percentage of the income tax base. Dependability of income to the states and localities was eroded by a five-year time limit in the bill.
2. Several extremely complex distribution formulas were established. A state got its share according to one of two formulas, whichever benefited the state more. One formula was based on population, general tax effort, and relative income. The other formula included these items, plus urbanized population and state income taxes. There were also formulas for determining the allocation of money to localities within a state.
3. The local-government share of the money was two-thirds. The state share was one-third.
4. While states were allowed to use the money as they wished, local governments were limited to public safety, environmental protection, public transportation, health, recreation, libraries, social services for the poor or aged, and financial administration. Welfare was specifically excluded.

What was the track record for those first five years? Virtually the only strings attached for local spending were the priority categories, revenue sharing having been sold partly on the understanding that communities would use the money to fund services similar to those funded previously by categorical grants. But that is not what happened.

Mistrusting the permanence of the program, local officials were much more attracted to one-shot projects than to the institution of services for which they might later have to dig up local monies. Instead of funding social services and health care, most local areas spent their money on street and road repairs and public safety; many used it to cut taxes or avoid a tax increase. A large percentage of all local revenue-sharing money went to new capital improvements.[18] Even after the program had been renewed, there was little apparent change in expenditure patterns. For 1981, public safety (police and fire) expenditures accounted for a reported 41 percent of funds, while health and social services accounted for only 4 percent.[19]

These actions have provoked both praise and blame. Some praise the cities' use of funds, saying that revenue-sharing money saved the day, allowing cities to deliver vital services that would otherwise have been squeezed by inflationary costs and other fiscal pressures. But critics of the revenue-sharing performance charge that the moment there was an easing of the pressures built into many categorical-aid programs designed to meet the needs of the poor and minorities, officials ignored social goals. Even the cities that wanted to spend for social services found their share of the pie smaller under the new system, because the pie has been portioned out to *all* localities, not just to those where the need was greatest.

[18] Richard P. Nathan, Allen D. Manvel, and Susannah, E. Calkins, *Monitoring Revenue Sharing* (Washington, D.C.: The Brookings Institution, 1975), pp. 198-206.

[19] David A. Caputo and Richard L. Cole, "City Officials and General Revenue Sharing," *Publius*, Vol. 13 (Winter 1983), p. 45.

The way that communities have spent their money has raised some doubt about a favorite American political myth—that "the closer to the people, the more responsive and responsible the government will be." Many local governments around the country used revenue sharing for frills. For example, some wealthy suburban communities used the money to build golf courses, or horseback-riding trails. Denver, Colorado, spent funds on movable stands for Mile Hi Stadium. Burlington, Vermont, spent $300,000 on uniforms for the municipal band and $160,000 on an ice rink and bathhouse. Aside from the frivolous, some localities spent money in an irresponsible fashion. After voters in Baton Rouge, Louisiana, had twice defeated bond referendums to build a coliseum, the city used its revenue-sharing money to build one. (It is fair to note that categorical-grant programs have also sometimes been wasteful.)

A telling criticism of revenue sharing points to the 1972 formula, claiming that it was unfair to central cities with the greatest need. Not only did relatively affluent jurisdictions get a piece of the pie, they got a disproportionate piece. While central cities received more money on a per capita basis than other areas, they fared badly when need entered the comparison. The most populous jurisdictions also received less assistance in relation to the revenue effort they made. In addition, it was argued that the population of central cities was undercounted by the Census Bureau, adversely affecting the population factor in the formula.

The civil rights provisions of revenue sharing were enforced limply, and studies have documented discrimination in employment and in service delivery funded by revenue sharing. For example, a federal investigation found hiring discrimination in the Chicago police department. And black residents of Ouachita Parish, Louisiana, charged that funds were used to repave roadways in white neighborhoods rather than to pave the dirt and gravel roads in black neighborhoods.

Finally, revenue sharing has been short on citizen involvement even though it was touted as a way to bring government closer to the people. Unlike other federal programs of the last decade, it had no citizen participation mechanism.

When Congress renewed revenue sharing in 1976, some changes reflected these criticisms, although some provisions remained the same:

1. The dollar amount was now tied to the level of federal income tax collections, as had been originally proposed. In theory, this means that as income tax collections rise, the dollars available for distribution will also rise. In practice, this provision had no immediate impact because Congress took away with the right hand what it gave with the left by imposing an annual ceiling of $6.85 billion per year.
2. Despite the widespread criticism of the allocation formulas, they were not changed.

3. Instead of increasing the pressure on local governments to spend in the specified categories, Congress eliminated the categories.
4. New provisions were designed to increase citizen participation in the program. Officials must now report on the actual use of revenue-sharing money, the relationship of shared revenues to the local budget, and proposed uses of the monies. Public hearings on proposed uses and on the local budget are required, with published advanced notice. After budget adoption, records must be available for public inspection. These changes constitute a kind of bare concern with citizen participation; no citizen participation procedures beyond public hearings have been added as requirements.
5. A number of changes toughened civil rights enforcement provisions.

An ongoing study of General Revenue Sharing by Caputo and Cole shows that GRS has achieved remarkable popularity among urban chief executives. Despite revisions in the program, GRS clearly remain one of the most, possibly *the most* popular program with these officials.[20] As part of the same study, citizen participation in GRS was examined; a mixed picture emerged. The public hearings which are held to discuss GRS can be useful, but they are not sufficient. Effectiveness wanes as "broader fiscal and social conditions constrain local decision makers and especially as interest levels of citizens, themselves, decline."[21] Both conclusions are important ones. The Reagan administration has proposed the end of GRS, but strong support from state and local officials has kept the program alive. If the program survives, states will be asked to provide their own guidelines for citizen participation.

The kind of revenue sharing discussed to this point is classed as *general* revenue sharing. Closely related is *special* revenue sharing, another name for block grants such as those established under the Community Development Block Grant program. Created by the Housing and Community Development Act of 1974, this program replaced categorical grants from the 1950s and 1960s. Like general revenue sharing, block grants give localities budget flexibility. And since local matching requirements have been eliminated, local priorities are not skewed by the grant game. The Reagan administration block grant consolidations of 1981 are essentially special revenue sharing.

DIMENSIONS OF FISCAL FEDERALISM

As the federal financial role decreases and battles are waged over requirements that federal monies be targeted on specific programs and clienteles, debate increases. Much of this debate is about the nature of the federal

[20] David A. Caputo and Richard L. Cole, "The Public Hearing as an Effective Citizen Participation Mechanism, *American Political Science Review* 78 (June 1984), 404-416.

[21] Richard L. Cole and David A. Caputo, "The Impact of Citizen Participation: A Case Study of the General Revenue Sharing Program" (paper prepared for delivery at the 1982 annual meeting of the American Political Science Association, Denver Hilton Hotel), p. 36.

system and the capabilities of states. If power is successfully devolved to the states and localities, there are significant implications. First, state and local government might prove more attractive for those with political ambition, as their powers are enhanced. Second, there will be more conflict at the state level. What does that imply?

If programs are turned back to the states, old concerns reemerge. The old arguments that the states are corrupt, racist, unprofessional, and reactionary (or, at least, not innovative) have again appeared.[22] Critics of state governments overlook the fact that the legislative and executive branches in the fifty states have thoroughly modernized in recent years.[23] The classic concerns about state government may miss the point in the 1980s. One key question may well be the administrative capacity of state governments to manage programs in areas where they have little (or no) bureaucracy, and limited expertise. For example, if you examine the nine new block grants created in 1981, it is certain that states are strong in educational and social services policy and administration. However, what are the states' capacities in health, community development, community services, and energy assistance?

An even more important question may be the biases of state government. These governments are more professional, to be sure, but in a conflict, will professional bureaucrats side with poor people, or with the business lobbies, which are traditionally strong in the state capitals? Will states help the cities, as their need increases? As we have seen, many older and needy cities are declining in population—and therefore in electoral power. How will states divide their assistance between the needs associated with growth and the needs associated with age and decline?

The issues are manifold. A larger role for states means a larger role for the level of government that depends most on sales taxes and regressive forms of revenue production. The high mobility of business investments inclines states to promote policies favored by business interests. What about the special tie between federal officials and community groups? We can speculate that at best there will be an uncertain and hazardous future for the many community action and nonprofit agencies which have served as quasi-public entities at the local level. These organizations dispense social services, largely with federal dollars. In considering their future, it is wise to remember that the federal government became involved in many of these policy areas because the states weren't doing much for the needy. The interplay of these fiscal influences will be demonstrated through two case studies—one of New York City, and the other of Jacksonville, Florida.

[22] See, for example, Greg Easterbrook, "50 Miniature Washingtons—the flaw in Reagan's New Federalism," *Washington Monthly* 13 (January 1982), p. 11.

[23] See David H. McKay, "Fiscal Federalism, Professionalism, and the Transformation of American State Government," *Public Administration* 60 (Spring 1982), 10-22.

CASE STUDIES IN FISCAL INFLUENCES

The New York City Budget Crisis

New York's battle with bankruptcy is now a familiar story: 40,000 workers laid off; a freeze on the city budget; a takeover of the management of the city's finances by the state government and the business community; emergency loans from the federal government; a 1976 state court ruling that the moratorium on the city's debt was unconstitutional; an economic recovery fueled by tourism in the late 1970s, and a limited return to the bond market in 1982; amidst the seeming recovery and prosperity, an ongoing fisal crisis, and poor economic conditions, especially in the city's outer boroughs. Above all, key actors in the process believed that the city must avoid bankruptcy, at all costs. To this point, the city has not defaulted.

In discussing the New York City situation, everyone has a favorite villain. New York politicans and political activists often blamed the federal government. Former Mayors Lindsay and Beame believed that the federal government should take over many of the city's expenses. New York Senator Daniel P. Moynihan argued that the city's economic ills are substantially the result of national government policies. Richard Morris, a New York political consultant, notes that the fifteen states of the Northeast sent to Washington $44 billion more in taxes than they got back in spending in a recent year. In contrast, "The fifteen states of the sunbelt get back from Washington $36 billion more in spending than they pay in *taxes*. [Emphasis in original.] Such a gap between the regions is the true cause of the urban fiscal and economic crisis."[24] In this view, it is federal government policy, especially the distribution of grants-in-aid and regional policy, which brought about the fiscal crisis of New York and other older industrial cities in the East and Midwest. Some students place the blame on macroeconomic factors, such as the recession of the 1970s, the general decline of manufacturing and the white flight to the suburbs in the 1950-1970 time span. Other observers disagree.[25] In this view, New Yorkers must not look to Washington for blame or solutions but must look at themselves.

New York City politicians themselves can be blamed. As revenues declined (relatively), New York politicians borrowed to cover current account deficits, rather than lay off workers or reduce services. Eventually, the city's short-term debt was astronomical. Moreover, city officials used a number of budgetary gimmicks in an attempt to paper over harsh realities. New York financial institutions and the municipal bond market forced some of the city's difficulties. The two major bond rating services first

[24] Richard S. Morris, *Bum Rap on America's Cities: The Real Causes of Urban Decay* (Englewood Cliffs, N.J.: Prentice-Hall, 1980).

[25] Ken Auletta, *The Streets Were Paved With Gold: The Decline of New York—An American Tragedy* (New York: Random House, 1979), p. 144.

downgraded, then belatedly restored, the city's "A" (good) rating. Why? It seems obvious that the two bond rating services used poor information in their assessments or were susceptible to political influence—or both. Lending institutions found the city to be a highly profitable customer and did not discourage borrowing. Perhaps the clearest statement of this viewpoint comes from Jack Newfield and Paul DuBrul, two longtime observers of New York City politics. They blame the fiscal crisis on New York's "permanent government," an elite group consisting of bankers, bond underwriters, members of public authorities, big insurance companies, political fund-raisers, publishers, law firms, builders, judges, backroom politicians, and some union leaders. The power of the "permanent government" is based on the control of money, property, the law-making process and institutions.[26]

Still other observers would argue that New York's internal problems stem from the stranglehold that New York's municipal employees have on the city. In detailing the causes of New York's fiscal crises, for example, Auletta cites the introduction of collective bargaining for municipal employee unions in 1958 as an early step towards the city's fiscal plight. Auletta also discusses the growth of pensions for municipal employees, such as retirement after twenty years work at half pay. The transit strike of 1966, immediately after Mayor Lindsay took office, set a pattern in which public employees broke state law without punishment and ultimately received very high settlements as a reward.[27] Auletta added that the policy of pay parity between firemen and police, and the city's concession of power to outside mediators, both contributed to ultimately costly settlements in labor disputes.[28] The municipal employee unions may have been unfairly singled out, however. Economist William Tabb points out that average city pensions and salaries were in line with other large cities.[29] Bellush and Bellush conclude that municipal unions paid a substantial price during the city's fiscal crisis: "cuts in salaries and fringe benefits and layoffs which shattered the historical sense of security for civil servants."[30]

Related to this argument is the fact that New York City overextended itself fiscally by providing a level of services that could not be found in other municipalities. Morris discusses the growth and development of the city's municipal hospital system and the city's university system in the

[26] Jack Newfield and Paul DeBrul, *The Abuse of Power: The Permanent Government and the Fall of New York* (New York: Viking Press, 1977), p. 75.

[27] See Charles R. Morris, *The Cost of Good Intentions: New York City and the Liberal Experiment*, 1960-1975 (New York: W.W. Norton, 1980), pp. 83-90.

[28] Auletta, *The Streets Were Paved With Gold*, pp. 66-68.

[29] Tabb, *The Long Default*, pp. 61-65.

[30] Jewel Bellush and Bernard Bellush, "Collective Bargaining, Leadership and the Fiscal Crisis," paper prepared for delivery at the 1981 Annual Meeting of the American Political Science Association, New York Hilton, Sept. 3-6, 1981, p. 34.

1960-75 era as indicative.[31] The city's excellent university system was free to residents of New York City. In 1960, full-time enrollment in the system was 36,000 (with total enrollment of 93,000). Admission to the universities was restricted by high school grade average. For example, a student seeking admission to Queens College in 1960 needed an average in the high 80s. In 1970, the city declared a policy of open enrollment for the city's students in the university system. Registrations rose to a high point of 271,930 in 1974. Full-time personnel grew from 4,300 in 1960 to more than 20,000 in 1974. We would not argue the need for access to higher education in our society. There are two points here, however. First, very few cities have such an extensive system of universities (and the same could be said of hospitals, subways, and museums). Second, as Morris points out, the city's fiscal capacity never entered into the discussion of open enrollment. Since the fiscal crisis, tuition was imposed in the city university system, the state government assumed a major financial role, and the number of students decreased.

It is clear that the city possessed greater budgetary responsibilities than other cities. The city paid for numerous programs and services which aren't ordinarily municipal expenses in the United States. Some expenses were mandated by the state government, most notably the requirement that the city pay 25 percent of the cost of welfare and Medicaid. Welfare and Medicaid expense alone added almost a billion dollars to the city's budget, at the time of the worst fiscal crisis in the mid-1970s.[32]

Finally, some have blamed New York's fiscal crisis on management. Charles Morris, who worked in the Lindsay administration in several policy-making positions, believes that the fault lies with the rationalist approach to urban problems. Lindsay and his staff believed that "the most daunting problems would respond to enthusiasm and intelligence."[33] If only the right structures and processes were adopted, urban problems would be solved. Lindsay reorganized the ninety-odd city departments into ten superagencies. Linday argued that "with each (of the new superagencies) taking charge of a definite and integrated fund, and with clear lines of control and communication, I could know what's going on all the time. And we can save a lot of money that way, too."[34] There is little evidence that the superagencies provided better information or saved the taxpayers money. The city promoted numerous efforts in rational scientific analysis—the adoption of the PPBS (Planning-Programming-Budgeting System) approach to budgeting, analyses of urban problems by the New York City

[31] Morris, *The Cost of Good Intentions*, pp. 38-46.

[32] Andrew Polsky, "New York City: Managing Without Democracy," *Democracy 1* (July 1981), 111.

[33] Morris, *The Cost of Good Intentions*, p. 31.

[34] Quoted in *ibid.*, p. 46.

RAND institute and other consultants. While some of these studies were elegant methodologically, the techniques ultimately failed the city government in its attempts to deal with the complexity of urban problems in the 1960s and 1970s.

To provide a contrast with the New York City situation, we will examine a different kind of case. We will look at Jacksonville, Florida, and the growth and subsequent decline of federal aid.

A CASE STUDY: JACKSONVILLE, FLORIDA[35]

Jacksonville is known most widely to political scientists and public administrators for the consolidated government of the city of Jacksonville and Duval County. As a result of the 1967 consolidation, Jacksonville has 570,981 people (1980 census figure) spread out over more than 800 square miles. The old central city (or inner city) has approximately 138,000 residents. The outlying areas (suburbs in most U.S. settings) have more than 400,000 residents. Duval County grew only slightly (3 percent, approximately 42,000 people) in the 1970-80 decade. The growth occurred in the early years of the decade, and the county actually lost population in the last years of the decade. In the meantime, the four small outlying counties in the metropolitan area (Baker, Clay, Nassau, and St. John's) had growth rates of 60 percent-100 percent from 1970 to 1980. Total population in the Jacksonville SMSA (Standard Metropolitan Statistical Area) grew from 621,827 in 1970 to 737,519 in 1980. Twenty-six percent of the county population is non-white. This figure is close to the SMSA figure of 23 percent non-white population. Jacksonville is situated in northeastern Florida on the Atlantic coast, and serves as a general trade and service center for a broad region in northern Florida and southern Georgia. The city is a regional insurance and financial hub, an important seaport and industrial area, and the location of three large naval installations. Jacksonville is a city in which machine-style politics (of the southern courthouse variety) still predominates. A tightly centralized power structure, in the old southern tradition, makes major decisions.

For a long time, Jacksonville was not overly interested in federal aid programs. As in many southern cities, there was a tradition of autonomy from the federal government. Suspicion of the federal government was fueled by the anti-civil-rights attitudes of many whites which persisted into the late 1960s. For example, Jacksonville declined to take part in the Model

[35] We are greatly indebted to Professor David Swain of Edward Waters College for his assistance with this section. See his articles, "Block Grants Make Little or No Difference: A Local Perspective," *Public Administration Quarterly* 7 (Spring 1983), 4-21; and "Nonprofits, Federalism, and Reagan Social Policy, *Journal of Health and Human Resources Administration* 6 (Spring 1984), 407-424.

Cities program. More recently, the city has pursued federal aid vigorously. This has especially been the case since the election of former Mayor Hans Tanzler, who was elected after the city-county consolidation in 1967. The city maintained an office in Washington for several years, and now retains Washington consultants who assist with federal funding possibilities.

Federal aid to the city of Jacksonville increased tremendously in the 1970-80 decade. In the 1971-72 annual budget (the first year in which such figures were kept), federal program aid was only $1,575,000. In the 1980-81 annual budget, federal grant aid provided $114,092,000. In percentage terms, federal aid rose from about 2 percent of the overall city budget in the early part of the decade to a consistent 10 percent in the latter years of the decade. These figures undoubtedly greatly understate the case, since they do not include grants to independent agencies and boards, the judiciary, private agencies, and state agencies.

Much of the federal aid went for capital expenditures and the purchase of equipment. For example, the Jacksonville Port Authority received money for the rebuilding of a runway at Jacksonville International Airport, and the Jacksonville Transportation Authority received funds for a new bus maintenance facility. The Sheriff's office used LEAA money to buy new, sophisticated communications equipment. Most Community Development Block Grant (CDBG) money went for capital expenditures.

However, much of the federal aid went for human service expenditures, too. The local community action agency received substantial sums for job training, legal assistance, and other human reource programs. CETA funds were used for educational and job training activities and job creation.

From this brief description, we can see that the impact of federal aid in Jacksonville is obviously substantial. While it is difficult to generalize about a decade of federal aid experience, we make the following observations:

1. Federal monies were often used to purchase equipment. They were frequently one-time purchases. Some of the expenditures in law enforcement were typical of this trend.
2. Much of the federal aid was used to pay salaries and to create new positions. This was especially true in the CETA program. Still, the city workers in these positions understood that their jobs depended upon the continuation of federal grants. In addition, there are some situations where people who started as grant workers became permanent employees.
3. Federal general revenue sharing (GRS) money is used to support and maintain University Hospital, a public hospital. The city turns over its $12 million share (in 1983-84) of GRS money to the hospital.
4. Audit reports showed substantial shortfalls in federal grants received as compared with those anticipated in the budget. For example, in total, federal grants amounted to $101 million in the fiscal year 1978-79 budget compared with receipts of only $42 million, a shortfall of $59 million.

The precise impacts of Reagan administration budget cuts in Jacksonville are still impossible to ascertain. The 1983-84 city budget is predicated on a loss of about $40 million in federal funds. While definitive answers are impossible, we can attempt an assessment which parallels the national outlook.

1. *Finances*—The state-local revenue picture is dynamic, in relation to federal cutbacks. The homestead exemption has been increased to $25,000 for all homeowners. The state sales tax is now 5 percent, with half the money going to local governments. In the first year, 40 percent (and reducing amounts in the next two years) must be used for property tax relief. Jacksonville responded in 1982-83 by decreasing the *ad valorem* millage by 2 mills. In 1983-84, the millage went back up 1.75 mills. Thus, in 1982-83, sales tax revenue increased, while property tax revenue decreased. In 1983-84, the budget projects increased state sales tax revenue and property tax revenue.

The impact of federal cutbacks is coming, but it has been phased and gradual. This is primarily because the authorization period for grants varies from program to program and because excess funds are carried over from year to year. Generally, Jacksonville's response is to ratify the cuts by discontinuing services provided by reduced or discontinued federal funding. This finding agrees with the results of a nationwide study, which noted that "states and localities on the whole have ratified the Reagan cuts, *i.e.*, passed them along to the recipients of the federally aided services and activities.[36]

2. *Services*—Jacksonville lost 1,277 city and public-service jobs when the funding for CETA was reduced. Certain CETA titles, including Public Service Employment, were eliminated. Some of these employees were put on the city payroll, but most of the jobs—including many library aides—were eliminated.

The Jacksonville public services most affected by the federal cuts are transportation (reductions in city bus runs), and the library system (reduced hours in most branch libraries). Indirectly, non-profit agencies which employed CETA workers (such as theater and arts groups) are suffering from the cutbacks.

3. *Population Groups and Geographic Areas*—The poor are being affected by the budget cutbacks. AFDC (Aid to Families With Dependent Children) and Food Stamp cuts are hurting them. City welfare caseloads and private agency caseloads are increasing, with the addition of people serviced by the reduced (or discontinued) programs. Some cutbacks, such as the reduction of library hours, affect the middle class.

4. *Institutions and Processes*—It is really premature to talk about impacts here. However, it may be that the focus of the city's political activity for higher-level funding may shift somewhat from Washington to Tallahassee, the state capital. In this regard, Jacksonville is well positioned in the short run because Mayor Jake Godbold maintains one of the strongest political

[36] Richard Nathan, et. al., *The Consequences of Cuts: The Effects of the Reagan Domestic Program on State and Local Governments* (Lawrenceville, NJ: Princeton University Press, 1983).

organizations in the state. The mayor is a political ally of the current governor, who was re-elected in 1982.

Jacksonville, as well as New York City, suggests that the intergovernmental system is changing. The financial role of the federal government seems now to be declining after a rapid rise in the 1970s. The state role seems sure to grow, but how much and with what priorities are unanswered questions. Much of the burden of coping with budget stringencies will fall on the local governments themselves. How they respond will, of course, depend on the nature of their politics. It is fitting, then, that we now examine the evolving character of politics in urban communities.

SUGGESTED READINGS

AULETTA, KEN. *The Streets Were Paved With Gold: The Decline of New York–An American Tragedy*. New York: Random House, 1979.

BAILEY, ROBERT W. *The Crisis Regime*. Albany, NY: State University of New York Press, 1984.

BURCHELL, ROBERT W. and DAVID LISTOKIN, eds. *Cities Under Stress: The Fiscal Crises of Urban America*. Piscataway, N.J.: Center for Urban Policy Research, 1981.

CAPUTO, DAVID and RICHARD COLE, eds. *Revenue Sharing: Methodological Approaches and Problems*. Lexington, Mass.: Lexington Books, 1976.

CLARK, TERRY N. and LORNA C. FERGUSON. *City Money: Political Processes, Fiscal Strain, and Retrenchment*. New York: Columbia University Press, 1983.

DOMMEL, PAUL R.and ASSOCIATES. *Decentralizing Urban Policy: Case Studies in Community Development*. Washington, D.C.: Brookings Institution, 1982.

IVERSON, TOM. "General Revenue Sharing Dependency in Kentucky: A Fiscal Strait Jacket." *Public Administration Quarterly* 7 (Fall 1983), 262-273.

LEVINE, CHARLES H. and PAUL L. POSNER. "Austerity and the Intergovernmental System." *Political Science Quarterly* (Spring 1981), 67-85.

MELTSNER, ARNOLD. *The Politics of City Revenue*. Berkeley: University of California Press, 1971.

MORRIS, CHARLES R. *The Cost of Good Intentions: New York City and the Liberal Experiment, 1960-1975*. New York: W.W. Norton, 1980.

NIVOLA, PIETRO S. "Apocalypse Now?: Whither the Urban Fiscal Crisis." *Polity*, 14 (Spring 1982), 371-394.

RUBIN, IRENE S. *Running in the Red: The Political Dynamics of Urban Fiscal Stress*. Albany: State University of New York Press, 1982.

SBRAGIA, ALBERTA M., ed. *The Municipal Money Chase: The Poitics of Local Government Finance*. Boulder: Westview Press, 1983.

SCHWADRON, TERRY, ed. *California and the American Tax Revolt: Proposition 13 Five Years Later*. Berkeley: University of California Press, 1984.

SHEFTER, MARTIN. "National-Local Interaction and the New York City Fiscal Crisis in Douglas E. Ashford, ed. *National Resources and Urban Policy*. New York: Methuen, 1980, pp. 185-213.

TABB, WILLIAM K. *The Long Default: New York City and the Urban Fiscal Crisis*. New York: Monthly Review Press, 1982.

WOLMAN, HAROLD. "Understanding Local Government Responses to Fiscal Pressure: A Cross National Analysis." *Journal of Public Policy*, 3 (August 1983), 245-264.

chapter 6

Village Politics

History is sometimes defined as the study of the unique. But history can also uncover trends and identify patterns of change and development. Our concern here is with history in this latter sense. Setting aside specifics of person and place, we will sketch a sequence of four basic patterns in local politics. The four patterns—village politics, machine politics, reform politics, and postreform politics—are not "true" snapshots of any one place and time. But the models, or types, will simplify and help to make sense of the very complicated particulars of evolving urban life in America. In so doing, they will be useful as tools for understanding political change.

In the next several chapters we will look at urban politics to see how it has changed over time.

As we examine the four patterns, we shall see that leadership roles and leadership behavior vary with time and circumstance. Over time, political relationships have largely shifted from an individual basis to a collective basis. Village and machine politics were highly personalized forms of politics. Political life in the modern city is, however, a life of organizaitons and movements. Race, religion, and occupation are cornerstones of political activity. Rights and obligations no longer rest strictly on a personal basis, but now also grow out of the collectivities of which the individual is a part.

By focusing on the phenomenon of political change, we can use the historical perspective to see how political relationships shape the way communities make policy choices. The historical perspective also gives us some sense of where we are now and what forces may have brought us here. Our view is that the contemporary urban community represents two powerful long-term trends: toward the democratization of American life and toward increasingly complex political, social, and economic structures.

As we trace the urban political experience in America, we see evolving efforts to cope with the complexity of modern life. The urban community is not just a place with many people, it is a complicated social system—and becoming more so. Urbanization is more than a movement of people into cities and their suburbs. As people leave farms, they gradually shed a rural way of life. Values and behavior patterns change, sometimes slowly, but they do change. Industrialization first and now the coming of postindustrial society have transformed political and social life as well as economic life. Specialization and interdependence have advanced radically. Family relationships are no longer intertwined with work life. Neighborhood attachments, while important in some ways, are quite different from and sometimes subordinate to attachments based on workplace.

As urbanization proceeds, remote, indirect, impersonal relationships gain in importance. Our lives are increasingly affected by large institutions, bureaucratic organizations, and various forms of mass behavior. Problems are caused by people we may never see. Assistance frequently comes in forms that are purely institutional. Plans are often so long-term and esoteric that they mean little to the average citizen.

Urbanization is also a democratic force—and a volatile force—increasing social mobility, raising aspirations, and weakening traditional status distinctions. Moreover, because urban communities are socially and economically diverse, they contain numerous friction points. And a democratic thrust does little to lessen friction. Urban politics is therefore inevitably concerned with channeling and managing conflict.

For any community, a major question is whether or not cooperation can be achieved, and, if it can, by what means? On what are loyalties based? In this part of the book we will look at how leaders operate, asking such questions as: Who is involved in making official decisions? On what basis are they involved? What concerns are uppermost in the minds of decision makers? What ideas, institutions, and practice shape the behavior of decision makers and channel outbreaks of popular dissatisfaction? Is organized competition and conflict regarded with approval or disapproval? On what is leadership based? How is support mobilized?

The answers, as we shall see, vary with the times. The changing patterns of urban leadership reveal some of the stresses and strains of modern political life as they have taken shape. By understanding these stresses and strains, perhaps we can begin to come to terms with the need to reconcile democracy

and complexity. We should aim for no less. The city is a political testing ground for us all—here, now, and in the future. Let us then turn to past, present, and projected trends in urban political life.

Village politics is obviously more a phenomenon of the past than of the present. Its importance lies not in widespread current practice but in a tradition that still affects our thinking.

A village is the polar opposite of a fast-changing metropolis. As a preurban settlement, a village is small and intellectually isolated. The center of commerce for a surrounding area of farmland, it is likely to be politically and socially as well as economically interdependent with the agricultural area.

Village politics is the small town politics of relatively homogeneous and stable communities. Relationships are personal and informal. Obligations, and enmities too, build up between individuals—not as advocates for competing sets of interests but as specific individuals, each with a particular place in the social fabric of the community.

Civic life is not a sharply separate area of village life but simply a sphere into which ongoing personal relationships sometimes spill when the duties of citizenship are being performed. Voting and jury duty are activities open to ordinary individuals. But governance, the exercise of executive or legislative authority, is a matter which the community's "natural" leaders—its social and economic notables—are deemed most capable of handling. The attributes of leadership are most likely to be found, it is believed, in "men of education and fortune."[1]

While political leadership is an ambition that few people have, it is not a specialized occupation. Village officeholding tends to be an honorific duty or avocation, not a career that one fulfills by long study, careful apprenticeship, or the cultivation of a mass following. Political leadership falls to those with "leisure and ability."[2]

In communities as diverse as Chicago; Oberlin, Ohio; and Springfield, Massachusetts, scholars have found that in an earlier era prominent business figures held the important public offices (as well as the high offices in church and community organizations). Such dominance went unchallenged. It was, after all, the place of "leading citizens" to lead.

Even in small towns today, ordinary citizens rarely challenge leadership by the social and economic notables of the community, and policy making is the preserve of the big taxpayers. Village politics is not an arena in which the interests of the propertied and propertyless are set against one

[1] Stephan Thernstrom, *Poverty and Progress* (Cambridge, Mass.: Harvard University Press, 1964), p. 41.

[2] Oscar Handlin, *Boston's Immigrants* (Cambridge, Mass.: Harvard University Press, Belknap Press, 1959), p. 22.

another. Rather there is an assumption that various community interests are more or less in harmony with one another.

Perhaps because small towns and villages tend to be socially closeknit, conflict and open competition are frowned upon. So, village politics is a politics of consensus. Petty squabbling and personal rivalry may be inevitable, but they are nevertheless regarded as improper. Historically, small-town life has not accommodated competition and dissent, nor have things changed much in the contemporary village.

Public discussion is feared as divisive. One writer describes this cast of mind as an "unwillingness to confront issues squarely."[3] Even political campaigning, which is expected to be minimal, rarely involves substantive issues. In the village, political support has always been more a matter of obliging friends than of choosing policy alternatives.[4] One author characterized his home town's politics as one in which "a vote against a candidate is generally regarded as a personal affront, and a vote for a candidate is both an acknowledgement of past favors and a bid for favors to come."[5] Even in a context of partisan elections, politics is largely personalized. For most people in small towns, politics is mainly a spectator sport, an election a conversation topic, and controversies no more than arguments over personalities or small irritants.

A study of small-town life in Connecticut found that there was not much interest in substantive issues, but that "questions of personal and public morality have been a source of constant delight, consternation, and general conversation for Putnam politicians."[6] Sexual and financial indiscretions are apparently the favored topics of conversation but, of course, the conversations are private and informal.

Candidates for public office are no more expected to air the personal shortcomings of their opponents than they are to debate the great issues. One writer offered this description of campaigning practices in the small town where he lived:

> Candidates for the more important offices go from house to house, each carrying a box of cigars and cigarettes and a box of candy bars. After every member of a family has had his pick, the candidate sits down and talks, usually about the weather and other neutral topics. If his host makes any comment on political affairs, he deals with it to the best of his ability, and he may bring up a political issue on his own initiative, but more often than not he leaves without directly mentioning the campaign.[7]

[3] Granville Hicks, *Small Town* (New York: Macmillan Co., 1946), p. 140.

[4] Michael Zuckerman, *Peaceable Kingdoms* (New York: Alfred A. Knopf, 1970), pp. 169-71.

[5] Hicks, *Small Town*, p. 109.

[6] Everett C. Ladd, Jr., *Ideology in America* (New York: W. W. Norton, 1972), p. 191.

[7] Hicks, *Small Town*, p. 187.

Even in their public deliberations, official bodies conduct business in a way that by-passes any exchange of views over a sharply focused issue. Typically, they operate on the principle of unanimity in decision making. The village leaders consult informally before meetings to generate agreement. By common understanding, officials may consider it improper for anyone to bring up an unannounced issue or even to introduce a point not mutually agreed upon before meeting time. Surprise threatens the ritual of consensus and harmony. Even if agreement is not worked out beforehand or if discussion does take an unexpected turn, the unwritten rule is to discuss until there is unanimity. Rather than take a vote on a divisive issue, many official bodies simply postpone making a decision.

Because the village is small and intimate with campaigning conducted on a personal basis, there are no distinctly recognized constituency interests. There is no penalty for failing to bring up an idea or to promote a group's interests. The risks are all in being divisive. The tendency is to remain safely within areas of general agreement. One study found village legislative practice to be that in which "no member irrevocably commits himself on an issue and, hence, [he] does not alienate himself from the other members of the board with whom he must deal from month to month and in his daily living on a 'friendly' basis."[8]

Even among those who do not hold public office, social solidarity takes precedence over the focused attempt to meet a community problem. Discussion in community meetings is full of anecdotes, contradictions, and irrelevancies. So long as talk is only talk, and not directed toward community action or decision, it is a pleasant social exercise. Sustained argument, however, is a threat to good feeling, an unwanted intrusion into ceremonies of harmony and solidarity.

POLICY CONCERNS

Especially in an earlier era, towns were ruled by citizens who regarded government in a narrow way, as an enterprise best held subordinate to the interests of taxpayers. Frugality, even stinginess, was the watchword. The early days of a Massachusetts town have been described as a time in which the local government "was asked to do little, did little, and generally was reluctant to do very much more, concerned as it was with the interests and values of taxpaying property holders."[9]

[8] See Arthur J. Vidich and Joseph Bensman, *Small Town in Mass Society* (Princeton, N.J.: Princeton University Press, 1958), p. 130.

[9] Michael H. Frisch, *Town into City* (Cambridge, Mass.: Harvard University Press, 1964), p. 44.

With conflict minimized and leadership honorific, policy making is unlikely to be a dynamic process. Village governments tend to be caretaker governments. They do the least that can be done, and leave the the rest for private charity, for a higher level of government, or for business enterprise. In a classic study of small-town life, Joseph Lyford found the Chamber of Commerce, not Town Hall, to be the center of community activity in Vandalia, Illinois. Lyford observed further that it was a few wealthy, paternalistic businessmen who "had the ideas and [gave] the money for the community parks and the library."[10] In a small town, when citizens occasionally ask their governments to act, the action sought is likely to be a personal favor, not a systematic program of improved service. "Do-nothing" governments engender no wide expectations. Demands on government may be unfelt because they may be nothing more than the privately expressed grumbling of individual citizens. Grumbling is not necessarily an antecedent to action. Granville Hicks relates an incident from his small-town experience:

> For many years we heard that the road superintendent used the town's equipment and the town's men for the conduct of his private business. There was plenty of complaint, but the complainers voted for the man year after year. After all, he was a Republican, and he had done or might do favors for them and their relatives.[11]

Village residents are not unwilling to ask publicly for some action of particular benefit to themselves. Petitioning the government for some sought-after personal advantage is a practice of long standing.

Yet, even in the small town, some collective business has to be conducted, some decisions made. Not everything reduces to individual rivalry or the pursuit of personal gain. And, indeed, it is often possible to identify different leanings among a community's civic activists. Even where thrift and economy have been raised to the level of moral imperatives, there is still some room for differences in interpretation of general principles. The leadership circles of many communities are thus divided into vaguely differentiated categories of "stand-patters" and "progressives."[12] Some are more inclined than others to see a need and to entertain the possibility of spending public money to meet that need. Occasional disputes break out between the hard-line defenders of minimum taxes, minimum expenditures and the proponents of "true economy" who argue that "procrastination is not economy."[13] Repair-the-old-village-pump versus buy-a-new-one is a legitimate issue between individuals equally possessed by the

[10] Joseph P. Lyford, *Talk in Vandalia* (New York: Fund for the Republic, 1962), p. 42.

[11] Hicks, *Small Town*, p. 190.

[12] Ladd, *Ideology in America*, pp. 207-15.

[13] Frisch, *Town into City*, p. 96.

virtues of thrift. Similarly, devotees of low taxation may differ with one another over the wisdom of expenditures to develop property and stimulate commerce. Economic decline is sometimes as much feared as high taxes.

By and large, however, the village is a place of stability. The boomtown mentality is alien to the village public mind. The prevalent mode of thought is the psychology of scarcity. Since extravagance is a danger thought always to be lurking near the public till, precedents for spending money are established only with great caution. Any expenditure is always suspect as giving rise to another expenditure; it is also suspect as a means for private gain. Rumor and suspicion can easily fuel an inborn resistance to purchasing new equipment or undertaking an improvement.

The psychology of scarcity is more than ingrained conservatism. It is a frame of mind that serves well the interest of small-town businessmen. The typical village economy is not a rapidly growing one. Business practices are based on the need to cut costs. Capital expansion is rare. Small-town business operations, as Vidich and Bensman have observed, "are based on the careful and jealous guardianship of a limited and local market."[14] Customers are attracted and held not by the wonders of advertising, the glamor of a new shop, or the mass volume of a streamlined sales procedure but on the basis of personal loyalty. To gain the maximum out of a fixed market, costs must be cut, and taxes are a cost to be kept to a minimum. Thrift and the avoidance of unnecessary expenditures lead to public savings as well as private savings. Public savings are seen as especially virtuous because they protect the interests of all property owners.

Since private savings are often invested in property, and the property tax is the major source of public revenue, minimum governmental expenditures are crucial to economic success and security. Higher expenditures would mean higher taxes, and higher taxes are believed to be a threat to hard-working and thrifty citizens.

"RUGGED INDIVIDUALISM" AND SOCIAL SOLIDARITY

In small towns and villages, "rugged individualism" thrives in the economic sphere, but it is not widely approved in other areas of life. Personal morality is a matter of public concern. Temperance and prohibitions on the sale of alcoholic beverages are cases in point. Dry towns still abound. Sex education and "smut" are still publicly condemned. Alcohol, sex, or other "vices" are hardly absent from the small-town setting, but there are clear standards of public conduct—standards that are set more by social pressure than by the actions of government officials.

[14] Vidich and Bensman, *Small Town in Mass Society*, pp. 116-17.

Public life itself is very much under the guidance of community sentiment. Traditionally, the public school system has been a major instrument of social control. One school committee report described the public schools as "moral and intellectual machines which spin and weave the very 'warp and woof' of a well-regulated and order-loving community."[15]

Teachers are expected to lead exemplary lives. One student of small-town life reported that a group of teachers received a reprimand for "laughing noisily in a local restaurant." One of the teachers commented that members of her profession were "expected to act like small, grey mice." And, she added, "We do."[16]

The maintenance of social solidarity depends greatly on who instructs the young, and how. After all, the appearance of new role models and the transmission of new ideas could endanger an established way of life. Thus, teachers are recruited and reappointed with the same care that is given to other matters of grave importance.

In one upstate New York village, social origin was reported to be a major consideration in the appointment of teachers. The village's sociological observers reported that "preference is shown for native daughters who return to the community from college."[17] In the absence of native candidates, candidates reared in a rural or small-town setting were favored. Teacher selection was conducted so as to perpetuate tradition and "minimize innovative tendencies."[18]

Why, it may be asked, is there is such a concern with values and standards of conduct? The answer, we think, lies in the fact that the village is a place of intimate contact. People interact in a highly personal way only when the responses are predictable and reassuring. Clashing values make for unpredictability, and they leave people ill at ease. The personal and intimate character of village life leads inexorably toward conformity.

VILLAGE POLITICS IN TRANSITION

Village politics has proved vulnerable to a number of forces, most having to do with growth. Once a community begins to expand in population and size, the low-key rule of the "notables" is difficult to maintain. In some communities, the old leaders were overwhelmed by industrialization and immigration. In others, they were caught up in the boom-times mentality themselves and became too absorbed in making profits to spare time and

[15] Thernstrom, *Poverty and Progress*, p. 50.

[16] Lyford, *Talk in Vandalia*, p. 28.

[17] Vidich andBensman, *Small Town in Mass Society*, p. 179.

[18] Ibid., p. 180.

thought for civic duty. Government by the leisure class can only occur if the temper of the times affords some leisure.

Growth was a powerful force. It overran the caretaker outlook and squelched the psychology of scarcity. New facilities had to be built and services expanded, but profit opportunities were so abundant that revenue needs could easily be met through soaring property values.

Growth also meant immigration. As social homogeneity yielded to cultural diversity, the collision of divergent value systems undermined the unified standard of morality that had been one of the foundations of political harmony. Public crusades for temperance, for instance, served only to broaden group conflict. Religious diversity provided an institutional context in which political conflict could grow. The very fact that churches were usually centers of social life meant that religious differences took on wide significance. Especially in the industrializing towns of the northeast, the conflict was sharp; and, as one historian observed, " . . . the line was drawn not between capitalist and laborer, well-to-do and poverty-stricken, but between Protestant American and Catholic immigrant."[19]

Group consciousness fed a yearning for a voice in city government. In many a New England town, the political mobilization of the Irish ended the Yankee Protestant dominance of public life. In the struggle, previously repressed hostilities found open expression. The day of unorganized, low-key conflict passed as growth impelled one-time small towns into the unsettling status of cities.

Growth overwhelmed traditional governmental procedures and gave rise to new organizations and practices. New facilities and expanded services could not be provided by meandering discussion, unending delay, and prayerful hopes of unanimity. Overseeing the public business could no longer be an occasional civic duty. When politics became a full-time occupation, many business leaders simply withdrew from public officeholding. The time was auspicious for the emergence of the career politician. Rapid physical development and expanding public employment brought abundant opportunities to wheel and deal in favors. Politicians could build personal followings, reward loyal supporters, and feather their own nests in the process. Growth, industrialization, and immigration thus paved the way for the organized exploitation of patronage opportunities, a style of politics dominated by the machines and their bosses.

SUGGESTED READINGS

BANOVETZ, JAMES. *Small Cities and Counties.* Washington, DC: International City Managers Association, 1984.

[19]Constance McLaughlin Green, *Holyoke, Massachusetts* (New Haven: Yale University Press, 1939), p. 50.

Frisch, Michael H. *Town into City.* Cambridge, Mass.: Harvard University Press, Belknap Press, 1964.

Green, Constance McLaughlin. *Holyoke, Massachusetts.* New Haven: Yale University Press, 1939.

Hicks, Granville. *Small Town.* New York: Macmillan Co., 1946.

Robertson, James and Carolyn. *The Small Towns Book: Show Me the Way to Go Home.* Garden City, NY: Anchor Books, 1978.

Swanson, Bert E. et al. Small Towns and Small Towners. Beverly Hills, CA: Sage Books, 1979.

Thernstrom, Stephan. *Poverty and Progress.* Cambridge, Mass.: Harvard University Press, 1964.

Vidich, Arthur J., and Joseph Bensman. *Small Town in Mass Society.* Princeton, N.J.: Princeton University Press, 1958.

Zuckerman, Michael. *Peaceable Kingdoms.* New York: Alfred A. Knopf, 1970.

chapter 7

Machine Politics

Machine politics, like village politics, is personalized, but it is high rather than low keyed. It has the hustle and bustle, the hard-sell air of the market place. Trading favors is not just an occasional act of friendship but an ongoing business process.

Machine politics is organized but not bureaucratized. Bargains are often explicit, yet transactions take place on an informal, face-to-face basis. Many personal contacts are based on business calculations, but they are nonetheless *personal.* Sentiment as well as profit works to hold the organization together. A political machine, then, is a network of personal obligations—regularized to some extent but, even so, shaped by the particular persons who make up the organization.

In this chapter we will first look at the nature of the machine. Then we will examine the connections between machine and ethnic politics. Next we will consider the machine's nonideological orientation toward policy and the reasons for this orientation. After that we will attempt an assessment of machine politics, and will conclude with a discussion of the decline of the machine.

THE NATURE OF THE POLITICAL MACHINE

The machine is a political organization devoted to the pursuit of material gain, and its leaders are mainly concerned with the control and distribution of the "spoils of office." Machine politics thus revolves around patronage—jobs, contracts, and favors in the administration of the law—manipulated for the partisan advantage of a political organization.[1] The machine has many aspects; historically it bestowed recognition on the immigrant masses. But the heart of its operation is the use of divisible, material rewards to perpetuate the organization.

Sustaining the machine is like running a business—but a family business, not a modern corporation. The vast array of party workers, favor seekers, and officeholders who make up the machine operate by informal understanding. They are not bound together by contract nor do they sign collective agreements. Their relationships are defined by no organizational charts. It is trust that forms the basis of the relationships. Machine politicians cultivate personal bonds, promote sociability, and, above all, foster loyalty and friendship. In sum, while machines depend heavily on material incentives, they do not rely on them exclusively.

While patronage and political favoritism are practices that have run throughout history, machine politics did not assume its mature shape until the latter part of the nineteenth century and the early years of the twentieth century—a time of rapid growth both in the economy and in urban population.

Most machines have been organized through the device of the political party. All have been organized on a geographic basis. Typically, the organization is elaborate, reaching from the precinct worker at the bottom to the boss at the top. Not all, however, have been centralized; some have been coalitions of ward-based organizations. But discipline is an identifying characteristic of them all.

The machine is both narrower and broader than the party organization. It is narrower in that the heart of the system is an informal organization that controls the party organization. Holding party office is usually but not always important—the boss may hold no formal position. The machine is broader than the party in that the bosses and their lieutenants are at the center of a web of relationships involving three groups. One is the party organization, which controls nominations and can deliver a dependable set of voters. The second is officeholders, the object of party activity being to control public office for patronage, favors, and inside information. The third is a variety of businesses and other private interests, licit and illicit, seeking favors. The organization is the middle man between public officeholders and these private favor seekers.

[1] Raymond Wolfinger, *The Politics of Progress* (Englewood Cliffs, N.J.: Prentice-Hall, 1974), p. 99.

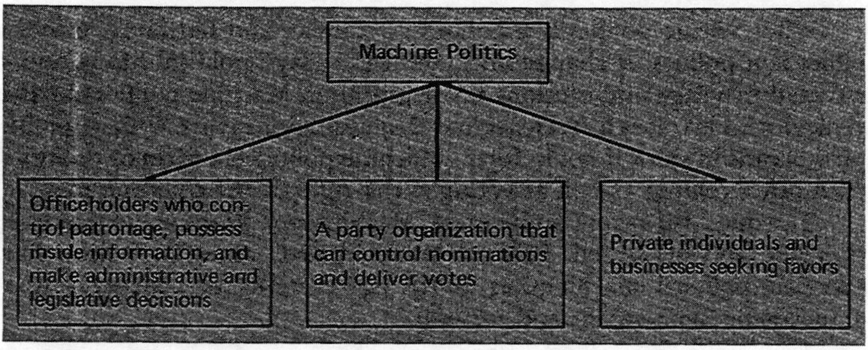

FIGURE 7-1. Web of relationships in machine politics.

Some organization leaders and workers may also hold public jobs, but there is no necessity for them to do so. And being on the public payroll may not be the same as working at a public job. The manhole inspector who spends his time getting out the vote is not just a myth. Machine transactions can also be complicated, involving public favors for private jobs; a private employer may agree to placing individuals in private employment in exchange for favorable treatment at the hands of governmental officials.

Machines have differed in important respects. Some have been highly centralized and tightly knit organizations. Others have been loose alliances of petty chieftains. Some bosses stuffed the ballot box, but others could trust to their personal popularity. Some have been openly venal. Others have avoided the open and indictable forms of corruption in favor of honest graft.

Many top-level machine politicians have followed the philosophy: "Thou shalt not steal, but thou shalt not blow the whistle on anybody who does."[2] Boss Richard Croker explained to muckraker Lincoln Steffens why police graft was tolerated in New York City:

> Police graft is dirty graft . . . We have to stand for it. If we get big graft, and the cops and small fry politicians know it, we can't decently kick at their petty stuff. Can we now?[3]

Under machine politics, control of public office is a business opportunity. Personal gain is widely acknowledged to be a prime motivating force behind the choice of politics as a career. In an earlier era, most bosses freely admitted that they made money out of politics. Boss Croker confessed to Lincoln Steffens, "I work for my own pocket all of the time".[4]

[2] Mike Royko, *Boss* (New York: Signet Books, New American Library, 1971), p. 53.

[3] Lincoln Steffens, *The Autobiography of Lincoln Steffens* (New York: Harcourt, Brace and World, 1931, 1958), pp. 237-38.

[4] Ibid., p. 238.

While village politics is a politics of stability and harmony, machine politics is a politics of change and conflict. Village political life is one of restricted privilege and cautious favor granting. Machine politics expands privilege and involves a freewheeling dispensing of favors. Village politics is aristocratic in spirit if not in form. Machine politics is a form of politics in which officeholding as well as voting is the right of the common man.

The quest for favors is universal. Machine politicians make that quest systematic and organized. Edward Banfield and James Q. Wilson have described political machines as party organizations that depend upon "inducements both *specific* and *material*."[5]

A specific inducement would be, for instance, a spot on the party slate that can be offered to one person and withheld from another. It is an inducement that can be offered on the basis of favoritism or as an individual reward. It can provide a basis for reciprocal obligations and can be used to establish a high degree of control over personal behavior.

A material inducement is one that involves some tangible reward—a job, a chance to make a profit, reduced taxes, or avoiding some costly regulation. The desire for material gain is a powerful force.

Specific and material benefits are the lifeblood of the political machine, motivating some people to make politics a full-time career. As the redoubtable George Washington Plunkitt of Tammany Hall explained:

> No other politician in New York or elsewhere is exactly like the Tammany district leader or works as he does. As a rule, he has no business or occupation other than politics. He plays politics every day and night in the year, and his headquarters bears the inscription, "Never closed."[6]

In more recent times, a Chicago politician offered his assessment:

> What I look for in a prospective captain . . . is a young person—man or woman—who is interested in getting some material return out of his political activity. I much prefer this type to the type that is enthused about the "party cause" or all "hot" on a particular issue. Enthusiasm for causes is short-lived, but the necessity of making a living is permanent.[7]

Experienced party workers are expected to know their districts thoroughly, to know everyone's likes and dislikes, strong points, and weaknesses, who belongs to which organization, how people vote, and whether they vote only in general elections or also in primary elections. They do favors, put in a good word, attend weddings and funerals, and try to draw people into the social life of the organization. Plunkitt explained his mode of operation:

[5]Edward Banfield and James Q. Wilson, *City Politics* (New York: Vintage Books, Random House, 1963), p. 115.

[6]William L. Riordon, *Plunkitt of Tammany Hall* (New York: E. P. Dutton and Co., 1963), p. 90.

[7]James Q. Wilson, *The Amateur Democrat* (Chicago:University of Chicago Press, 1962), pp. 70-71.

> For instance, here's how I gather in the young men. I hear of a young feller that's proud of his voice, thinks that he can sing fine. I ask him to come around to Washington Hall and join our Glee Club. He comes and sings, and he's a follower of Plunkitt for life. Another young feller gains a reputation as a baseball player in a vacant lot. I bring him into our baseball club. That fixes him. You'll find him workin' for my ticket at the polls next election day.[8]

Plunkitt has his counterparts in the modern era. Alderman Vito Marzullo, long a pillar of the Democratic organization in Chicago, operates much as Plunkitt did. In the twenty-fifth ward, Marzullo and his captains perform favors for their constituents. Like Plunkitt, Marzullo knows his district intimately, and his organization keeps up good relations with social institutions in the ward. Marzullo showed one political observer the ward organization checkbook, with the following comments: "We give a donation to thirty-five churches in the ward every year . . . look at some of the donations—$100 to the City of Hope, $20 to St. Stephen's Holy Name Society, $20 to the Bennett Playground, $200 to St. Michael's Church, $100 to the American Legion, $125 to the West Chicago Florists, . . . $25 to the New Trier Baseball Club."[9] In return, Marzullo's organization gets the support of many of these organizations. Party workers are expected to know who is and is not a neighborhood or ethnic leader, and they are expected to cultivate the good will of those whose word carries weight.

Local political clubs. Local party organizations in the United States have long maintained political clubs. The most famous, like Tammany Hall, have had central machine clubrooms in which the city-wide bosses made their headquarters. But by far the largest number of clubs and those reaching the greatest number of individuals have been the neighborhood or ward clubs. In the 1920s, as many as one million people were enrolled in two thousand clubs by one estimate.[10] These clubs were as much social as political. Typically a clubroom included a pool table, a card room, and a bar, as well as a large meeting room. Dues were nominal, and not collected with diligence. The bar and a modest rake-off from the nightly poker games were more important sources of club revenue. Membership was inclusive rather than exclusive: *all* Democrats or *all* Republicans were eligible. The clubs sponsored sports events, dances, picnics, excursions, and other activities, many of them free.

The club was a place for informal gathering, for entertainment or the exchange of gossip. But it was also a place where party workers and constituents could see one another, to give and get favors without embarrassment or

[8] Riordon, *Plunkitt of Tammany Hall*, pp. 25-26.

[9] Milton Rakove, *Don't Make No Waves, Don't Back No Losers* (Bloomington: Indiana University Press, 1975), p. 121.

[10] Frank R. Kent, *The Great Game of Politics* (Garden City, N.Y.: Doubleday, 1923), p. 68.

awkwardness of any kind. The ward boss could keep informed about public opinion, and even if a favor could not be granted, convey the feeling that someone cared.

Clubs are not entirely a relic of the past. They still remain, even in this era of television campaigning and media politics. A recent study of political clubs in New York City found the clubs to be remarkably resilient institutions!

> The parties and dances continue, people still come for help and to some of the clubs for jobs and offices. In 1972, New York City had approximately 300 political clubs; a majority of these had memberships of 100-500 people.[11]

There is a romanticized view of machine politics as a form of unlimited benevolence to the needy. Martin Lomasny explained to Lincoln Steffens, "I think . . . that there's got to be in every ward somebody that any bloke can come to—no matter what he's done—and get help. Help, you understand; none of your law and your justice, but help."[12] But running a machine is a matter of bargaining, of trading favors. Most people have only one thing to offer the machine, their vote. And that vote is important to the machine.

Many poor voters, however, have supported the machine out of friendship for party workers or simply out of loyalty to the neighborhood or ethnic group. Sometimes the friendship and loyalty have been based on small favors, often only on tokens of recognition. Machine officials make unending rounds of family events and social gatherings. Plunkitt explained why the machines were attentive to the personal and immediate needs of the poor: "The poor are the most grateful people in the world, and let me tell you, they have more friends in their neighborhoods than the rich have in theirs."[13]

Despite a dependence on the poor for votes, the machine is oriented toward wheeling and dealing with substantial businesses and other large private interests. The machine is a broker in favors. Those who can do big favors get big favors in return. The utility company that can make a sizeable campaign contribution and hire the machine's constitutents is in a position to exact substantial concessions. So too can the individuals who can deliver large blocs of voters. But because brokers always operate on the basis of a mutual exchange, those who can do small favors or deliver few votes get little in return. The individual voter thus bargains from a weak position, and most of the poor can offer only their own votes or a few from family and friends.

[11] Norman M. Adler and Blanche D. Blank, "The Political Clubs of New York Revisited" (Paper presented at the 1972 meeting of the Northeastern Political Science Association, Amherst, Mass.).

[12] Steffens, *Autobiography*, p. 618.

[13] Riordon, *Plunkitt of Tammany Hall*, p. 28.

MACHINE POLITICIANS AND ETHNIC POLITICS

Machine politics is a politics of growth, expanding opportunities, and uninhibited struggle for success. Historically, it was a politics in which the underdog rose, Catholic immigrants took power from Protestants, and the explebes displaced the social and economic notables. A political careeer was an avenue of economic advancement and public recognition. Poor ward heelers became wealthy, and the sons of immigrant parents became big-city mayors. Persons who began life in poverty parlayed their political contacts into positions as insurance agents, real estate operators, and owners of construction firms.

Not everyone who tried and played the game moved up the ladder. Nor have those who won power been ready to share it with new immigrant groups. For example, the Irish Catholics who broke the Yankee Protestant monopoly on office have held on to power in the midst of great ethnic diversity. In many communities, Italians found the business world to be more open than the world of politics.

Machine politics is combative politics. Competing groups are a challenge. Efforts are made to outpoll, outmaneuver, and in general outdo the opposition. Apocryphal stories abound about rival precinct captains racing to see who is first at a fire or who gives the finest wedding gift to the daughter of the popular neighborhood leader.

Competitiveness is not the same thing as chaos. Open struggle can take place between disciplined contenders. The machine's appeal, especially to businessmen, lay in its ability to establish order and provide predictability, to pick as candidates straight organization men who would "vote right" and "stay hitched."[14]

The persons who imposed order on chaos were the bosses, who, like their counterparts in the business world, wanted to maximize their own con trol of the situation. They preferred to subdue the opposition, make its workers dependent upon them, and if possible, establish a monopoly. Grabs for political monopoly were widely supported and approved of because it made the times of rapid change and rugged individualism more manageable.

In background and outlook most city bosses have resembled self-made businessmen. What frequently distinguished them, however, was that the boss was more likely to be a power seeker. A few bosses were well born and brought fortunes to, rather than made them in, politics. But they were individuals who liked politics for its own sake and were good at it. In contrast with the honorific office holder, the machine boss was likely to be characterized by a "single-minded dedication to the quest for power, political position and prestige. . . ."[15]

[14] Kent, *The Great Game of Politics*, p. 58.

[15] Alex Gottfried, *Boss Cermak of Chicago* (Seattle: University of Washington Press, 1962), p. 351.

The competitive atmosphere enveloping machine politics was not restricted to individuals and political parties; it was also intertwined with ethnic politics—the struggle for group recognition by immigrant groups. Of course, the struggle was a struggle because the native-born resisted the social and political advances of newer groups. Job discrimination was rampant. "Irish need not apply" accompanied many an employment notice, and "No Roman Catholics" was written on more than one application form. Religious identity and ethnic identity were both powerful forces of reaction against such old-stock discrimination. Indeed, because churches were an organized and vital force in community life, religion and nationality reinforced one another as sources of group conflict.

In the face of rising immigrant militancy, the old-stock population inconsistently continued their discrimnatory practices while urging acculturation for the nation's newcomers. Old-stock Bostonians, for example, complained that" . . . our foreign population are too much in the habit of retaining their own national usages, of *associating too exclusively with each other*, and living in groups together."[16]

Nationality and religious cleavages inevitably spilled over into specific issues, such as Wets versus Drys. And conflict on such specific issues reinforced the separatist feelings of various groups. In this climate, appeals to group pride and consciousness proved to be an efficient means for mobilizing voters, and the scramble for votes speeded up the process of naturalization and rapidly extended the franchise to new constituents.

The ethnic appeal became self-perpetuating to a considerable extent. Once group consciousness became a campaign resource, political leaders had a stake in maintaining group solidarity. Members of nationality groups were encouraged to retain feelings of separateness, and they responded favorably to leaders who maintained close identity with their nationality groups. Anton Cermak was such a leader for the Chicago Czechs, who, "at the same time that they accepted American, middle-class standards and values, insisted upon retaining their cultural individuality . . . Thus, a cardinal reason for Cermak's three decades of leadership of the Czechs was his willingness to remain one of them and among them."[17]

Voter rejection of assimilationist leaders in favor of the Cermak type signified that ethnic conflict was genuine. It occurred between immigrant groups as well as between immigrant and old-stock populations. It was, then, a significant part of the combative atmosphere in which machine politics flourished. Machine politicians skilled in the practice of "divide and rule" could and did establish their dominance in ethnically diverse communities. In the cross-nationality struggles some groups were slow to achieve recognition.

[16]Oscar Handlin, *Boston's Immigrants* (Cambridge, Mass.: Harvard University Press, 1959), p. 185.

[17]Gottfried, *Boss Cermak of Chicago*, p. 341.

Machines are, of course, not a purely ethnic phenomenon or a Catholic phenomenon or a Democratic phenomenon or even a city phenomenon. Contending nationality groups were not the only background against which the bosses plied their skills. County machines were once probably as numerous as city machines, and they often were, and to a degree still are, rural, Republican, and WASP. But they played a different role in the lives of their adherents. These machines were less likely to be avenues of upward mobility, and their bosses were frequently prominent citizens. Whether city or county, whether headed by the prominent citizen or the upwardly mobile ethnic, machine politics has always been a rough-and-tumble politics of patronage and keen competition for control of public office.

A NONIDEOLOGICAL ORIENTATION TOWARD POLICY

Machine politics is nonideological politics. To be sure, an occasional boss, James Michael Curley for one, has campaigned against "big-business control." When the temperance issue was prominent, many bosses opposed prohibition. But on the whole, machine politicians have not been committted to social and economic reform. In fact, they have not been issue-oriented at all. Issues can be dangerous; they can create enemies. Typical of the bosses, the late Mayor Richard Daley believed that voters could be influenced best "by ministering carefully to their daily and personal needs." He regarded the "great social issues" as "secondary at best and irrelevant at worst, in comparison to the day-to-day problems of the individual voter."[18]

Machine politicians are not indifferent to government activity, however. They like a growing city, and do everything possible to encourage physical expansion. A building city is a place where profits can be made and favors freely exchanged. It is a city that needs an extensive public works program, and for obvious reasons, machines are happy to pursue a bricks-and-mortar policy.

The construction of roads and bridges, the erection of new public buildings, redevelopment projects, and changes in land use offer abundant opportunities to provide and collect on favors. Officers in the machine, of course, take full advantage of their inside information, their influence, and their contacts to pursue their own material advancement.

A machine-controlled government is not necessarily an activist government, or a high-priced one. Some machine politicians pride themselves on keeping taxes low. And the machine's easygoing standards for service delivery may cost less than a rigorous and professional approach. Some machines, of course, have been highly extravagant spenders of public monies.

[18] Rakove, *Don't Make No Waves*, p. 68.

Machine politicians are often hesitant or unwilling to pioneer in social policy. For the most part, they are politically cautious individuals, attached to things as they are, with no far-reaching visions of how things might be. They fear that abstract issues only cause hard feelings, and they shy away from social engineering. They see it as divisive, as costing the organization support without providing tangible benefits in return. Many of the bosses have been conservative, reluctant to alter the status quo, and unwilling to lead a revolt against other power centers in the community. The machine approach is to come to terms with power wielders, not to confront or challenge them.

Even if many of the bosses were not personally conservative, they still would not be social reformers. They have always viewed with suspicion any issue that did not provide the specific and material benefits that are the coin of exchange. Benefits that accrue to everyone, friend and foe alike, (what the economists call "public goods") offer no advantage to the machine. Clean air, neighborhood parks, and a vice-free city fall in this category; their benefits cannot be allocated on the basis of favoritism.[19]

What motivates the machine politician is neither ideology nor desire to serve the community. The machine politician, *qua* machine politician, is concerned with maintaining the organization, and that means having favors to dispose that can be traded on a particularistic basis for other favors. To the machine leaders, politics is a matter of running an organization. They want good will and popular favor, but above all they want a dependable corps of workers and a loyal band of supporters.

Because machine politics is based on *mutual* exchanges of favors, members of the organization cannot afford to deplete their supply of favors for nothing more than generalized good will. To seek service from someone else is to incur an obligation; the more time and resources involved in the service, the bigger the obligation. Obligations have to be met on a basis of reciprocity.

From the perspective of the machine politician, providing constituents with collective benefits, such as parks or other neighborhood improvements, is an unproductive enterprise. For a project such as a neighborhood park, a precinct worker must establish contact with the head of the Parks and Recreation Department and perhaps with an alderman or the mayor as well. In the process, the worker incurs political debts. But the neighborhood park provides little in return. It is of great personal benefit to no one person. Consequently no one feels a lasting obligation to the precinct worker for the effort.

Similarly, a vice-free community may offer some collective benefit but generates no strong obligations to political officeholders. An antivice policy may also be risky. It may engender the deep enmity of those whose live-

[19] See Matthew A. Crenson, *The Un-Politics of Air Pollution* (Baltimore: Johns Hopkins Press, 1971), pp. 133-58.

lihood or profit margins depend upon a lax administraton of liquor or gambling laws. Tolerance of "human frailties," on the other hand, is a relatively cost-free way of providing favors and building support.

A DEROMANTICIZED VIEW OF MACHINE POLITICS

Assessments of machine politics have moved full circle from unfavorable to favorable back to unfavorable. The impact of machines on city life is not easy to determine. When machine power was at its peak, muckrakers and reformers attacked boss politics for being corrupt, irresponsible, and inefficient. Later writers found that the city machines performed a number of latent functions (that is, unstated and even unintended ones) that were helpful to a society undergoing the stress of rapid urbanization and heavy immigration. More recently, writers have observed that the machines were not helpful enough to make real inroads on deprivation, misery, and discrimination. Indeed, one reason that Congress, during Lyndon Johnson's administration, declared "war on poverty" and enacted the Community Action Program was to meet the needs of the urban poor—needs that were being unmet even in those cities where machine politics had not withered away.

While extending only token help to the poor, the bosses were fully accommodating to business interests. Unwilling to rock the boat of established economic relationships, they made numerous deals with business, big and little. Many writers have traced the connections between bosses and businessmen, which have always been both close and complex. In some cities, the first bosses were saloon keepers who had need of government favors to protect and promote their businesses. But big business also played a major role in the early days of machine politics—a time when businesses, especially those needing franchises, were expanding rapidly. But as growth slowed, and when the Great Depression hit, big businessmen became less concerned with the acquisition of new privileges and more concerned with holding what they had. As their interest in individual favors declined, their support of the machine also declined. Machine politics has, however, always had a wider base of support than big business. The bias of machine politics is not a big-business bias but a bias toward privilege-seeking businesses (licit and illicit), which could pay for the favors they wanted.

Many have argued that putting up with politics based on purchased privilege was a small price to pay in exchange for an organization that enabled new groups to integrate into the political system and become acculturated to urban life. Certainly machine politics was a means by which immigrant groups gained recognition, new residents were quickly enfranchised, and many individuals experienced a phenomenal degree of upward mobility. But the group recognition gained was as much a matter of competitive politics as one of machine politics. In other words, the two-party system rather than the machine system may have produced group recogniton. Moreover, the speed with which acculturation and social integration took place can easily be exaggerated. It was a slow process, and many other agents were involved besides political machines, including the networks of self-help organizations that most nationality groups formed.

The machines were, in fact, unconcerned with the collective interests of the poor, and remained that way even in the post New Deal era. Significantly the machine bosses were less sympathetic to dissident spokesmen for working-class interests than reform mayors have been, and the more militant strains of organized labor have never found ready allies in the heads of political machines. Bosses have invariably regarded third-party or radical spokesmen for have-nots as a threat to the machine—as individuals who are to be discredited and defeated. Thus while the precinct workers of political machines have always been most active in lower-class areas, the organizations have been internally incapable of becoming channels through which the collective interests of the lower class could be represented.

One of the conditions believed to encourage machine politics is the fragmentation of governmental authority. The long ballot, weak executives, numerous boards and commissions, and cumbersome legislative procedures characterized local government at the time that political machines gained such wide ascendancy. Rapid growth, cumulating problems, and rising demands for service and assistance served to generate a need for some means of expediting governmental action. Though the machine was an extragovernmental organization, it nevertheless had the capacity to control officeholders; it provided a means by which exercises of authority could be coordinated and action expedited. In all likelihood, this capacity to facilitate governmental decision making did enhance the power of the machine. Unarguably, the machine offered a way around road blocks and red tape.

For some, machine politics still looks attractive as a way of establishing some degree of popular control over the actions of autonomy-seeking administrative agencies. But the more general verdict has not been so favorable. On close examination, machine politics is inefficient. Operating largely on the basis of a network of personal obligations, the machine can handle only a very limited number of demands for action. The absence of routine procedures also leads to a degree of arbitrariness in decision making. Furthermore, machine politicians have not always dealt with constituents on a plane of benevolence. The stick as well as the carrot has been used as an inducement to support the organization. Earlier bosses, like "Boss" Hague of Jersey City, used strong-arm methods. Later techniques tended to be more subtle.

Mike Royko gives an account of how support for Mayor Daley's opposition could be costly to the small businessman in Chicago. The following events took place when a restaurant owner put up a sign supporting a 1963 opponent of Daley, Ben Adamowski:

> The day it went up the precinct captain came around and said, "How come the sign Harry?"
>
> "Ben's a friend of mine," the restaurant owner said. "Ben's a nice guy Harry, but that's a pretty big sign. I'd appreciate if you'd take it down." "No, it's staying up."
>
> The next day the captain came back. "Look, I'm the precinct captain. Is there anything wrong, any problem, anything I can help you with?" Harry said no. "Then why don't you take it down. You know how this looks in my job." Harry wouldn't budge. The sign stayed up.
>
> On the third day, the city building inspectors came. The plumbing improvements alone cost Harry $2,100.[20]

Because it is an extravagant operation, machine politics flourishes best in boom times or periods of growth. As long as profits abound, opportunities to provide favors also abound. If an economic recession strikes, however, the machine like many other operations must retrench. Ironically, the machine is best able to help the poor when they least need it and least able to help the poor when they most need it. The Great Depression was a severe blow to many big city machines because they could not cope with such massive want, and city governments had to cut payrolls and decrease services in order to stay solvent.

Even in prosperous times the machine's capacity to facilitate governmental action is a selective capacity. Because the machine is held together by a system of favors and personal obligations, some actions are more likely to be taken than others. The machine can promote development and expedite growth, but it has no penchant for providing high quality services, such as in health or education, and little concern with social problems. The capacity of the political machine to make the system of government work is therefore a capacity that is restricted by the nature of the times, and it applies to some issue areas but not others.

Finally, the capacity of the machine to make the system of government work is a capacity that is easily expended. Public tolerance of extravagance, self-enrichment, and favoritism is limited, and the practices associated with machine politics tend eventually to discredit public office holders. As public officialdom loses respectability, there is real danger that the competence and ability of officials will decline. Citizens become reluctant to entrust the government with additional responsibilities. Because they are held in low repute, public officials are reluctant to sponsor new programs, and no one ex-

[20] Royko, *Boss*, p. 131.

pects government under their leadership to be infused with an innovative spirit. Machine politics eventually weakens the capacity to govern by instilling in citizens a feeling of uninterested cynicism about public affairs.

THE DECLINE OF MACHINE POLITICS

The machine is no longer the dominant form of organization in the politics of cities. A number of conditions that prevailed at the turn of the century enabled the machine to prosper, but changes in these conditions—socioeconomic, cultural/attitudinal, and political/structural—paved the way for the decline of machines.

The Socioeconomic Milieu

Machines flourished under paradoxical conditions: the general economic expansion and prosperity that we associate with industrialization in the late nineteenth and early twentieth century, alongside widespread individual poverty. Economic expansion meant jobs, contracts, licenses, franchises, and business contacts that could be traded for the political support needed to maintain an active organization. The widespread poverty provided the machine with a large clientele willing to barter away its voting power for immediate help and tokens of social acceptance. Yet, in many places today, poverty and growth still occur side by side without their sustaining a machine style of politics. We must look then to the other possible explanations for the decline of machine politics.

Attitudes

Economic misery was highly visible. The rapid growth, the heavy influx of immigrant groups, and the shift from an agricultural to an industrial order had other social consequences that were not so immediately observable. A sense of community, especially because ours was still a relatively new nation, was weak. Immigrants had loosened their ties to the "old country" and had not had the time to develop broad social bonds in the new. Although social ties sometimes extended to coreligionists or fellow ethnics, socializing was often confined to family, friends, and neighbors. These kinds of particularistic social relationships provided few curbs on a general atmosphere of opportunism and graft.

As we assess the rise and decline of machine politics, we need to be careful, however, about assigning too much weight to the impact of immigration. It seems unlikely that a lower-class and largely unsettled group could by numbers alone set the dominant tone for a community's politics. The immigrant had, after all, come to places where a frontier spirit encouraged "freewheeling individualism and pragmatic opportunism."[21] Most histories of urban communities conclude that all classes partook of a "private-regarding" ethos and provided support for machine politics.

The weak sense of community and the air of opportunism extended throughout the social structures of growing, industrializing towns. Lincoln Steffens saw the desire for privilege—wherever it cropped up—as the corrupting force that generated machine politics. He quotes a St. Louis prosecutor: "It is good businessmen that are corrupting our bad politicians; it is good business that causes bad government—in St. Louis,"[22] The bosses were tolerated, condoned, and backed so long as they met strongly felt needs of many subgroups, including those of important leaders in finance and industry.

Structural Factors

The same winds of change that brought industrialization, brought increased urbanization and with it the demand for an active and responsive public sector. The shortcomings of local governments structured for village life were plain to see. Formal authority was widely dispersed; procedures were antiquated; and local officials on their own were incapable of quick and decisive action. The political machine put together the Humpty Dumpty of local authority, making government action at least somewhat predictable, dependable, and consistent. By providing an informal means of managing public affairs, the boss system put governance on a "business basis."

Government reorganization was an obvious alternative to the patchwork of machine politics, but real reform could come only after or where political support for machines weakened. Until then, the machine could either stop structural change or continue to manage affairs by manipulating reform institutions. As we shall see in the next chapter, reform was more than a new way of arranging public positions and defining official responsibilities. It was also an expression of moral outrage, and its adherents devised elaborate platforms of institutional restructuring through which to disestablish the hated bosses. But reform was as much a symptom of the decline of the machine as a cause of that decline.

CONCLUSION

If machines had such a stong edge in resisting reform, we are brought back to the question of why machine politics has become the anachronism it is—especially in those communities where there is still a large disadvantaged

[21] Fred I. Greenstein, "The Changing Pattern of Urban Politics," *Annals of the American Academy of Political and Social Science* 353 (May 1964), 3.

[22] Steffens, *Autobiography*, p. 271.

population. One fact of urban life is that, with slowed growth, cities now have a smaller pool of benefits than they once had through which to sustain political organizations. Fewer benefits means less capacity to mobilize voters. However, a declining urban economy is at best only one factor at work: the more prosperous and still-growing cities have fewer, not more, remnants of traditional politics. The fact is that technical and social complexity have overrun the personalized transactions of city bosses. The machine, *qua* machine, cannot undertake vast projects, provide services to a mass citizenry, and hold in check the competing group aspirations that characterize the fully modern city. Although the machine is an effective form of organization in the short run, it contains weaknesses. In circumstances where available benefits do not match popular expectations, the machine can maintain control only by limiting participation and excluding the demands of some. It is not highly responsive to social change.

The Chicago experience is instructive. Under Mayor Daley, the Democratic organization in Chicago relied heavily on voting support from a coalition of white ethnics and blacks. In Daley's initial election and the early years of his administration, black precincts were a key voting bloc for the machine. But when office holding, the distribution of patronage, and the direction of city housing and education policies continued to be tilted toward white ethnics despite growth of the black population, black support for the Daley organization waned.[23] In 1979, blacks voted heavily against Daley's successor for mayor. And in 1983, Harold Washington, a non-machine black candidate, won the Democratic nomination and the mayoralty.

In the face of a changing city population, the machine under Daley and his successors continued to provide disproportionate benefits to whites, adopt policies intended to stem white exodus to the suburbs, and give special attention to the concerns of white neighborhoods.[24] The Chicago machine under Daley and his successors was a semi-closed group that lost its capacity to mobilize a growing element of the city's population. While the ward-based organization that Daley once headed remains a formidable force, it no longer controls mayoral elections. Instead of adapting to a changing population, the machine sought to keep control in the hands of established leaders and continued to play to a diminishing base of support. The personal network of ward chiefs could not match the

[23] Kathleen A. Kemp and Robert L. Lineberry, "The Last of the Great Urban Machines and the Last of the Great Urban Mayors?" in *After Daley: Chicago Politics in Transition*, ed. Samuel K. Gove and Louis H. Masotti (Urbana: University of Illinois Press, 1982), pp. 1-26.

[24] See, for example, David Koehler and Margaret Wrightson, "Inequality in the Delivery of Urban Services: A Reconsideration of the Chicago Parks," paper prepared for delivery at the annual meeting of the American Political Science Association, Chicago, IL. September 2, 1983.

mass appeals to politically conscious groups made by non-machine candidates for city-wide office.

The patronage politics of the machine, like the personal politics of the village, has ben overwhelmed (though not eliminated) by a rising tide of change and complexity. As a dominant mode of conducting public affairs, machine politics proved to be only a transitional stage. It held sway as a bridge between the simple, slow-paced life of village politics and the complicated, fast-paced life of modern organizations and large collectivities. While the machine style (reciprocal obligations reinforced by personal bonds of friendship and loyalty) is by no means extinct, it rarely serves now as a method for mobilizing a mass following.

SUGGESTED READINGS

EISINGER, PETER K. "Ethnic Political Transition in Boston, 1884-1933: Some Lessons for Contemporary Cities." *Political Science Quarterly* 93 (Summer 1978), 217-39.

ERIE, STEVEN P. "Two Faces of Ethnic Power: Comparing the Irish and Black Experiences." *Polity* 13 (Winter 1980), 261-284.

ERIE, STEVEN P. "The Organization of Irish-Americans into Urban Insitutions: Building the Political Machine, 1840-1896." Paper prepared for delivery at the annual meeting of the American Political Science Association, September 1-4, 1983.

FUCHS, ESTER R. and ROBERT Y. SHAPIRO. "Government Performance as a Basis for Machine Support." *Urban Affairs Quarterly 18 (June 1983), 537-550.*

GOVE, SAMUEL K. and LOUIS H. MASOTTI, eds. *After Daley: Chicago Politics in Transition.* Urbana: University of Illinois Press, 1982.

GUTERBOCK, THOMAS M. *Machine Politics in Transition.* Chicago: University of Chicago Press, 1980.

JOHNSTON, MICHAEL. "Patrons and Clients, Jobs and Machines." *American Political Science Review* 73 (June 1979), 385-98.

JONES, BRYAN D. "Party and Bureaucracy: The Influence of Intermediary Groups on Urban Public Service Delivery." *American Political Science Review* 75 (September 1981), 688-70.

KAHN, MELVIN A. andFRANCES J. MAJORS. *The Winning Ticket.* New York: Praeger, 1984.

RAKOVE, MILTON. *Don't Make No Waves, Don't Back No Losers.* Bloomington: Indiana University Press, 1975.

SHEFTER, MARTIN. "The Emergence of the Political Machine: An Alternative View." In *Theoretical Perspectives on Urban Politics,* eds. Willis D. Hawley and others. Englewood Cliffs, NJ: Prentice-Hall, 1976.

YEARLEY, CLIFTON K. *The Money Machines.* Albany: State University of New York Press, 1972.

chapter 8

Reform and Modernization

Reform means different things in different contexts. It implies an abuse that gives rise to a demand for change. In the urban context, "reform" refers to a specific movement beginning early in this century. That movement was especially bent on eliminating the evils of machine politics. When reformers promised "good government," they often had in mind structural changes that would eliminate some of the practices used by bosses to perpetuate their power. Yet the boss was not only the object of frustration to those who sought to improve ways of running local government. In fact, some reformers were more concerned with inefficiency and backwardness than with corruption and favoritism, especially since local governments were often slow to respond to the need for greater technical competence. Reform was as much a break with the traditionalism of village politics as a break with the practices of the machine; it was an effort to modernize local government and set up procedures suited for getting the most out of twentieth-century life.

Different though village and machine politics were in some respects, they were alike in being very personal styles of governance. Both were firmly rooted in a traditional outlook. Reform, by contrast, heralded the coming of a new and more impersonal style of governance; and it was rooted in what is termed here a modern outlook.[1]

Reform can be examined on several levels. First, one can examine some of the specific measures that the reform movement developed and supported: the short ballot and the merit system, then the city manager plan, and later on, metropolitan reorganization. Second, one can examine the premises on which each reform measure was based. Third, reform can be examined as the early wave of a new orientation toward society and how it should be governed. Reformers had a new and distinct outlook on political affairs. "Good government" reform was one wave of a profound transformation of society, a shift from a traditional to a modern system. The clash with the machine bosses was at heart a clash of values, a conflict born of differing ways of looking at and responding to the world.

To get the broadest canvass, we will take up this last perspective first, then examine the structural changes advocated by reformers and the principles underlying them. Finally, we will look at reform in action and its consequences for the citizens of urban communities.

THE CLASH OF VALUES

Traditional political actors tend to see public affairs in personal and immediate terms, to be more conscious of local traditions and of past relationships and loyalties. And they make decisions within this frame. Modern political actors take a more impersonal and abstract view. They are more aware of national trends and are more inclined to apply the impersonal standards of a profession or ideology and to weigh long-term consequences.

In the traditional orientation, the object is not only to take care of one's self but also to see that family, friends, and associates benefit from the opportunities that exist. Those obligations might extend to include the neighborhood or the ethnic group, but strongly felt obligations rarely extend to some impersonally defined group or community.

The traditional sense of obligation is based on strong personal feelings, a shared sense of destiny, a common outlook on life, and it is intertwined with the need for trust and mutual support. The traditionalist outlook is captured well in the advice of an immigrant father to his son:

[1] The terms "traditional" and "modern," as used here, parallel several other pairs of terms ranging from the "gemeinschaft and gesellschaft" of Ferdinand Tönnies through the "public regarding and private regarding ethos" of Edward Banfield and James Q. Wilson to the "cosmopolitanism and provincialism" of Everett C. Ladd. Of the various discussions, the one by Ladd seems to be the most useful in understanding contemporary urban politics. See Ladd, *Ideology in America* (New York: W. W. Norton and Co., paperbound edition, 1969, 1972), esp. pp. 166-74.

> The only protection was to take care of yourself and to make sure you had friends you could count on when the time came. Pop always said that he trusted Italians more than Americans, Sicilians more than Italians, his *paisani* more than other Sicilians, but most of all he trusted his family.[2]

Among traditional politicans, loyalty is the ultimate virtue. On the death of Richard Daley, *Washington Post* columnist David Broder paid perhaps the supreme tribute to the Chicago mayor when he wrote, ". . . unlike many others who inhale great power, Daley never abandoned his basic loyalties—to his neighborhood, to his city, to his party, to his own code."[3]

Traditionalists practice favoritism because it is a way of building and maintaining in-group solidarity. With the machine as in the village, reciprocity in the granting of favors is the other side of the coin of loyalty. People interact as whole persons, not out of formal role relations. If a constituent is a friend or neighbor, then an official feels obligated to give her or him special attention. To do otherwise would be a discourtesy. Traditional politics can be calculative and exploitive, of course, just as friendships in any era can be. But the calculations are based on the view that personal favors generate and sustain reciprocal loyalties. Sentiments and feelings are not to be avoided but cultivated.

Modernists are oriented more toward the larger community, taking into account universal principles and general considerations. Society is too large and too complicated to be reduced to purely personal terms; sentimental attachments carry less weight because they are considered an impediment. Loyalties are based on membership in an impersonal collectivity or on adherence to a set of ideas. Many business and professional relationships are impersonal, hence much of the conduct of public affairs tends to be impersonal. Often individuals interact in narrow and delimited ways, as one formally defined role with another. Much interaction is not even face to face—it is by newsletter, telephone, memoranda, recorded messages, and even the exchange of quantitative data. Of course, the personal does break through, and it is sometimes used for manipulative purposes. But compared to the traditionalist, the modernist administrator, for example, tends to be professional, nonemotional, and impersonal.

The traditional outlook is prescientific and nonideological. Traditionalists rely mainly upon firsthand knowledge, personal experiences, and inside dope. Knowledge is personal and intuitive. The modern outlook is more scientific and abstract. Modernists, believing in formal knowledge, professionally learned procedures, and objective analysis, enjoy poking fun at the actions of traditionalists. A favorite anecdote of one of the authors comes from a conversation with a city planner in Atlanta about why the city

[2] Francis A. J. Ianni and Elizabeth Reuss-Ianni, *A Family Business* (New York: New American Library, 1972, 1973) p. 80.

[3] *Washington Post*, December 26, 1976.

was using federal planning funds to map its water and sewer system. With a mixture of amusement and anxiety, the planner explained that there was no existing map of the system other than the one embedded in the remarkable memory of an aged employee of the Public Works Department. The conversation occurred in 1968!

Thoroughgoing modernists find it hard to conceive of doing things in an unsystematic or purely intuitive manner. Problems are solved by correct procedure, sound principles, and careful planning, which take into account remote and indirect consequences. To the traditionalist, local government is mainly an association through which friends and neighbors can be taken care of and in-group solidarity maintained. Long-range consequences of actions are not a major consideration. To the modernist, local government is a mechanism through which collective problems can be solved, services provided, and social change directed.

The two value orientations described above are logical constructs, highlighting contrasting tendencies. As we shall see later, modernity itself contains differing strains. In the everyday world of politics, behavior is mixed. Traditionalist public officials are, of course, constrained by some general considerations and expectations. Modernists certainly are not without personal feelings and impulses: they are not above individual favor seeking, and they sometimes make decisions based on personal likes and dislikes. Above all, it is important to remember that the terms used here are not moral judgments. The word "modern" is not meant to imply something superior, or "traditional" to suggest something inferior. "Modern" is used only to mark a break with the value orientation of both village and machine politics. It does not signal the reaching of a higher ethical plane.

The conflict between the machines and the reform movement was not so much a battle between morality and immorality as a contest between different modes of thinking. Despite some strong propensities to see it that way, local politics rarely unfolds as a dramatic struggle between good and evil. To be sure, corruption and inefficiency were rampant in traditionally run cities. But, as we shall see later, modernization has given rise to its own form of corruption and inefficiency. Likewise, while many reformers were well intentioned, so too were many traditional-minded officeholders.

A PREFATORY NOTE ON LOCAL GOVERNMENT STRUCTURE

The conflict between value systems is one level of analysis. At another level, there is an array of governmental and electoral arrangements, some of which were especially accommodating to traditional (unreformed) politics and others of which were devised and promoted by advocates to reform. Before looking at the principles of reform, it might be helpful to contrast reform and nonreform *styles* of governance. Then it might also be useful to consider the alternative ways in which local government can be organized formally. It should be remembered that while forms of government can be bent and manipulated to operate in more than one way, some forms do lend themselves more readily than others to the reform style of governance. Formal structure and style of governance thus are not unrelated, and students should be acquainted with the essential features of the four basic forms of local government and also with alternative methods of conducting elections. Perhaps the contrast between reform and nonreform styles of governance may highlight some of the possible connections between structure and procedure.

As a procedure of government, the reform style relies heavily on experts, tends to be administratively centralized, and usually provides some show of nonpartisan or community-wide support. As an illustration of reform politics in operation consider the following description by one city manager of how he handled potentially controversial matters:

> If I am trying to get in a particular code, like a housing code, I have the expert, such as the building inspector, explain the code at a private meeting, then with the council's agreement, bring the matter up at the next council meeting; and inasmuch as this is a very controversial matter, ask the council to appoint a citizens committee to study the code. The citizens committee is likely to be influenced by the evidence developed by the staff, and a broad foundation of public sentiment is developed.[4]

By contrast, ward politics, a typical style of unreformed politics, is folksy and little concerned with the trappings of either expertise or civic respectability. A reformist study of early twentieth-century politics in Janesville, Wisconsin, noted that the ward politicians who ran the city government "enjoyed handling the public relations of the city in street-corner gatherings, saloons, and other centers of social life of the less prosperous and less enterprising half of Janesville."[5] (That reform proponents were not unbiased in their reporting of local politics is readily apparent.) In this same study of Janesville, the authors observed that the ward politicians made "no distinction . . . between political and administrative functions. They looked after their wards and administrative departments alike." But the authors also noted that in Janesville, unlike some of the more notorious cities, there was "no evidence of dishonesty in the aldermen's handling of municipal affairs," and "the 'shakedown' was unknown."[6] Janesville was criticized more for its antiquated and cumbersome procedures than for its

[4] Quoted in Clarence E. Ridley, *The Role of the City Manager in Policy Formulation* (Chicago: International City Managers' Association, 1958), p. 15.

[5] Harold A. Stone, Don K. Price, and Kathryn H. Stone, *City Manager Government in Nine Cities* (Chicago: Public Administration Service, 1940), p. 6.

[6] Ibid., p. 6-7.

corruption. The fragmented and unprofessional character of an unreformed system is captured in this description:

> The city clerk-comptroller, the treasurer, and the attorney were elected; the street commissioner and the city engineer were appointed by the council; the fire and police commission, the water board, and the board of health were appointed by the mayor. The mayor had little power; the council committees and the independent boards were in control of administration.
>
> The council's procedure was involved and painfully slow. . . . Petty matters called for debate, discussion, and formal resolution; the minutes record that "Alderman Dulin moved that the chairman of the police committee see that the traffic policeman on the corner of Main and Milwaukee Streets be equipped with a traffic policeman's whistle," and that the motion was duly carried. Long squabbles over salary scales, with protests and petitions from employees and their friends pouring in, were matters of course as fiscal plans were debated.
>
> In this maze of procedure, those aldermen were most influential who looked most carefully to the welfare of their wards, and who knew most thoroughly the intricate rules of the game.[7]

Let us consider now alternative governmental structures and electoral forms.

Weak-mayor system. Under the weak-mayor system, administrative power is shared by the mayor and the legislative body (generally called either the council or the board of aldermen). Separation of powers is therefore more apparent than real. Members of the legislative body may control the appointment or removal of some administrative officials, or they may exercise direct administrative control of departments through legislative committees. Some department heads may be separately elected. While the mayor may be an influential figure informally, the formal distribution of authority favors a dispersion of power, particularly among members of the legislative body.

Strong-mayor system. Under the strong-mayor system, the mayor is chief executive in fact as well as in name. The mayor appoints and removes department heads and exercises direct administrative control of all departments. Separation of powers is therefore distinct, and the mayor monopolizes administrative authority. Recently some county governments have adopted this system, though an elected county executive is not referred to as the mayor but as the executive.

Commission system. The commission form combines legislative and administrative power in a small elected body (three to seven, often five

[7] Ibid., p. 7.

members). Each commissioner may exercise detailed supervision over one or more departments. With relatively few traditional service responsibilities, many county governments have utilized the commission system as a matter of course.

Council-manager system. Like the commission form, council-manager government disregards the separation of powers principle. Only the council is elected, (if there is a separately elected mayor, that role is mainly ceremonial), and it possesses all legislative powers as well as ultimate administrative power in the form of the authority to appoint and dismiss the city manager. However, the city manager appoints all department heads; and the council is expected to stay out of day-to-day administrative matters. It is sometimes referred to as the city manager system because the city manager is the chief administrator, but the council-manager label is preferred by its architects, to emphasize that ultimate control is in the hands of an elected legislative body. Some counties have adopted the form, and in that setting it is often referred to as the county manager plan. The manager is considered a professional—a specialist in administration rather than a politician.

The National Municipal League, a reform organization, recommends that the charter provision describing the position of city manager read as follows:

> The City manager shall be chosen by the council solely on the basis of his executive and administrative qualifications with special reference to his actual experience in, or his knowledge of, accepted practice in respect to the duties of his office. . . . At the time of his appointment, he need not be a resident of the city or state . . .[8]

The League also recommends that the council under the council-manager plan be a relatively small body, preferably elected at-large and on a nonpartisan basis.

At-large and district elections. At-large and district elections refer to methods of electing members of the legislative body. The terms are self-explanatory. At-large elections are city-wide or county-wide. District elections refer to the system of breaking the city or county up into separate geographical constituencies or election districts, sometimes called wards. (The term "ward politics" is used to refer to political practices in which council members or aldermen are oriented mainly toward actions of benefit to their own districts and the constituents of their respective districts.) Commission and council-manager governments typically (but not universally) have at-large elections. Mayor-council governments can be either.

[8] *Forms of Municipal Government* (New York: National Municipal League, 1973), p. 8.

Members of legislative bodies can also be elected by a mixed system—some from districts and some at-large; and they can be chosen in a system of nomination by district (the city or county is divided into districts, each of which is to be represented by one or more legislators who *reside* in that district) but *balloting* for each seat is at-large.

Partisan and nonpartisan ballots. Party labels may or may not be allowed on local election ballots. If party labels are prohibited, then the ballot form is nonpartisan. While political parties might still engage openly or discreetly in campaign activities, the intent is to free local elections of the influence of state and national political parties. On a partisan ballot, candidates are identified by party affiliation, and partisan activity is therefore given full encouragement. In some systems regarded as genuinely nonpartisan, local organizations unrelated to the state and national political parties do perform such party-like functions as recruiting candidates and campaigning for them.

PRINCIPLES OF REFORM

Despite the inefficiency, corruption, and cynicism that abounded in American cities, the early proponents of reform were basically optimists. They held a generally benevolent view of humanity; and they were confident that urban communities could be directed along paths of cooperation, good will, and collective accomplishments. From the beginning, these advocates of "good government" were sure of our collective ability to understand the problems facing us and to prescribe effective remedies. They had a virtually unshakable faith in experts, and strongly supported activities such as the city planning movement.

Proponents of reform were convinced that with a continuing rise in the level of education, the populace would become increasingly enlightened. Progress could be made. The abuses around them reformers attributed more to faulty institutions and bad procedures than to any inherent defects in human nature. Richard S. Childs, one of the leading theorists of "good government" reform, stated, "The difficulties of democracy . . . are mechanistic, not moral, and respond to mechanistic corrections. . . ."[9] One leading textbook in municipal government (written as many of them were by advocates of reform) proclaimed: "Bad city government in the United States has largely been the result of unsound theory."[10]

[9] Richard S. Childs, "Civic Victories in the United States," *National Municipal Review* 44 (September 1955), 402.

[10] Austin F. Macdonald, *American City Government and Administration*, 6th ed. (New York: Thomas Y. Crowell Co., 1956), p. 133.

With municipal institutions based on "sound theory," the reformers argued, people could be united in the pursuit of their common interests. Reformers did not regard conflict as something based on natural antagonisms in the urban community.

The optimism of the reform movement is associated with some basic assumptions about the nature of local government. And the structural changes advocated by reformers were the concrete expressions of these same assumptions. Therefore to understand both their optimism and their program, it is necessary to examine the reformers' premises. There are three separate but interrelated principles of "good government."

1. There is an overriding public interest that is superior to the particular interests of the various segments of the urban community.
2. This general interest is more easily discovered through cooperation than through conflict and competition.
3. Technical problem solving is the central task of local government; "politics" is therefore to be minimized.

Let us look at these principles as they were elaborated and applied by the proponents of reform.

The public interest. First of all, whether they were attacking the corruption and extravagance of the machine or the standpattism and backwardness of the village outlook, reformers have always argued that there is a general interest of the whole community that should guide the actions of government officials on all occasions. Reformers were impatient with bargaining for neighborhood or ethnic advantage, which they regarded as a failure to subordinate particular interests to the general welfare. In their minds, bad government was government by petty favors. Favor seeking, they believed, would be unnecessary if cities would simply offer their citizens a high level of efficient service. They were confident that transcending the special interests of the various parts of the community is an easily identified interest of the entire community. As they saw it, the public interest is not simply an aggregation of partial and segmental interests. Instead, they held what might be termed a unitary conception of the public interest.

As proponents of a unitary conception of the public interest, reformers have stood for the consolidation of authority by means of a number of specific changes:

Executive reorganization. Throughout the century, the reform movement has consistently backed executive reorganization as a means to consolidating executive power and thereby promoting unity of command. By contrast, scattered authority was seen as grist for the machine politician's mill. Bosses could induce unity on an ad hoc basis, but only by favor trading. Efficiency and consistency of program, the reformers argued, could come only when a chief executive's authority was commensurate with the responsibility to see that the general welfare is served.

The short ballot. One of the earliest planks in the reform platform called for a short ballot. The long ballot lends itself to ticket balancing, ethnic representation, and the kind of special interest bargaining so abhorrent to reformers. The reformers reasoned that the average voter could not possibly be well informed on the actions of a host of minor officials—sheriffs, coroners, magistrates, recorders of deeds, registrars of wills, city clerks, prosecutors, judges, and others. Therefore public accountability would best be served by consolidating authority in a few major elected positions.

*Metropolitan reorganization.*Another way of consolidating authority is metropolitan reorganization, which creates an area-wide government to replace multiple existing units. Again, the argument has run, voters cannot hold accountable a multitude of officials with overlapping jurisdictions. Further, so long as officials represent only segments of the metropolitan community, then, the reformers argue, they will never take a broad and inclusive look at the community's needs. In each case, the concentration of authority can be justified by the same argument—the argument that the community has an overarching set of common interests and that government should be structured in such a way as to promote these common interests in a unified and authoritative manner.

At-large elections. The "good-government" platform has also favored at-large elections. Reformers have considered them to be a device through which the link would be broken between elected officials and the "selfish," parochial interests of constituents. District elections, reformers have feared, provide a basis on which deals could be made and practices such as logrolling (you support my project and I'll support yours) could flourish. By no longer representing separate segments of the city, reformers believe, victors in at-large elections could promote the discovery of general community interests. At-large elections thus embody the principle that the public interest is a unitary phenomenon. Clearly the reform movement treats governance not as a matter of representing the diverse interests of constituents but as a matter of discovering the best way to solve the problems of the whole community.

Cooperation over conflict. Because community well-being can easily be overlooked in the heat of factional battle, reformers frown on conflict, especially of a partisan or organized kind. They see the search for the public interest as a nonemotional and disinterested search—one conducted in an atmosphere of mutual cooperation and unhampered by "artificial" divisions in the community. Indeed, reformers maintain that a community should be organized politically so as to discourage public figures from thinking about and promoting the particular and immediate interest of their constituents. For them, the ideal leader is one who is beholden to no special interest, who has no particular obligations to any organization or segment of the community. Voters should therefore select candidates who are best qualified to act the statesman's role and should not vote for candidates on the basis of partisan affiliation, ethnic identity, or a place of residence.

Reformers, concerned with weakening the hold of machine politics on local elections and equating partisan competition with the search for favors and partronage, became strong supporters of *nonpartisan elections*. Though they sometimes form local organizations to recruit and support candidates for local office, they have always thought of these efforts as nonpartisan in spirit as well as form. How, they have reasoned, could an organization be partisan if it was set up to defend the common good?

Reformers aimed for more than an end to party-dominated elections. They sought a general lessening of the competitive spirit. In many communities, the proponents of reform regarded controversy and argumentation as obstacles to progress. They considered such behavior regressive, a throwback to the selfishness and factionalism of prereform days. Competition and conflict, far from being seen as paths to a fuller understanding of the issues, were seen as sure signs that some minds were closed off to the best way to serve the public interest.

Expertise over "politics." In the reformers' eyes, government is not a matter of representing and reconciling conflicting interests. In fact, reformers tend to dismiss as "politics" such functions as interest representation and conflict mediation. And to them as to many Americans, "politics" is a derogatory term. Reformers have conceived of government as a process through which sound, expert judgment would be applied to technical problems. As the reformers see it, building a transportation system, for example, is not a political problem but an engineering problem. (They started the old saw about there being no Democratic or Republican way to pave a street.) Further, reformers have made no distinction between the physical and the social problems of the city—both alike were regarded as amenable to expert analysis and solution.

Reformers have always displayed great confidence in fact finding. As one city manager put it, "The body of municipal knowledge has grown to the point that an increasing number of problems is resolved factually, and this has been accepted and even demanded by the public."[11] Typically, citizens were expected not to question the judgment of experts. One writer explained how the city manager should be regarded:

[11] C. A. Harell and D. G. Weiford, "The City Manager and the Policy Process," *Public Administration Review* 19 (Spring 1959), 104.

> No matter what politician selects a manager, it goes without saying he's a better man than the politician. That's that.
>
> He knows how to manage things the professional politicians barely suspect exist—bonds, refinancing, machinery, short-term paper, pinochle-playing bums in the outlying municipal offices and plants, traffic, welfare, the works. City management always does it better. . . .
>
> If you take your car to the garage or your liver to the doctor's office, you go prepared to accept a judgment. The garage man says there's a perforation in the fuel-pump diaphragm, and you yield. The doctor says he is going to half sole your liver. Ah, well, you say. You do not observe that this is authoritarianism. You don't ask who the hell he thinks he is, because you know.[12]

School superintendents, chiefs of police, transportation planners, finance officers, personnel administrators, and other municipal experts presumably are to be treated with equal deference so long as they possess and act on a body of expert knowledge.

Merit hiring. If government is primarily a technical exercise in problem solving and if competence means expertise, then it follows that government personnel should be chosen on merit and given job protection through civil service tenure. Reformers have predictably backed extensions of the merit system. And to them, merit is often best measured by such means as written tests or formal credentials. They have therefore been active in efforts to professionalize various public service occupations—that is, to organize them so that job holders have either formal training or at least the kind of expertise that can be demonstrated on written tests.

Council-manager system. After a brief affair of the heart with the commission plan, municipal reformers settled on the council-manager plan as the ideal form of government (along with nonpartisan, at-large elections). The commission form was flawed in principle in that it failed to unify executive authority. Moreover, it mixed politics and administration by having elected officials head major administrative departments. In practice, machine politicians could and did easily manipulate the plural executive structure of the commission plan.

The council-manager plan, while it could be subverted in practice, is pure reform in principle. No administrative officials are elected. Instead, the executive function is headed by a professional administrator, whose claim to office is expertise and disinterest in any private advantage. As professionals, city managers presumably are dedicated to their work and seek no gain beyond a salary. The manager is therefore supposed to be uninvolved in politics and fully capable of overseeing processes by which technical problems are identified and solved in the one best way.

[12] William A. Caldwell, "Inevitable Urge to Be Bright," *National Municipal Review* 42 (May 1952), 222.

Who controls policy? The theory of council-manager government calls for the city council to determine policy. The city manager is, of course, allowed to make recommendations, and always prepares the budget. The power to formulate proposals, combined with a command of the technical details of city governance, gives the manager a wide opportunity to put a personal imprint on city policy—theory notwithstanding. And policy and administration cannot be neatly separated. The discretionary judgment that administrators must exercise as they apply broad policy directives to concrete situations involves considerable opportunity to shape the actual content of policy. This inevitable blurring of policy and administration in practice has never disturbed proponents of municipal reform because they have not regarded policy making as necessarily a political exercise. Keeping elected officials out of the details of program administration has mattered more than restricting the policy role of administrators.

Reformers, in fact, have been somewhat ambivalent about popular control. The short ballot and other concentrations of authority have always been defended as mechanisms through which accountability could be sharpened and popular control enhanced. Yet, in the name of keeping politics out of various phases of local government, reformers have sometimes devised ways of diffusing administrative authority in order to insulate specific programs from constituency pressures. In reform communities, appointive citizen boards and commissions—composed of civic leaders or blue-ribbon members—have often served as buffers between elected officials and administrative agencies such as those for planning, redevelopment, and even public safety.

Education has been a touchy area that reformers have tried hard to insulate from popular influence. School boards often are not elected. Even when they are, school board members are expected not to be "politicians" but instead to be capable of ignoring aroused community groups. The reform movement looks on the school board, the PTA, and other education-related organizations more as supporters for the programs of professional educators than as independent sources of educational ideas and programs.

Even the holders of regular elective offices are expected to be willing to defy any sudden upsurge of popular feeling, should the vagaries of public opinion threaten sound governmental practices. Ideally, officials would be individuals with no personal stakes in the outcome of any issue. And model officeholders would also be uninterested in a political career, so that their personal ambitions would not sway their judgments in a time of controversy.

Caveats. A few caveats are in order about reform principles and practices. Reformers have never been 100 percent true to their principles. On occasion, they have harbored both personal and partisan resentment against their opponents. Class and ethnicity clearly were interwoven into many of the conflicts between reformers and bosses, reformers typically being middle-class and Protestant while machine supporters were mostly lower class and Catholic. A reform group in Michigan, for example, once celebrated their victory by holding a reception at the Masonic Temple. Subsequently they fired all Catholic employees of the city and replaced them with Protestants, and as a final slap at their opponents, they took liquor licenses away from saloons and gave them to hotels.[13]

Reformers, no less so than others, are capable of inconsistency. Robert Moses, after a long career of crusading for civil service reform, once in office shrewdly cultivated alliances with figures in the financial and construction industries. No system has ever functioned without an element of personal wheeling and dealing. Furthermore, technical problem solving obviously cannot be separated neatly from matters of policy preference. Expert know-how inevitably spills over into issues on which there are no neutral positions. Yet, when all of the caveats are said, the need for technically skilled and professionally committed public servants must still be acknowledged. Modern communities cannot be run without them.

THE POLITICAL CONSEQUENCES OF REFORM

Reform structures have not been universally adopted. By and large, they have been introduced most readily in those communities where traditional politics has been least firmly entrenched. Older and large cities that were heavily populated by immigrant groups and those that have not experienced high population mobility have been notably resistant to reform structures. Conversely, newer and middle-sized cities, especially those that have grown rapidly, have been the most willing to embrace reform. But reform is not an all-or-nothing proposition. Civil service has diminished the range of patronage in all parts of the country. Procedural requirements everywhere tend to move in a direction that gives less room for the more blatant forms of favoritism. And even where professional city management has not been instituted atop the administrative branch of government, the trend is to provide the mayor with a chief administrative officer (CAO) or an assistant under some title who excels in the skill of management. Moreover, in those cities that have been unwilling to adopt the council-manager system, reform efforts have been directed at strengthening the office of mayor. Thus, even unreformed structures bear the imprint of a general movement toward reform and modernization. While the movement is halting and uneven, it has left few parts of the urban landscape untouched.

[13] Stone, Price, and Stone, *City Manager Government in Nine Cities, pp. 221-23.*

One of the most profound consequences of the reform movement has been in the appointment of department officials. Even in cities with an elected chief executive, a partisan ballot, and a ward system for choosing legislative representatives, traditional political values have ceased to control administrative appointments. Ethnic and geographical balancing as well as reward for party service have lost ground to technical expertise. In places where patronage is still practiced, career specialization and affiliation with the proper professional and skill groups are often essential qualifications for top administrative positions.

The reform mentality does not lead to distrust of the outsider. The "best person for the job" does not have to be a loyal member of the in-group, but can be "best" on the basis of formal education and professional training. Communal solidarity and feelings of fraternalism are traditional considerations; they carry small weight among the practitioners of reform.

The decline of traditional considerations in administrative appointments has important consequences. As civil service coverage is extended upward and as professional credentials become essential for the leaders of departments, agencies inevitably gain greater degrees of autonomy. To a large extent, departmental bureaucracies become self-directing forces in city affairs. They also become self-centered; top-level officials are usually individuals who have risen through the ranks of the department (in some other place if not in the hometown). They are expected by their departmental colleagues to see that outside interference is minimized and that professionals are largely free to pursue their own ideas about how best to conduct the work of the agency. As one observer drily summed up the situation, "The departmental bureaucracies are not neutral, they are only independent."[14]

The rise of professionalism also chokes off a path of upward mobility, in which the less-educated, ethnic, or other minority groups lose entree. With this trend, bureaucratic leadership becomes more and more the preserve of upper-status groups.

Reform not only makes departmental administrators less representative of the citizens they serve but also tends to weaken the representative role even of local legislators:

1. Voting for the "best qualified" candidate—for example, the one with the most education and civic experience and with the least personal interest at stake—is likely to mean voting for the upper-status candidate.
2. Nonpartisan ballots, if they are genuinely such, eliminate the political party as a recruiting agent for legislative candidates, and often the void is filled by civic associations and business organizations.
3. Nonpartisan and at-large elections tend to enhance newspaper influence, and candidates who have civic respectbility and some city-wide visibility tend to be favored by the press over those whose base of support is in a particular area or ethnic group.

[14]Theodore J. Lowi, *At the Pleasure of the Mayor* (New York: Free Press, 1964), p. 207.

The vitality of legislative representation is weakened in other ways, too. Reform institutions and practices tilt the balance of power sharply away from the legislative branch toward the executive branch. Amateur, spare-time legislators usually prove no match for professional administrators, with their near monopoly of the technical knowledge needed to legislate effectively. Further, few administrators are averse to making alliances. In fact, they regard the building of support as an integral part of the job; and they have the time and resources to do so. They just do not call it politicking. In routine matters, civil service protection, combined with a thumbs-down view of "political interference" gives agencies virtual autonomy. Even the budget, which is one form of influence and control, is more an executive instrument than a legislative one.

Perhaps the key factor in executive dominance under reform politics is the decline in legislative bargaining. Logrolling (you support my project, I'll support yours) and ward courtesy (I decide who gets what in my ward, you decide in your ward) were the backbone of machine politics. With their decline, alternative methods of generating support for policy action have had to be developed. Public relations and media promotion replace (or at least supplement) bargaining in caucus as a way of bringing together the needed backing. If a new proposal is afoot, it must first be legitimized by the experts, via a report showing that it is technically feasible and that it will be good for the community. The next step is endorsement by influential lay figures—persons representing the groups that would be most directly affected or general civic leaders or both. In the meantime, since most policy innovations are likely to involve either some foundation funding or some federal money, administrators are negotiating to bring together the money people and action agencies around a commonly agreed-upon program. The final major step is publicity. The officials bring in news media to publicize the proposed program, get civic organizations to sponsor meetings, and pull together ad hoc citizens' committees to mobilize additional public support and press for adoption of the program. A citizens' committee may even oversee its implementation. The city council's legislative role in the process is reduced to one of giving rubber-stamp approval to a project that it neither initiated nor promoted. Rarely does the city council have a genuine opportunity to modify the proposal; only the mayor or city manager is likely to play a key part in the process.

In general, then, reform politics weakens the representation of particular groups, especially if those groups are of lower status, have no city-wide base of operation, or rank low in civic prestige. Citizen participation in making policy tends to occur through blue-ribbon committees, that is, committees composed mainly of upper-status business and professional persons. Legislative influence decreases, and agency autonomy grows.

Reform politics appears in its purest form in affluent suburbs. The homogeneous, middle-class setting produces the least tension between reform institutions and the clientele that those institutions serve. In a large-city setting, the story is different. Because reform structures and practices are not attuned to the diversity of city life, minorities, especially those of lower status, have no easy avenues of political expression. Reform represents majority views more easily than the views of discrete segments of a large community. Moreover, by weakening overtly political institutions, reform dims the public voice of the lower class. Middle- and upper-class groups retain a channel of expression through various civic organizations, but the lower class has need for direct political representation—for the personal link between constituent and representative.

POLICY

In its early days, reform was touted as a way to achieve economy and efficiency. However, reform does not necessarily lead a local government to spend less money. The professionals, so valued in reform government, often turn out to be spenders. Career success comes to those who put a personal imprint on a program. Professionals are receptive to new ideas; they maintain contact with other professionals and tend to be informed about the latest developments in the field. Indeed, occupational standing often hinges on making innovations. A research and planning division, the usual hallmark of an up-to-date administration, institutionalizes activism and innovation.

There are other dimensions to the reform impact on policy. A study that was made of traditional and reform styles of law enforcement is illustrative.[15] The study showed that traditional police departments are most likely to have a caretaker outlook—"the watchman style." They favor the status quo. Since traditional departments have little specialization and few incentives to promotion-seeking, they understandably place no great weight on formal training. Performance is not measured by any technical standards. In fact, the prevailing norm seems to be that of "don't rock the boat."

Traditional departments accommodate to the environment by being flexible about legal standards and by pursuing the course of least resistance. As a consequence, the police are lenient about many forms of misconduct, and they prefer to settle problems informally. They do not hesitate to use irregular procedures, ranging from curbstone justice to talking off the record to a juvenile's parents. The traditional style tends to privatize the law. Actions are judged less by what the law says about them than by who did them and in what circumstances. Because of their influence, "notables" may be excused. By contrast, "nobodies" can expect harsh treatment. On the other hand, if the actions in question can be defined as private, then no matter who is involved, "the police tend to overlook the violation, to handle it

[15] James Q. Wilson, *Varieties of Police Behavior* (Cambridge, Mass.: Harvard University Press, 1968). Page citations below are to the Atheneum edition, 1973.

informally, . . . or to allow . . . aggrieved parties to resolve it between themselves . . ."[16] Thus, while the traditional department practices leniency in many matters, it is likely to perpetrate inequities because it does not apply a uniform standard to everyone.

Reform departments, in contrast, may pursue either a legalistic style or a service style. Though there are significant differences between the two styles, there are also some important similarities. Both are characterized by formal training, written rules and reports, and specialization. Both tend to employ strict rules, and both try to minimize opportunities for favoritism. Legalistic departments insist on observance of fixed standards, and even service-oriented departments, while perhaps more flexible, are likely to set uniform standards. The accent is on formal processes and on specialized and professional services. Career advancement is tied to objective measures of performance. And in a legalistic department especially, arrest rates are apt to be high: they "emphasize *technical* efficiency; that is, they try to produce as much output as possible, no matter how it is valued, for a given cost."[17]

Reform politics, no less than traditional types of politics, is an adaptation to community environment. The service style of law enforcement, for example, is practiced because it conforms to expectations. One observer of reform politics commented:

> Politics in general is regarded, at least by the politicians, as providing services and amenities to persons clearly able to afford them. Though taxes are an issue, the politicians believe that people are willing to pay for programs that improve the quality of community life beyond what is minimally necessary. Government, besides keeping the streets clean and putting fires out, is also expected to sustain a prosperous business life, provide excellent schools, hire courteous and obliging public officials, and maintain the "character of the community."[18]

That kind of reading on what government should do is not likely to lead to frugality in public spending. Reform practices are most likely to be encouraged where there is a desire for a high level of services, not just any services but those that are amenities and improve the quality of life. Reform politics tends to conform in substance and procedure to middle-class tastes.

EXECUTIVE LEADERSHIP AND THE "NEW CONVERGENCE OF POWER": REFORM AND THE SEEDS OF AN URBAN REVOLT

Reform has assumed a distinctive character in the big-city setting. It could not take on the nonpolitical appearance possible in smaller and more homogeneous communities. Thus it centered to a great degree on the

[16] Ibid., p. 142.
[17] Ibid., p. 185.
[18] Ibid., p. 250.

office of mayor. Furthermore, big-city reform took shape from the need to come to terms with the economic condition of older communities.

By the end of World War II, urban government had become too complicated and too costly to be run on the basis of reciprocal personal obligations. As issues became more complex, they could not be handled simply by the exchange of favors and courtesies among the representatives of various geographic and ethnic groups. While patronage, favors, and opportunities for boodle did not disappear, they remained as political resources largely at the disposal of the chief executive. Ward-based leaders became creatures of the past, content to live off what emanated from city hall. They made no large demands and received no great rewards.

Ward-based leadership atrophied, in part, because it served a passive and changing lower-class constituency. In the early years after World War II, many white ethnics moved out of the lower class and loosened their traditional political ties. At the same time, the growing number of lower-class blacks and Spanish-speaking minorities gained only limited access to the ward structure of leadership. While petty favors, ethnic recognition, and personal loyalty continued to mobilize some supporters, almost everywhere voter turnout declined.

Conditions were ripe for the rise of executive leadership. Legislative leadership was waning and administrative agencies had not yet developed independent bases of political support. They needed executive backing to expand their budgets, and to buttress autonomy against "political" intervention by ward bosses.

While happy to fill a political vacuum, many post-World War II mayors had no secure political base of their own. As party organizations declined in strength, the news media became an important link between chief executives and their constituents. Favorable media treatment required that a mayor adopt a "good government" posture, cultivate an activist image, and promote projects—such as downtown revitalization—in which the major newspapers were interested. It was good public relations to appear respectable—get blue-ribbon committees to endorse projects, use experts to justify new ventures, hire the best qualified managers regardless of place of residence or political affiliation and use the private sector extensively in order to remove the taint of patronage politics.

Reform-minded observers of the big city political scene were quick to praise the leadership potential of the mayor's office. While not as theoretically clean as the council-manager form, a strong-mayor system was an acceptable second best. Besides, some reform proponents were realistic enough to see that in a big city of great diversity, there had to be something other than professional expertise, some centripetal force to foster community-wide interests. They seized upon the office of mayor as the centralizing instrument required. The mayor's political skill could be used constructively to cajole, concede a point now and then, and in the long run outmaneuver the parochial-minded advocates of various special and particular interests. In the parlance of public administration, neutral competence as an administrative principle was subordinated to an alternative principle–executive leadership.

Reform is, of course, more than a matter of executive structure, and the big-city changes were more than cosmetic. Mayors emerged as the central figures in a new alliance with business leaders. Old-line Democratic politicians put aside considerations of party and allied themselves with Republican business leaders in order to renew the health of the central city. And both partners in the coalition appeared eager to employ the analytical and management skills of professional administrators. As this "new convergence of power" coalesced, mayors became more problem oriented and public agencies more professionalized.[19] Though it was sometimes mostly a ritual bow to science in a technological society, comprehensive planning became a fixed part of policy formation. The good of the city as a whole, deference to expertise, and a dedication to technical problem solving—all principles of reform—infiltrated the rhetoric and perhaps the thinking of big-city political leaders. Not everything that went on was strictly according to the reform book, but enough conformed to reform expectations to get the blessings of "good government" advocates.

What was at the heart of this alliance? The new convergence was as much one of interest as of power. The growth of suburban shopping centers, changing modes of travel, major population shifts, and a general process of aging were ample grounds for widespread apprehension over the economic future of the central city. The businessmen involved came from the firms with the greatest stake in the central city, firms whose financial standing is often tied to property values in and around the main business district. Public officials had (and still have) cause to be worried about the economic health of the city and the strength of its tax base.

Out of their mutual concerns, the elements composing the new convergence responded to central-city deterioration with a variety of measures. Traffic and transportation, the amelioration of socially disruptive problems, and redevelopment became top items on the public agenda for most large cities. And business leaders, political executives, and professional administrators agreed on the prescription for curing the ills of the central city: slum clearance, economic development, and making the central city attractive to the affluent.

The new convergence represented an apparent consensus among important segments of the urban community about how to combat core-city decay. Its approach was in many ways true to the spirit of the reform movement: a problem-solving endeavor in which technical experts, promi-

[19] Robert H. Salisbury, "Urban Politics: The New Convergence of Power," *Journal of Politics* 26 (November 1964), 775-97.

nent citizens from the business community, and political leaders were joined together to produce the "best" remedy for the ailments of the city.

As programs took shape, however, it became clear that not all segments of the community were going to be equally well served. The consensus was a shaky one. Somewhere between Plunkitt of Tammany Hall and the new convergence, poor people lost favor among the nation's urban politicians. Plunkitt looked on the needs of poor people as opportunities to win friends, cultivate votes, and maintain his influence. Latter-day politicians view the needs of the poor mainly as a threat to the city's fiscal solvency.

Overtly, revitalization programs centered on promoting downtown commercial activity and making urban life attractive to the affluent. Older areas were cleared to make way for office buildings, luxury apartments, hotels, and civic centers. Efforts to relocate the displaced poor were often inadequate. Covertly, the policy objective often was not just to provide room for commercial activity but also to move the lower class away from the commercial center, away from high-status institutions, away from affluent residents. Though much rhetoric about human renewal accompanied efforts at physical renewal, the rhetoric often proved empty. The members of the new convergence had few incentives to try social programs that might be costly, controversial, or worse yet, so successful as to attract new throngs of poor to the city.

Although big-city mayors depended on votes from lower- and working-class groups, the connection between the mayors and their constituents was a tenuous one. In cities with locally active party organizations, votes could still be delivered on the basis of patronage and favoritism, but the mayor did not usually seek the *counsel* of grass roots politicians on matters of policy. Many of the resources needed by mayors did not come from constituents—funding for key projects and national recognition came from foundation executives and career professionals in federal agencies. Thus as traditional bases of support for city hall receded in importance, other lines of access gained in importance; and policy decisions followed the shifting balance of influence. Even though blacks were the mainstay of the local party organization in many big cities, the grass-roots black politicians were not the power figures that their ethnic predecessors had been. Blacks received few benefits but incurred much of the cost involved in combatting the decline of the central city. Considering that grass roots politicians are the group closest to and most sympathetic toward the minority poor, the reform impact in the big city was a political disaster for the lower class.

Reform was by and large elitist. Its programs took little account of what the little people wanted. Key positions in the city government were no longer a reliable route for upward mobility. Even the benefits of such programs as urban renewal, expressway construction, and the promotion of economic growth were too indirect to offer much aid and comfort to the lower strata of urban society.

Inevitably, discontent built up in the neglected neighborhoods of large cities. Their leaders had no readily available lines of access to governmental decision makers. Their life conditions were not improving despite city hall rhetoric and program activity. Indeed, conditions often worsened. Without direct representation in the process of governance, the left-outs came to distrust the motives of top-level officials. To blacks, "good government" was a smoke-screen for subordinating their well-being to that of a vague but strongly disliked white power structure.[20] The emotional distance between city hall and neighborhood was increasing at a time when black aspirations were on the rise. When programs like urban renewal worked no wonders for the big cities, "good government" got low marks from many blacks. The stage was set for a period of conflict, out of which is emerging a postreform era in city politics—but not just in city politics. For the suburbs are uneasy neighbors of the core city and they too are places of change and political conflict.

SUGGESTED READINGS

CARO, ROBERT A. *The Power Broker*. New York: Knopf, 1974.

CONWAY, M. MARGARET, and FRANK FEIGERT. "Motivation, Incentive Systems, and the Political Party Organization." *American Political Science Review* 62 (December 1969), 1169-83.

DUTTON, WILLIAM H. and AND ALANA NORTHROP. "Municipal Reform and the Changing Pattern of Urban Party Politics." *American Politics Quarterly* 6 (October 1978), 429-52.

LADD, EVERETT C. *Ideology in America*. New York: W. W. Norton and Co., 1969, 1972.

LINEBERRY, ROBERT L., and EDMUND P. FOWLER. "Reformism and Public Policies in American Cities." *American Political Science Review* 61 (September 1967), 701-16.

LOWI, THEODORE J. *At the Pleasure of the Mayor*. New York: Free Press, 1964.

LYONS, WILLIAM. "Reform and Response in American Cities." *Social Science Quarterly* 59 (June 1978), 118-32.

SALISBURY, ROBERT H. "Urban Politics: The New Convergence of Power." *Journal of Politics* 26 (November 1964), 775-97.

SCHUMAKER, PAUL D. and AND RUSSELL W. GETTER. "Responsiveness Bias in 51 American Communities." *American Journal of Political Science* 21 (May 1977), 247-81.

______. "Structural Sources of Unequal Responsiveness to Group Demands in American Cities." *Western Political Quarterly* 36 (March 1983), 7-29.

STILLMAN, RICHARD J., II. *The Rise of the City Manager*. Albuquerque: University of New Mexico Press, 1974.

WILSON, JAMES Q. *Varieties of Police Behavior*. Cambridge, MA: Harvard University Press, 1968.

[20]See, especially, Ernest Patterson, *Black City Politics* (New York: Dodd, Mead and Company, 1974).

chapter 9

Suburban Politics: Change and Paradox

More Americans live in suburbs than in any other kind of community. As we saw in Chapter 1, suburban dwellers are now more numerous than central-city dwellers. Yet, from the mass media—and despite our own experience living and working in suburban communities—many of us have a stereotyped image of suburbia. We think of suburbia as a place where only affluent white middle-class citizens live. The suburbanites of our image are conformists—inane, dull, and promiscuous—more concerned with backyard barbecues than with intellectual discussions or pressing social issues.

Stereotype and reality, however, are not the same. The stereotyped image first developed in the 1950s, when suburbia as we know it had come into its prime—the product of postponed residential building and family formation during World War II. In reality, there are many kinds of suburbs and suburbanites. Yet, as compared to central cities or the traditional small towns, the individual suburb is a relatively homogeneous community. In the smallest suburbs, sometimes a single social group is completely dominant. In larger and growing suburbs, there are often two or three distinct social groups. However, even in the largest suburbs, rarely is there the wide social mix that makes up the typical city. As suburbs grow and mature, they may gradually lose their social homogeneity, but for now that continues to be an identifying trait.

Suburbs, though they are by definition outside the central city, are part and parcel of the urban scene. It takes both "urb" and "sub-urbs" to make a metropolitan area. Their economic interdependence is the cement that binds them together. Until recently, the home-to-work flow was almost all one way, but now the pattern is more complex.

If economic interdependence is one hallmark of the typical metropolitan area, suburban political independence is the other. In any metropolitan area, there is a multiplicity of suburban jurisdictions—municipal governments, counties, towns, school districts, and other special districts. Generally speaking, these jurisdictions jealously guard their independence against annexation by the central cities and, for that matter, against any form of area-wide governance.

There is diversity *among* suburbs, which come in all shapes and sizes. Many were rural villages, whose older residents feel threatened by the forces of urbanization and modernization. A growing population creates demands for services, in particular for more and better schools. Older residents may fear tax increases and oppose new growth. Suburbs, however, are not just places of new growth. The spillover of the central-city poor into adjacent geographical areas has brought whole suburban counties face to face with the kinds of problems that used to be on the agenda only in central cities. There are also satellite cities—suburbs only by having been engulfed by metropolitan growth through the years—which have their own centers of industry and commerce. Some of these satellites contain new plants, offices, and housing developments. But many are older communities experiencing the same set of problems as the core city—a decaying business district, declining tax base, and fixed-income population. In many of these communities, traditional politics is still the dominant practice.

Some suburbs specialize in retailing. They are literally built around shopping centers, and their politics and tax base reflect that fact. There are other kinds of suburbs that depend on a specialized economic function—tourist trade, a university, or even organized crime, gambling, and other illicit activities. Some suburbs are trying to build their job and tax base by attracting office buildings, developing convention and entertainment facilities, or building coliseums and stadiums. Recent years have also brought the rise of planned suburban communities and "new towns." While thought of originally as alternatives to suburbia, they nevertheless are suburban communities, though with distinctive, planned environments.

Finally, there are stereotypical residential suburbs: the homes of the affluent white middle class. Even among these residential suburbs there is more diversity than the analysts of the fifties indicated. It is these residential suburbs, however, that ultimately have stamped politics in suburbia with its special character: social homogeneity *reinforced* by political independence. Social homogeneity is not peculiar to suburban neighborhoods; city neighborhoods also tend to be homogeneous. But city neighborhoods lack political independence. In the distinctive suburban imprint—communities with narrow social and economic spectra dependent on the city and the larger metropolitan area for jobs and income, yet independent when it comes to taxes and services—lies a huge potential for service inequalities and unresolved problems; and much of that potential has come to fruition.

THE "GOOD GOVERNMENT" ETHOS

Although they resist metropolitan area-wide governmental integration, suburbs, in particular the more affluent ones, have been the heartland of "good government" reform. There is a shortage of specific studies on suburban governmental forms, but it is possible to do some generalizing:

1. Nonpartisanship is widespread, indicating a belief that political parties bring corrupt machines and dirty politics.
2. Among suburbs generally there is a trend toward the council-manager form of government, another of the basic reform institutions. It is most prevalent in the affuent, white-collar, well-educated upper-middle-class communities of suburbia and in those with a younger, rapidly growing, mobile, white population.
3. In suburbs there is a degree of grassroots democracy that is hard to achieve in large cities. Indeed, the suburbs have often been characterized as a rather ideal example of citizen participation in political life. Citizens tend to accept an obligation to take part in public affairs. And the scale of political action enables citizens, acting on their own, to reach a consensus about the public good. Smallness and homogeneity make all that possible, and because they do, suburbanites jealously guard their smallness and homogeneity.

All these possibilities come to fullest flower in the affluent, middle-class communities of our stereotype, whose residents have been called hyperactive in such activities as voting, contacting public officials, and doing campaign work.[1]

The suburban desire for no-party politics and widespread participation has another face, though—one that poses a great danger for grassroots democracy. Suburban governments (like the central cities) have dealt with the pressures of growth and change by professionalizing greatly in recent years: witness the trend to the council-manager plan. The suburban ethos says this is fine; bureaucrats will administer things on a nonpartisan and professional basis. The problem lies in reconciling grassroots democracy with the aloof and sometimes introverted behavior of professionalized bureaucracies.

[1] On this point, see Joseph Zikmund II and Robert Smith, "Political Participation in an Upper Middle-Class Suburb," *Urban Affairs Quarterly* 4 (June 1969), 443-58; and James E. Skok, "Participation in Decision Making," *Western Political Quarterly* 27 (March 1974), 60-79.

Once again, the affluent suburbanite has all the best of it, as Herbert Gan's classic study, *The Levittowners*, documents. The modest-income, not-highly educated suburbanites are immobilized by the expertise of school administrators and other professionals; in contrast, upper-status suburbanites are quite aggressive. They do not seek direct control of decision making, but they do seek administrators with compatible values.[2]

POLITICAL CONFLICT IN SUBURBIA

The suburban ethos also includes the view that political disputes should be settled by consensus—part of the American middle class's general distaste for conflict. Abrasiveness and conflict should be muffled; amiability should prevail. As in the village setting, citizens are reminded that they should not tear the community apart. Ideally the combination of reform institutions and professional management should keep things running smoothly and efficiently.

Consensual politics may be the ideal but it is hard to avoid conflict, so the gap between ethos and reality is significant. One sociologist makes the point that rancorous conflict tends to occur when one relatively homogeneous set of leaders is threatened by a new leadership group.[3] The point is that suburbs can often be consensus oriented because they are relatively homogeneous, but a change in composition that tilts the balance of power is perceived as more of a change than it would be in city politics. Conflict therefore tends to be total because it is felt to involve the whole community's life style. Since suburbs are still growing, there is a repeating pattern of change and of conflict between old and new residents and between commuters and stay-at-homes (local businessmen within suburban communities). These cleavages are likely to be reinforced when they coincide with religious, ethnic, or especially, class differences. Unlike city politicians, who are accustomed to managing intergroup conflict, suburban officials are often uncomfortable in the role of mediator. Politics may thus take on a winner-take-all cast and intensify conflict.

Zoning is a specific issue that makes people forget about consensus. In a question of land use and location, as in few areas of policy, political leaders are frequently forced to make an either-or choice—often between the demands of activated citizens' groups and the demands of local elites such as real estate developers and banks. In such a situation, appeals to the general good are of little avail. Even compromise is extremely difficult.

[2] Herbert J. Gans, *The Levittowners: Ways of Life and Politics in a New Suburban Community* (New York: Random House, 1967), especially ch . 5, "The New School System."

[3] William A. Gamson, "Rancorous Conflict in Community Politics," *American Sociological Review* 31 (January 1966), 71-81

Land-use decisions provoke a particularly high level of conflict when they involve the movement of a lower-class population into a middle-class area. Suburban communities behave pretty much the same, whether they are adjacent to Washington, D.C., or Stockholm, Sweden,[4] over an issue such as the location of a public-housing project.

Conflict often replaces consensus as a mode of operation when schools are the issue, too. We are all aware of the many disputes over busing in recent years. Supporters of busing feel that education has been a traditional avenue of social mobility in this country and that systematically excluding blacks and other minorities from schooling in "better" neighborhoods forecloses that mobility. Opponents are apt to feel that purchase of a home carries with it the privilege of restricted social access to a neighborhood and the institutions that serve it. In any case, controversies over busing clearly illustrate conflicts over social access.

Other suburbs have fought over such issues as sex education, the size of the school budget, and curriculum orientation. It is not unusual for issues to be fought over which books should be permitted in school libraries. When the school board in the Long Island suburb of Island Trees, New York, dominated by "locals," banned such books as Kurt Vonnegut's *Slaughterhouse Five*, Bernard Malamud's *The Fixer*, Desmond Morris's *The Naked Ape*, Eldrige Cleaver's *Soul on Ice*, "cosmopolitans" ran for the school board and filed a court suit to prevent the banning.[5] These kinds of conflicts are widespread because few modern communities are so homogeneous as not to have people with very different personal values and philosophies.

While some suburbanites are concerned mainly with the image and prestige of their community as a symbol of their own importance, others have the kind of social conscience that makes them uneasy with social homogeneity. As a result, even in one-class affluent suburbs, there can be conflict over change and social access. Still, when the chips are down, protection, prestige, and amenities usually prevail. One study of Bloomfield, Connecticut, analyzed a number of controversies centering on the race issue. There were significant splits over school busing and urban renewal between liberal "cosmopolitans" who were strongly concerned about social problems and conservative "cosmopolitans" who were strongly concerned about protecting their property and life style. The views of the conservatives prevailed, but the conflict was a drawn-out and intensely fought contest.[6]

[4] Thomas J. Anton, *Governing Greater Stockholm: A Study of Policy Development and System Change* (Berkeley: University of California Press, 1975), ch. 3, pp. 64-95.

[5] Kay Bartlett, "The Right to Read," AP wire dispatch, printed in the *Atlanta Journal and Constitution*, February 20, 1977, p. 22B.

[6] Everett C. Ladd, *Ideology in America: Change and Response in a City, a Suburb, and a Small Town* (New York: W. W. Norton, 1974), pp. 224-79.

PARTICIPATION AND THE EMERGENCE OF IDEOLOGY

Many of these ideological differences in a suburban community grow out of new patterns of political participation. Of the two basic types of political activists, most suburbanites tend to be "amateurs," who participate because they are issue oriented and want to bring about changes in government policy. They are ideologues who participate in a wide range of civic affairs and who have entered politics for idealistic reasons. The amateurs tend to be middle-class, highly educated "cosmopolitans." The other type, the "professionals," are in politics for material rewards and are interested in winning elections for patronage purposes. They are usually "locals."

In contemporary suburban politics, the amateurs clearly prevail; they are important as officeholders and even as activists within the two major political parties. In the Democratic party suburban amateurs played a key role in the presidential campaigns of a number of figures beginning with Adlai Stevenson in the 1950s. They have also been active in the election campaigns of a number of liberal Democratic suburban congressmen. In the Republican party, they were especially influential in the presidential campaigns of Barry Goldwater in 1964 and of Ronald Reagan more recently. Minor parties also conform to the pattern; a study of the Conservative party in New York State shows its members to be highly educated amateur cosmopolitan types.[7] The amateurs have set the parties' ideological tone in recent elections. At times, the views of the amateurs have not gone down well with their professional colleagues in the party, but the amateurs appear to be the ascendant force.

SUBURBS IN TRANSITION

Population Trends

The white flight to suburbia has been widely noted. Most large central cities lost white population beginning in the 1950s and the 1960s while the suburban rings were registering huge increases in white population. In the 1980s whites are still leaving central cities for suburbia. In the period after World War II, blacks began a huge migration to the central cities, and the black proportion of central-city population increased greatly.

Recent population trends indicate a small but perceptible black flight to the suburbs.[8] Blacks generally are moving into areas in the suburbs that already have other blacks as residents; thus, black enclaves are forming in

[7] Robert A. Schoenberger, "Conservatism, Personality and Political Extremism," *American Political Science Review* 62 (September 1968), 868-77.

[8] Reynolds Farley, "Components of Suburban Population Growth," in *The Changing Face of the Suburbs*, ed. Barry Schwartz (Chicago: University of Chicago Press, 1976), pp. 3-36.

the same manner as enclaves of other ethnic groups. Though it is mainly younger, middle-class blacks who are moving, this movement is especially significant for the older inner suburbs closest to the central city.

The poor also are moving outward, in numbers large enough to signal a measurable geographic shift in the poverty population. One Massachusetts study found that the central-city share of metropolitan poor had dropped from 80 percent in 1950 to 45 percent in 1967.[9] Significantly, problems of coping with a poverty-level population can prove even more difficult for a suburb than for a central city. Many suburbs lack the economic base that central cities have—extensive central business districts and other large taxpaying properties. In the future we may even see sharp divisions between rich and poor suburbs.

The Economy, Housing, and Education: Issues in Suburbia

The gaps are growing not only in terms of residents but also in terms of the economy, with central cities in a state of decline while in many suburbs business has been booming. A study by Berry and Cohen indicates that the trend is not a new one; the large central cities of the east and midwest lost manufacturing jobs between 1947 and 1958, while their suburbs gained manufacturing jobs.[10] In many cases, the best known, quality manufacturers were the very ones that moved to the suburbs. The picture in retail sales is similar. Sales in central cities declined, while the suburban shopping malls registered a tremendous percentage increase in retail sales. The story has been the same in construction; a very large share of private nonresidential construction has been in the suburbs. For example, over 80 percent of recent new industrial building in the Boston SMSA and 98 percent of all new community facilities in Dayton, Ohio, were constructed in the suburban ring.

The downward spiral of the central city, disparities between central cities and suburbs, and racial polarization and separation are likely to continue in the near future. A report issued by the U.S. Commission on Civil Rights provided an incisive explanation of why that is so, with particular emphasis on the private and governmental forces at work in the housing market. Particularly important in this process were the behavior of real estate agents, including such practices as steering (showing whites homes in overwhelmingly white neighborhoods and blacks homes in transitional neighborhoods) and the lending practices of major financial institutions.

[9] David L. Birch, *The Economic Future of City and Suburb* (New York: Committee for Economic Development, 1970), p. 24.

[10] Brian L. Berry and Yehoshua S. Cohen, "Decentralization of Commerce and Industry: The Restructuring of Metropolitan America," in *The Urbanization of the Suburbs*, Masotti and Hadden, P. 439.

Government institutions at all levels have failed to provide low-income housing in the suburbs.[11]

Since there isn't a coherent national policy, people concerned with central-city/suburban disparities have increasingly turned to the courts. Suits attacking exclusionary suburban zoning have been argued in both state and federal courts. The court suits challenging exclusionary zoning—largely the work of "concerned" cosmopolitans—presently seem to be part of a suburban deadlock. Their impact is balanced, even cancelled, by the efforts of other "concerned" cosmopolitans to halt suburban growth, protect the environment, and maintain their current life style. Petaluma, California, has passed an ordinance that establishes a housing quota of 500 new units per year. Other communities have passed population ceilings and moratoria on building permits. One suburban executive even proposed to restrict the building of homes in his jurisdiction to those over $85,000 in value.[12] The effect, if not the intent, of these antigrowth measures is to prevent low-income minorities from moving into these communities.

Education is another area in which the disparities between central cities and suburbs have been attacked in the courts. In the case of *San Antonio School District* v. *Rodriguez* (1973), the U.S. Supreme Court rejected the argument that "equal protection of the laws" included equalization of disparities in the fiscal capacities of school districts. The issue of equalizing disparities in school financing has been left to the states for the time being. In 1974, in the case of *Milliken* v. *Bradley*, the Supreme Court rejected a metropolitan school-busing plan for the Detroit area. Chief Justice Burger wrote the opinion for a 5-4 majority, on the basis that the suburbs were not charged with violating any state education laws.

Despite the initiatives of activist citizens, many suburbanites react to proposals for change in these areas with indifference or hostility. One conclusion reached by a number of commentators on suburban politics is that suburban residents have retreated into personal and family concerns. They "simply want to be left alone, to have secure economic [home] investments, and to ensure their family's safety. . . . In many ways, the politics of suburbia . . . emerges as a consequence of sincere people's seeking to achieve the goals of privacy, well-being and safety."[13] These goals run head on into such goals as equality and social justice. The question is, how will we resolve the conflict between jurisdictions over who will house and educate and otherwise serve the poor, and who will pay what share of the costs (social and economic) of providing metro-wide services?

[11] U.S. Commission on Civil Rights, *Equal Opportunity in Suburbia* (Washington, D.C., 1974), pp. 2-49.

[12] *Washington Post*, September 30, 1979.

[13] Joseph Zikmund, "A Theoretical Structure for the Study of Suburban Politics" *Annals of the American Academy of Political and Social Science* 422 (November 1975), 59.

Much of our analysis has focused on conflict *within* suburbs, and as we have pointed out, such conflict is at odds with the "good government" ethos to which suburbanites subscribe. The issues of zoning, housing, and education show that there is also conflict *among* competing jurisdictions,and it too is at odds with the "good government" ethos. While embracing the rhetoric of reform (government should serve the good of the whole communtiy), the suburb is in reality a monument to the pursuit of particular and partial interests: it wants moderate taxes for *its* citizens, good schools for *its* children, and low-density living for *its* residents. In their external relations, suburban governments have been undaunted champions of the interests of their particular citizenries. Though the rhetoric and the institutional practices of suburbia represent a full flowering of the reform movement, suburban governments in fact have emerged as strong advocates of particular, geographic-based interests. As such, they served as models for those who came to question the superiority of reform ideals.

In the next chapter on postreform politics, we will see that the proponents of black power and of community control for central-city neighborhoods draw a parallel. They argued that they only wanted for the inner-city poor what the suburb provided the affluent middle class—neighborhood control over key service-delivery institutions. The rhetoric of reform in suburbia did not hide from them the reality of a competitive pursuit of private aims.

CONCLUSION

The suburbs are places of change and conflict, despite an ethos favoring stability and consensus. The tensions between myth and reality show up in a number of paradoxical situations:

Paradox: Individually, suburbs are relatively homogeneous; but, collectively they are quite varied and diverse.

Paradox: Suburbs are a place of growth and newness—new housing, new commercial establishments, new job opportunities, new public facilities. Indeed, one of the persistent problems of suburbs has been to provide for new and growing neighborhoods. Yet suburbs are facing the problems of aging. Some, for example, are beginning to struggle with the problems of a declining school-age population and the need to close down some school facilities.

Paradox: Some suburbs are noted for willingness to innovate and to pursue a high level of amenities and top-quality services. But others are backward looking and traditional, especially if they are declining in population and are not affluent and/or if they have a sizeable older population living on a fixed income.

Paradox: Suburbs, especially affluent ones, are thriving centers of the "good government" reform ethos, of modernization, of "cosmopolitanism." But in many significant ways suburbanites are highly provincial. Wanting small, stable, and homogeneous communities, they resist strongly the costs and discomforts of change.

Paradox: Suburbanites are on the whole, deferential toward technical and professional expertise. But many upper-status suburbanites, who have high expectations and high levels of self-confidence and efficacy, are aggressive and assertive when dealing with their officials.

Paradox: Most suburbs have a "village" regard for "keeping things smooth." But now the suburbs have to deal with conflict: internal debates over the proper balance among social, environmental, amenity, and privacy concerns and external disputes over how the costs and burdens of metropolitan life are to be shared.

Paradox: Suburbanites, especially affluent ones, have a sense of civic duty and feel an obligation to participate in public affairs. Still, the allurements of privacy, isolation, and self-concern are strong.

SUGGESTED READINGS

DANIELSON, MICHAEL N. *The Politics of Exclusion*. New York: Columbia University Press, 1976.

GANS, HERBERT. *The Levittowners: Ways of Life and Politics in a New Suburban Community*. New York: Random House, 1967.

KAPLAN, SAMUEL. *The Dream Deferred: People, Politics and Planning in Suburbia*. New York: Seabury Press, 1976.

LADD, EVERETT C. *Ideology in America: Change and Response in a City, a Suburb, and a Small Town*. New York: W. W. Norton, 1972.

MASOTTI, LOUIS, and JEFFREY HADDEN, eds. *Suburbia in Transition*. New York: New Viewpoints. 1974.

———. *The Urbanization of the Suburbs*. Urban Affairs Annual Reviews, Vol. 7. Beverly Hills, Calif.: Sage Publications, 1973.

MILLER, ZANE L. *Suburb: Neighborhood and Community in Forest Park, Ohio, 1935—1976*Knoxville: University of Tennessee Press, 1981.

MURPHY, THOMAS, and JOHN REHFUSS. *Urban Politics in the Suburban Era*. Homewood, Ill.: Dorsey Press, 1976.

SCHWARTZ, BARRY, ed. *The Changing Face of the Suburbs*. Chicago: University of Chicago Press, 1976.

WIRT, FREDERICK, et al. *On the City's Rim: Politics and Policy in Suburbia*. Lexington, Mass.: D.C. Heath and Co., 1972.

WOOD, ROBERT C. *Suburbia: Its People and Their Politics*. Boston: Houghton Mifflin Co., 1959.

ZIKMUND, JOSEPH. "A Theoretical Structure for the Study of Suburban Politics." *Annals of the American Academy of Political and Social Science* 422 (November 1975), 45-60.

chapter 10

Postreform Politics

A NEW STYLE IN GOVERNING

Reform politics brought technical problem solving to urban government. The postreform period has surrounded that problem solving with an aggressive and open style of politics, a style that we, as a nation, are not entirely comfortable with. Most Americans retain the reformer's aversion to politics and politicians, associating political activity with favoritism and crass acts of self-advancement. But there is more to politics than this stereotype suggests. It is the process through which individuals and groups struggle to gain and maintain support for a variety of objectives—some altruistic, some self-serving, some broad, some narrow, some open, some hidden. Political actors usually have multiple goals and mixed motives.

Reformers have had difficulty grasping these basic political facts, and as a result, they failed to anticipate the rising demand for representation in a diverse society. But what reformers shunted aside could no longer be ignored in the 1960s. Postreform politics is an open recognition that we are a society of diverse interests, that these interests expect to be represented, and that politics, the activity through which this representation is obtained, is an inescapable part of modern life.

In a real sense, reform contained the seeds of its own destruction. It gave rise to an active government, and an active government cannot maintain a nonpolitical pose for very long. The more that government becomes openly involved in mobilizing resources and solving problems, the harder it is to preserve a low-intensity political atmosphere. An active government means that priorities have to be set and choices must be made, and the resulting decisions visibly affect things people care about. The interplay of conflicting goals and objectives cannot be avoided—nor can the conflict be hidden. Technical problem solving cannot serve indefinitely as a cover for official decision makers to hide behind. Of course, today's policy makers do require a great deal of technical information, and they often apply complex formulae and procedures. But they *are* making choices about who benefits and who pays. Since some gain and some lose with each decision, decisions are not neutral, no matter how technically proficient the experts. And in the end, the public understands that fact.

CHARACTERISTICS OF THE POSTREFORM PERIOD

Ever-broadening efforts to solve problems coincided with, and probably gave encouragement to, the political awakening of several groups—principally the poor, public employees, blacks, and other minorities. The political awakening, in turn, set in motion still greater change. As the pace of change has escalated, groups have shed traditions of deference and submissiveness. Democracy has come to mean much more than universal suffrage or equality under the law. The nation is perhaps undergoing what sociologist Daniel Bell calls a "revolution of entitlements"—a growing insistence that government should guarantee everyone a wide range of minimum rights and benefits.[1] "Have-nots" want prosperity to be widely shared, and they expect government to redistribute society's benefits. "Haves," too, are inclined to see government as active—as a force in planning and promoting a prosperous society. With such clamor for government activity, expectations have inevitably come into sharp conflict.

Predictably, the reform notion of a single overarching community interest, best served by technical experts and highly trained professionals, has been widely challenged. Politics has become too high-keyed for that. Few groups are quiescent; most are eager to have direct and vociferous representation. Reform institutions—especially those that do not reflect social and economic diversity—have come under great pressure from all quarters.

The reform movement probably reached its prime in the 1950s. But given the active and involved governments it encouraged, diversity and political change were bound to assert themselves. Conditions were ripe for the tumultuous and aggressive politics that flourished so openly in the

[1] Daniel Bell, "The Revolution of Rising Entitlements," *Fortune*, April 1975, pp. 98ff.

1960s. The sit-ins of civil rights demonstrators, the protest-oriented activities of Saul Alinsky and other community organizers, the unionization of public employees, the outbreaks of disorder, the militancy of Black Power advocates and others demanding drastic social reform, the flowering of radical dissent among academicians, and the appearance of such new schools of analytical thought as the public-choice approach—all marked the dissolution of the era of "good government" reform.

The postreform style is a volatile and still-changing mode of politics. Tactics wax and wane. Personalities come into prominence and then fade from the scene. Hopes swirl around new devices and then dissipate.

Still, despite the flux and change, it is possible to identify some enduring themes. Only the future can tell what will be long lasting, but we can be certain that there will be no simple return to the past. The 1960s with its violence and disappointments marked us in ways that will not be easily erased; they left us all a little more conscious of the darker side of human nature. Moreover, the last years have made us aware that the resources at our disposal have limits and that human knowledge, too, is limited. If the 1970s brought us back to a more passive time, it was a passivity born less of contentment and optimism than of frustration, cynicism, and pessimism.

Though the break with the past is never absolute, major and fairly persistent political trends that surfaced in the postreform 1960s marked a visible departure from the rhetoric and practice of "good government" reform:

1. The service-providing agencies of local government became the direct target of efforts to make government more responsive and effective.
2. A relatively high level of overt social and political conflict was encouraged in part by the view that the benefits and opportunities of modern life are limited and competition is therefore inevitable. Moreover, some groups took the position that conflict and competition are not only inevitable but healthy and beneficial.
3. A variety of politically conscious groups emerged, each seeking maximum direct influence in and on the decisions of government.
4. There was growing recognition that problem solving, especially if it involves person-to-person activity, is to some degree culture bound and is, in any event, heavily intertwined with value choices. Once this perception gained currency, the decisions of experts and professionals, no longer protected by the claim of being politically neutral, became fair game for political attack.
5. More and more people embraced the view that "the" public interest is best conceived of as the satisfaction of a maximum number of the diverse groups found in a community. They moved away from the view that there is an overarching interest of the whole community.

This list is not a set of absolute principles. It simply highlights some related features of patterned reaction to the reform movement. In this chapter we will lay out two facets of this reaction:

1. Disenchantment with public-service bureaucracies and the professionals who staff them began to surface in the 1950s, among the professionals and bureaucrats themselves.
2. The emergence of militant community organizations in the 1960s, marked by a high level of intergroup conflict, furthered the idea that various segments of society need their own advocates. These groups did much to popularize the idea of consciousness raising and to call into question the assumptions underlying "good government" reform.

In the next chapter, we will concentrate on the experiences of two major postreform movements—black political mobilization and public-employee unionism:

1. As the ideology of black political mobilization in the 1960s, Black Power was the most thoroughly developed alternative to "good government" reform. In a direct challenge to its principles, Black Power rejected the idea that problem solving could be neutral, it embraced a conflict strategy, and it explicitly repudiated the unitary conception of the public interest.
2. The more-or-less concurrent rise of public-employee unionism, another contemporary monument to conflict strategy and all that it entails, also signaled open acceptance of a series of once-heretical concepts—the competitive nature of social relationships, the need for all kinds of interest groups to be politically aware, and the legitimacy of using a full range of power tactics in exerting influence.

By looking at the experience of black officeholders and of public-employee unions, we can see some of the dilemmas of the postreform era. Conflict is never easy to deal with, but postreform officeholders must tread an especially difficult path. They have to contend not only with the turbulence of the postreform style itself but also with the continuing presence of the reform ethos. Officeholders thus face conflicting expectations—some based on the pressures from postreform forces, others based on the still significant influence of the reform outlook. The postreform era thus represents not complete abandonment of the reform ethos but the appearance of a countervailing set of forces that challenges its dominance.

For their part, public-employee unions have found conflict to be a two-edged sword. It is a useful strategy, but an overly aggressive use of it can provoke a backlash effect. Conflict entails risks, not the least of which is the birth of competing and even stronger forces.

PUBLIC-SERVICE AGENCIES AS TARGETS OF DISCONTENT

"Nothing works" is a common complaint, and bureauracies—the organizational structures through which programs are implemented—are ready targets for blame when programs fail. Of the five points identified as characteristic of the postreform period, concern about effectiveness and responsiveness in service-providing bureaucracies goes most directly to the heart of the reaction against reform. The account of how that concern grew and gave rise to efforts to organize poverty neighborhoods reveals much about the nature of postreform politics.

It began with the bureaucrats themselves. Long before bureaucracy became a topic of general public concern, staff members in key government and foundation offices had developed a keen interest in revitalizing the performance of urban service agencies. In the late 1950s and early 1960s, initially in the Ford Foundation's Gray Areas project and a little later (after John Kennedy's election), in the President's Committee on Juvenile Delinquency, a group of idea entrepreneurs laid the groundwork for what was to become the Community Action program in President Johnson's War on Poverty. The Community Action Program was devised as a major assault on the institutional conservatism of agencies servicing the central-city poor. The poor themselves were to have an integral part in the running of the program.

These idea entrepreneurs were known to one another as "guerillas" because, as they saw it, they lived "off the countryside of the government and foundations" while seeking to bring about "revolutionary" social change.[2] Despite the rhetoric of revolution, these proponents of social reform had not at this stage come into full conflict with the tenets of "good government" reform. They were still guided by a belief in an overriding general good of the community. They saw themselves as "facilitators, analysts and catalysers, crystallizing the good intentions of many people about a common endeavor. . . . "[3]

These benign "guerillas" were especially concerned about social conditions in the nation's large cities. Urban renewal had brought no improvement in the lives of the poor. Delinquency rates were rising. Unemployment was high. Educational institutions and job-training programs were having no appreciable impact. To the "guerillas," the villain on the set was bureaucractic inflexibility. Urban service agencies, they believed, were too conservative and too parochial to adapt to the changing and growing needs of the inner-city poor. The cycle of poverty and despair, as the "guerillas" anlayzed the problem, gave birth to a deep-set apathy among the poor that reinforced their lack of opportunity. Only a broad and imaginative assault on the cycle of poverty could break the pattern. But the urban service agencies were too rigid, too set in their ways to meet the challenge facing them.

[2] Richard Blumenthal, "The Bureaucracy: Antipoverty and the Community Action Program," in *American Political Institutions and Public Policy*, ed. Allan P. Sindler (Boston: Little, Brown & Co., 1969), p. 133.

[3] Paul N. Ylvisaker, quoted in Daniel P. Moynihan, *Maximum Feasible Misunderstanding* (New York: Free Press, 1969), p. 39.

In the first place, they were unresponsive to individuals. A bureaucracy functions under a set of impersonal relationships guided by formal regulations—as such it serves well the "good government" goal of preventing favoritism. Professionalism too tends toward impersonality. Consequently, service-providing professionals, even those with a large zone of autonomy and discretion, were regarded as aloof—and as so committed to established procedure that they did not respond openly and warmly to the people they served.

As the "guerrillas" assessed their urban targets, the problem lay deeper than bureaucratic impersonality. Service agencies are not adaptive. Their employees, as in all bureaucracies, are specialized. In a sense, they are narrow-minded—seeing clearly and valuing only those activities of which they are a direct part. Almost inevitably they fail to see their activities as means to larger ends. In this way they are provincial. Moreover, in a hierarchical organization, coordination is important. Therefore loyalty and unquestioning obedience tend to be rewarded. Following established procedure is the safe road to advancement. Set ways of operating go unquestioned, even if conditions change and agency performance lags. In the eyes of the change-minded "guerillas," urban institutions failed for lack of imagination more than for lack of money, and lack of imagination was due in part to a bureaucractic atmosphere of caution.

Urban service agencies tend not to be adaptive for still another reason. Institutions, like people, have a survival urge. As a result they are wary about their established program areas. So, while an agency may be reluctant to try a new program, it has no reluctance about fighting off an intrusion into its domain. As the "guerillas" devised their strategy for change, they realized that real change was unlikely to come about simply by proposing new programs or even new agencies.

The "guerrilas" had one foot firmly in the old "good government" camp. Still clinging to the unitary conception of the public interest, they sought to facilitate change by inducing local communities to undertake comprehensive social planning and by encouraging broad coalitions among the various groups and organizations concerned with social programs. They also encouraged experimentation and called for rigous evaluation of service projects (signs that faith in science and objective analysis had not faltered). However, as the performance of urban agencies was examined more and more closely, other concerns emerged that were not as compatible with the tenets of "good government" reform. The "guerillas" also had one foot stepping toward a conflict-ridden future.

Beyond the conservatism and rigidity of bureaucratic agencies, they saw a built-in middle-class bias and paternalistic assumptions guiding the professional administration of many services. Rules and procedures were often abrasive to clients. Residents of renewal areas complained that they were planned *for*, not planned *with*. Some services appeared to be a "white man's burden," motivated by "superiors" helping "subordinates." One welfare director was quoted as stating of his agency's clientele:

> Society stands in the same relation to them as that of parent to child. . . . Just as the child is expected to attend classes, so also the "child-adult" must be expected to meet his responsibility to the community. In short, "social uplifting"—even if begun on the adult level—cannot expect to meet with success unless it is combined with a certain amount of "social disciplining"—just as it is on the pre-adult level.[4]

There was among the critics of bureaucracy a strain of antiprofessionalism at work. And some of the "guerillas" strongly supported the employment of residents of poor neighborhoods in social agencies, to lessen the paternalism and middle-class bias. But a more profound idea was also at work—the idea that delinquency, apathy, and various forms of deviant behavior were traceable not to the shortcomings of individual personalities but to the shortcomings of society: deviance was prevalent among the poor because their aspirations were blocked by a lack of opportunity. Within this framework of thought, social workers and other members of the "helping" professions were criticized for treating symptoms (the behavior of individual poor persons), but ignoring the real problem (an inadequate opportunity structure in society.)

Ghetto Schools: Neglect and Deterioration

The school system, too, was a matter of keen concern. Psychologist Kenneth Clark and others involved in developing the Haryou program in Harlem (one of the earliest community action programs), spelled out a pattern of teacher and system indifference. Closer to the local scene than the largely Washington-based "guerillas," they documented a deteriorating school performance in ghetto communities and laid much of the blame on the indifference of professionals and the bureaucracy.

Clark showed that I.Q. scores, supposedly a constant measure of intellectual potential, showed "a sharp drop for ghetto children between third and sixth grades."[5] The Haryou group strongly dissented from the "cultural deprivation" explanation for poor academic performance in ghetto schools. They offered instead the view that school officials and teachers alike held a defeatist attitude toward education in Harlem, expecting little and therefore setting in motion a self-fulfilling prophecy. Clark cited pilot projects indicating that a child expected to learn does so but that "the child of whom little is expected produces little." He concluded, "Stimulation and teaching based upon positive expectation seem to play an even

[4] Quoted in Charles E. Silberman, *Crisis in Black and White* (New York: Random House, 1964), p. 314.

[5] Kenneth B. Clark, *Dark Ghetto* (New York: Harper and Row, 1965), p. 121.

more important role in a child's performance in school than does the community environment from which he comes."[6]

Clark and others described a vicious cycle. Lowered expectations meant lowered standards. Lowered standards reinforced negative stereotypes. Administrators concurred in, and perhaps encouraged, the bad image of ghetto schools. The bad image helped assure that the ghetto would get the worst-qualified and least-experienced teachers. In a place where there was need for a caring and nurturing response, the Clark critique continued, there was a growing reliance on custodial and order-maintaining activities. Discipline problems were intensified, psychologist Clark argued, because students saw the school system as a "deep and pervasive attack upon their dignity and integrity as human beings."[7]

In language stronger than most "guerillas" would have felt comfortable with, Clark stated:

> The clash of cultures in the classroom is essentially a class war, a socio-economic and racial warfare being waged in the battleground of our schools, with middle-class and middle-class-aspirng teachers provided with a powerful arsenal of half-truths, prejudices, and rationalizations, arrayed against hopelessly outclassed working-class youngsters.[8]

Summary

Though the "guerillas" were fully aware of the notion of middle-class bias, they never developed their ideas into a theory of class conflict. They were certainly keenly aware that the nonpoor would resist paying higher taxes for antipoverty programs, and they realized that institutional change could not come without friction. But they believed that the system would be responsive to pressures for change. Urban society was, in their view, "a benevolent anarchy."[9] Therefore, even the conservatism of bureaucratic institutions and the self-protective reflexes of middle-class Americans should yield to properly applied leverage. Despite some occasional rhetoric of revolution, the "guerillas" were themselves too close to the "good government" reform tradition to see that some differences might be irreconcilable; but their efforts had let the genii of group conflict escape the reform bottle. The idea had been loosed that the poor and discriminated against needed their own advocates. Change-minded social reformers unerringly moved in the direction of pressure-group politics and the need for the poor to develop their own political resources. In that setting, the

[6] Ibid., p. 132.

[7] Ibid., p. 129.

[8] Ibid.

[9] Peter Marris and Martin Rein, *Dilemmas of Social Reform*, 2nd ed. (Chicago: Aldine Publishing Co., 1973), p. 52.

Community Action Program was born, and a long-time proponent of militant community organization, Saul Alinsky, gained national visibility.

PRESSURE POLITICS AND COMMUNITY ORGANIZATION: ADVOCATING THE INTERESTS OF THE POOR

One of the central elements of President Johnson's War on Poverty was the Community Action Program. Architects of community action had as their general goal the mobilization of public and private resources in the fight against poverty and the improvement of service delivery to the poor. They hoped that federal funding for local organizations, called community action agencies, would better the position of the poor politically as well as economically. Indeed, some of them hoped to improve the economic lot of have-nots by making the poor into an effective political pressure group. The designation, community action, signified that these agencies were to be active on behalf of the poor, providing some services themselves but more than anything else advocating the interests of the poor.

Early proponents of community action were agreed that the poor themselves should be involved in the antipoverty effort, and some saw the program as a way of making the poor into a self-directed political force. Thus, while most agencies in practice used a traditional social service approach, there was a great deal of rhetoric about the need to organize the poor so they could exercise power on their own behalf. Significantly, then, the 1964 legislation creating a Community Action Program contained the enigmatic phrase, "maximum feasible participation." Whatever intent surrounded its inclusion in the legislation, this phrase shaped, or rather came to be surrounded by, a body of ideas that shaped our way of looking at the urban political scene. It was a phrase that merged with Saul Alinsky's theory of community organization to alter conceptions about how society operates and to provide an outlet for many frustrations. What was this body of ideas and what has been the experience with efforts to organize poor communities?

The proponents of advocate-style community organizations look upon the local community first and foremost as a political arena, a place in which competing interests exercise power to promote their own ends. Like the poor they seek to champion, militant organizers tend toward a cynical view of life. Alinsky, one of the most colorful and articulate of these organizers, remarked in obvious disdain for the mentality of "good government" reform, "In this world laws are written for the lofty aim of 'the common good' and then acted out in life on the basis of the common greed. . . . It is a world not of angels but of angles, where men speak of moral principles but act in power principles."[10] To the radical organizer, society is an aggregation of competing interests. Alinsky commented that "to question the force of self-interest that pervades all areas of political life is to refuse to see man as he is."[11]

Power, understandably, occupies a central place in the thought processes of militant community organizers. It is a word Alinsky insisted on talking about in blunt terms, referring to the "conflict-ridden, grimy, and realistic power-paved highway of life."[12] For him the choice lay between organized and unorganized power. To ignore power or to leave it in an unorganized state, he believed, was to fail to come to terms with the struggle for justice. "So-called power institutions get away with a lot because they're not challenged."[13] The ghetto he conceived of as a political creature, that is, something created and maintained by prevailing power arrangements, and as he saw it, the ghetto was something that could be changed only by mobilizing a counter force. Various advocates of community organization saw the contemporary poor as being at a disadvantage because, unlike the immigrant poor of the past, they were not politically organized. The message spread—only power, not moral suasion or right reason or accumulated facts, could bring about change.

As Alinsky and others saw it, power in a neighborhood had to be exercised by the people themselves. If pursuit of self-interest is pervasive, only the poor can protect their own interests. They should be organized to identify problems as they see them, to determine what courses of action they wish to pursue, to mobilize and use their own resources, and to make their own assessments of what is good or bad. Citizen participation became one of the catchwords of community action. Alinsky, for his part, believed that

1. community organization should be democratic, that is, controlled by the people of the neighborhood, and representative of virtually all of the interests and subgroups located in the neighborhood being organized;
2. professional organizers have a crucial role to play in getting a community organized, but they should not come into a neighborhood unless invited by a cross-section of the people who live and work there; and
3. a community organization would be effective only if the organizers saw themselves as employees of the neighborhood.

Thus, he told members of The Woodlawn Organization (TWO), a neighborhood organization his Industrial Areas Foundation (IAF) helped form

[10] Saul D. Alinsky, *Rules for Radicals* (New York: Random House, Vintage Books, 1971), p. 13.

[11] Ibid., p. 54.

[12] Ibid., p. 90.

[13] Marion K. Sanders, *The Professional Radical, Conversations with Saul Alinsky* (New York: Harper and Row, Perennial Library, 1970), p. 57.

in Chicago, that the only way they could be certain their aims would be carried out was to "get the organizers off my payroll and onto your payroll. Then you can tell them what to do, and if they don't do it, you can fire them and get someone who will."[14] The IAF followed this operating principle to encourage the neighborhood organization to become self-sufficient within a few years, financed by the community itself, and with indigenous spokespersons assuming active leadership.

"Tactics," Alinsky explained, "means doing what you can with what you have."[15] That might mean to embarrass, protest, harass, inconvenience—whatever was needed to create a climate for change. Laughter, ridicule, and the outlandish could be turned to account as political weapons. He once proposed feeding a hundred kids a baked beans dinner before sending them off to a Rochester Symphony concert. Another time he threatened to use demonstrators in a literal sit-in to tie up the toilets at O'Hare Airport in Chicago. When a department store was recalcitrant about hiring blacks and a boycott proved ineffective, Alinsky proposed the opposite—a buy-in. His plan called for busing in three thousand blacks who would inundate sales clerks with questions about the price and quality of goods, make endless exchanges and returns, order a large number of items C.O.D., and then refuse to accept delivery. When the plan became known, results came fast. "Overnight, 186 new jobs were opened. For the first time, blacks were on the sales floor and in executive training."[16]

Alinsky was an unapologetic Machiavellian, believing that if the end was important enough, the means could be justified. As he put it, "*The means-and-end moralists or non-doers always wind up on their ends without any means.*"[17] Far from having qualms about a strategy of conflict and confrontation, he believed that controversy was beneficial and that polarization was a necessary step before any issue could be resolved.

The basic Alinsky tactic, widely though sometimes faintheartedly copied, was to send organizers through a neighborhood to locate grassroots leaders and find out what grievances they had. Organizers would then get the leaders together to talk about the problems and frustrations that most bothered the neighborhood.

> The organizer dedicated to changing the life of a particular community must first rub raw the resentments of the people of the community; fan the latent hostilities of many of the people to the point of overt expression. He must search out controversy and issues, rather than avoid them, for unless there is controversy people are not concerned enough to act. . . . An organizer must

[14] Quoted in Silberman, *Crisis in Black and White*, p. 326.
[15] Alinsky, *Rules for Radicals*, p. 126.
[16] Ibid., p. 148.
[17] Ibid., p. 25.

stir up dissatisfaction and discontent; provide a channel into which the people can angrily pour their frustrations.[18]

Conflict thus serves multiple purposes:

1. It is a means for overcoming apathy and producing a climate of activity and excitement. It is also cathartic, giving people who have lived long with pent-up frustrations a chance to air those feelings. Alinsky argued that the TWO area in Chicago was riot free because grievances were not pent up.
2. As a means of attracting attention, arousing interest, provoking reactions, and involving people in a significant struggle, conflict can instill new pride and self-esteem.
3. Above all, it sustains an organization. If controversy ceases, interest slackens. Conflict is fuel on which the community organization engine runs. If people are not active, there is no organization. If there is no organization, there is no power to be exercised. If there is no power to be exercised, the cycle of apathy and despair again dominates the community.

CONFLICT STRATEGY AND NEIGHBORHOOD ORGANIZATION: AN ASSESSMENT

The success of the conflict strategy in organizing poor neighborhoods depended on two factors. One was the ability to overcome divisions within the neighborhood. The other was the capacity to garner a succession of victories in the struggles with City Hall and other institutions of the larger community. That protest groups and militant community organizations have not been as evident in recent years as they were in the 1960s is an indication that the conflict strategy has encountered major difficulties. And, indeed, protest groups and neighborhood organizations have had difficulty both in maintaining internal unity and in sustaining a winning streak of any duration.

Neighborhoods, especially older and nonaffluent ones, can be incredibly complex. They may house diverse ethnic and racial groups. They may contain wide-ranging age groups. They almost always have a substantial economic mix. Contrary to popular misconceptions, intermingled in even very poor neighborhoods are families who have steady incomes, own homes, and have long-established ties to the community, alongside those who are transient and poverty stricken. There are proprietor-run businesses as well as those run for absentee owners. Churches and hustlers sometimes occupy the same streets. Despite an outward appearance of apathy and disorganization, organizations may abound.

[18] Ibid., pp. 116-17.

Internal division is always a possibility. Change and new activity can be threatening to leaders, institutions, or property owners in a slum, just as much as in other kinds of neighborhoods. Older, poorer neighborhoods seem particularly prone to cleavage between homeowners and renters. Conflicting group interests are sometimes intertwined with personal rivalries between leaders. And, in fact, there is substantial evidence that poorer neighborhoods are especially open to leadership rivalries. Recognition is, after all, a scarce commodity and is therefore jealously guarded. Neighborhood effectiveness requires leaders who have substantial skills and wide connections, but the more such leaders emerge, the more likely is conflict between them. Moreover, as leaders sharpen their skills and enhance their base of support, they may arouse suspicions, especially suspicions that they are active mainly for personal gain. One survey of four highly active neighborhoods concluded:

> Each of the neighborhoods displayed a saddening amount of inter-leader antagonism. In some ways it might have been functional—by encouraging eclecticism and representation—but all too often it bred self-destructive bitterness, recrimination and even violence. Constant jockeying for position and power sapped community energy and frequently led to irrational acts.[19]

Still, neighborhoods can be rallied into joint action against threatening activities. Divergent groups can agree readily on their opposition to expressway construction through the neighborhood, or they can join together to battle clearance by the urban renewal bulldozer. But it is much easier for people to agree on what they dislike than to agree on what should replace it.

As soon as community organizations shift from a negative to a positive program, they run a risk of foundering on the rock of disunity. If a new facility is to be built, no one wants it built in her or his block. If new housing is to be built, homeowners want moderate-income housing to stabilize or upgrade the community. Renters want low-income housing so they can have an opportunity to escape the slum landlords but stay in the area. Some of the same issues that produce conflict with the larger community also crop up in smaller scale to divide neighborhoods.

The community action agencies developed in conjunction with the War on Poverty, like their privately sponsored counterparts, proved vulnerable to internal dissension. One study concluded that directors of neighborhood centers appeared highly insecure about their positions.[20]

[19] John H. Mollenkopf, "On the Causes and Consequences of Neighborhood Political Mobilization" (Paper presented at the 1973 Annual Meeting of the American Political Science Association, New Orleans, September 4-8, 1973), pp. 21-22.

[20] André L. Delbecq and Sidney J. Kaplan, "The Myth of the Indigenous Community Leader," *Academy of Management Journal* (March 1968), 11-25.

Some, lacking formal training or prior work experience that would have made them expert in managing their centers, handled staff relationships poorly. Their inexperience in management techniques led them into relying heavily on formal authority and thereby antagonizing and frustrating their subordinates. Resentments and frustrations in turn undermined the director's authority and left subordinates uninhibited in the pursuit of their personal ambitions. Because of divisive undercurrents like these, few community action agencies became highly cohesive organizations.

External resistance was an even more serious problem than internal dissension. Community action or other government-funded agencies could not go far along the protest route before encountering powerful opposition. Some community action agencies appeared to be independent of city hall, but that independence was more apparent than real. City halls were uniformly uninterested in social revolution or in any significant redistribution of power.[21] The more a community action agency was oriented toward mobilizing political power, the stronger the official resistance. Once the mayors became upset, government-funded "revolution" was at an end. Whatever sentiments federal antipoverty staffers might have had about empowering the poor, the Congress and the president were much more closely attuned to city hall than to poverty neighborhoods. Of course, most community action agencies never embarked on a path of militancy, but of those that did, most were tamed and some were eventually destroyed. Daniel P. Moynihan described a four-stage sequence for militant agencies:

> First, a period of organizing with much publicity and great expectations everywhere. Second, the beginning of operations, with the onset of conflict between the agency and local government institutions, with even greater publicity. Third, a period of counterattack from local government, not infrequently accompanied by conflict and difficulties, including accounting difficulties, within the agency itself. Fourth, victory for the established institutions, or at best, stalemate, accompanied by bitterness and charges of betrayal.[22]

The community action agencies won some victories, of course, but the going got increasingly tough once the easy targets were out of the way. Demands for drastic change were met with countercharges of extremism and irresponsibility. When protests could not be discredited, they could usually be outwaited. A protest organization is a highly unstable phenomenon. Individual community organizers, especially if employed in government-funded programs, were highly vulnerable. They had no civil

[21] J. David Greenstone and Paul E. Peterson in their study point out that some progressive mayors did hope that community protests would help curb the power of service bureaucracies. See *Race and Authority in Urban Politics* (New York: Russell Sage Foundation, 1973), especially pp. 133-34.

[22] Moynihan, *Maximum Feasible Misunderstanding*, p. 131.

service tenure. The administrative inexperience and an air of laxity, which characterized many community action offices, left a number of organizers open to counterattacks of mismanagement. And of course, few such agencies were generously funded. Most were in fact dependent on the cooperation of other agencies for some of their program activity, and a strategy of conflict could cost them much-needed sources of support.

Many employees in community action programs, both public and private, rediscovered Sam Rayburn's maxim, "To get along you have to go along." It is not easy to maintain a conflict strategy in the face of a long and possibly unsuccessful struggle when the fruits of accommodation are immediately available for plucking. Long periods of frustration make it easy for individuals to reason that they could be more effective inside the establishment than outside. Leadership is, after all, more easily maintained if leaders have benefits they can bestow on supporters. Eager for recognition and genuinely wanting to offer substantive help to their constituents, churches and other organizations found it easy to abandon prolonged conflict for opportunities to deliver services instead. "The many jobs, contracts, development rights, housing grants, relocation benefits, and subcontracts controlled by redevelopment authorities, city agencies, mayors, and even business firms give them a strong hand with community groups."[23] Further, once a group switches from conflict to accommodation, a switch back to conflict is most difficult.

Mobilized neighborhoods did, then, gain some concessions, and some attempted to raise wider and more substantial issues. But fighting for the wider issues requires a broad coalition and a sustained struggle. Prolonged conflict proved costly, and the costs fell on a population that could little afford them. So instead of leading to a succession of victories, conflict led to some short-term victories, some devastating defeats, and many piecemeal compromises. City Hall and the old-line agencies learned quickly that they could disaggregate most protest movements.

Even such a skillfully organized Alinsky-style group as TWO found it hard to pyramid their victories. After its initial successes, TWO was able to mobilize hundreds of people for regular community meetings and even larger numbers for special meetings and demonstrations. Moreover, it became a formally constituted and durable organization, able to attract as many as one thousand delegates to its annual convention. Yet it suffered at least three major defeats—it could not sustain its controversial youth program, it failed to get a hearing on its Model Cities plan, and it could not secure support from the school system for its experimental educational program.

[23] Mollenkopf, "On the Causes and Consequences of Neighborhood Political Mobilization," p. 19.

Before it was ten years old, TWO had shifted strategy from conflict to coexistence (as the organization newspaper proclaimed, "From Protest to Programs.") Other organizations underwent a similar change. For example, when North Side Forces, a neighborhood group in Paterson, New Jersey, was unable to develop a mass political base, it forsook its political goals and evolved into a service-oriented body. It operated several neighborhood programs, including a dental clinic and two day-care centers.[24]

Such organizations gave residents significant employment and job-training opportunities. Yet a community organization that can attract and administer programs is much different in style and leadership from a protest organization concerned with raising political consciousness and activating mass support. Management skill gains central importance. To illustrate, of TWO's changed character, it was noted:

> The intricacies of development corporations, special funds, health care systems, housing rehabilitation schemes, and business ventures have become so complex and sophisticated that knowledgeable participation is beyond the reach of all but a few residents and TWO is increasingly dependent upon the insights and advice of its staff, consultants, and specialists.[25]

Protest could hardly be a permanent strategy for an organization based in a poverty neighborhood. Immediate needs are too great and resources too short. The change from protest to providing service is almost inevitable. And there are questions about service provision that remain to be answered. Services directed at improving the quality of life in non-affluent neighborhoods are quite vulnerable to fiscal stringency. All in all, the fruits of protest appear not to be long lasting.

SUGGESTED READINGS

ALINSKY, SAUL D. *Rules for Radicals.* New York: Random House, Vintage Books, 1971.

BAILEY, ROBERT, JR. *Radicals in Urban Politics: The Alinsky Approach.* Chicago: University of Chicago Press, 1974.

BROWN, MICHAEL K. and STEVEN P. ERIE. "Blacks and the Legacy of the Great Society." *Public Policy* 29 (Summer 1981), 299-330.

CLARK, KENNETH B. *Dark Ghetto.* New York: Harper & Row, 1965.

FAINSTEIN, NORMAN I., and SUSAN S. FAINSTEIN. *Urban Political Movements.* Englewood Cliffs, N.J.: Prentice-Hall, 1974.

FISH, JOHN HALL. *Black Power/White Control.* Princeton, N.J.: Princeton University Press, 1973.

[24] Norman I. Fainstein and Susan S Fainstein, *Urban Political Movements* (Englewood Cliffs, N J.: Prentice-Hall, 1974), pp. 130-47.

[25] John Hall Fish, *Black Power/White Control* (Princeton, N.J.: Princeton University Press, 1973), p. 298.

GREENSTONE, J. DAVID, and PAUL E. PETERSON. *Race and Authority in Urban Politics*. New York: Russell Sage Foundation, 1973.

LIPSKY, MICHAEL. *Protest in City Politics*. Chicago: Rand McNally, 1970.

MARSHALL, DALE ROGERS, ed. *Urban Policy Making*. Beverly Hills, CA: Sage, 1979.

METROPOLITAN APPLIED RESEARCH CENTER. *A Relevant War Against Poverty*. New York: Metropolitan Applied Research Center, 1968.

MOLLENKOPF, JOHN H. *The Contested City*. Princeton, NJ: Princeton University Press, 1983.

O'BRIEN, DAVID J. *Neighborhood Organization and Interest Group Processes*. Princeton, N.J.: Princeton University Press, 1975.

chapter 11

Postreform Politics Continued

BLACK POWER: A VITAL FORCE FOR CHANGE

Of all the forces for change and intellectual ferment that emerged in the 1960s, none has been more potent than the civil rights movement. While the idea entrepreneurs who promoted community organizations and drafted the Community Action Program made a significant contribution, profound social change could not have come about without a popular base of some kind. The black community, as the repository of accumulating frustration, provided mass support for efforts to promote change. Its leaders, especially those who were proponents of Black Power, made by far the boldest strides toward new political thought. They, far more than the predominantly white "urban guerillas," made a frontal assault on the intellectual underpinnings of the reform outlook.

Blacks understandably were the segment of the population least enamored with the rhetoric of reform. They had the least grounds to believe that society, its government, and its laws operated fairly and impartially. The experience of discrimination taught blacks that people were judged not on their merits but on the basis of their race or social position. Significantly, in the post-World War II period, while black educational attainment advanced rapidly, black income continued to lag. Travel on the road to success (study hard and get ahead) was beset with difficulties. Black aspirations ran high, but so did black disappointment.

Black disappointment was not restricted to the shortage of opportunities for personal advancement. It also extended to the performance of the government. Throughout the 1960s, surveys showed that blacks consistently judged government services—schools, parks, recreation, garbage collection, and above all, the police—to be less adequate than whites, even city-residing whites, did. Blacks were also more likely to believe that government officials were *not* making a strong effort to solve city problems. For example, when one survey asked about how hard the mayors of selected cities were trying to solve the major problems of their communities, fewer than half (47 percent) of blacks said the mayor was "trying as hard as he can." Nearly two-thirds of the whites (65 percent) gave that answer. At the other end of the scale, 24 percent of blacks but only 13 percent of whites responded that the mayor was not trying hard at all.[1]

In numerous surveys conducted during the riot years in the 1960s, blacks displayed a low level of trust in government. A Newark survey, for example, revealed that among blacks *not involved* in riot activity, only 14 percent said they felt they could trust local government "most of the time"; 34 percent indicated they could "almost never" trust local government. Among those *involved* in riot activity, alienation was even higher: a mere 5 percent said they could trust government "most of the time"; 44 percent said "almost never."[2]

Such alienation pointed to something more than dissatisfaction with a particular set of incumbents or a particular package of programs. Rather, it indicated a root dissatisfaction with political and governmental arrangements. Blacks could see no evidence of government in the interest of the whole community. Instead many blacks believed there was government in the interest of the white, the powerful, and the privileged. The black community was ready for its own ideology, its own approach to righting what it saw as wrong in American society. Black Power filled that need.

Black Power as a Political Ideology

The Black Power catch phrase, first used in the mid-sixties, gave new meaning to the civil rights movement, transformed some of its basic goals, and helped unleash a potent new force in urban communities throughout the nation. Perhaps more than any other development, the emergence of Black Power gave strength to the idea that people should, in fact, be able to influence the decisions that bear most directly on their lives.

[1] *Supplemental Studies for the National Advisory Commission on Civil Disorders* (Washington, D.C.: Government Printing Office, July 1968), p. 41.

[2] Joe R. Feagin and Harlan Hahn, *Ghetto Revolts* (New York: Macmillan Co., 1973), p. 41.

The Black Power movement itself did many things. Foremost among them, it challenged head-on the reformer's notion that there is a unitary public interest to which all separate group interests should be subordinate. Black Power advocates, like the Alinskyites, saw society as a multiplicity of competing and even antagonistic interests.

Like most catch phrases, Black Power defies exact definition. It carries a heavy load of emotional baggage, and therefore its meaning depends somewhat on the person, place, and circumstance. Yet there are some central ideas that give the term meaning and strength. For blacks, the term serves as a symbolic expression for a set of interrelated beliefs about their place in society—what it should be, what it is, and how the "should" and the "is" could be brought closer together. In brief, Black Power is more than a slogan; it is shorthand for a political ideology appealing to the black masses. While the term itself has fallen into disuse, the ideas behind it continue to have a significant impact.

Independence, solidarity, and pride—these are the bases on which the Black Power ideology rests. Each of these key words itself has several dimensions.

Independence

Independence above all means that there are separate black interests that should be represented by blacks who speak firmly and unequivocally for the social, political, and psychological well-being of blacks.[3] Black Power was in part a reaction to practices labelled "white colonialism." Stokely Carmichael and Charles Hamilton, for example, attacked what they saw as an American version of indirect rule, by which they meant practices whereby whites picked leaders to represent the black community who were more responsive to the white leaders who selected them than to the black populace.[4] Such black leaders, according to Carmichael and Hamilton, have no real power. They are beholden to groups outside the black community and thus cannot represent the interests of blacks. The skills and abilities they have are squandered on a showpiece role rather than being devoted to a genuine representative role. Malcolm X put the matter plainly in a 1960 Freedom Rally in Harlem:

> We want to get behind leaders who will fight for us . . . leaders who are not afraid to demand freedom, justice, and equality. We do not want leaders who are handpicked for us by the white man. We don't want any more Uncle Toms.[5]

[3] Tobe Johnson, *Metropolitan Government: A Black Analytical Perspective* (Washington, D.C.: Joint Center for Political Studies, 1972), p. 14.

[4] Stokely Carmichael and Charles Hamilton, *Black Power* (New York: Random House, 1967), p. 10.

[5] Quoted in John H. Bracey, Jr., August Meier, and Elliott Rudwick, *Black Nationalism in America* (Indianapolis: Bobbs-Merrill Co., 1970), p. 416.

According to Black Power ideology, only those whose base of support rests in the black community can represent black interests. It is not enough that a leader be black. As Carmichael and Hamilton put it, "Black visibility is not Black Power . . . The power must be that of a community, and emanate from there."[6]

Direct representation is necessary because people are guided by self-interest, and the interest of one group seldom coincides with the interest of other groups. Liberal or labor groups, for example, have concerns and priorities that differ from those of the black community. Coalition with such groups therefore runs the risk of subordinating black interests to those of other, more influential groups.

Black Power advocates are inclined to see self-interest as the overriding force in politics and in other human relationships. "Politics results from a conflict of interests, not of consciences."[7] Moral appeals carry little weight at City Hall or on Main Street. There the pertinent questions are, "Can you buy, can you sell, how much and how many votes can you deliver?"[8] Advance, then, comes to those groups who can bargain from a position of economic or political strength.

Interests, according to this argument, are not protected by morality, benevolent coalitions, or civic mindedness. They are protected, Black Power advocates and Alinskyites alike argue, by having and using a power base. Consequently, most blacks do not see political independence as a step toward racial separatism—in fact, one study indicates that separatist sentiment is weaker among blacks than among whites.[9] Blacks have looked upon political independence as a means of guaranteeing self-preservation and promoting group advancement in a competitive and far-from-altruistic society.

Independence has also entailed a willingness to use unconventional tactics. Even before Black Power came into being, Martin Luther King had unstintingly defended the virtue and necessity of direct action. Though not disdainful of moral appeals, King argued strongly for the need to precipitate crises in order to bring defenders of the status quo to the bargaining table. King was as aware as any labor leader that negotiations are effective only if the aggrieved party works from a base of strength.

Black Power advocates moved even further away from the tactics of moderation and accommodation. They were even more willing to embrace new tactics and call for new political forms—no matter how controversial.

[6] Carmichael and Hamilton, *Black Power*, p. 46.

[7] Ibid., p. 75.

[8] Ruth Turner Perot, "Organizing the Black Community for the Purpose of Promoting the Interests and Concerns of the Black People," reprinted in *Black Nationalism in America*, Bracey, Meier, and Rudwick, p. 467.

[9] Joel D. Aberbach and Jack L. Walker, *Race in the City* (Boston: Little, Brown & Co., 1973), p. 68.

Carmichael and Hamilton urged an end to fears of white backlash, and in a sideswipe at older leaders, they called for the abandonment of "the old language" of love, suffering, and patience.[10] They argued that "black people must make demands without regard to their initial 'respectability' precisely because 'respectable' demands have not been sufficient."[11] Avoiding controversy was one of the ways the status quo was perpetuated.

Solidarity and Pride

The more-militant black leaders saw power, not persuasion, as the key to political success. A prerequisite to that power was a high level of group consciousness. Solidarity is therefore the second major theme in Black Power ideology. Black leaders, pointedly calling attention to the ethnic character of American politics, reminded blacks that they have a shared experience and a collective fate. Black Power therefore "calls for black people to consolidate behind their own, so that they can bargain from a position of strength."[12]

Solidarity could not come, however, without a third ingredient—pride, the final complement in the Black Power ideology. The point is not a new one. Many years ago, Alain Locke argued for "developing race-pride and stimulating race-consciousness."[13] Because they have been relegated to a subordinate social position, blacks have not had the psychological freedom to develop a healthy and unfettered group identity. To counter society's tendency to associate blackness with inferiority and dependency, Black Power proponents called for a revival of the designation "black" and urged a celebration of the black heritage. The contributions and achievements of individual blacks should be recognized, it was argued, first because they have been unduly neglected, but, more to the point, because it is important for black children to have estimable black role models to identify with.

Race pride, though, is not purely a matter of celebrating or encouraging individual accomplishments. Black Power calls for recognition that the black community, as a collectivity, has strength and therefore has contributions to make to the nation. The Black Power ideology asserts that the American culture is pluralistic and that the distinctively black component of that culture is not inferior. The black perspective is therefore not to be sacrificed on the altar of assimilation but is something to be preserved and valued.

Because black life had been depicted as inferior and inadequate, proponents of Black Power felt that one of their major objectives was to

[10] Carmichael and Hamilton, *Black Power*, p. 50.

[11] Ibid., p. 166.

[12] Ibid., p. 44.

[13] Alain Locke, *The New Negro* (New York: Albert and Charles Boni, 1925), p. 8.

develop what Kenneth Clark termed an ego- and culture-building approach.[14] The strong and emotional attack on white liberals that was a key feature of the early days of the Black Power movement was in part a repudiation of what blacks regard as paternalism. The revolt against "welfare colonialism" was a reaction to the view that blacks were weak and dependent—in need of benevolently bestowed help. As Alain Locke argued, the black "resents being spoken of as a social ward or minor, even by his own, and being regarded as a chronic patient for the sociological clinic, the sick man of American Democracy."[15] In place of such paternalism, the proponents of Black Power stressed collective self-help and enlarged opportunities for group self-expression. The needs of blacks thus were largely political—they especially needed the opportunity to control and direct their own destinies.

According to Black Power doctrine, American society had left blacks with a weakened sense of self-worth, a damaged group psychology, and a somewhat warped perspective. The cure for these problems was a self-directed program of cultural rehabilitation. In the words of Malcolm X, "We must launch a cultural revolution to unbrainwash an entire people."[16]

Without a self-grown feeling of pride there could be no sense of community, no solidarity, and no real independence. Pride could not come without asserting independence, but independence could not be maintained without developing pride. It is not surprising then that Black Power advocates joined others in attacking social service agencies as well as in castigating the members of the "helping" professions who staffed those agencies. At one point Carmichael and Hamilton depicted the issue as a form of class struggle, charging social agencies with perpetuating client dependency so that they could enlarge their programs and still continue "their operation through professional organization."[17]

What the Black Power rhetoricians were doing is, of course, no different from the tactics long employed by union leaders, community organizers, and others. The rhetoric of conflict is a way of raising political consciousness, broadening the awareness of issues, and promoting in-group unity.

Again, there is a reciprocal relationship between objectives. A heightened political consciousness is necessary to increase participation, and participation is necessary to overcome the badge of inferiority and instill pride. Greater pride, in turn, can increase participation, just as higher participation can increase pride.

[14] Clark, *Dark Ghetto*, p. 107.

[15] Locke, *The New Negro*, p. 10.

[16] Quoted in Bracey, Meier, and Rudwick, *Black Nationalism in America*, p. 427.

[17] Carmichael and Hamilton, *Black Power*, p. 148.

It is important, then, to see the Black Power ideology as a guide to action. While it was also a reaction to frustrations, it was far more than an emotional catharsis. It involved a strategy for both long-term social change and some fairly concrete and immediate objectives. The Black Power example almost surely provided lessons to feminists and gays as they became more assertive of their rights and sought to heighten political consciousness. Similarly, anti-abortionists, religious fundamentalists, and others on the Social Right also experienced a growing political consciousness and, in the postreform climate, developed a new appreciation of the value of political power and a willingness to exert power in an open and aggressive manner.

Community Control

Blacks, for their part, realized that it was not enough to participate more in existing institutions and political structures. They called for a search for new forms and, if necessary, the creation of parallel community institutions" controlled by blacks.[18] The interest in parallel institutions was, in turn, linked with the move for community control. As Carmichael and Hamilton explained, "We must begin to think of black community as a base of organization to control institutions in that community."[19] That control might come about, numerical strength permitting, by outvoting other groups and gaining control of existing elective offices, but where districts were gerrymandered or where at-large elections foredoomed blacks to a permanent minority status, new structures could be necessary.

Community control is not easily defined. It is not a precise structural arrangement, like the council-manager plan. But it does involve acceptance of the principle of *political* decentralization and thus runs directly counter to the kind of centralized structures with area-wide constituencies advocated by the "good government" reform movement.

Community control is overtly political. Its proponents view the protection and promotion of group interests as a legitimate and necessary objective. And they deny completely the reform movement's dichotomy between politics and administration. As they see it, all groups—including program professionals—seek to maximize self-interest and can therefore be checked only by other groups that are equipped to protect their own interest. Community control is thus a frontal assault on the mystique surrounding professionalism and technical competence. For example, Carmichael and Hamilton argued, "Control of the ghetto schools must be taken out of the hands of professionals, most of whom have long since

[18] Ibid., p. 43.
[19] Ibid., p. 166.

demonstrated their insensitivity to the needs and problems of black children. These 'experts' bring with them middle-class biases, unsuitable techniques and materials. . . ."[20] Social workers, police, city planners, and other employee groups were equally criticized.

To the proponents of Black Power, control of community service institutions was a necessary step in promoting independence, solidarity, and pride. Black control could increase group consciousness, promote unity, and in this way, maximize political influence. It would also serve to develop a sense of efficacy, provide role models, and eventually replace residual feelings of inferiority with feelings of pride. But for these things to come about, the objectives of the black community would have to replace professionally derived objectives. In addition, procedures and techniques would have to be those prescribed by or at least acceptable to the black community. Blacks were too cynical about broken promises, neglected priorities, and bureaucratic noncompliance to put confidence in anything less than ample and firm neighborhood authority over all administrative decisions. Community control left little room for professional autonomy. It asserted neighborhood hegemony over those matters of greatest concern to the neighborhood. Advocates were not just criticizing the *performance* of community service agencies; they were challenging the *legitimacy* of these institutions. Legitimacy would come only when blacks gained effective control over the activities of public institutions working in black communities.

Failures and frustrations. In the main, the community-control experience has been a variant of the community organization experience. Indeed, in some cases, the groups seeking community control originated as protest groups. TWO in Chicago, for example, tried to gain neighborhood control in the school system and also in the Model Cities program. The limited impact of protest activities may well have been one of the factors that led such groups to seek a more direct say in the running of public agencies. However, community-control efforts, like the community organization activities that often preceded them, foundered on the rocks of external resistance and internal divisiveness.

Community control is, after all, a radical notion. It involves a drastic change in set ways of doing things. It requires a redistribution of authority, and is thus likely to be resisted by city hall. Even when a mayor, like John Lindsay of New York, saw such a move toward decentralization as a way of lessening the power of established bureaucracies, the agencies themselves could be counted on to offer strong resistance. In New York, for example, teacher strikes dealt the coup de grace to the community-control experiments in the school system.

[20] Ibid.

Democracy operating at the neighborhood level is no more exempt from obstacles than when operating at other levels. Internal divisiveness limited black political effectiveness even when community boards provided black neighborhoods with a political voice. Furthermore, serving on a board requires time. Programs are often complicated; and information, especially technical information, is hard to acquire and, when acquired, hard to assimilate. Just as legislatures have difficulty overseeing administrative agencies, so have neighborhood boards.

Take the case of a decentralized school system. It may be less complex than a centralized one, but education is still a complicated process to oversee. Recruitment and supervision, purchasing and distributing supplies, integrating social relevance with the teaching of basic skills, site selection or remodeling and building maintenance, teacher and curriculum evaluation, class size and special education needs, student safety and individual spontaneity, food and health care programs, community service activities and the allocation of scarce resources—each of these is an intricate problem in itself. How much oversight can a lay board with limited time manage? Not much. One study of the school decentralization experience concluded that, while new changes had been induced, the neighborhood boards had not produced "tangible, visible impacts."[21] If requirements such as elaborate procedures, extensive consultation, open meetings, and a formal system of election are added to a broad task like school governance, then the burdens of participation are still greater. Under such circumstances the chances of maintaining an active and united board are not very good. Significantly, studies of citizen participation have concluded that the wider and the less focused the mandate of a citizens' board, the more likely conflict is to break out. In the words of one writer, "An ill-defined agenda can be a source of conflict."[22] General, long-range, and diffuse objectives are the least manageable and the most likely to breed internal conflict. On the other hand, when a citizen board "is busy with clearly defined tasks, . . . members seem more likely to keep . . . grievances to themselves, and the likelihood of 'personalized' conflict is diminished."[23]

The validity of these generalizations is borne out by the few success stories that community control has to tell. According to one of the more thoroughgoing assessments of the decentralization experience, a neighborhood board is more likely to do well when it is clearly focused on a specific and concrete service-delivery problem—running a health clinic or a day-care center—than in governing the school system or planning a coordi-

[21] Douglas Yates, *Neighborhood Democracy* (Lexington, Mass.: D. C. Heath and Co., 1973), p. 63.

[22] Matthew Crenson, "Organizational Factors in Citizen Participation," *Journal of Politics* 36 (May 1974), 372.

[23] Ibid., p. 373.

nated and multifaceted attack on urban decay.[24] Success also depends in part upon the presence of sympathetic professionals inside the target agency. If neighborhood leaders and at least some agency professionals have a shared interest in innovation, then they can give one another mutual support. Neighborhood leaders can create a climate of change; professionals, who possess expertise, can legitimize change in the eyes of their more cautious colleagues. There is no guarantee, of course, that a given agency will contain sympathetic professionals. "There is no reason to assume that bureaucrats will react constructively to a crisis created by client rebelliousness; it is quite likely that they will respond with panic, defensiveness, and symbolic gestures."[25]

Though the community-control movement is now largely a matter of history, the Black Power thrust is not at an end. It has simply shifted targets. The attempt to create new and parallel institutions no longer seems as timely as it once did. Now it seems more urgent (and possible), to gain and use traditional centers of power in local government. A push for conventional positions of authority—the mayoralty, high-level administrative positions, city council posts, and membership on school boards, planning commissions, and the like—has become the major outlet for Black Power aspirations. Public sector activity is so important, especially to minorities, that blacks inevitably are concerned with local government; they see it, among other things, as an avenue of political development. Holding public office is in part a symbolic achievement, and as such, it can heighten group identity and self-respect. But public-office holding is more than symbolic. It can lead to policy gains, and it offers practical opportunities to sharpen political skills, to develop experience and sophistication, and above all to exercise the kind of leadership that unites and mobilizes a group.

As blacks attempt to consolidate power through the ballot box, countervailing forces keep the outcome in question. Racial gerrymandering is still a problem, despite federal prohibitions against it. And though blacks have won some top posts, even in cities like Los Angeles, Chicago, and Philadelphia, where blacks are not a majority, frustrations still abound. Moves toward metropolitan consolidation—a legacy of the reform movement—make most blacks uneasy. They see it as a thin veneer for yet another round of white domination, domination brought about by engulfing black city majorities with a sea of suburban white voters.

These fears are not eased by the small numbers of actual consolidations—not more than four major ones at this time. Regional planning bodies do exist. While such bodies have relatively little authority, they do have some powers of review. And in all too many cases, central cities—and therefore blacks—are underrepresented on these bodies. Because repre-

[24] Yates, *Neighborhood Democracy*, p. 66.

[25] Fainstein and Fainstein, *Urban Political Movements*, p. 214.

sentation on them is not based on population, small suburban jurisdictions easily outweigh their central city partners. Small wonder that regional planning agencies often do not give a high priority to central-city problems. Efforts to increase central-city representation or to alter priorities may generate friction. In the Cleveland area, for example, when Mayor Carl Stokes tried to increase city representation, the suburban-dominated regional planning board retaliated by refusing to okay Cleveland's application for $750,000 to develop twenty-seven small city parks—a program that had no significant effect on the suburban jurisdictions.

In other places, blacks fear that state government may be used to curtail city authority. Baltimore, which now contains a black majority, has relinquished its airport to state control—ostensibly for financial reasons. The Port Authority is also under state control. State financing for the public transit system and for a new convention center is an indication to some observers of further signs of diminished city authority.

Black mayors—problems and achievements. Despite the storm signals, blacks have made substantial political gains. The increasing number of black mayors is one indicator. Office holding, especially the top executive post, is not, however, without frustrations. Black mayors, even in predominantly black cities, though certainly more so in cities without a black majority, are vulnerable to intense political crossfire. Their black constituents have high expectations; their white constituents have easily triggered anxieties. Should the mayor advocate black interests and give them high priority, or should the mayor alleviate the anxieties of white business people and white residents by leaning over backwards to prove racial impartiality? The spirit of Black Power (indeed of the postreform style) leads to the first alternative. The reform outlook, which continues to exert much influence, favors the second.

Two of the first black mayors of large cities, Richard Hatcher of Gary, Indiana, and Carl Stokes of Cleveland, offer some insight into Black Power politics as waged through conventional positions of city authority. Both men were elected in 1967. At this writing Hatcher is still mayor of Gary. Stokes, unable to come through the maelstrom of Cleveland politics, retired after two two-year terms. In 1967, Gary's population was about half black, half white, while Cleveland's population was only about one-third black.

In their 1967 campaigns, both Hatcher and Stokes appealed to black pride and sought to mobilize the votes of a cohesive black community. Both succeeded. Hatcher got almost 93 percent of the black vote, Stokes 96 percent. Both men were overwhelmingly opposed by white voters, although their electoral margins did include some white votes.

Even though they were winners in racially polarized elections, both appointed some whites to high level administrative positions and both, with limited success, sought the cooperation of the white business community. Both were criticized within the black community for not being more thoroughgoing in the pursuit of black aspirations. Yet it was quite evident that the two mayors brought new priorities to office. Many blacks were appointed to positions long occupied by whites. Black contractors and suppliers increased their business with both cities. Whereas their predecessors had built little or no housing for the poor, Stokes's administration built more than 5,000 units of low- and moderate-income housing, and Hatcher in his first term oversaw the development of 4,500 new units. Using the leverage of his new office (administrative control of the placement of city deposits totaling about $50 million), Stokes was able to persuade Cleveland banks to embark on a program of small-business loans to black entrepreneurs. Hatcher, with the aid of large amounts of federal money, launched massive job-training programs, programs linked to the city's various housing and physical development programs.

Mayor Hatcher pursued an independent course of action, refusing throughout to ally himself with the white machine politicians of the Lake County organization. He also would not move to create his own machine of patronage-supported precinct workers. Instead, when seeking reelection in 1971, Hatcher relied heavily on his record, and used professional organizers and a political consulting firm to run his campaign. He was able to project a favorable image as capable, honest, and progressive, gaining 25 percent of the white votes as well as solid black support. In the 1971 Democratic primary, there was a 70 percent turnout among the black registered electorate whereas the white turnout was only 60 percent—a decisive index of his success in appealing to black pride.

In a white-majority city, the political career of Carl Stokes ultimately foundered on the shoals of racial polarization, even though he was not without strengths and some notable accomplishments. Besides doing some ad hoc coalition building and inevitable bargaining, Mayor Stokes organized the Twenty-First Congressional District Caucus so that blacks would have an independent political base. And he used the powers of his office to the hilt. But there were so many issues at stake that Stokes was forced to fight a multifront war, while most of his opponents enjoyed the luxury of single-issue conflict. In only a four-year span, Stokes was beset by conflicts with the local Democratic party, organized labor, his own police commissioner, his own police chief, rank-and-file policemen, the city council, the white news media, the county prosecutor's office, the suburban jurisdictions around Cleveland, and several members of the business community—all of this in a community where newspaper editors and civic leaders deplored conflict. Ultimately a violent confrontation between blacks and police in the Glenville area eroded his already embattled position. As Stokes concluded, "Politics is no box of crackerjacks. . . ."[26]

[26] Carl B. Stokes, *Promises of Power* (New York: Simon and Schuster, 1973), p. 280.

Both mayors proved that it is possible to mobilize the black masses and to do so without inducements of machine politics. In office as well as on the campaign stump, they exercised leadership oriented toward the collective well-being of blacks. They delivered programs of tangible benefit—housing, jobs, and improved services. Though it is hard to measure and document, in all likelihood black pride was also advanced. Certainly, heightened voter turnout as well as available survey results would indicate such advance.

The recent election of Harold Washington, Chicago's first black mayor, is ample evidence of the importance of mobilizing voting strength. For many years, voter participation in Chicago's black neighborhoods had declined. The Daley machine was content with low turnout in these areas.[27] But as the black population and Latinos came to represent a potentially determining bloc, interest in a black candidacy heightened. The fall, 1982, state election saw more than 100,000 black voters added to the rolls. With a city primary due in February 1983, an additional mobilization increased black registration by another 100,000, bringing the number of blacks up to 41 percent of the city's electorate. With black participation no longer lagging, Washington was able to win the Democratic primary and subsequently the general election. The contest generated a voter turnout of about 80 percent of the eligible electorate—a phenomenally high turnout, especially for a local election.

The large voter turnout came about in part because racial antagonisms and fears were at a high level. In the general election especially, racial feelings ran strong, and public employees made little pretense of neutrality. The police department, 75 percent white and 25 percent black, divided sharply along racial lines.[28] Race was a stronger factor then party affiliation; at least eight Democratic ward bosses endorsed Republican candidate Epton, one did so saying it was a matter of racial pride.[29] Harold Washington refused to waver in his strong and close identity with a black constituency. He explained that he was running as a black candidate "because the people in my community were not getting out of [the Daley machine] what they were putting into it."[30] At a rally, he unapologetically said: "We've waited patiently, voted for white candidates over and over. It's our turn now."[31] To Washington, his strategy was nothing more than a continuation of long-standing Chicago practice. In responding to news media questions about a racial appeal, he stated:

[27] Gove and Masotti, *After Daley*.

[28] *Washington Post*, April 9, 1983.

[29] *Nation*, March 12, 1983, p. 295.

[30] *New Republic*, February 28, 1982, p. 12.

[31] *Nation*, March 12, 1983, p. 295.

> We try to push our own and everybody asks for an explanation: "Why would you push your own? Are you racist or something?" Any politician will stress his base. Is there something wrong with a black base?[32]

As the Washington campaign proceeded, and it became apparent that blacks had become a major electoral force in Chicago, white anxieties and hostilities reached a high level. Racial slogans and appeals to "white solidarity" emerged as significant features of the campaign. Voting followed racial lines. Washington won with 51 percent of the total vote, achieved by receiving 99 percent of the black vote, 80 percent of the Latino vote, and 18 percent of the white vote.

The Chicago experience is by no means typical. In the same year that Chicago was electing its first black mayor in a racially divided campaign, Birmingham, Alabama, was reelecting its first black mayor in an election characterized by racial harmony. Although the black incumbent faced a white challenger, all campaign committees and election slates were biracial. Perhaps because the city had a history of racial antagonism, the opposing mayoral candidates jointly formed a Committee for a Fair Campaign to prevent racial appeals from dominating the campaign.[33]

As we consider black participation in urban politics, it is important to keep perspective. Elections are, of course, important, but they are only one element in gaining the power to govern. Moreover, the mayor's office is only one position of authority out of several. As mayor of Chicago, Harold Washington has been confronted by a hostile and uncooperative majority on the city council. Atlanta's first black mayor, Maynard Jackson, experienced eight years of tension with the city's white business community.[34] His successor, Andrew Young, acknowledged that he could not govern the city without the cooperation of the business community.[35]

Frustrations abound. The urban condition is not easily changed. Aging physical structures, a declining economy, and deep-rooted social problems characteristic of so many older cities are not easily dealt with. As one observer noted, even the successful black mayor can do little more than "improve conditions at the margin of daily life."[36] Still black electoral power is on the increase. From 1972 to mid 1983, the number of black mayors grew from 86 to 247.[37] Among the nation's largest cities, Phila-

[32] *Newsweek*, April 11, 1983, p. 21.

[33] *Washington Post*, October 13, 1983.

[34] M. Dale Henson and James King, "The Atlanta Public-Private Romance: An Abrupt Transformation," in *Public-Private Partnership in American Cities*, ed. R. Scott Fosler and Renee A. Berger (Lexington, MA: Lexington Books, 1982), pp. 293-337.

[35] *Atlanta Constitution*, July 24, 1983.

[36] Charles H. Levine, *Racial Conflict and the American Mayor* (Lexington, Mass.: D. C. Heath and Co., Lexington Books, 1974), p. 81.

[37] Figures courtesy of the Joint Center for Political Studies.

delphia and Chicago as well as Charlotte, North Carolina, and Flint, Michigan, joined that list in 1983, bringing to nineteen the number of cities over 100,000 in population headed by black mayors.

The area where black political leadership has made the most visible difference is in public employment. Without a doubt, black elected officials matter.[38] Affirmative action programs are pursued more vigorously, and the number of blacks appointed to high-level administrative and professional positions increases dramatically. In Atlanta, for example, in the five years after the election of a black mayor, the number of blacks in professional positions more than doubled—from 19 percent to 42 percent.[39] The overall increase in black employment in the total classified service was more modest, from 42 to 56 percent, but nevertheless significant. Thus, while the channeling of Black Power aspirations into conventional lines is not without frustrations, it is also not a hollow exercise.

PUBLIC-EMPLOYEE UNIONISM: A SUCCESS STORY IN CONFLICT STRATEGY

Neighborhood groups and Black Power advocates were not the only ones to pursue a conflict strategy in the 1960s. Public employees were quick to follow the tenor of the times. Their unions emerged as a major force, willing to use work stoppages, demonstrations, and organized political activity to further their aims.

As public employees came more and more to see collective bargaining as a right, public employee unions underwent an astounding growth spurt in the 1960s. In that decade, the American Federation of State, County, and Municipal Employees (AFSCME) more than doubled in membership. In that same ten-year period the American Federation of Teachers (AFT), perhaps the most aggressive of the teacher organizations, grew to more than three-and-a-half times its 1960 size. Other organizations also experienced rapid growth. By the 1970s, about two-thirds of the personnel in local government were represented by some type of employee organization.

Changing Strike Policies

Public-employee unionization not only grew in the 1960s, it became more militant. Before then, most such unions proclaimed a no-strike policy. During the 1960s, constitutions were changed, new policies were

[38] See Peter K. Eisinger, *The Politics of Displacement* (New York: Academic Press, 1980). On budgetary consequences, see Albert Karnig and Susan Welch, *Black Representation and Urban Policy* (Chicago: University of Chicago Press, 1981).

[39] Eisinger, *Politics of Displacement*, p. 161.

announced, and union leaders became more outspoken. Reversing earlier positions, one-time conservative organizations like the National Education Association and the American Nursing Association withdrew opposition to strikes by their local affiliates. The sensitive area of public safety was no more immune to worker militancy than were other areas. AFSCME removed its prohibition against strikes by law-enforcement officials, and the somewhat more staid International Association of Fire Fighters also removed the no-strike clause from its constitution.

Though sometimes called job actions to avoid the word "strike," work stoppages have hit almost all phases of local government in the last decade. With few exceptions, strikes by public employees are illegal. Nevertheless, they occur and have remained at a high level since the 1960s.[40] There were more strikes in 1968 alone than there had been in the entire period from 1958 to 1965.[41] Teacher strikes have become especially prevalent, and "sick outs" and "blue flu" for police and "red rash" for firemen are strikes in all but name. However unprofessional they may have seemed a few years ago, strikes are now part and parcel of labor relations in the public sector. They have spread to all parts of the country and to all sizes of jurisdictions.

Strikes are not the only kind of job action a public-employee organization can take. Police, for example, may report to work but refrain from enforcing some or all of the laws they normally enforce. Maryland State Police, for example, proposed to write fewer traffic tickets and thereby cut state revenue by 3.8 million dollars. And police officers in one county engaged in a work slowdown by writing detailed reports on such matters as displaced manhole covers, alarms sounding off, and recovered stolen bikes. The Social Service Employee Union in New York City once instructed its members to report to work, but, "Do not answer phones. Do not pick up pen or pencil. Do not go to intake. Do not go to the field." As the union president explained, "We'll think about our cases, think about our problems, and talk about them with our coworkers until the time when the Department comes to its senses."[42] Another tactic is to follow rules and procedures rigidly, making no exceptions and taking no short cuts. If followed closely, most prescribed procedures are cumbersome enough to snarl the flow of work.

But the strike or the threat of strike is the basic weapon of public unions as it is of private ones. Union leaders, public and private, agree that without the strike there is no genuine collective bargaining, and management has no incentive to enter into real negotiations. Though the strike is

[40] Clark and Ferguson, *City Money*, p. 154.

[41] See Sheila C. White, "Work Stoppages of Government Employees," in *Collective Bargaining in Government*, ed. J. Joseph Loewenberg and Michael H. Moscow (Englewood Cliffs, N.J.: Prentice-Hall, 1972), pp. 251-60.

[42] Quoted in Sterling D. Spero and John M. Capozzola, *The Urban Community and Its Unionized Bureaucracies* (New York: Dunellen Publishing Co., 1973), p. 181.

admittedly coercive, labor leaders regard it as an essential guarantee of a free labor market. Antistrike measures, as public-employee unions see them, serve only to relegate public employees to the status of second-class citizens.

Union militancy is typified by the union leader who is willing to defy an injunction and go to jail to defend the right to strike. Under these conditions, jailing seldom discredits leaders or weakens their position. Quite the contrary, it seems to enhance the leader's position and strengthen the resolve of the union to bring the city or county to the bargaining table. In New York City, for example, Albert Shanker, then president of the United Federation of Teachers and later an officer in the AFL-CIO, gained national attention as well as local support by being jailed during the 1968 strikes. Private sector unions may lend their support to their fellow unionists in the public sector, particularly if the right to strike itself seems to be at issue.

Though attitudes toward union activity are highly volatile, they have been permissive enough to make some antistrike measures ineffective. However, while courts tend to be supportive of the right of association and other First Amendment freedoms, the legal situation for public employees varies from state to state. Moreover, the political climate is also variable. Some elected officials sense political gain to be had from an anti-strike stance.

Politics and the Unions

If war is diplomacy conducted by other means, then a strike is politics conducted by other means. And just as diplomacy is far more common than warfare, so noncoercive union political action is more common than strikes. Public-employee unions are involved in a variety of political activities. They lobby. They conduct public relations efforts. Moreover, with proscriptions against campaign activity by civil servants on the wane, they support candidates for office.

Candidates recognize that public-employee unions are one of the most vital forms of political organization. They have many of the features of traditional party organizations. Unions publish newspapers and journals. They have campaign funds and campaign workers.

One former Tammany leader declared, "The best political machine in New York City is John DeLury's Sanitationmen's Union." And, he added, he would rather have them "with me in an election than half the party headquarters in town."[43] The union has direct contact with an estimated 150,000 voters. It also has a card file on every member, former member, retired member, and spouse of a deceased member. Moreover,

[43] Edward N. Costikyan, "Who Runs City Government?" *The New York Times Magazine*, May 26, 1969, p. 45.

members are available to work in each election district in the city as well as in centralized activities. All in all, the members and their families constitute a substantial block of probable voters themselves, and they have a significant capacity to mobilize an even larger vote.

Unions have also shown that they know how to use the mass media. When they wanted to get authorization for a civilian review board repealed, the Policemen's Benevolent Association in New York City poured nearly a million dollars into a media campaign. They won in a referendum that had the mayor and both U.S. senators lined up on the other side. Public-employee unions have thus proven skillful in using multiple techniques to dramatize issues, secure friends, and punish enemies.

While public-employee unions have not won every contest they have entered, they have won often enough to become a recognized and even feared political force. Union aggressiveness can go too far, though, and generate a backlash, as it has in one-time union strongholds like San Francisco and Seattle. Nevertheless, their aggressiveness has bred political success, and political success has reinforced union aggressiveness.

The Unions and Employee Benefits

Though it is hard to establish any firm and specific connection between union activity and employee benefits, most people do attribute higher salaries, improved pensions, and other benefits to increased unionization. Clearly, salaries have gone up rapidly during the recent years of heightened union activity. For example, in the 1960s—relatively low-inflation years—teachers' salaries went up about 8 percent annually, a rate approximately twice as high as the Consumer Price Index increases in that period.[44] Police work hours have been going down while salaries have been going up.

These kinds of changes take on special significance in light of the fact that well over half of the typical city budget goes for salaries and fringe benefits. Much of the recent resurge in government expenditures is traceable to personnel costs—an estimated 80 percent, in the case of public schools. To be sure, the number of people employed by local governments has increased, but salaries have gone up much faster. In the important 1950-1968 time span, local-government payrolls more than quadrupled even though the number of employees only a little more than doubled.[45]

Public-employee union activity is by no means restricted to narrow money matters such as salaries and pensions.

Public-employees unions have sought improvements in the quality of public services, and they have emerged as prime defenders of agency

[44] Richard A. Cloward and Frances Fox Piven, *The Politics of Turmoil* (New York: Random House, 1974), p. 325.

[45] Spero and Capozzola, *The Urban Community and Its Unionized Bureaucracies*, p. 218.

autonomy. Public-employee victories have thus been far ranging. Some of the most spectacular examples have come from New York City, notably the teachers' strike against community control in Ocean Hill-Brownsville and the police defeat of civilian review mentioned earlier. In both instances employees successfully defended their autonomy against attempts to increase citizen oversight and influence.

Nor are victories confined to large cities. A Huntington, New York, contract with teachers, negotiated by collective bargaining, states that "the members of the teaching profession have a special expertise which entitles them to participate in determining policies and programs designed to improve educational standards."[46] Teachers' working conditions—matters not easily separated from broad questions of educational policy—are covered in great detail by contracts. Class size, the number of teaching hours, free-time periods for class preparations, and freedom from certain custodial and supervisory responsibilities are also specified in a number of collective bargaining agreements. An East St. Louis, Illinois, contract stipulated, "No change in teaching conditions shall occur within a building unless a majority of teachers desire the change."[47] Other agreements spell out teacher rights in textbook selection, curriculum planning, and academic freedom. Some steps have been taken toward granting teachers the right to elect department heads. Increasingly common are detailed regulations covering matters such as transfers, grievance procedures, the school calendar, and even free athletic passes.

The Policemen's Benevolent Association in New York City even objected to the appointment of an independent commission to investigate charges of corruption, fearing that it might lead to "greater expense, harassment, and inconvenience" for police officers.[48] The police have sought to specify such details as the number of officers assigned to a patrol car. The sanitation workers' union in New York City was able to bring about changes in the city's air pollution regulations. Employee unions sometimes bargain for added staff to handle the work load, and they are greatly concerned about measures that might cut local-government payrolls. The Detroit AFSCME, for example, negotiated a restriction on the city's ability to contract out work.

Unions have ranged so far in negotiating work conditions that some writers see them as codeterminants of public policy. Certainly personnel administration has become increasingly subject to the process of collective bargaining. Nor does the matter end with the signing of an agreement. Setting up grievance procedures and implementing contract provisions almost of necessity require some sharing of supervisory prerogatives with union representatives, known as shop stewards or office representatives.

[46] Quoted in ibid., p. 175.
[47] Quoted in ibid., p. 177.
[48] Ibid., p. 185.

The extent and quality of the gains made by public-employee organizations should not be exaggerated. Aside from salary increases, the most spectacular victories have come largely at the expense of racial minorities seeking change. Salary increases themselves have been partly a matter of catching up with the private sector: now that those gains have been registered and budgets have tightened, resistance by the general public to further increases has greatly intensified. Moreover, recent research suggests that increased compensation has been achieved by trading off for a decreased number of employees.[49] Nevertheless, public-employee unions have been far more successful than neighborhood groups were with the same conflict strategy. Why?

Divisive Forces

Like neighborhoods, unions, contain some forces that unify and others that fragment. The common, unifying interests in higher salaries and improved working conditions are obvious enough. Less obvious, but quite real, are certain fragmenting forces. In the first place, there is considerable competition among unions for members. Each wants to be recognized as the bargaining representative for as wide a segment of the work force as possible. So while there is a facade of union solidarity on such matters as the right to strike, there is an undercoat of rivalry and competition. Even within a given union there are divisive forces at work. Older workers may be more interested in pensions, younger workers in salaries. Or the drive for higher salaries may conflict with the desire to avoid personnel cutbacks. Lower-echelon employees often have different priorities from employees with supevisory responsibilities.

But no factor is potentially more divisive than race. In some instances, race reinforces other divisions—blacks may be newer members or hold subordinate positions in a given work force and as a result may feel doubly disadvantaged. Blacks and Puerto Ricans, for example, led the way in forming a dissident group, the Rank and File Committee for a Democratic Union, to challenge the old-line Irish leadership in the Transit Workers Union in New York City. Further, where there is friction between blacks as a client population and service-providing employees, black employees may identify more strongly with the client population than with their co-workers. Under these circumstances, black employees—who are generally a minority of the work force—may form a separate organization or set up a caucus within the union.

Generally, though not always, divisiveness is held in check. Two major factors work to promote unity. First of all, especially at negotiating time, unions operate in an environment of conflict and struggle that encourages

[49] Clark and Feruguson, *City Money*, pp. 160-5.

members to close ranks. Indeed, drawing on long experience in the private sector, union leaders in the public sector deliberately foster an atmosphere of strife. Belligerent demands, indignant rejoinders to the "intransigence" of management, and a bravado stance often characterize union leaders when they begin the bargaining process. Appealing largely to the emotions of their followers, union leaders stoke the fires of fear and resentment. In this way, they can maintain rank-and-file support, even if the hardships of a strike must be borne. The pattern has been reenacted frequently enough to become known as the script. Its dramatic ending calls for the union to gain "hard-won concessions" from a "tough and stubborn" management team. While union leaders approach the bargaining table in an unemotional and reasonable manner, public histrionics serve to heighten the us-against-them feelings of workers. In this way internal divisions are subordinated to the external struggle with management.

Emotional appeals aimed at bolstering union solidarity would, of course, be ineffective if union leaders did not gain tangible concessions. An AFSCME leader explained to his members: "They may like the idea that Vic Gotbaum bangs the table and gets aggravated, but if I labor and bring forth a mouse, they are not going to be impressed."[50] On the other hand, delivering improved benefits can do wonders for solidarity. Transit Worker Union success in garnering sizeable pay and pension increases, for example, substantially weakened the challenge from the Rank and File Committee for a Democratic Union.

Unions are in a position to gain benefits that are immediate, specific, and concrete. By contrast, neighborhood improvements tend to be longer in coming, and when they come, their consequences are usually diffuse and less tangible than a bigger paycheck. For example, bringing about decentralization of authority to the neighborhood level or inducing an agency to adopt new procedures does not translate directly enough and fast enough into improvements in the lives of people to generate durable support. Even when a neighborhood group wins in getting something tangible like a new clinic, it may lose when the problems of site location generate disunity. And, of course, neighborhood organizations never reach that financial plum of compulsory membership dues. Unions, on the other hand, that gather enough momentum to negotiate an agency shop have a fixed source of income through which to sustain the organization.

So far, conflict strategy has worked far better for civil servants than for neighborhood organizers. The ironies are rich: in many cases, public-employee union wins are made in opposition to, or at the expense of, the less-potent community groups. But circumstances change. Unions may face strong resistance and declining rates of success. After all, local budgets

[50] Quoted in Spero and Capozzola, *The Urban Community and Its Unionized Bureaucracies*, p. 111.

are much tighter now than they were a few years ago. As citizens become more tax-conscious, elected officials can mobilize their support against public-employee unions and win. Those who pursue a conflict strategy always run the risk of provoking a counterforce, and unlike the laws of physics, a counterforce in politics may be even greater than the original force that prompted it.

If union victories become smaller and less frequent, union solidarity may become more difficult to maintain. Because our experience with public-employee unionism is still unfolding, it would be a mistake to assume that past patterns of influence or effectiveness will necessarily carry over into the future.

DURABLE SIGNS OF A POSTREFORM POLITICS

Despite repeated postreform assaults on the citadels of "good government," the urban landscape is by no means barren of reform ideas and practices. Indeed, one might well wonder whether the various waves of postreform politics have had any lasting effects. Neighborhood protest groups are less evident now than earlier. The community-control movement is largely spent. Black Power has taken the nonradical tack of pursuing control of conventional positions of authority. And even though public-employee unionism remains a viable and active force, it faces a less than friendly environment. Was the turbulence of the 1960s a brief interlude, signifying some temporary difficulty in assimilating social change but leaving untouched our basic political processes? We think not. Many of the ideas and political styles engendered in the 1960s have proved to have staying power. Our manner of governance has altered: perhaps of equal importance, the issues now on the public agenda are fundamentally different from the issues that grew up around the reform movement.

Some of the politically expressed concerns of the 1960s have gained academic trappings and have taken on more formal expression. The verdict of public-choice theorists is that bureaucratic agencies are cumbersome instruments for giving urban citizens the services they want and need—a conclusion quite compatible with the postreform outlook. The limitations of large-scale organizations combined with diversity in citizen preferences have led some public-choice theorists to advocate political and administrative decentralization. They oppose metropolitan consolidation and make a plausible case for neighborhood participation in shaping and overseeing government programs—especially those involving human services. Related developments, especially the growing interest in program evaluation, also indicate that the level of doubt about bureaucratic performance remains high.

There is also a growing acceptance for the view that preferences and priorities differ from group to group. Government, it is recognized, has not only to govern and make binding decisions; it has also to represent diverse groups. Consequently, one can find evidence of a growing concern with interest representation. For example, there is renewed sympathy for district rather than at-large elections. And affirmative action plans for hiring women and minorities are justified not simply on grounds of equalizing opportunities for individuals but also on grounds of representativeness. Moreover, the argument for representativeness is not mere window dressing. A study of black officeholders in a variety of New Jersey communities concluded that "they make a difference"—that they have an impact on both the formulation and implementation of a wide range of policies. Significantly, this same study concluded:

> . . . black elected officials sensitize their white associates not only by overt proposals but simply by their presence. Paradoxically and perversely, the tendency among whites to believe that black interests were well represented was greater in communities with no elected blacks than in those that had elected them. This was true for citizens and officials. . . .[51]

In general, the sentiment that groups should be represented in the programs directly affecting them has gained a large measure of acceptability. It has extended beyond the initial beachhead of antipoverty programs to other areas. A few jurisdictions even have high school students on school boards. And the emergence of consumer protection agencies in local governments constitutes a kind of recognition that consumer interests are entitled to specific representation.

Aside from any official representation of various segments of the community, groups continue to display a high level of political consciousness. Looking back over our recent experience, we conclude that heightened political consciousness by one group heightens the political consciousness of others. By now the process is irreversible. As political commentator David Broder has observed, ours is an era in which people "increasingly believe that they can best protect their interests by raising their voices and casting their votes."[52] An abundance of assertive groups has come to characterize the contemporary political condition. While the representation of specific interests, no matter how elaborately done, must still be reconciled with the need to govern, official decision making is now infused with the process of representing divergent interests to a degree beyond the ken of early reformers.

[51] Leonard A. Cole, *Blacks in Power* (Princeton, N.J.: Princeton University Press, 1976), p. 222.

[52] *Washington Post,* July 21, 1983.

CONCLUSION

What, then, can we say overall about the postreform style of politics, as it has emerged and endured?

Even with the fading away of the urban "guerillas" and the evolution of the Black Power movement, postreform politics is still characterized by a strong concern with the performance of service-providing agencies.

Moreover, politics remains overtly competitive. Neighborhood groups, unions, and minority groups have been joined by many others in openly seeking to further their interests through political action. Groups continue to organize, to be concerned about consciousness raising, and to seek representation in the decision-making process of government.

And, as we shall see in more detail in later chapters, the problem-solving efforts of public agencies and professional groups are no longer protected from popular pressure. Once the urban "guerillas," Black Power advocates, and others pulled aside the protective shield of expertise, even routine governmental actions, such as teaching and policing, were revealed as inherently value-laden. Consequently, much of contemporary politics continues to be concerned with the behavior of program administrators.

Finally, we seem to have moved irretrievably away from universal acceptance of the unitary conception of the public interest. Black Power advocates made the argument forcefully: many interests are competitive, and promoting the well-being of one segment of the population, even a majority, does not guarantee that the well-being of other groups will advance. From the proponents of the public-choice approach, we also hear the argument that individual citizens are the best judge of their own interests, that citizens are most appropriately thought of as consumers of government services, and that benefits can therefore best be calculated in terms of user preferences. Moreover, because citizens do not have uniform preferences, the public interest involves different groups being satisfied in different ways. In much the same manner that the Black Power ideology does, the public-choice approach calls for decentralization and diversity.

Again, we emphasize that reform ideas have not disappeared, but other ideas have now appeared on the urban landscape. And the appearance of these ideas means that reform no longer has an intellectual monopoly. Other ways of looking at and running urban government have gained acceptability and are likely to have a continuing impact. The impact of these alternative ideas and practices marks the postreform imprint.

SUGGESTED READINGS

BELLUSH, JEWEL and BERNARD BELLUSH. *Union Power and New York*: Praeger Publishers, 1985.

BROWNING, RUFUS P., DALE ROGERS MARSHALL, and DAVID H. TABB. *Protest Is Not Enough.* Berkeley: University of California Press, 1984.

BRYCE, HERRINGTON J. *Black Mayors of Medium and Large Cities: How Much Statutory Power Do They Have?* Washington, D.C.: Joint Center for Political Studies, 1974.

COLE, LEONARD A. *Blacks in Power*. Princeton, N.J.: Princeton University Press, 1976.

EISINGER, PETER K. *The Politics of Displacement.* New York: Academic Press, 1980.

HAMILTON, CHARLES V. "The Patron-Recipient Relationship and Minority Politics in New York City." *Political Science Quarterly* 94 (Summer 1979), 211-27.

HOLLI, MELVIN G. and PAUL M. GREEN, eds. *The Making of the Mayor: Chicago, 1983*. Grand Rapids, Michigan: William B. Eerdmans Publishing Co., 1984.

JOHNSON, SUSAN M. *Teacher Unions in Schools*. Philadelphia: Temple University Press, 1984.

JOHNSON, TOBE. *Metropolitan Government: A Black Analytical Perspective.*Washington, D.C.: Joint Center for Political Studies, 1972.

KARNIG, ALBERT and SUSAN WELCH. *Black Representation and Urban Policy*. Chicago: University of Chicago Press, 1981.

LEVINE, MARVIN J. and EUGENE C. HAGBURG. *Public Sector Labor Relations*. St. Paul: West Publishing Co., 1979.

METHE, DAVID and JAMES PERRY. "The Impacts of Collective Bargaining on Local Government Services." *Public Administration Review* 40 (July/August 1980), 359-71.

MORRIS, ALDON D. *The Origins of the Civil Rights Movement*. New York: The Free Press, 1984.

NELSON, WILLIAM E., JR. *Black Politics in Gary*. Washington, D.C.: Joint Center for Political Studies, 1972.

PATTERSON, ERNEST. *Black City Politics*. New York: Dodd, Mead and Co., 1974.

PRESTON, MICHAEL B., LENNEAL J. HENDERSON, JR., and PAUL PURYEAR. *The New Black Politics: The Search for Political Power*. New York: Longman, 1982.

SPERO, STERLING D., and JOHN M. CAPOZZOLA. *The Urban Community and Its Unionized Bureaucracies*. New York: Dunellen Publishing Co., 1973.

WOODY, BETTE. *Managing Crisis Cities: The New Black Leadership and the Politics of Resource Allocation*. Westport, CN: Greenwood Press, 1982.

YATES, DOUGLAS. *Neighborhood Democracy*. Lexington, Mass.: D. C. Heath and Co., 1973.

chapter 12

Emergent Trends

We have traveled now from the quiet, stable, conformity-demanding political life of the village to the fast-paced, volatile, nearly irrepressible political life of the postreform city. While the journey is, in part, one through time, change does not come with equal force to all communities. Some change sooner than others. Some change more profoundly than others. Political style, as we have tried to emphasize, reflects community setting—social, economic, and cultural.

We should, of course, remember that our four basic patterns of politics—village, machine, reform, and postreform—are abstractions from real-world complexity. Communities may, and do, mix patterns. Further, no pattern is impervious to change. Postreform politics in the 1970s has already taken on new forms and shapes and is still evolving. Let us look first at what trends the four patterns represent. Then we can consider some of the still-emerging facets of the contemporary urban political scene.

A TYPOLOGY OF URBAN POLITICAL PATTERNS

In tracing our four patterns of politics, we have followed two basic themes. One reflects the trend from a traditional to a modern outlook. The other—less evident but equally important—centers on the way people look at what is at stake in the governance of the community. We will call it an interest orientation. It indicates whether politics emphasizes common interests or competing interests. If politics focuses on the community as a unit and what people share in common, then public life does not concern itself much with how the interests of various segments of the community are differentiated from one another. Village politics, for example, works to reinforce social solidarity, and reform practices purposefully discourage public conflict. By contrast, some styles of politics are highly competitive, and they accentuate differentiation of interest among various segments of the community. Machine politics, for example, is not only highly partisan, but it also deals with geographic and ethnic diversity. Its emphasis on loyalty is justified as a way of maintaining unity among an ingroup in its competitive struggle with others. The postreform style openly celebrates diversity of interests, and, as various groups mobilize, they do so by accentuating their unique interests and how they may conflict with the interests of other elements of society.

The trend from a traditional to a modern outlook represents a broad shift over time. Interest orientation represents a seesawing back and forth, with nondifferentiated interests first being ascendant under village politics, then giving way to competing and differentiated interests in the machine era, then still later regaining ascendancy with the reform style, and finally giving ground again with the rise of postreform politics. Under the one pattern—ascendant in village and reform politics—the emphasis is on concord and shared well-being. Under the other pattern—evident in machine and postreform periods—diversity of interests and overt conflict are more openly accepted. Again, we emphasize, the different styles of politics represent different *tendencies*, not absolute differences.

The overall set of patterns can be represented in a two-by-two diagram, giving us a typology of four styles of politics.

There is no simple formula to explain the dynamics of political change. The shift from a traditional to a modern outlook represents an adaptation to changes in the scale of life, which in turn are related to changes in technology and the organization of the economic system. The seesawing back and forth between interest orientations is harder to explain. The general process of change and growth seems to give rise to new aspirations that find an outlet in the political arena. Thus the emergence of new aspirations means the formation of new political groups and the transformation of old ones, a process that is bound to disrupt an established sense of shared well-being.

In preindustrial villages, the political dominance of the propertied element was guaranteed by tradition, social stability, and perceived scarcity. Industrialization brought greater social diversity and expanding profit opportunities. As aspirations for upward mobility and hopes for recognition grew, control of publc office came within the reach of industrial

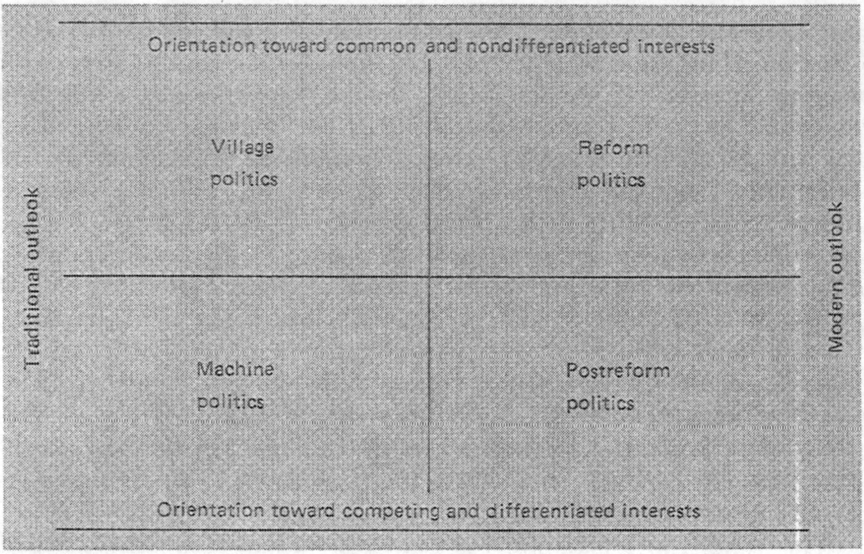

FIGURE 12-1. Four styles of politics.

society's ex plebes. Machines flourished during this time. Later, a new outlook and the complex needs of modern society ushered in an era of deference to professionals and technical experts. Reform and modernization disoriented the lower strata and undermined the ward-based political institutions they were attached to. But as government became more openly involved in planning and managing the quality of life, it became clear that government was a prime bestower of benefits. Meanwhile traditional barriers to equality weakened. The aspirations of minorities, especially of blacks, were rising just as the importance of governmental decision making was becoming more apparent. Thus, in our recent experience, even though government actions sometimes disappointed and even antagonized lower-status groups, the search for recognition and new opportunities through the public sector nevertheless increased.

With an active government not meeting expectations, trust in government declined but aspirations remained high. The postreform era arrived on that paradoxical note of expecting more and trusting less. Caught in a crossfire of competing demands and discordant objectives, the reform mystique weakened, and the reform ethos yielded ground it could not recapture from the new postreform spirit.

The cycle of interest orientations is shorthand for a very complicated process of political change. We are not talking about a predetermined path of development, but political arrangements that reflect the efforts of various institutional elites and popular leaders to reshape practice in the world around them. This is not to suggest that either established elites or leaders of new movements foresee all the consequences of their actions. It is to suggest that political arrangements are socially constructed, not spontaneously generated. Individual aspirations, social identifications, and shared visions of a just society are some of the forces that motivate actors intent upon shaping political arrangements. As actors compete and cooperate with one another in building, maintaining, and modifying a set of political arrangements, their impact depends upon the resources they can command, the skill with which they use these resources, and the alliances they form. But leadership is not a matter of managing a fixed body of resources; leadership is a creative activity. It involves the capacity to take a given situation and redefine it so that new possibilities become evident. It is Martin Luther King, Jr., questioning the morality of racial segregation and unleashing mass feelings of pride and hope through his display of courage and dignity. He showed that intimidation and coercion can be overcome. But leadership may also involve the use of coercion—President Reagan firing air controllers after defining their demands as unreasonable and illegal. Leadership is business executives making alliances with machine bosses in order to inaugurate a "new convergence of power" and launch programs of redevelopment. It is Tammany Hall expanding and using an elaborate network of clubs to garner the support of New York's foreign-stock voters away from the United Labor party.[1]

Is there any pattern to the myriad acts of leadership and the cycle of interest orientations? Yes, but only at a general level. First, there has been a "circulation of elites." Older paths to power have given way to newer paths; older bases of authority have been supplanted by or at least supplemented by newer bases of authority. But no revolution has occurred. When ex-plebes used machine politics to gain positions of power, they didn't overthrow established property elites. They reached accommodations with them. When reform brought professional expertise into big city administration, the transformation was gradual and incomplete. Indeed, what happened is that politicians more adept at working with and making use of program professionals eventually replaced those less adept. Today, the process of gradual change continues. As black mayors assume control of city hall, they come to terms with established centers of power and often make special efforts to court the business community.

Thus the process of change can best be described as one of absorption rather than substitution. New elites join but never totally replace old elites. It is easy to see why the circulation of urban elites takes a nonrevolutionary form. Public officials control only limited resources and need the cooperation of those who hold substantial private resources. Hence they are drawn toward accommodation.

[1] Martin Shefter, "The Electoral Foundations of the Political Machine: New York City, 1884-1897," in *The History of American Electoral Behavior* ed. Joel Silbey, and others (Princeton, NJ: Princeton University Press, 1978), pp. 263-98.

Beyond the gradual and partial circulation of elites, we can talk about a second general point—the institutional instability of the competitive interest orientation. While conflict can readily be defended as a source of innovation and as a prompter of adaptation to new conditions, it is hard to cope with. Even combatants—labor and management, for example, generally agree on rules to narrow the scope of hostile behavior in collective bargaining. Those who exercise public authority tend to justify that authority as in furtherance of some common good. While protest leaders are less constrained, they too tend to point to a future time when community will prevail over conflict. At the 1963 march on Washington, Martin Luther King's "I have a dream . . ." speech was so stirring because it painted a vivid picture of a future of racial concord.

As is evident even with such well-organized contenders as labor unions, the proponents of conflict and competiton are always at something of a disadvantge. Their actions, though they may be defended as in support of a general principle, are disruptive and inconvenient. Disorder inevitably generates a counter move.

Looking back at the era of machine politics, we can see that its strength was due, not to its competitiveness, but to its capacity for disciplined control. In Chicago politics, Mayor Daley was such a durable figure because he was so adroit at managing conflict, brokering among power centers, and promoting the image of Chicago as "the city that works."[2]

Chicago also illustrates the political weakness of the "mature" machine. Conflict management often comes about by leaving some interests unrepresented. Elites maintain order through arrangements that bring together selected interests in support of a system of exchange and mutual support. But other interests may be excluded or, as in the case of blacks in Chicago, provided only meager benefits. For those who are part of an ongoing system of exchange and mutual support, governance appears to be in support of the general welfare. For those who are excluded or underrepresented, the system is one of exploitation and favoritism. Reformers attacking the early machine sought to replace favoritism with a more inclusive notion of community. Postreformers challenging the "mature" machine have questioned its representativeness and have heightened awareness of the differentiated interests that make up the contemporary urban community. But they have had difficulty institutionalizing a new and more inclusive system of order. Conflict and competition can induce change, but they are not bases on which governance rests. John Lindsay's mayoralty in New York eventually gave up its postreform agenda and became preoccupied with efficient management.[3] In Boston, Kevin White

[2] Ester R. Fuchs and Robert Y. Shapiro, "Government Performance as a Basis for Machine Support," *Urban Affairs Quarterly* 18 (June 1983), 537-50.

[3] Clarence N. Stone, "Complexity and the Changing Character of Executive Leadership," *Urban Interest* 4 (Fall 1982), 29-50; see also Morris, *The Cost of Good Intentions.*

also started as a mayor with postreform ideas. However, he soon abandoned his program of decentralized responsiveness to neighborhoods in favor of a program of centralized executive control and business-oriented redevelopment.[4] In Atlanta, Maynard Jackson's attempt to focus on the policy concerns of blacks generated strong opposition in the business community and in the news media.[5] Obviously it is no simple matter to come into office and represent previously underrepresented groups.

The contemporary picture is unclear. We are not simply reverting to reform politics. In Boston, for example, Kevin White faced decreasing popularity and declined to run for a fifth term. Moreover, his successor, Raymond Flynn, ran on a platform of renewed responsiveness to neighborhoods.

As we attempt to discern what is emerging in the post-reform era, we need to focus on two considerations: one is the long-range trend toward greater modernization; the other is the interplay between a competitive interest orientation and the need for conflict management.

THE TREND TOWARD GREATER MODERNIZATION

As we consider the consequences of greater modernization, it is important once again to bear in mind that we are talking about a relative matter—greater degrees of some things and lesser degrees of others. As discussed here, modern politics is a highlighting of trends, not a complete description of a complex reality. What can we say, then, about modern politics as a composite of still-emerging trends? Compared to traditional politics, it is less personal, less intuitive, and less sentimental. It is more bound by formal rules and procedures. Above all, modern politics is a politics of collectivities—of organized interest groups, mass movements, and hierarchically arranged institutions. Consequently, at the mass level it is a politics of impersonal loyalties and obligations. As politics becomes more impersonal, indirect relationships and formal groups become more important.

Formal groups have thus gained an importance totally alien to traditional politics. Whereas the machine, for instance, thrived on the immediate individual favors it could provide supporters, modern politics centers more on the search for group benefits—benefits that often can be secured only after some form of collective action can be launched. To cite one example, individual public employees no longer ask for raises. They join and support unions that bargain for higher employee benefits.

[4] Martha W. Weinberg, "Boston's Kevin White," *Political Science Quarterly* 96 (Spring 1981), 87-106.

[5] Henson and King, "The Atlanta Public-Private Romance," in Fosler and Berger, eds., *Public-Private Partnership in American Cities*, pp. 293-337.

Impact of the media. Reciprocal loyalties and favor swapping have not entirely become relics of the past, but consider how political campaigning has changed. The machine activated networks of personal connections—the strongholds were the "delivery wards," the places where ward heelers and precinct captains could use their personal contacts to deliver the vote. The upper-income precincts, where the machines were weakest, were known as newspaper wards—the places where voters responded to the impersonal appeal for "good government," an appeal made typically through the mass media. Now the mass media carry messages not to an affluent minority but to the vast majority. The last hurrah of traditional politics has yielded to the modern techniques of image making. Now, when candidates announce for public office, there is as much interest in which advertising agencies they have hired as there is in who their backers are.

Only in a few places has the traditional party machinery proved durable. Elsewhere, in election after election, party officials demonstrate an ever-lessening capacity to deliver the vote. For major offices, leading candidates generally employ skilled media consultants, and often they have inspired followings of enthusiastic volunteers motivated in no small part by the appeals of issues and ideology. More and more campaigns are a matter of projecting the images and raising the issues that carry well over the mass media. Direct personal contact has, of course, not disappeared completely, but it is no longer a dominant campaign technique.

Protests and direct-action techniques also are geared toward the mass media. Initiating a rent strike, for example, may be inspired more by a desire to dramatize an issue than by a desire to see specific families aided. Visibility, not the pursuit of tangible and immediate gains, is the way to reach a mass audience. With the spread of movement politics across the social landscape, dissident activists concentrate on raising political consciousness rather than on gaining redress of particular grievances. Machine politicians, by contrast, were rarely concerned with general issues; they lived and prospered by the concrete and particular actions they could perform. Almost totally unconcerned with political consciousness, they trafficked mainly in direct favors that they could do for past and prospective supporters.

The use of the mass media illustrates an important point about modern politics and its complexity. Actions are not based just on their direct and immediate consequences. The projection of a campaign image, for example, is a matter of style, of how a whole pattern of speeches and actions are perceived and regarded. It is not mainly a matter of making specific promises or even proposing a concrete program. Instead, it is more a matter of discerning a public mood and assuming a symbolically important stance. Similarly, raising political consciousness involves calculations about how to make an issue salient. Typically, consciousness raising involves foregoing possible short-run gains in anticipation of long-range advance. Sensational but unrealistic demands may beget a backlash effect, but protest leaders willingly run such risks. They see their ultimate goal as one of heightening awareness of an issue. If their actions make an issue more visible and arouse the concerns of previously quiescent supporters, they are willing to incur some short-term hostility.

Campaign issues. Modernization has not necessarily made mass politics more rational and issue directed. Yet, some of the old obstacles to issue politics are gone. Personal and sentimental attachments no longer cement political organizations, and the friends-and-neighbors appeal carries an ever-decreasing weight. Still, the politics of electoral contests and of popular movements often serve as arenas of emotion, arenas in which vague discontents find nonrational expression.

No matter how much we might wish it to be otherwise, candidates for office find substantive policy issues to be both difficult and risky to talk about. But why? For one thing, policy decisions are complex. Because few events take place in isolation, every decision has indirect and delayed effects.

Every issue has broad implicatons. The more these implications are spelled out and made concrete, the more apparent it becomes that various groups have competing interests at stake in the outcome. While officials may, under some conditions, pursue a strategy of polarization, generally they try to avoid public stances that will antagonize any group of constituents. So rather than detail the costs and benefits of alternative courses of action they wage campaigns of image, style, and personality.

Problems of modern officeholders. The complexity of modern policy poses other problems for popular participation and control. In the first place, program execution has gotten to be such a long and involved process that elected officeholders seldom have time for careful planning and sustained oversight before the next election comes up. Nor do they often have the time or the patience for following a program through a long and tortuous path of implementation.

In the second place, technical expertise is hard to cope with. Modern governance calls for a high degree of expert decision making, and we are unable to dispense with it. Experts, by the nature of the situation, know more about their work than ordinary people do; and modern life has become so technically complicated that a wide variety of experts is necessary. Yet we have long since learned that experts, profesionals, and other holders of administrative office are neither all wise nor disinterested and impartial participants in the decisions they make. Thus, while they see secondary effects of decisions, they see some effects more clearly and urgently than others. They see problems narrowly, in terms of their own limited areas of expertise *and* in terms of their own agency's institutional self-interest. Rarely will they sacrifice or neglect the particular interests of their own departments. And, far from being apolitical, they do battle over competing priorities, carry on interagency rivalries, and go through countless deceptions to protect (or increase) a budget allocation.

Modern bureaucracies thus contain the same competitive, self-serving urges that motivated the traditional political machines. Whereas the ward bosses pursued their career goals by promoting the particular interests of neighorhood and ethnic groups, modern administrators pursue their career goals by promoting the particular interests of departmental and professional specialty groups. However, the circumstances surrounding the pursuit of self-interest have changed. Modern executives, unlike the bosses of yesteryear, do not have patronage (or its equivalent) to any great extent. That is, they lack divisible, unrestricted benefits to induce cooperation. Nor do they have intangible appeals they can use as inducements. As rational, specialized, and hierarchical institutions, bureaucracies are not amenable to appeals of sentiment and mutual loyalty to the same degree that many of the political machines were.

Controlling the activities of bureaucratic organizations tests human ingenuity to a greater extent than machine politics did. As actors in a modern society, we face a dilemma. Although complex interdepartmental planning and programs seem to be necessary, they are managed only with great difficulty.

A further barrier to popular control lies with the citizenry itself. Most people will follow only a few issues that have a direct bearing on their lives. Even when citizens become active and are afforded opportunities to serve on neighborhood boards and advisory committees, they deal best with narrowly defined responsibilities for concrete, uncomplicated service programs. However, problems overlap. Attempted solutions to one have an impact on others.

This is not to say that citizens are totally unconcerned with secondary effects. But concern, when it occurs, may be in an emotionally charged and hard-to-manage context. Particularly in a time of scarce resources, citizens may feel that there are more losers than gainers. In a study of the impact of racial conflict on mayoral leadership, one writer found that racial polarization heightened concern with secondary effects.[6] For example, as conflict intensified, racial groups showed a keen interest in the symbolic significance as well as the substantive importance of the decisions made. The race of an appointee to police chief or school superintendent can serve as an indicator of the stance of the entire city government. A highly charged political atmosphere can also lead racial groups to increase their concern with what the economists call opportunity costs—resources expended on

[6] Charles H. Levine, *Racial Conflict and the American Mayor* (Lexington, Mass.: D.C. Heath and Co., Lexington Books, 1974), pp. 23-24.

one alternative are not available for other alternatives. Furthermore, once antagonistic groups are aroused, they become concerned not only with what they gain or lose but also with what they gain or lose relative to their antagonists. An increase in a white-dominated police department's budget can be a defeat for blacks if the budget of the black-dominated school system does not increase by an equal proportion. After groups become preoccupied with such secondary effects, agreements are harder to negotiate; and cooperation is harder to secure.

Summary

In summary, modernization has bequeathed us a number of difficult problems. The interrelatedness of modern society means that efforts to solve one problem unavoidably have consequences for a wide range of people, some of whom have competing goals and different priorities. After all, postreform politics finally burst forth because these conflicting goals and priorities could not be suppressed indefinitely in a democratic society. Though it did not begin on that note, modern politics is a politics of conflict between collectivities. And as in the case of racial polarization, conflict between collectivities is not easy to manage. It restricts the range of official action and makes issue resolution difficult. Yet, while a certain amount of conflict is inevitable, conflict is not uncontrollable. How conflict is managed is thus a crucial feature of postreform politics and of the political future in front of us. We therefore turn next to a discussion of conflict management.

CONFLICT AND ITS MANAGEMENT

Political conflict is inevitable. It is also disturbing to any system of governance. Once competing interests are differentiated as they were in the rise of both machine and postreform politics, some means is needed for channeling competition and keeping it within bounds. Competition generates a felt need for some restraining mechanism, some system of conflict management. Unbridled competition is rarely tolerated for a long period of time.

Conflict can be managed in many ways. It can be strongly discouraged and virtually suppressed. More often it is restricted to certain channels and simply held in bounds. It can be shifted to less volatile forms of expression, or diffused and localized so that it does not grow in scope and intensity.

Methods for managing conflict can come about in any of a number of ways. Often, politics seems to evolve, almost naturally, into certain patterns of conflict management. Yet, no method of conflict management is politically neutral, and groups are constantly trying to alter the system of conflict management in order to further their interests. Thus, conflict management is not only something that grows out of circumstances, but also something that contending forces seek to manipulate.

In the present section, we will look at conflict management in the past as a cue for what to expect in the future. Changing patterns of conflict management should tell us much about how new power groups arise. Perhaps these patterns can also give us some useful insight into the still-unfolding characteristics of postreform politics.

In village politics, conflict was minimized for the sake of social solidarity. Because most people sensed a need for harmony, no elaborate system of conflict management was needed. By general understanding, conflict was avoided.

Conflict could be contained rather easily in the stable and homogenous villages of preindustrial America just as it still can in contemporary small towns. Conflict was prevented by perpetuating cultural homogeneity. Our real experience with *urban* conflict management began with the growth of industrialization and the movement of massive waves of immigrants into the rapidly developing cities of the nineteenth century. Social turmoil, uninhibited economic competition, and intense value conflict simply overwhelmed the formal instruments of government. It remained for the political machines and the bosses who headed them to prove that conflict need not be suppressed to be managed. It could be tamed, channeled, and rendered predictable. Partisan competition between machines welded the opposing groups into powerful organizations that could make the wheels of government turn in an orderly and well-regulated manner. In searching for ever-larger material benefits, ambitious individuals synchronized their efforts so that industrial growth and the accompanying development of public facilities could take place with phenomenal speed. We need not romanticize the machine nor disregard its considerable shortcomings to appreciate Robert Merton's insight that the political machines performed latent functions as well as manifest functions. And we should not ignore the use of party organization and political clubs to preempt labor militancy.[7]

The machines averted some conflict by allowing for diversity. Whereas small communities, because they are relatively homogeneous, can suppress value conflicts by exacting conformity to a single standard of morality, large cities cannot readily use the same technique. What they can do, and what the machine with its ward system of organization is admirably suited for, is to accommodate diverse life styles. In disregard of efforts by prohibitionists and other do-gooders to uplift the behavior of the urban masses, the machines privatized morality—tolerating (sometimes at a price) the weaknesses of human nature. Laws regarding gambling, alcohol, and sex were either enforced selectively or not enforced at all. The police, as we have seen, fol-

[7] Shefter, "The Electoral Foundations of the Political Machine," in *History of American Electoral Behavior*, pp. 263-98.

lowed what James Q. Wilson has called the watchman style.[8] Watchman-style police officers intervene only to quell public disorder or to prevent serious crimes. In general their disposition is to avoid involvement to the extent possible, and if intervention becomes necessary, to resolve problems with an informal, or familial, approach. Tolerance and privatization of the law thus served to reduce conflict in a heterogeneous and volatile society.

In the reform era, conflict was managed by techniques faintly reminiscent of the preindustrial village. Reform rhetoric called for cooperation and consensus, and the reform movement was aimed more at stifling conflict than at channeling it. In deference to professionals and technical experts, reformers sought to isolate program administration from the pressures of the electoral process. By insulating the management of administrative agencies from the intervention of elected officeholders, they facilitated the modernization of government service. A mystique of professionalism and expertise served to fend off outbreaks of popular discontent against planners and administrators as well as to parry the patronage ambitions of party politicians.

The contemporary urban community resembles in some ways the early industrial city on the verge of the machine era. We are confronted, as we were then, with a major need to manage conflict. Social diversity and interest cleavages abound. Demands for governmental action are high, but the capacity to act is limited.

The basic problem is that contemporary conflicts generate demands for governmental action but also hamper the capacity of the urban governmental system to respond. What, then, may be in the offing? Whatever the eventual postreform solution to conflict management, we can expect it to be consonant with a modern outlook just as machine politics was consonant with a traditional outlook. We should not expect a revival of bossism, not even in new garb. Social, economic, and political arrangements have become too large in scale to be managed through reciprocal personal loyalties and obligations. Instead we should look for conflict to be restrained by means consistent with the modern outlook.

CONFLICT MANAGEMENT IN THE POSTREFORM CITY

Not everything about postreform politics is new. Postreform politics resembles the machine era in that the electoral arena has regained some of its importance. There is a difference, however. While the new era, like the machine period, is one of increased demand for service, the postreform age is one of relatively scarce resources. Still, as ours has become a time of scarcity,

[8] James Q. Wilson, *Varieties of Police Behavior* (Cambridge, Mass.: Harvard University Press, Atheneum, 1968), pp. 140-71.

organized groups who want benefits realize that they must influence the process of setting priorities, and priority setting is done under the aegis of elected officials. Despite a continuing stigma around the role of politician, elected officials are gaining in stature as more groups come to see them as fulcrum points for policy setting.

A wide array of people for a variety of reasons now support the principle that the power and authority of elected officials should be strengthened. Two examples will suffice. The Nixon administration's New Federalism strategy called, in part, for chief executives at the state and local levels to exercise greater control over social programs. That thrust has been maintained by later administrations because it promotes administrative convenience. Federal officials have little desire to interact with a host of local officials and interest-group leaders. They want to deal with individuals who can speak definitively and act authoritatively. Change-minded groups have similar wants. For example, as more blacks are elected to mayoral and council offices, the black community can see obvious advantages in strengthening these offices. Understandably, then, the Black Power movement has shifted orientation from community control of urban service agencies to a greater concern with capturing elected office.

Focusing attention on elected officials serves a purpose beyond administrative convenience or increasing the influence of minorities. It channels conflict. Confrontation and strident conflict, while useful in dramatizing new issues, are somewhat out of place as tactics to gain support in the electoral process. Protest leaders, black or white, who shift their energies to the electoral arena, find that their appeals have to be tempered to reach a broader constituency. They moderate their demands in order to bargain more effectively with their fellow power holders. We are coming to realize anew that elections can serve as regularized channels for *resolving* competing demands for change and action.

Focusing more attention on elected officials and enhancing their authority will not necessarily restrain conflict. Election campaigns sometimes are fairly stormy, and elected officials occasionally intensify rather than moderate their demands. So, if the 1970s and 1980s have proved to be less tempestuous than the 1960s, we must consider some other factors. Let us look to see what is particularly modern and contemporary about postreform conflict management.

First of all, the highly emotional conflicts of the 1960s have yielded much ground to more formal debate and analysis in the later decades. Elected officials have become increasingly concerned with ways to monitor and evaluate the performance of line agencies. Policy analysis and program evaluation have emerged as ways of using the techniques of scientific analysis in the identification and evaluation of policy alternatives. Undoubtedly elected officials will maintain their own intuitive preferences about program priorities, but they want more reliable estimates of both program costs and program benefits. In all likelihood, they also want to deflate the rancor of charges and countercharges by shifting the tone of the debate toward a more nonemotional examination of the facts. Just as the practices of political machines did for an earlier era, policy analysis and program evaluation may for us fulfill latent as well as manifest functions.

In any event, the increased reliance on formal techniques of analysis enhances the capacity of elected officials to set priorities and regulate the conduct of service-providing personnel. And these formal methods of analysis do serve to absorb some of the friction of intergroup competition; they lower the temperature of any policy debate and remove some elements from the throes of partisan contention. We can therefore anticipate that despite pressures to hold down the level of government employment, elected officials will increase the number of staff people involved in planning, budgeting, and evaluation activities. The modern age remains one in which expertise plays an important role.

While formal analysis can decrease the friction in any given issue, it does not decrease the number of issues. As competing interests have become more differentiated and assertive in the postreform period, local governments have come face to face with more demands than they can cope with. Indeed. one version of the urban predicament is "demand overload," a barrage of demands that confront officials with an unending series of crises to which they must react but that run beyond their capacity to control.[9] What we should expect to find, then, is a modern move parallel to the machine's privatization of the law. Specifically we can predict that postreform officials will make an effort to lessen the scope of conflict by reducing the number of issues engaging city hall's attention.

One of the obvious ways local officials can lessen conflict is to reduce the range of their responsibilities. In fact, the outlines of such a strategy are already visible. Local governments have already begun to spin off some functions to higher levels of government. A recent survey by the Advisory Commission on Intergovernmental Relations found that large cities especially are prone to transferring responsibilities for functions to special regional districts and to higher levels of government.[10] Activities as diverse as sewage treatment, property assessment, and some specialized social services have been shifted permanently to other governments. Business groups often support the removal of transportation and other development activities from electoral control.

If no other alternative is available, cities may treat some problems as unsolvable and simply let them go unattended. Nothing provides a star-

[9] Douglas Yates, "The Future of Urban Government," *New York Affairs* 3 (Winter 1976), 8-19.

[10] Advisory Commission on Intergovernmental Relations, *Pragmatic Federalism: The Reassignment of Functional Responsibilities* (Washington, D.C.: 1976).

ker contrast with the optimism of the reform era than proposals such as a recent call for "planned shrinkage."[11] Fiscal stringency is highly useful as a counter to group demands.

Some functions can be neither transferred nor abandoned. Nevertheless, officials can lessen their conflict potential by decentralization. Such human-service activities as education and law-enforcement—program areas where the evaluation of performance is highly subjective and the demand for neighborhood diversity is strong—can be administered on a basis other than city-wide (or county-wide) uniformity. As neighborhood conditions differ, so do subjectively defined needs. Varying populations have varying preferences and priorities, so city halls are likely to follow the aphorism, "Different strokes for different folks."

In general, what we can detect is a decrease in the number of programs for which local governments are willing to be responsible. And many of those for which they retain an involvement are administratively decentralized or even run by nongovernmental groups.[12] By lessening the number of functions performed and by adjusting to demands for diversity, officials have decreased the overall amount of conflict and localized some of the rest. Much as the machines privatized the law and allowed for diverse moralities, postreform officials have experimented with various ways of accommodating the varied preferences of an urban population. Administrative decentralization, sundry forms of citizen involvement, and contracting out services to neighborhood groups and nonprofit organizations have all been tried in a number of cities.

EMERGENT PATTERNS AND ISSUES

As we look back over our brief survey of conflict management, we can see that each new pattern has produced a new group of power wielders. Each group of power wielders, in turn, promotes some policy interests to the neglect of others. We can debate whether or not a particular system of conflict management is just or necessary; we cannot argue that it is neutral. Some partiality is inevitable.

In the village setting conflict was managed by social disapproval and the development of informal procedures of decision making. Both techniques encouraged consensus. That system was linked with a policy of caretaker governments—governments that levied minimum taxes and pro-

[11] Roger Starr, "Making New York Smaller," *New York Times Magazine* (November 14, 1976), pp. 32ff. For a similar argument, see also William C. Baer, "On the Death of Cities," *The Public Interest*, no. 45 (Fall 1976), pp. 3-19.

[12] On depoliticized service provision, see Charles V. Hamilton, "The Patron-Recipient Relationship and Minority Politics in New York City," *Political Science Quarterly* 94 (Summer 1979), 211-27.

vided minimum services. It was a policy quite suited to the interests of large and established property holders. It helped them maintain positions of wealth and esteem.

The machines managed conflict by subordinating individual competition and conflict to the needs of the party organization and by privatizing the law, especially in areas of personal morality. The new power wielders were the political bosses who rose from the ranks of the immigrant and lower status population. Yet their power was not exercised to uplift the masses of poor people. The maintenance needs of the machine dictated otherwise. The bosses learned quickly to work hand-in-glove with business interests. The patronage needs of the machines brought them especially close to those businesses concerned with the growth and development of urban communities.

The reform movement cast an ideological shadow on organized forms of partisan conflict, and it worked to restructure local government in such a way as to insulate decision making, particularly administrative decision making, from partisan and ward-based interests. Reform created a set of professional administrators, heading the line agencies of local government. They were reform's new cadre of power wielders. They, too, supported economic growth, but their special hallmark was a high level of services and amenities aimed mainly at those citizens able and willing to underwrite the budgets for such programs. In short, they served well the interests of the affluent middle class.

With postreform politics, the pattern is still emerging and therefore less clear. Conflict management seems to be taking the shape of (1) a reemphasis on institutionalized electoral competition, (2) a greater reliance on formal methods of analysis, (3) using financial stringency to eliminate some programs, and (4) a restructuring of service provision by local government to devolve some functions to other levels of government or to insulate them from electoral control.

Who are the newly emerging power wielders, and whose interests will they promote? The answers to these questions must be matters of conjecture, but we can venture some tentative answers at the present time.

Whereas the machine system managed conflict with individual rewards and informal means, the postreform system appears to rely more on collective arrangements and formal means. In this way, it has continuity with the reform methods of managing conflict. Postreform politics has, however, tilted the balance of power away from the line administrators of urban service programs. The emergent group appears to be staff members engaged in planning, budgeting, and evaluation activities. Their specialities are formal knowledge and managerial control. In a time when the overriding concern is with directing the actions and assessing the performance of service-providing agencies, they possess the requisite skills and the strategic position to become new ingredients in the power equation.

The kind of formal and impersonal analyses they do carries its own scientific authority and, because of their staff positions with the major officeholders, their scientific authority is linked to the authority of high governmental position. Hence, they have the power as well as the opportunity to become a significant influence on public policy.

What bias may these knowledge-and-control experts be expected to display? From their position as central-office staff members and from their stock in trade of formal analysis, one can speculate that they will be inclined to favor programs that further some overall community goal, that have tangible and quantifiable effects, and that produce relatively quick, sure, and clear-cut results. Neighborhood-oriented human service and other social programs are not likely to fare well at their hands. They are programs that primarily benefit a particular area and population; they are often subjectively valued and not easily measured by objective standards; and they produce results that may be long-term, often are uncertain, and can be evaluated only in tentative and conditional kinds of ways.

Pervasive pessimism about the workability of public programs and continuing distrust of public bureaucrats and program professionals have served to enhance the position of those who specialize in managerial control and policy evaluation. Yet, ours is no technocratic regime. Whatever their formal credentials, experts must render their judgments in a form and manner acceptable to elected politicians,[13] and it is politicians who excel at sensing and shaping public moods and mobilizing popular support.[14]

Moreover, power-wielding is not restricted to those who occupy governmental positions. Those who initiate political movements and mobilize politically assertive groups often do not hold political office. Further, not all power-wielders are new. As we have seen, the circulation of elites has not been so extensive as to the end the prominent role played by business executives and the directors of non-profit institutions.

The power situation is sufficiently complex to convince many observers that no one is in charge, that ours is a time of fragmented leadership and volatile alignments. Movements develop and then dissipate. Many incumbent officeholders experience short tenure. But does postreform politics mean a completely fluid pattern of power and decision making? Hardly. We need to remember that the postreform era is a layer resting on the bedrock of previous arrangements and earlier practices.

Emerging political styles do not displace past practices. From the machine-to-reform era, consider two examples. In Chicago, Mayor Daley

[13] Charles E. Lindblom and David K. Cohen, *Usable Knowledge* (New Haven: Yale University Press, 1979).

[14] Joel D. Aberbach, Robert D. Putnam, and Bert A. Rockman, *Bureaucrats and Politicians in Western Democracies* (Cambridge, MA: Harvard University Press, 1981).

headed a patronage-based organization, but ran it in a tight, executive-centered manner. He cooperated extensively with the city's business community in a vast program of redevelopment, and when faced with a police scandal, he didn't hesitate to bring in a law-enforcement professional to manage the police department. In several ways, he gave his administration a reform imprint. Moreover, Daley cultivated the image of his organization as an effective deliverer of services. The Daley machine was thus in reality a blend of machine and reform practices, and that blend was integral to the organization's electoral success.[15]

In New York, Robert Moses began his career as a principled reformer and staunch opponent of Tammany. Yet he became czar of an administrative empire, while maintaining the image of uncompromising reformer, by working out arrangements with various dispensers of special favors. He came to work closely with New York's "retainer regiment" and learned to play the inside patronage game extraordinarily well.[16] To talk about mid-twentieth century urban politics in terms of machine-versus-reform is to miss at least as much as one reports.

Patterns of policy making have changed. In most places decisions are no longer made by ward bosses, endowed with a patronage pool and engaged in working out a "logroll" or respecting the practice of "ward courtesy." The scale of modern activity and the complexities of modern life have outrun such simple and direct exchanges. Furthermore, those who head personal networks of supporters are no longer major actors. The scale of activity and the complexity of life have thus largely overshadowed the machine style of organization.

The scale of activity and the complexity of life do more, however, than contribute to the passing of machines as the means through which the masses are organized politically. They also stand as a barrier to the decentralization of policy making and dispersion of power that some postreform movements have sought. That black political mobilization should be redirected from controlling community or neighborhood institutions to the winning of city hall is no happenstance. It represents a learning experience about the durability and effectiveness of power bases.

Further, while it is the case that "no one is in charge" in the sense that no one is in a position to command obedience from a subject population, that does not mean that power is hopelessly fragmented or completely fluid. Large development projects are carried out, and an extensive array of services are provided. Much is done routinely by large bureaucratic enterprises, many of which are linked intergovernmentally to state and federal agencies with the same set of functional responsibilities. And new projects as well as a variety of innovations in service provision are very

[15] Fuchs and Shapiro, "Government Performance as a Basis for Machine Support."

[16] Caro, *The Power Broker*, esp. pp. 703-54.

much a part of the contemporary urban scene. Indeed, a preoccupation with innovation seems endemic to public affairs. Elected officials, career administrators, and movement leaders all tend to be caught up in the search for visibility by launching new policy initiatives.

These policy initiatives, especially if launched by public officeholders, tend to bear a reform-style imprint. Typically, new programs are touted as being in the interest of the whole community, and they call for the use of experts committed to appropriate professional norms. Most such programs emanate from or at least involve a major role for the executive branch. As political actors bring ideas to fruition, they must mobilize a variety of resources, organizational and economic. It is vital to have personnel with specialized skills in such activities as: obtaining legal clearance, arranging for credit, managing finances, negotiating endorsements, and promoting a favorable public image—all of these in addition to the specialized skills involved in implementing the actual program itself.

Program innovation often involves both public and private institutions, and different levels of government within the public sector. It is a process in which the representatives of large organizations are dealing with the representatives of other large organizations. Like the "logrolls" of ward politics, these negotiations entail efforts to aggregate support from diverse interests. The difference is in the scale of the interests represented and the complexity of the terms of negotiation.

The emergence of a postreform style has not displaced this executive-centered, interorganizational pattern of policy making. What the postreform era has witnessed is a proliferation of the sources of policy ideas; the political landscape is now populated with a large number of politically conscious groups. These groups often lack access to an aggregation process. They push their own separate agendas, believing that their continued existence as organized groups depends upon having a visible and therefore distinct agenda. Many groups are only loosely organized or have weak means for overcoming the collective action problem on a long-term basis. Some are not clearly focused on concrete and achievable goals. Most are not large-scale organizations; they lack stable resources and the full range of experts needed to launch and monitor a policy initiative. While they often have skills in idea promotion, their officers and staff members may lack detailed knowledge of how the policy making system operates (what some observers call "maze wisdom").

It is easy to conclude from the large number of policy demands never enacted or, if enacted, never implemented that the postreform era is one of political overload and policy impasse. That, however, is a superficial view. Not all policy initiatives are vetoed; new projects are being carried out; and significant changes do occur in service delivery. Public business is not at a standstill, though some activities are easier to sustain than others.

The emergence of a postreform style has brought new actors to urban politics. It has not overthrown the past but has modified it in ways that are still unfolding. To discern what is genuinely new and emerging, we should turn now to topics of power and leadership. Then we can examine various arenas of urban policy.

SUGGESTED READINGS

AARON, HENRY J. *Politics and the Professors*. Washington, DC: Brookings Institution, 1978.

BEER, SAMUEL H. "The Modernization of American Federalism." *Publius* 3 (Fall 1973), 49-95.

______. "Political Overload and Federalism." *Polity* 3 (Fall 1977), 5-17.

BELL, DANIEL. *The Coming of Post-Industrial Society*. New York: Basic Books, 1973.

CARROLL, JAMES D. "Noetic Authority." *Public Administration Review* 29 (September/October 1969), 492-500.

FAINSTEIN, NORMAN I. and SUSAN S. FAINSTEIN "The Future of Community Control." *American Political Science Review* 70 (September 1976), 905-23.

HUNTINGTON, SAMUEL P. "Postindustrial Politics: How Benign Will It Be?" *Comparative Politics* 6 (January 1974), 163-91.

KATZNELSON, IRA. *City Trenches*. Chicago: University of Chicago Press, 1981.

LOCKARD, DUANE. "Stranded Cities." *Democracy* 3 (Winter 1983), 34-42.

POLSKY, ANDREW J. "New York City: Managing Without Democracy." *Democracy* 1 (July 1981), 109-22.

ROGERS, DAVID and NORMAN H. CHUNG, *110 Livingston Street Revisited*. New York: New York University Press, 1983.

SCHUMAKER, PAUL D. "Policy Responsiveness to Protest-Group Demands." *Journal of Politics* 37 (May 1975), 486-521.

SCHWARZ, JOHN E. *America's Hidden Success*. New York: Norton, 1984.

STONE, CLARENCE N. "The Implementation of Social Programs." *Journal of Social Issues* 36 (Fall 1980), 13-34.

chapter 13

Group Power and Individual Leadership

This section is concerned with power and leadership. The present chapter contains a largely theoretical discussion of power, a discussion that covers the parts played by both individuals and groups. The main point of this discussion is that power is relational. It is not a substance possessed by an individual or even by a group of individuals. While power is often based on resources, it is not a body of resources held in isolation.

Resources form the core of any system of cooperation. They provide a capacity to act purposefully. It is in this sense that they empower. Brought together in the right way and under the right circumstances, resources enable some actions. They may also be used to prevent other actions or to combat rival groups and their efforts. Because the present chapter is somewhat theoretical and abstract, it will be helpful to keep in mind earlier discussions such as those of the Daley organization in Chicago and other executive-centered coalitions in various cities. Machine politics and executive-based coalitions are examples of governmentally-centered elements in broad systems of social cooperation.

Power relationships are not to be understood in strictly personal or individual terms. Resources, after all, are group based. Different groups control different resources. Some may represent large voting blocs. Others may be prestigious, or they may command valuable expertise. Still others may hold wealth or be capable of extending credit or providing useful forms of protection.

Combined into a coalition, groups may have considerable capacity to act in pursuit of their shared aims. A coalition is powerful in that sense; coalescence enables it to act. But there are also power relationships within coalitions. Because some groups control resources vital to the coalition, other groups are dependent upon them. The dependence of one group or individual on another creates a power relationship. Dependence need not be one-sided, of course. It can be mutual. If so, it still constitutes a relationship of power. The exchange of resources or the conditions under which resources are brought into a common pool are thus at the heart of the power relationship.

The next chapter in this section concentrates on leadership, especially the role of elected executives. In this next chapter, we give special attention to the constraints surrounding executive leaders. Although they can put together groups of supporters in various ways, elected officials are not free to pursue all coalition-building strategies with equal ease. Some alignments are readily put together and maintained. Others are not.

It matters in many ways what kinds of coalitions are assembled. Policy formation reflects the kind of support elected executives can and do put together. Indeed, policy leadership is inseparable from political leadership. Policies can be pursued only by building bases of support for them. This is not to suggest, however, that political actions always and inevitably rest on precise calculations about policy consequences. Much that happens is unintended. Because political actors often concentrate on the immediate and particular consequences of their actions, longer term and more general consequences often go unheeded. After all, coalitions are, among other things, systems of exchange in which individuals and groups participate because they receive benefits, both material and psychic. And coalition participants tend to be especially mindful of the immediate benefits they themselves enjoy. Other consequences are given little sustained attention. In summary, what we can say is that coalition partners support certain forms of cooperative activity (for a variety of reasons), and cooperative actions have policy results—some of which are intended but others are not.

The process of coalition construction is enormously complicated. Leaders—that is, individual political actors of strategic importance—play a part in shaping and defining the terms on which groups cooperate. Put another way, the activities orchestrated by leaders determine which groups are politically relevant. Groups don't simply exist and await discovery. They are brought into political being and oriented by the actions of political leaders. A political machine or an executive-centered coalition is not simply discovered, nor does it arise spontaneously. Each set of political arrangements is built by the actions of political entrepreneurs. Leaders construct a base of support and fashion the manner in which the different elements in a coalition cooperate and coexist. It is therefore important to know something about the constraints and inducements at work in the world of political leaders, especially the world of elected executives. Why are they drawn toward some cooperative arrangements, but not others? Why are some alliances more appealing than others? These are questions that need to be addressed in understanding the connections between politics and policy. Let us start by addressing the connection between group power and individual leadership.

Politics involves a paradox. People have divergent interests, yet they are better off cooperating than not cooperating. While there is no natural harmony among people, our finest achievements grow out of community. When diverse groups act in pursuit of cooperative aims and overcome their differences, they are acting as a political society. But the key question is, on what terms will they cooperate? That is *the* political question, and the answer to this question is where power and leadership come in.

Power is, of course, a capacity to act. The most basic form of power, however, is the capacity to set the terms on which cooperation will occur. It is intertwined with leadership.

Leadership is the ability (1) to envision arrangements through which cooperation can occur, and (2) to have those arrangements put into place. Individuals with extraordinary skills and ability often play a vital role in bringing about and directing means of cooperation. For this reason, it is useful to think of leadership in terms of individual political actors.

However, because setting and maintaining arrangements through which cooperation can occur is not the activity of isolated individuals, it is perhaps appropriate to think of power in group terms. Often people act on the basis of shared concerns. Consider some hypothetical examples of groups—the courthouse gang, the firefighters' union, the downtown business association, the black community, the alliance of neighborhood organizations, the port authority, the first metropolitan bank, university hospital, the fraternity of gun users, the association of families with handicapped children, the assembly of Latin organizations, the taxpayers league, and environmentalists united. This list illustrates the myriad contenders for power. Some are occupation or business groups and may have been organized for those purposes and not explicitly for political action. Others may have been organized as political action groups. Some are bureaucratic structures organized to perform business or service functions, but nevertheless are major political actors. Others may not be formally organized but share a common political consciousness and a loose network of communications. Let's look further to understand why it is helpful to treat power as group-based.

POWER

While individuals are important in mobilizing groups and in creating, maintaining, and altering organizations, it is groups that provide the resources on which cooperative action is based. It is from giving, withholding, combining, and using resources that power derives. Individuals are important, but they play their parts as representatives for various constituency groups. Still, individuals are not locked into a given role. They may expand or change the constituency they represent. As they accumulate experience, they may come to represent different or larger and more encompassing groups and coalitions of groups. Note, however, that they are not isolated actors. It is as representatives that they command resources.

Other things being equal, those groups that control or represent more resources are more powerful than those that control or represent fewer resources. A large voting bloc is more weighty than a small one. Control of large amounts of investment capital is more attractive than control of small amounts. Being able to mobilize many precinct workers is better than being able to mobilize only a few. Large campaign contributions have stronger impact than small ones. The capacity to execute a large and highly visible project is more highly valued than the capacity to execute a small and scarcely visible project. The ability to offer large amounts of credit is weightier than the ability to offer only modest amounts of credit. This is true in each instance—other things being equal.

Other things are rarely equal, however. Consequently power defies precise measurement. Resources never stand alone. Establishing and maintaining a system of cooperation require combinations of resources. It is for this reason that power—the capacity to act in furtherance of some set of purposes—often comes through coalitions of groups. Of course, individual leaders play important roles in forming, occasionally in dissolving, and frequently in reshaping coalitions. No doubt that is why, in the popular mind, power is associated with individuals. Leadership is vital, but leaders are engaged in bringing resources together. They are constrained by the capabilities of the groups they work with.

Politics is a complex game. The paradox of having both common and divergent interests occurs within coalitions as well as within the larger community. Coalitions are conglomerations of groups that share some interests but not others. If all the coalition members enjoyed only shared interests, they would not be a coalition but a single group. But they do diverge on some matters. Consequently there are two interconnected power contests going on all of the time—the contest for influence within the coalition, and the contest between the coalition and its competitors in the larger community. Moreover, members in a coalition are not bound together in all actions. They are partners in some cooperative arrangements, but not in others.

Thus, in some ways, power is a very fluid phenomenon. It depends upon who is brought together, for how long, and for what purpose. Power has many dimensions. Among them are domain and scope. Domain has to do with the size of a jurisdiction in which the writ of power runs. The alliance of neighborhood organizations might be influential with the city council and the news media but not with others. University hospital, for its part, might be influential with the mayor's office and federal health administrators, but it might carry little weight with anyone else. Scope has to do with the range of issues affected by a power group. The downtown business association might be very influential in shaping policy for development but unable to have much impact on metropolitan reorganization. Working-class suburbs might be able to veto metropolitan reorganization but have no control over transportation planning.

Limitations of domain and scope are among the reasons coalitions are created. As resources are combined, the potential for a larger domain and scope grows. But it is not just a matter that big combinations of resources are more potent than small aggregations of resources. There are strategic advantages too, advantages that have to do with the permanence and durability of power. Group members, and especially their leaders, are not just interested in influencing particular issues as they arise, they are interested in being a part of the process through which policy goals are set and pursued. While they may have much keener interest in some issues than in others, they are mindful that in a world of interdependence and scarce resources everything potentially affects everything else. It is important, then, to be a part of a system of cooperation through which policy is made. All groups want a say in the policy agenda—a chance to promote their own concerns and to guard against threats to their interests. Groups therefore come to be concerned not with just the content of particular decisions but also with the arrangements through which decisions are made. Their concerns do not end with substantive interests in such matters as taxation, spending priorities, transportation planning, and police protection. Their concerns also extend to how they are governed—the arrangements through which policy is formed and carried out.

Leaders are, of course, more keenly aware of governing arrangements than are ordinary members. And they may regard themselves not only as leaders of particular groups but also as members of the governing group. If so, they have a stake in these governing arrangements—perpetuating what they are a part of and perhaps bending these arrangements in a way that corresponds with their understanding of what is appropriate.

Leaders thus come to be disassociated to some extent from the individual groups in the coalitions they head. Even leaders who start out as representatives of a specific constituency may be drawn into concurrent membership in that set of people responsible for maintaining the system of cooperation. Labor union representatives who become part of a governing coalition, or black precinct officers who rise to leadership positions in the city-wide machine may find themselves with dual sets of concerns, and some of these concerns are not closely tied in with the immediate constituency from which they came. Participation in overall power arrangements can cause some leaders to be regarded as having forsaken their original backers.

Leaders who take part in governing coalitions balance two sets of responsibilities. They heed the interests of constituent groups in the coalition, but they also pay attention to the cooperative arrangements which the coalition supports. Leaders are guided by several considerations—their own career ambitions being one. But there are others. They also have notions of what is right and just, and they have an understanding of what is feasible. These views may change over time and with the accumulation of experience, but at any one time, they shape leadership behavior.

Participation in the system of cooperation through which a community is governed may make an individual leader aware of a broader or different constituency. If a leader becomes part of the governing arrangements as representative of a particular constituency or even as representative of an alliance of constituent groups, this leader may develop a broader or different view. As he or she sees the system of cooperation in operation and comes to see its uses, the leader's ideas may undergo change.

When Richard Daley was elected mayor of Chicago, he was no longer merely the leader of a cadre of precinct workers. He was part of a governing coalition which was in need of the active mobilization of a variety of resources including private investment capital and credit for public expenditures. Although his origins were working class and his political party base was Democratic, he cultivated an active partnership with Republican business executives. When reformer Robert Moses became a park administrator in New York, he saw that the building and use of a park system was but a segment of a larger pattern of development. His own activities soon led into a growing role as a transportation czar. As his own administrative empire grew, he discarded reform principles in favor of pacts of reciprocal support with patronage-minded politicians and their business and labor allies.

The Daley and Moses examples suggest that accumulated experience does not necessarily enable leaders to develop more refined notions of justice. As they are caught up in the need to see things happen, coalition leaders may feel a strong pull in the direction of accommodation with others who control valuable resources and who head their own enclaves of cooperative activity. The Moses example, in particular, illustrates how reform principles and aspirations can founder on the desire to expand a system of cooperation.

While there are good reasons to broaden the base of support for a coalition and to perpetuate the coalition as a system of cooperation, disintegrative forces are also at work. Conditions change; populations shift; and new issues emerge. Moreover, individual ambitions collide. It is, therefore, no easy matter to hold a body of support in place. And the more diverse a coalition, the harder the task may be.

Issue conflicts and competition among aspiring leaders occur against a background of tension within coalitions and potential group struggle. Power alignments sometimes sunder and, then, are put back together in altered form.

Consider the rise in black electoral participation. As blacks become an increasingly large constituency in America's cities, their capacity to control electoral office increases. Black political leaders have emerged to mobilize that capacity and become major figures in the governing coalitions of urban communities. But blacks and whites often see themselves as having separate interests. Schools, housing, and access to service are issues on which racial groups sometimes divide. Sometimes they compete for scarce resources. Budgets, after all, are tight; and not all requests for expenditures can be honored. Job opportunities are highly valued, and racial groups may differ sharply over the rules by which job placements and employee retention occur.

Chicago politics provides an example of how racial divisiveness can undercut a system of cooperation. The Daley machine was a formidable instrument of power, but its top operatives were largely based in the city's white ethnic neighborhoods. Because many of these neighborhood concerns focused on blacks, the machine leaders found it difficult to accommodate to the reality of a growing black population. Black support for Daley tapered off.[1] After his death, it shifted temporarily to Jane Byrne. But when Byrne made peace with the machine operatives, she too became inattentive to the interests of blacks. In 1983, she was defeated by an upsurge of black voting for Harold Washington, who became the city's first black mayor. However, white ethnics still control a majority of the city's legislative body, and at this writing, no stable accommodation between black and white leaders has emerged. The power situation remains somewhat volatile. There is no broadly encompassing system of cooperation comparable to the Daley machine.

Power is thus hard to track. It is never possible to say precisely who has how much power over what range of issues and for how long. Sometimes arrangements are stable, but sometimes they go through periods of wrenching change. Tensions pervade most coalitions, and coalitions contract and expand as circumstances change.

[1] See Gove and Masotti, *After Daley*.

RESOURCES

There are some constants in the power picture, however. The changing position of individuals suggests more volatility than there is. Power is based on the resources of groups, and those resource distributions don't change much on a year-to-year basis. Yet resource distributions are not self-enabling phenomena. Individual leaders are instrumental in bringing groups together and in devising the means by which coalitions function as systems of cooperation. Power is thus manifest in the actions of individuals, and individuals do matter. Still, the actions of individual leaders should be seen as efforts to mobilize and sustain the use of resources. For that reason, political leaders do not operate independent of the social structure or of the nature of the economy. At the same time, social structures and economies don't devise and install political arrangements. That is the role of political leaders. Political leaders must work with the resources they can mobilize (and anticipate what competing leaders might be able to mobilize). At the same time, they are not confined to a single pattern of arrangements. Leadership is in part a creative exercise.

Although power is never completely stable and in any event is hard to measure, we can still make some general observations about the part that various groups play in the governance of urban communities. Groups are not equally attractive as coalition partners. The resources they provide vary along the following four dimensions:

1. Quantity
2. Range of resources
3. Durability of resource mobilization
4. Indispensability of resources

We tend to think mainly about quantity of resources, and that is a dimension along which groups can be ranked fairly easily. But power is not that simple. That Chicago's blacks are becoming more numerous and the city's white ethnics less numerous is a clear sign that *electoral* power is shifting. But the ability to win elections is only one resource. To sustain a system of governance requires multiple resources. It is relevant to ask to what extent the black community in Chicago can provide mobilizable resources that contribute to forms of cooperative action. If the mayor wants to launch a series of neighborhood-based child care programs, or the school system wants to inaugurate after-school and weekend tutorials, does the black community have the capacity to mobilize people to respond to city initiatives? What about money? Can the black community raise funds for political campaigns and local referendums? Does it contribute substantial amounts to United Way or various civic organizations? What kind of investment capital does it command? To what extent can it meet the credit needs of the city or lend money to voluntary organizations? In addition to money in its various forms, does it have people with professional skills and various forms of expertise? It is not enough for them to be around; they must be willing to be detailed to specific projects. Are they available to take part in promotional campaigns? Can they undertake assignments to see that projects don't falter because needed steps have not been taken?

As the above questions suggest, it is not just the amount of a given resource (number of voters, for example) that underlies group power, but it is also the range of resources that can be brought to bear. Groups are more powerful when they contribute multiple resources to a system of cooperation. Indeed, as was the case with Harold Washington's mayoral victory in Chicago, even the mobilization of electoral power requires more than large numbers of people. It requires organization, money, and the employment of a variety of skills. Or, to take another example, in cities such as Atlanta, where blacks were a significant political factor even before they gained numerical control of city elections, their influence rested on a range of resources.

Let us turn now to the third matter, the question of the durability of resource mobilization. Groups may or may not be organized. Those that are not organized suffer a power handicap. Without organization, the resources of groups are not easily mobilized. And even if they are mobilized on one occasion, they may not be available on a continuing basis. A system of cooperation cannot, of course, be maintained by a one-shot effort. Power is not based on a single show of strength but on the capacity to sustain an effort.

The fact that elections are won or lost by the turnout on a given day conveys a misleading impression. Elections make it seem that power can be exercised by an occasional mobilization of numbers. But winning elections is only the first step in governing a community. The successful candidate who fails to become part of a wide system of cooperation can accomplish little and, without accomplishments, cannot continue to win elections. On the group side, if membership participation ends with the election, the group is unlikely to reap any policy benefits. Elected officials are drawn to those who have mobilizable resources available on a ready basis. Groups that lapse into passivity lose their place in the governing coalition.

We come now to the fourth factor in group power—the indispensability of the resources controlled. Systems of cooperation come about through exchanges.[2] Each constituent group contributes to a coalition built around a system of cooperation. As a contributor, each group receives some voice in what the coalition does or does not undertake. And each has

[2] See Peter M. Blau, *Exchange and Power in Social Life* (New York: John Wiley & Sons, 1964). On organizations, a classic work is Richard Cyert and James March, *A Behavioral Theory of the Firm* (Englewood Cliffs, NJ: Prentice-Hall, 1963).

some say about the terms on which various projects are undertaken. Given some degree of discordant interests among coalition members, we can expect that there is much political pushing and shoving. Some participants may threaten to withdraw and perhaps even align themselves with an entirely different coalition. Other coalition members may be ignored or even encouraged to leave the coalition to make room for someone else. As an example of the threat to withdraw, there is the case of the business community in Atlanta during Maynard Jackson's mayoralty.[3] Disappointed with their limited access to city hall and unhappy over the mayor's strong emphasis on minority employment, the business community gave Atlanta's first black mayor an ultimatum—reach an accommodation with us or we'll close down our investment effort in the central business district. In the case of the election of Harold Washington as mayor in Chicago, Washington's candidacy represented a new and more aggressive step in black withdrawal from the Daley machine. Andrew Young, Atlanta's second black mayor, illustrates how a political leader can tilt the balance within a coalition. Strongly in favor of a program of economic development, Young has cooperated extensively with white business leaders and has distanced himself somewhat from the city's neighborhood groups. In that vein, he has largely phased out a special tie between the city planning department and neighborhood groups.[4]

What is it that makes a threat to withdraw effective? Or what is it that contributes to a leader's willingness to cut a group loose from its place within a governing coalition? The indispensability of the resources a group controls has a major part in the power of the group. Business is a valuable ally for many reasons, but a primary reason is its control of vast amounts of investment capital. No other group is an alternative source. Business support is, thus, indispensable for an economic development effort. Neighborhood groups, on the other hand, are power relevant primarily as sources of voting support. But they are only one of several sources of votes. Electoral majorities can usually be put together in any of several combinations. Voting alignments are fluid; those that prevail in one election may not hold together for a succeeding election. Blocs of support come and go. Elected officials are dependent on majority support, but in most cities they can bring that support together in alternative ways.

The indispensability of a group's resources depends on two conditions. The first of these is whether the group controls needed resources that are not readily available through another group. So long as there is an alternative source for what is needed, the group is not indispensable. The

[3] Henson and King, "The Atlanta Public-Private Romance: An Abrupt Transformation."

[4] Clarence N. Stone, "New Class or Convergence: Competing Interpretations of the Impact of Social Complexity on the Structure of Urban Power," in *Power and Elites* Vol. 1 (Fall 1984), pp. 1-22.

second condition is the unity of the group. Unless there is unity, the group *as a group* has little bargaining power. Without unity, resources are provided on the basis of particular arrangements with individuals, who act as individuals. General concerns of the group do not enter as a consideration, and the group is not in a powerful position. Without unity, a group is unable to make the availability of its resources contingent on attentiveness to the group's interests.

Consider some examples. To the extent that business is not united on such matters as what constitutes a favorable climate for business investment, the group is less powerful. Unless it acts in a unified direction, business exercises no monopoly control over capital as a resource. Investment decisions are ad hoc, and have no group impact. Similarly, a group divided in its voting preference has little electoral power.

Disunity can take more than one form. The most obvious is a split between coalitions, with some members of the group aligned with one coalition and other members aligned with a competing coalition. But even here, one must be careful. Alignments of support often diverge during election campaigns, but such a divergence does not mean a continuing split. After the election is over, all elements of a group may cooperate with the winning candidate, whether or not they backed the candidate in the election. Individual access may depend upon who supported whom, but group interests can be and often are represented by more than one individual. Indeed, it is to a group's interests to have access to all of the prospective holders of public office. Consequently, campaign contributions are often spread around to more than one candidate in order to protect future access. And different group members may be active in the campaigns of different candidates.

It is important to keep election campaigns in perspective. Governing coalitions do not transform each time a new mayor is elected. The mayor's office, after all, is only one element in any governing coalition. By no means is it assured of being the dominant element, even in a city like Chicago with a strong and centralized party apparatus. Patterns of candidate support are, therefore, not sure indicators of group unity.

Disunity is itself not a simple phenomenon. It need not take the form of division into competing coalitions. Disunity can also take the form of an incomplete mobilization. For example, if businesses in a given community organize no peak association and remain aloof from civic affairs while showing little interest in searching out investment opportunities (an unlikely combination of occurrences), then they fail to position themselves well as a power group. They fail to provide indispensable resources, thereby making it plain that business participation in city governance is not essential. Far more common, however, is the failure of other groups to mobilize themselves fully. Even voting in the highly charged Chicago election of 1983 amounted to participation by only two-thirds of the citizenry.

Looking over the general sweep of cities, one finds that business is almost always a part of the governing coalition. It may or may not be an integral part of the winning team in electoral contests. Often it is not. Business lacks numbers and seldom finds itself able to promote matters such as metropolitan reorganization, which depend heavily and directly on popular approval. The key to business power is that it controls a wide variety of resources, and it is more extensively organized than other segments of the community. Its extensive organization enables it to be a durable and dependable fount of resources. Some of these resources—investment capital, control of credit, and an ongoing capacity to wage promotional campaigns, for example—are virtually indispensable to a governing coalition. It is hard to maintain a system of cooperation without these resources. Business is an especially attractive coalition partner because no other group can provide some of these essential resources.

Neighborhood groups, racial groups, union members, and various single-interest groups are in a much different position. Except for employee unions, most are not strongly organized. They control a limited range of resources, and they are not in a position to make sustained contributions over long periods of time. They do mobilize for elections but, even then, imperfectly. Often no single group is a dependable majority, hence any group is at least partially dispensable over the long haul. Candidates are elected on pro-neighborhood platforms but, once in office, come to develop working arrangements that relegate neighborhoods to a minor role. Racial solidarity is sometimes a key to electoral victory, but even that is no guarantee of extensive power. Voting majorities are only one of several essential resources.

Further, numerical dominance is not the same as electoral dominance. As the bosses of political machines learned long ago, low electoral participation makes it easy for those in office to control elections with a relatively small number of dependable voters. Disunity among or imperfect mobilization of a numerically dominant racial group enables incumbent members of a governing coalition to maintain electoral control by enlisting the support of a fraction of the whole group. If one subelement gets restless, another may be enlisted.

Political leadership is an essential element in the overall picture because governing coalitions can be constituted in more than one way. Leadership consists in bringing groups together. Because most of these groups are imperfectly mobilized, their power is partial. The arrangements that leaders devise provide terms on which groups and fractions of groups participate in the governance of urban communities. Because elections are only a part of what governance is about, electoral support is only a part of what it takes to maintain a system of cooperation. Groups have power in proportion to their contribution to the system of cooperation and exchange. Political leaders have some leeway in who participates and on what terms, but their leeway is limited by the resources they require and the need to reciprocate a voice in governance in exchange for contributions to the system of cooperation.

Having taken a general overview of power and leadership in urban communities, let us turn now to a closer examination of executive leadership. Elected and appointed executives have emerged as the key public figures in governing arrangements. We should, therefore, look at the part they play and the constraints they operate under.

SUGGESTED READINGS

ANTON, THOMAS. "Power, Pluralism, and Local Politics." *Administrative Science Quarterly* 7 (March 1963), 425-57.

BACHRACH, PETER, and MORTON S. BARATZ. *Power and Poverty*. New York: Oxford University Press, 1970.

BALDWIN, DAVID A. "Power and Social Exchange," *American Political Science Review* 72 (December 1978), 1229-42.

DOMHOFF, G. WILLIAM. *Who Really Rules? New Haven and Community Power Reexamined*. New Brunswick, N.J.: Transaction, 1978.

ELKIN, STEPHEN L. "Markets and Politics in Liberal Democracy." *Ethics* 92 (July 1982), 720-32.

GAVENTA, JOHN. *Power and Powerlessness*. Urbana: University of Illinois Press, 1980.

LUKES, STEVEN. *Power: A Radical View*. London: Macmillan Press, 1974.

POLSBY, NELSON W. *Community Power and Political Theory; A Further Look at Problems of Evidence and Inference*. 2nd, enlarged ed. New Haven: Yale University Press, 1980.

SMITH, MICHAEL P. "Critical Theory and Urban Political Theory," *Comparative Urban Research* 7 (#3 1980), 5-23.

STONE, CLARENCE N. "Systemic Power in Community Decision Making." *American Political Science Review* 74 (December 1980), 978-90.

______. "Social Stratification, NonDecision-Making, and the Study of Community Power." *American Politics Quarterly* 10 (July 1982), 275-302.

WRONG, DENNIS H. *Power: Its Forms, Bases, and Uses*. New York: Harper & Row, 1980.

chapter 14

Executive Leadership

News accounts of urban politics tend to dwell on conflicts and personal rivalries, of which there are many. Sometimes it seems that impasse is more prevalent than action. However, large-scale projects are executed, services on a mass basis are provided, and disputes are resolved. In short, urban communities are governed. Coalitions bring disparate interests together, and these coalitions adhere around systems of cooperation. Group representatives, the officers in major businesses and nonprofit organizations, union chiefs, those who head charitable activities, and public officials develop compatible ways of pursuing their aims.[1] There are friction points, inefficiencies, and from time-to-time, temporary breakdowns at key points. Still, a complicated set of interdependent activities is carried on, and these activities sustain the urban community.

How does this happen? Who takes care of breakdowns in the system? How is the system adapted to change? Is anyone in charge?

First of all, some of the activity even in a large metropolis takes place informally within small groups on a face-to-face basis.[2] Complex systems

[1] For one explanation of how this occurs, see Norton E. Long, "The Local Community as an Ecology of Games," *American Journal of Sociology* 64 (November 1958), 251-61.

[2] Crenson, *Neighborhood Politics.*

rarely depend on area-wide coordination for all activities.[3] Second, much of the activity consists of market exchanges, and markets are highly decentralized. Although market transactions are regulated and shaped by numerous legal restrictions (zoning is an obvious example), and by various agreements among supposed competitors (dividing up market areas, for example), the urban economy follows no central set of directions. Even governmentally, the metropolitan community is fragmented into several jurisdictions. Within the core cities, central direction is quite limited. Most of the functional areas are, in practice, only loosely joined to one another.[4] While there are occasional jurisdictional struggles, turf fights are less common than is widely supposed.[5] Generally the prevailing view is "live and let live." Each agency is largely free to develop its own mode of operation and cultivate its own base of support.

Among the various actors on the urban scene, public and private, few take a broad and comprehensive view.[6] Most are concerned with their own particular goals. They are not obedient to any set of central directions. Cooperation develops through experience over time, and much of it comes about through negotiation. Many of the consequences of activities are unintended; they come about as the result of the interacting calculations of individuals concerned mainly with their short-term preferences. Racial segregation, for example, can come about without either the conspiratorial efforts of an elite or the deep prejudices of the many. All it requires is that individuals make uncoordinated moves to avoid being a greatly outnumbered minority.[7]

There are other examples of unintended consequences. Air pollution and traffic congestion come about through heavy reliance on automobiles for transportation. To some extent, these problems are the aggregate results of individuals pursuing their personal preferences within the options available to them. Some problems result from unplanned activity, or put another way, the "invisible hand" does not always have beneficial consequences.[8]

We should be careful, however, about assuming that all activities are unplanned. Not every actor in the urban community simply chooses among

[3] Cf. Herbert A. Simon, *The Science of the Artificial* (Cambridge, MA: M.I.T. Press, 1969), pp. 87 -103.

[4] Theodore J. Lowi, "Machine Politics—Old and New," *Public Interest* No. 9 (Fall 1967), 83-92.

[5] Roland L. Warren, Stephen M. Rose, and Ann F. Bergunder, *The Structure of Urban Reform* (Lexington, MA: Lexington Books, 1974).

[6] Long, "The Local Community as an Ecology of Games."

[7] Thomas C. Schelling, "On the Ecology of Micromotives," *Public Interest* No. 25 (Fall 1971), 61-98. See also, Harvey L. Molotch, *Managed Integration* (Berkeley: University of California Press, 1972).

[8] Garrett Hardin, "The Tragedy of the Commons," *Science* 162 (December 13, 1968), 1243-48.

the options available. Robert Caro describes key decisions in the New York metropolitan region through which mass transit was neglected while the expressway system was expanded.[9] No one intended the pollution, the sprawl, the congestion, and the neighborhood dislocation that the pattern of development brought about. But it would be misleading to say that it just happened. As Caro's prize-winning book, *The Power Broker*, details: Highway-oriented development occurred because it served the career aspirations of individuals like Robert Moses; it provided profit opportunities to developers and builders; it provided jobs for construction workers; it met the patronage wants of party professionals and the "retainer army" they gathered around them; and it fit the legal requirements of federal programs influenced by a nationally powerful automotive industry.

Large, organized interests such as financial institutions, contractors, utilities, and other major businesses are concerned with broad patterns of development. But their concerns reflect their particular interests in profit, investment, and business growth. While they are often integral parts of the system of governance in the local community, their concerns are partial and limited. Political scientist Norton Long described the urban community as "an ecology of games," suggesting that most urban actors are playing roles in particular games.[10] What happens overall is mostly the result of the interactions among these games *within a common territory*—hence "an ecology of games." Few actors are oriented toward a comprehensive look at the quality of urban life, and some of those that are so oriented command little organization power. Long comments: "The protagonists of things in particular are well organized and know what they are about; the protagonists of things in general are few, vague, and weak."[11]

In a real sense, then, no one is in charge. Some actors have considerable influence, but they may not take an overall view of the urban community. When they exercise their influence, it is to adjust the impact of urban conditions on the matters of particular concern to them—business executives seeking to protect investments, union officials trying to maintain an employment base for their members, or hospital and university officials attempting to reshape their immediate environment into one compatible with the needs of their institutions. These various actors take part in urban governance in order to protect particular interests.

But what about public officials? They are in a position to look out for the general welfare. After all, government is their official responsibility. And government differs from profit-seeking enterprises and even from nonprofit service institutions in possessing authority to act on the basis of the common and inclusive well-being of its citizens. Business executives and

[9] Caro, *The Power Broker*.

[10] Long, "The Local Community as an Ecology of Games."

[11] Ibid., p. 255.

other group representatives may take part in the informal coalitions that govern the community, but their private responsibilities tend to pull them in the direction of particular concerns. If general leadership is to be offered, it almost certainly must come from government.

PUBLIC LEADERSHIP

There are three categories of local officials who play leadership roles: elected chief executives (mayors and, for urban counties, county executives), legislators (who are, of course, also elected and who are known as council members or, in some cases such as Chicago, as aldermen), and professional administrators (for example police superintendents or directors of public safety, school superintendents, the heads of redevelopment and transportation agencies, and in the case of council-manager cities, city managers).

Professional administrators

Let us start by looking at the last of these sources of leadership. It is clearly the case that professional administrators are a significant source of policy leadership, and they play a major role in resolving the issues that confront their communities. The emergence of a postreform style of politics has by no means eliminated the influence of professional administrators. What it has done, however, is to remove some of the mystique from administrative leadership, and to leave professional administrators vulnerable to political attack. Opponents of the policy stances with which given administrators may be associated sometimes seek to have these administrators ousted from office. From all accounts, the tenure in office of school superintendents and top-level police administrators has shortened. Dismissal is no rare occurrence. And, even those officials who are quite successful in maintaining a strong set of allies find that the strains of office are enormous. Impressionistic evidence suggests that top administrators retire at younger ages than their predecessors did in the more low-keyed reform era.

Although professional administrators operate in a highly political environment, they are not without abilities to exert leadership. Many are quite skillful in coalition building. Significantly, a number of elected chief executives have backgrounds in law-enforcement administration. There are other sources as well. Philadelphia's current mayor, Wilson Goode, served as chief administrative officer to the previous mayor. In the postreform age, professional credentials are no guarantee one will prevail in a controversy or be regarded with great respect. But these credentials are still useful, as is the political experience of top-level administration.

In one study, the authors found that career administrators are guided significantly by professional norms.[12] Despite the group turbulence and issue conflict surrounding their work, administrators did not simply accommodate to public pressures. How could they? Some of these pressures are crosscutting so that the demands of one group are countered by the opposing demands of another group. Some pressures do not persist. Others are confined to a fairly specific issue of concern only to a small group, and then sometimes only for limited duration. As the authors of this study report, group demands are "often unfocused, confused, contradicted, and in time, lack persistence."[13] Professional administrators, by contrast, have concrete policy ideas, know procedures in great detail, have considerable experience in looking for (and in hiding) scarce funds, possess much savvy about the location of pitfalls, know much about coping with protest groups, and have usually had the opportunity to develop working relationships with an extensive network of individuals and organizations.[14]

The weakness of professional administrators as community leaders is mainly the limited scope of their activities. City managers, of course, have a wide scope of activity, but they are found mostly in small and medium-sized localities. Other professional administrators, by the nature of their work, are confined to specific policy areas. Moreover, they are expected to represent a particular set of functional interests rather than to provide general leadership. Norton Long described the attitudes of the officials of the Port of New York Authority toward the general problems of the metropolitan area as being "scarcely different" from those of executives in private firms.[15]

Heads of departments and agencies find the balancing of responsibilities difficult. Two examples from suburban Maryland illustrate the problem. Montgomery County recruited a police chief from Boston with a national reputation as someone willing to shake up his department and challenge police orthodoxy in order to build better community relations. Acting on that program in Montgomery County, he alienated members of the police department and was fired as soon as a new county executive was elected.

The second example comes from neighboring Prince George's County. A high ranking police administrator and prospective candidate for police chief had strong internal support to become head of the police department in his county, but the county's sizeable black community

[12] Frederick M. Wirt and Leslie J. Christovich, "The Politicization of American Local Executives," paper prepared for delivery at the Annual Meeting of the American Political Science Association, New York, September 3-6, 1981.

[13] Ibid., p. 17.

[14] Cf. Hugh Heclo, *A Government of Strangers* (Washington, D.C.: Brookings Institution, 1977).

[15] Long, "The Local Community as an Ecology of Games," p. 255.

regarded him as unsympathetic to their concerns about police conduct. He was passed over for the chief's position when the incumbent chief retired.

While many professional administrators navigate successfully between the expectations of department employees and groups in the larger community, they are nevertheless confined to a fairly narrow range of concerns. Some move on to exert wider leadership, but they do so by shifting to the electoral arena. General leadership, after all, is regarded as the responsibility of elected officials.

Elected officials

In the era of traditional politics, policy was made largely in the legislative arena. Leadership consisted of working out ways in which particular demands (often for a slice of the patronage pie) could be aggregated legislatively into a proposal with majority support. Hence, logrolling was common practice. Ward "courtesy" institutionalized the practice of legislative reciprocity—"you support my proposal affecting my district, and I'll support your proposal affecting your district." Now, aggregations of legislative support are only a small part of what it takes to launch a major new program, and legislative leadership has declined in importance. Legislators today command too few organizational resources to provide comprehensive and ongoing leadership. Further, in most communities council membership is a part-time position. Council members do have a public forum, and their visibility enables them to serve as critics of executive leadership, but leadership comes primarily from elected executives. As a leadership position, council membership serves primarily as a recruiting ground for candidates for executive office.

It is the chief executive who controls the organizational resources that make general policy leadership possible. The chief executive's office prepares the budget, manages finances, and arranges credit. The typical city council has little staff to even oversee these activities. The chief executive in a large jurisdiction is surrounded by a vast array of staff—press aides, speech writers, liaison officers with various community groups, specialists in intergovernmental relations, lobbyists in the state and national capital, special assistants, planners, directors of research, and a variety of issue specialists either from within the career bureaucracy or directly in the chief executive's office. Although any chief executive must use persuasion as well as the formal authority to command, it is the chief executive who presides over the local government's considerable administrative apparatus and directs most of the service agencies. Reorganization and the creation of new agencies fall to the chief executive's initiative.

With most sustained policy efforts growing out of dealings among the heads of large organizations, mayors are able to take their place in these activities. As commanders of substantial resources, they can negotiate with business executives, federal and state officials, union leaders, foundation representatives, and the directors of medical, educational, and other nonprofit service institutions. Local legislators, on the other hand, have few bargaining chips for participation in such negotiations.

Constraints

We talked earlier about America's strong tradition of privatism. Public authority is regarded with some suspicion, and, dating back at least to the day of machine politics, elected officials have not been highly regarded.[16] Their motives are widely suspect. Thus, while chief executives bring considerable resources to the task of building policy coalitions, they operate under numerous constraints.[17]

Not all of the constraints on authority are informal. Cities and counties have limited home-rule powers, especially in raising revenue. Many of their actions, particularly in the field of taxation, require state approval. And in some instances such as the tax-limiting referendums in California and Massachusetts, for example, major restrictions are not removable. A recent court ruling has raised the issue of antitrust liability, tightening the dependence of local government on state authorization. Most localities are also required to have a balanced budget and therefore possess limited borrowing power. They can, subject to the restriction of state law, issue bonds of various kinds, but the rate at which they can borrow is determined by their bond rating, which is set by private credit authorities.

One of the major constraints on local officials is the mobility of private investment. Particularly in this age of conglomerates and multilocational firms, capital is highly mobile. Few large businesses are dependent on a single location, and over time they can shift activities from inside the city to its periphery, or from one metropolitan area to another, or even overseas. City officials are dependent on business investments in a way that businesses are not dependent on location. Geographic mobility lies with business, not with local governments. Public officials are thus drawn in the direction of providing a favorable business climate.

Mobility is not restricted to capital investments. People are also mobile, and those who are most attractive as revenue-producers are the most mobile. Moreover, in a meritocratic society given to rewarding educational credentials and emphasizing an educated life style, social status coincides to a high degree with educational level, and a high educational level

[16] Peter B. Clark, "Civic Leadership: The Symbols of Legitimacy," in *Democracy in Urban America*, ed. by Oliver P. Williams and Charles Press (Chicago: Rand McNally, 1969), pp. 350-66.

[17] Peter A. Lupsha, "Constraints on Urban Leadership, or Why Cities Cannot Be Creatively Governed," in *Improving the Quality of Urban Management*, ed. by David Rogers and Willis Hawley (Beverly Hills, CA: Sage Publications, 1974), pp. 607-23.

often carries with it high mobility. Economic position and educational level are also correlated. Local officials very much want to attract and keep the educated and affluent middle class. The prospect that this population will move serves as a restraining force on governmental officials.

One of the most significant constraints on chief executives is the frequency of the election cycle. While the most obvious effect of popular elections is to make officials sensitive to sources of public satisfaction and dissatisfaction, elections also have less obvious consequences. Four-year terms of office and, even more so, two-year terms of office provide executives with little time to compile a record of accomplishment. Consequently, elected officials are drawn toward policy actions that offer quick and visible results. They have little inclination to engage in long-range plans to ameliorate complicated social problems. Building a new police station is immediately visible. Carrying out a plan to decrease juvenile delinquency is much less visible and not likely to produce immediate results. Methadone maintenance provides a ready count of people enabled to return to ordinary work life; searching out the causes of drug addiction offers no ready numbers and no promise of early success.[18]

Short terms of office also constrain coalition building. With a need for immediate accomplishments, elected executives have little opportunity to engage in long-term efforts to build organizations capable of making sustained policy efforts. They need allies who already have the capacity to act. Coalition building around groups already organized and endowed with staff capacities, money, and their own network of allies is much more attractive than starting from scratch with groups that are not highly organized.

In most communities, business interests hold a strongly superior organizational position. Individual enterprises are themselves significant organizations, and the large ones command resources that can be deployed on community projects. Moreover, business is typically organized into one or more peak associations. Usually the local chamber of commerce represents all businesses area-wide. In addition, many big cities have organizations of the major businesses with a stake in the central business district—"the Vault" in Boston, the Greater Baltimore Committee in that city, Atlanta's Central Atlanta Progress, and San Francisco's Bay Area Council are just a few of the business associations to appear on the urban scene.

Business itself engages in coalition building. Business executives take a leading part in forming and guiding a number of civic organizations. They usually play a major role in fund raising for cultural and charitable activities. They hold many of the board positions of educational, medical, and religious institutions. News media executives are an integral part of the business community—newspapers and broadcast companies are businesses

[18] See the case study in Diana R. Gordon, *City Limits* (New York: Charter House, 1973), pp . 63-106.

themselves and, of course, depend heavily on advertising. They are thus very much a part of the business culture of the community.

Including business in the governing coalition is, thus, the quick and almost irresistible way to link into a vast body of readily mobilizable resources. But what about other groups? Unions are an obvious source of ready organization. Municipal employee associations and the building trades, with their strong stakes in the city, are potential partners in a system of cooperation.[19] Their interests tend to be narrow, however.

Neighborhoods and racial/ethnic groups are also possible allies. But their organizational capacities are quite limited. As groups relying exclusively on volunteer participation, they have limited capacity to overcome the collective action problem.[20] Most of their potential membership has no individual inducement to make an ongoing contribution to the group effort. Consequently, these interests are largely unorganized, except for occasional bursts of interest that are prompted by the excitement of an election campaign. Or the immediacy of a threat, such as disruption by the development of a highway, might spark a high level of participation. But such protest activity tends to be short-lived, and it usually fades back into nonparticipation as soon as the threat subsides (or becomes an accomplished fact). Such sporadic participation, especially when backed with limited resources, is unappealing as a coalition component.

Elected executives are thus also constrained by the dynamics of coalition building. Faced with limited time between elections and restricted in their ability to provide resources from within the government itself, chief executives look for coalition partners who can enable them to achieve visible accomplishments quickly. The business community has resources and ready organizational capacity that no other group can match. Elected executives are thus drawn strongly toward partnership with business, even though their personal policy predilections may lie in a different direction.

Consider one example of how mayoral priorities shift. When Kevin White was first elected mayor of Boston, he ran as a progressive candidate.[21] His platform called for administrative decentralization and responsiveness to neighborhoods. And, indeed, his initial program was consistent with that platform. However, he soon shifted his policy priorities. Sixteen years after his initial campaign, when White announced that he would not run for a fifth term, his program accomplishments consisted primarily of redevelopment efforts in the central business district. White's successor,

[19] Jewel Bellush and Bernard Bellush, "Collective Bargaining, Leadership, and the Fiscal Crisis," paper prepared for delivery at the Annual Meeting of the American Political Science Association, New York, September 3-6, 1981.

[20] Mancur Olson, Jr., *The Logic of Collective Action* (Cambridge, MA: Harvard University Press, 1965). See also Russell Hardin, *Collective Action* (Baltimore: Johns Hopkins University Press, 1982).

[21] See Martha W. Weinberg, "Boston's Kevin White," *Political Science Quarterly* 96 (Spring 1981), 87-106.

Raymond Flynn, ran on a platform of redressing the imbalance in the city's priorities with renewed attention to Boston's neglected neighborhoods. The city's politics had come full circle, perhaps to repeat itself in the future.

Community development policy, as we shall see in greater detail later, is pitched toward "leveraging"—using city authority and resources to stimulate private development and private efforts. Business interests are well positioned for such cooperative activities. Neighborhoods are not. Campaign promises and popular appeals are hard to convert into concrete accomplishments, especially within the bounds of a short term of office. Governing is a different activity from winning election campaigns.

Stein Rokkan, a Scandinavian political scientist, made an acute observation, one as fully applicable to city policy making in America as to national policy making in Scandinavia: "Votes count but resources decide."[22] Mayoral dependence on private resources shapes the formation of governing coalitions and is a major constraint on the leadership of elected executives.

STYLES OF MAYORAL LEADERSHIP

Executives differ in temperament. Some are highly active and aggressive in initiating programs. Others are less so. Some assert authority freely and are quick to take charge. Others are more inclined to wait out a problem or controversy, and to intervene only if necessary. Some are flamboyant public figures. Others prefer quiet, behind-the-scenes negotiation. The public personality of a mayor may differ from her or his private personality. Leadership styles differ with the circumstances. As executives go about setting policy agendas, building and maintaining networks of support, and overseeing program implementation, personality and community context make a difference.[23] But no individual controls the flow of events. Much of the attention of any chief executive goes into crisis management, into reacting to events not of her or his choosing.[24]

Types of mayoral leadership reflect, to a considerable extent, the political setting in which executives operate. Mayoral types correspond in a general way with political styles. *The caretaker* type takes little policy initiative and is largely content to maintain traditional services and provide ceremonial leadership. Such leadership has a strong affinity with village

[22] Stein Rokkan, "Norway: Numerical Democracy and Corporate Pluralism," in *Political Oppositions in Western Democracies*. ed. by Robert A. Dahl (New Haven: Yale University Press, 1966), p. 105.

[23] John P. Kotter and Paul Lawrence, *Mayors in Action* (New York: John Wiley and Sons, 1974).

[24] See Martha W. Weinberg, *Managing the State* (Cambridge, MA: M.I.T. Press, 1977).

politics, and it is most feasible in smaller localities with the low-keyed life of the stable community.

The broker is not so much a policy initiator as someone who mediates conflicts. Brokers concentrate on negotiating agreements and devising compromises out of the public limelight. This style has its strongest affinity with machine politics. The bosses of patronage-based organizations have little need for visibility to a mass audience. Their support rests on a highly personalized network of support held together by the exchange of favors and mutual loyalties. Negotiating skills thus are at a premium. Performance skills, useful before a mass audience, are less useful. Public drama and conflict serve only to heighten awareness and perhaps involve the risk of unleashing volatile feelings that could interfere with settled arrangements.[25]

Of course, if patronage provides no mass basis of support, low-visibility leadership is less feasible. The entrepreneurial type of leadership centers on highly visible problem-solving efforts. Major projects call for the involvement of a variety of policy professionals and substantial private resources. These kinds of efforts are most easily launched where group conflict is subdued and promotion can center on community-wide benefits. Entrepreneurial leadership thus has an affinity with reform politics, and it finds easiest expression in projects designed to promote economic development. Such projects primarily serve business interests, but the promise of revenue gains and employment opportunities can be used to broaden appeals for support. Redevelopment of Baltimore's harbor area, for example, contributes significantly to Mayor William Schaefer's continuing electoral success in that city. Schaefer combines negotiating skill with a flair for public relations.

Economic development projects are, of course, challengeable. Critics question both the revenue gains and the generation of employment opportunities. And, as in the recent Boston election, an agenda concentrated on central business district revitalization is vulnerable to criticism. Other props of reform leadership are also subject to attack, now that group conflict has unleashed itself in the postreform manner. Testimonials by policy experts and program professionals do not ward off opposition.

As a period in which many groups are politically active and contentious, the postreform period has witnessed a variety of leadership styles. Starting in the mid 1960s, a number of mayors, including Kevin White in Boston, began as social reformers. *The social reform* types appeal strongly to conscience. They identify closely with the causes of minorities, the poor, and neighborhood interests. In the context of that time, the 1960s, administrative decentralization and various forms of citizen involvement provided ways of trying to reorient schools, police departments, and other service agencies. Chief executives sought mass support for policies intended to cor-

[25] Rakove, *Don't Make No Waves, Don't Back No Losers*, pp. 68-75.

rect past neglects and to open up opportunities to new groups. These efforts led to some changes in agency practice, and they opened up both elected and administrative careers to minorities, in particular, to those who had been excluded from many areas of public service.[26]

Social reform leadership, however, proved not to be viable in most cases. As we have seen, Kevin White in Boston reverted to reform style entrepreneurial leadership. When that proved to have waning popularity, he retired. In New York City, John Lindsay started off as one of the most aggressive social-reform executives on the urban scene but found himself beleaguered by conflicts with city police, and teachers, as well as middle-class neighborhoods opposed to scattered-site public housing. Although he was elected to a second term in 1969, Lindsay faced substantial opposition and a tightening financial situation.[27]

With a diminished capacity to practice social reform leadership, Lindsay shifted to a *managerial style*.[28] He began to emphasize technical issues such as productivity and touted such ideas as efficiency in traditional services. These are relatively low-keyed issues and enjoy broad popularity. Hence, the managerial style provides a way of avoiding intense controversy and staying out of the cross fire of competing groups. Other mayors, subsequently, have emphasized fiscal retrenchment and built support as proponents of economy in government.[29]

Managerial-style mayors narrow the problem-solving responsibility of government. Sometimes they make sharp distinctions between what is public and what is private in order to disclaim any obligation to correct ills in the private sphere. Lowering expectations is another way of lessening the intensity of conflict surrounding public decision making.

A shift toward expressive leadership?

As discussion of the managerial style suggests, the difficulties of consensus building under conditions of intense group conflict can serve to deflect mayors from broad assertions of leadership. There are other consequences. The difficulties of mobilizing mass support can divert mayors from a task-oriented approach to urban problems. New York City's current mayor, Ed Koch, specializes in a highly emotional form of leadership—

[26] Paul E. Peterson, "The Death of Maximum Feasible Participation," in *Urban Governance and Minorities*, ed. by Herrington J. Bryce (New York: Praeger Publishers, 1976), pp. 159-63; and Peter K. Eisinger, "The Community Action Program and the Development of Black Political Leadership," in *Urban Policy Making*, ed. by Dale Rogers Marshall (Beverly Hills, CA: Sage Publications, 1979), pp. 127-44.

[27] We are indebted to Ester Fuchs for findings on this point.

[28] Clarence N. Stone, "Complexity and the Changing Character of Executive Leadership," *Urban Interest* 4 (Fall 1982), 29-50. See also Charles R. Morris, *The Cost of Good Intentions* (New York: W. W. Norton & Co., 1980).

[29] Clark and Ferguson, *City Money*.

what may be termed expressive leadership. How does such leadership come about? On what is it based?

In sociological literature, there is considerable agreement that all social systems have two structures: a task (or instrumental) structure and an expressive (or socioemotional) structure. The task structure is oriented toward resolving conflicts within the group and creating commitment to it. In small groups, typically, one person serves as task leader while another person serves as socioemotional leader. Sociologists suggest that task leadership is important when goals are certain, but that expressive leadership attains greater importance when goals are uncertain.

How does this idea apply to cities? Small groups usually have both types of leadership, but cities are governed by one mayor. The mayor must embody both types of leadership and will undoubtedly act as task leader and as expressive leader for the city on different occasions. However, we must stress that our concern here is with leadership styles; some mayors will emphasize a task orientation, while other mayors will emphasize a socioemotional style. In the case of city managers or other career administrators, they are much more likely to be confined to task leadership. The assumptions underlying their positions include a high degree of goal certainty. City council members, on the other hand, are quite free to provide expressive leadership. They may even welcome the opportunity to take up an emotional issue.

The concepts of task and of expressive or socioemotional leadership are especially relevant when one considers urban leadership styles in recent years.[30] Whereas the reform period was characterized by goals that seemed reasonably clear and attainable, the postreform period has witnessed greater conflict and uncertainty about goals. Problems no longer appear as amenable to solution as they did in earlier times.

In accordance with sociological theory, expressive-oriented leadership has emerged in a number of city halls. Some mayors emphasize law and order and identify themselves with harshly repressive measures. When former Police Chief Rizzo was mayor of Philadelphia, he cultivated an image of toughness. Opposition to criminality is, of course, a no-lose stance. Rizzo went further—"You get them to the electric chair, I'll throw the switch myself." Capital punishment is a matter of state and federal law and not an issue that mayors control. Yet it has symbolic significance. Mayor Koch of New York City gives big play to his support for capital punishment. Not all symbolic gestures appeal to punitive sentiments. During her term as mayor of Chicago, Jane Byrne spent a weekend living in one of the city's public-housing projects to affirm her concern with the poor.

[30] Sevgi O. Aral and Robert K. Whelan, *Leadership Styles in Urban Societies* (Tucson, AZ: Institute of Government Research, 1974).

Yet, for all the importance of symbolic gestures and the contributions they can make toward group solidarity and loyalty to a particular leader or regime, expressive leadership is in some ways empty. It changes little. It is no substitute for task leadership, though it is attractive as a way of identifying oneself with widely popular sentiments.

Complex society is characterized by a large number of groups with crosscutting interests. Many concrete policy actions affect different groups in different ways. Some problem-solving efforts worsen conditions for some while improving them for others. Broad, shared interests are not immediately evident to a populace divided by race, nationality and language, religion, income, type of occupation, location of neighborhood, family status, age, sexual preference, general life style, and a number of other considerations. Such fragmented interests are both an opportunity and a frustration to elected officials. Majorities can be put together in numerous ways, but many electoral coalitions are unstable. The resources for instrumental leadership are most readily available in partnership with business, but that partnership is not always popular with voting public. Expressive appeals can garner majority support but, by themselves, leave one without a record of accomplishment. The managerial style can also command majority support. However, added economies are hard to come by, and service cuts have limited appeal. Social reform coalitions are highly unstable and lack a strong resource base.

Elected executives are, of course, able to mix kinds of leadership. They seldom assume a single leadership stance. However, the types of leadership identified here should serve to highlight the kinds of pressures and inducements elected executives respond to. These types of leadership should also direct attention to the conditions on which these responses are based.

CONCLUSION

General leadership in the urban community falls to the public sector, not the private sector. Yet, many of the resources needed to govern must be mobilized from private interests, particularly from the business community. As we shall see in more detail later, federal community development policy reinforces this dependence.[31]

Leadership within the public sector is exercised most broadly by elected executives. But they operate under many constraints. Their authority is restricted, and many of their potential allies are organizationally weak. The social complexity of modern society fragments the

[31] John J. Mollenkopf, *The Contested City* (Princeton, NJ: Princeton University Press, 1983).

urban public, leaving executives free to assemble support in a number of different ways. However, the fragmentation of the public along with the organizational weakness of many groups makes it hard for executives to draw together effective support for broad programs of urban governance. The shortness of the election cycle in the face of intractable problems also limits the policy efforts of urban executives. Some are attracted toward expressive leadership. Some adopt mainly a managerial agenda. Much of the urban public is itself poorly organized to share in the governance of the urban community. Without constituents organized to play a governing role and without a mobilizing conception of the public interest to guide the citizenry, elected executives have little opportunity to exert broad and sustained task leadership. Leaders, it seems, are only as strong as their followers.

SUGGESTED READINGS

CLARK, TERRY N. and LORNA C. FERGUSON. *City Money*. New York: Columbia University Press, 1983.

DAUGHEN, JOSEPH, and PETER BINZEN. *The Cop Who Would Be King: The Honorable Frank Rizzo of Philadelphia*. Boston: Little, Brown & Co., 1977.

GORDON, DIANA R. *City Limits: Barriers to Change in Urban Government*. New York: Charter House, 1973.

GREER, ANN L. *The Mayor's Mandate*. Cambridge, Mass.: Schenkman Publishing Co., 1974.

KOTTER, JOHN, and PAUL LAWRENCE. *Mayors in Action: Five Approaches to Urban Governance*. New York: John Wiley & Sons, 1974.

LEVINE, CHARLES. *Racial Conflict and the American Mayor: Power, Polarization, and Performance*. Lexington, Mass.: Lexington Books, 1974.

LUPSHA, PETER A. "Constraints on Urban Leadership, or Why Cities Cannot Be Creatively Governed," in *Improving the Quality of Urban Management*, ed. David Rogers and Willis Hawley. Beverly Hills, Calif.: Sage Publications, 1974.

MOLLENKOPF, JOHN H. *The Contested City*. Princeton, N.J.: Princeton University Press, 1983.

MORRIS, CHARLES R. *The Cost of Good Intentions: New York City and the Liberal Experiment*. New York: W. W. Norton & Co., 1980.

MURPHY, RUSSELL. *Political Entrepreneurs and Urban Poverty*. Lexington, Mass.: D. C. Heath and Co., 1971.

NELSON, WILLIAM E., and PHILIP MERANTO. *Electing Black Mayors: Political Action in the Black Community*. Columbus, Ohio: Ohio State University Press, 1977.

SHARKANSKY, IRA. "Mayor Teddy Kollek and the Jerusalem Foundation." *Public Administration Review* 44 (July/August 1984), 299-304.

STONE, CLARENCE N. "Complexity and the Changing Character of Executive Leadership." *Urban Interest* 4 (Fall 1982), 29-50.

WEINBERG, MARTHA W. "Boston's Kevin White." *Political Science Quarterly* 96 (Spring 1981), 87-106.

WOODY, BETTE. *Managing Crisis Cities: The New Black Leadership and the Politics of Resource Allocation*. Westport, CN: Greenwood Press, 1982.

YATES, DOUGLAS. *The Ungovernable City* . Cambridge, Mass.: MIT Press, 1977.

chapter 15

Poverty and Welfare Policy

To some observers, urban politics is a microcosm of state and national politics. There is no denying that there are similarities; politics, after all, is a universal game. Yet it would be a mistake to assume that urban politics is simply state or national politics writ small. Local governments are different in some important ways. They are, for one thing, legally subordinate to both of their larger partners in the federal system.

Parallels with state and national governments are, of course, much in evidence. Each is concerned with such issues as tax policy, expenditure levels, economic growth, health, education, public safety, recreation, transportation, civil rights, individual liberties, and welfare policy. But more than either of the others, local government is on the service-delivery firing line. That is, it is usually the city (or county) that has to provide services to citizens firsthand—build and run the schools, collect and get rid of the garbage, create and run a public transportation system, provide police protection, remove snow and ice so that winter traffic can move, and many more. Local government ultimately determines how good most of our services will be even though the states and the federal government have a large influence.

Plainly, we cannot discuss the full list or trace out all of the areas of decision making. Instead, we will put the spotlight on five policy areas of special significance for large urban areas: transportation, economic and com-

munity development, poverty and welfare policy, education, and law enforcement. The first two represent local government's strong involvement in land use. The latter three represent local government's equally strong involvement in human service-delivery programs. The first two, especially transportation, represent program areas that the economists call capital-intensive (that is, a large proportion of their costs are tied up in physical plant and public works). The others are labor-intensive program areas (that is, most of their costs are personnel costs). Put even more simply, transportation, and economic and community development are concerned mainly with the physical aspects of the urban community; poverty and welfare policy, education and law enforcement are more concerned with the social and human aspects of community life. There is, be cautioned, no absolute distinction between the two. For example, though transportation is a physical program area, it has enormous social consequences.

As we look at these five policy arenas, we will examine the issues and policy alternatives in each. We will also be concerned with the mechanisms through which policies are carried out: How are programs planned and executed? How are programs structured and managed? How do citizens and public servants interact with one another? But in the present chapter and the four following chapters, our major concern is with substantive issues rather than with problems in service-delivery procedures. Still, substantive issues of policy cannot be neatly separated from the instrumentalities through which policies are carried out. Indeed, some of the key policy issues are those of how services will be provided. What part should other levels of government play in setting standards? Within cities, should citizen or neighborhood groups play a role? What principles should guide governmental action, and how much should government try to do? These are some of the major questions that surround the various arenas of urban policy.

In the 1960s, when the War on Poverty was declared, the battle was not a new one; it was not even a new venture for the national government. Efforts to relieve and eliminate poverty had been a major feature of Franklin Roosevelt's New Deal. And poverty problems had been a concern of state and local governments long before that time. In fact, programs of poor relief date back to the colonial era. Nor is the 1960s idea that education is a major weapon in the on-going battle against poverty a new one. Early proponents of public education conceived of it as a program of economic as well as moral uplift. The 1960s efforts thus marked not a new direction in government policy but the broadening of initiatives begun long ago.

Even though poverty did diminish under the policies of the Kennedy-Johnson era, social programs are not in high repute today. Accomplishments have not matched expectations; as a result, there is considerable skepticism about the effectiveness of government-operated programs. Moreover, budgetary concerns are at a high level. Many of the programs of the 1960s, both national and local, have either been phased out or merged with older programs.

Not all programs have failed by any means, but the disappointments have been great enough to raise important questions. Perhaps the best place to begin is with the nature of poverty. In this chapter, after starting with a consideration of who is poor and why, we focus on social welfare, that is, programs of public assistance to the needy. In income assistance, the administrative burden falls mainly on local governments while rule making and standard setting occur principally at the state level. As a source of funds and codeterminant of policy, the national government is also important. With that as a background, let us see who is poor, why, and what has been done about it.

WHO IS POOR?

Poverty in the United States is not a matter of severe physical deprivation. Few people are unable to get the bare necessities, though to be sure, some have nutritionally inadequate diets, and many lack adequate medical and dental care. Homelessness has become an increasingly visible problem. What the American poor lack, as a group, is a standard of living commensurate with the requirements of full human dignity in this country. In a society that measures worth by material success, those who are economically dependent bear the special stigma of failure. Though there are some people in material need, most deprivation is not absolute. Still there is a need for yardsticks. One writer suggests that poverty be defined as the "inability to obtain the goods and services sufficient to meet socially defined needs."[1] Another definition, which emphasizes the relative character of the deprivation, sets the poverty line at one-half the median income for the nation. The most widely used definition, one that estimates "socially defined minimum needs" in a very restrictive manner, comes from the Social Security Administration. This "official" definition is based on considerations such as family size and place of residence. In 1963, a nonfarm family of four required a minimum of $3,130 to meet food and other essential needs. By 1983, that amount had risen, through inflation, to $10,178. No doubt some people below that income level do not feel poor and many above it do feel poor.[2] Nevertheless, this poverty line gives us a

[1] Bradley R. Schiller, *The Economics of Poverty and Discrimination* (Englewood Cliffs, N.J.: Prentice-Hall, Inc., 1976), p. 13.

[2] A Boston survey indicated that the nonaffluent themselves set a figure nearly twice as high as the Social Security Administration figure. See John B. Williamson, *Strategies Against Poverty in America* (Cambridge, Mass.: Schenkman Publishing Co., 1975), p. 17.

usable definition through which we can identify the poor and talk about their characteristics.

In 1963, when poverty surfaced as a major national issue, about 20 percent of the population fell below the poverty line. A decade later, that figure was down to about 10 percent. By 1984, with unemployment proving to be a persisting problem, the figure had risen to more than 15 percent. Without some form of government assistance, at least a quarter of the American population would live below the poverty line.[3] Thus much of our success in holding people above the poverty level rests squarely on government aid.

In looking at poverty, it is important to distinguish between the characteristics of the poor (what proportion of the poor falls into various categories of age, race, employment status, and educational level) and the incidence of poverty (what proportion of a given population category falls below the poverty line). It is especially important in looking at data on poverty and race, which are so inseparably mixed in America. A large majority of the poor are white (69 percent), but the incidence of poverty among whites is only 10 percent. Conversely, only 31 percent of the poor are black or members of other nonwhite minorities, but the incidence of poverty among *these* groups is nearly one-third.

Probably the greatest change in the profile of poverty in America is that is has become feminized. In 1979, half of all the poor families, almost 13 million people, were headed by women. Between 1970 and 1977, while the number of poor families headed by men declined by 25 percent, there was an increase of almost 40 percent in the number of poor families headed by women.

The largest single category of the poor are children; nearly half of the poor are under 18 in age. And, of all children in the nation, at least one out of six lives in a poverty household. The number of children in a family is also associated with poverty; 30 percent of the families with six or more children fall below the poverty line.

Contrary to popular beliefs, a majority of poor families are headed by someone who is in the work force. Nearly one-third of the heads of poor households work full time, all year around; another quarter or more work at least part time. In some cases, more than one family member is in the work force and income still does not exceed the poverty level. Many other families stay above the poverty line only by having more than one member of the household employed; one income won't do it. For this and other reasons, being poor is concentrated in female-headed households. Job and salary discrimination against women, of course, also contributes to this pattern. Predominantly female occupations continue to be among the lowest paid.

[3] Robert D. Plotnick and Felicity Skidmore, *Progress Against Poverty* (New York: Academic Press, 1975), p. 170.

Obviously, having a job helps, if one does not want to be poor. But 71 percent of the poor, as former Secretary of Health, Education and Welfare Joseph Califano has reminded us, are people we do not normally ask to work: children and young people under 16, the aged, the severely disabled, students, or mothers with children under six. Only 2 percent of the 26 milion poor people statistically resemble the mythical welfare stereotype of able-bodied men who "loaf." And most of this 2 percent are either near retirement age (62 to 64), ill, or actively looking for work.

Jobs are no panacea, though. One reason the incidence of poverty is so high among blacks is that work has not yielded the same economic benefits for blacks as for whites. Among poor households headed by males, 71 percent of the blacks are employed but only 59 percent of the whites are employed. A similar pattern exists among female-headed poverty households; 49 percent of the blacks hold jobs compared to 39 percent of the whites. Even though they work, their incomes are still below the poverty line.

Education is highly related to employability and salary rate. There is, then, a close association between poverty and the level of education of the head of household. Among households headed by someone with less than an eighth-grade education, 25 percent are poor. By contrast, among the heads of household who have finished high school but have no college, the proportion who are poor is only 5 percent. The college-educated are even less likely to be poor.

It is not enough, however, to look at poverty in terms of single characteristics. Economic disabilities such as a large family, minority status, and a low educational level tend to be cumulative. The more handicaps a family has to overcome, the greater the likelihood it will fall into the poverty class. For example, 73 percent of the families that have seven or more members and are headed by black females live in poverty.[4]

Poverty, however, is not a fixed state. Over a third of those who fall below the poverty line one year rise above that line the following year. At the same time, more than a third of those who are poor in a given year were not there in the previous year. By one estimate, only 3 percent of the American population is persistently poor.[5] Others set the figure higher, and certainly a large proportion of the population, at least a quarter, either lives close to the poverty line or falls below it at some point. One recent estimate of the long-term poor puts the figure at 10 million, and sees this group as a permanent underclass responsible for a disproportionate amount of crime, welfare costs, and social hostility.[6]

[4] The figures used here are based on the 1970 census, and are drawn mainly from the analysis by Williamson, *Strategies Against Poverty in America,* pp. 9-12.

[5] *The New York Times,* July 17, 1977.

[6] Ken Auletta, *The Underclass.*

THE CULTURE-OF-POVERTY DEBATE

At one level, poverty is easy to understand. Some people do not make enough money because they are prevented from working by mental or physical disabilities. Households with small children may lack a wage earner because of death or desertion. In many cases, people work but get wages too low to lift them out of poverty. Still others do work that is too seasonal to generate an adequate annual income. And some, of course, are thrown out of work by fluctuations in the business cycle or by the decline of particular industries.

Some of these conditions are temporary. Many families thrust into poverty recoup their earning power, sometimes by putting a second family member to work. Even so, a number of people appear to be locked into a life of low income. Why? Over this question there is now and always has been much debate.

Styles of life do vary with income level. Some maintain that there is a distinct culture of poverty—a set of values that tends to be perpetuated from one generation to another.[7] Other observers argue that there is no single style of life among the poor but several. Still others contend that the behavior traits of the poor differ only in degree, not in kind, from the social strata immediately above them and that there is no hard evidence of unique culture of the lower class. Still another group maintains that though there is no separate "culture" of poverty there *is* a distinctive lower-class style of life that is a functional adaptation to reality. The situation of the poor, they explain, consists objectively of inadequate opportunity. Subjectively, it means having to cope psychologically with economic failure in a society that measures worth by occupational success.[8] Let us look more closely at the issue.

Oscar Lewis, originator of the culture-of-poverty concept, described it as more than an adaptation to a set of objective conditions. He argued:

> Once it comes into existence, it tends to perpetuate itself from generation to generation because of its effect on the children. By the time slum children are age six or seven, they have usually absorbed the basic values and attitudes of their subculture and are not psychologically geared to take full advantage of

[7] The leading proponent of this idea, Oscar Lewis, was a student of life among the poor in Mexico and Puerto Rico. See *Five Families* (New York: Basic Books, 1959); *The Children of Sanchez* (New York: Random House, 1961); and *La Vida* (New York: Random House, 1965). Edward Banfield, with his argument that the lower class is characterized by a "present-time orientation" is perhaps the major popularizer of this view. See *The Unheavenly City* (Boston: Little, Brown & Co., 1970); and *The Unheavenly City Revisited* (Boston: Little, Brown & Co., 1974).

[8] A particularly incisive study of street-corner life is Elliot Liebow, *Tally's Corner* (Boston: Little, Brown & Co., 1967). A thoroughgoing critique of the culture-of-poverty thesis is Charles A. Valentine, *Culture and Poverty* (Chicago: University of Chicago Press, 1968).

the changing conditions or increased opportunities that may occur in their lifetime.[9]

Lewis and other supporters of the culture-of-poverty thesis thus argue that the poor hold and pass on a distinct set of values and aspirations. Some maintain, for example, that the lower class have a different set of "focal concerns"—concerns such as masculinity, toughness, physical prowess, and smartness (the capacity to outwit or con others) and that these values not only constitute a rejection of middle-class values but also tend to lead the lower class into a high rate of delinquency and law breaking.[10]

Such a concept has some serious implications for policy. In education it might suggest an emphasis on cultural enrichment. Or, more pessimistically, it might suggest that little more can be done in lower-class schools than to try to maintain order. Similarly, if lower-class values perpetuate poverty regardless of objective circumstances, then efforts to develop new economic opportunities or provide income guarantees are of little avail. Indeed, it might follow that nothing can be done. Most proponents of the culture-of-poverty thesis would not take such an extreme view, but perhaps more important, there is another school of thought. Some writers reject the culture-of-poverty theory and look to other explanations with quite different policy implications.

In order to understand the critique of and alternative to the culture-of-poverty concept, it is important to keep two distinctions in mind. First, there is a difference between overt behavior on the one hand and values, goals, and aspirations on the other hand. Oscar Lewis, for one, does not distinguish between the former and the latter factors. In fact, most of the seventy traits he identifies as characteristics of the poor—traits such as fatalism, present-time orientation, weak family ties, transient relationships, cynicism, and a preoccupation with masculinity—have to do with behavior. Critics do not deny that lower-class *behavior* differs from middle-class behavior, though they would remind us that lower-class people do not all act alike any more than middle-class people do. But they would argue that middle-class *values and aspirations* are widely shared in even very poor inner-city neighborhoods.

Critics would argue that there is a difference between culture conceived of as a self-perpetuating set of values and culture conceived of as behavior adapted to the actual conditions that are part of life as a poor person. Thus, they do not deny that some of the poor, especially young males, display the kind of behavior that culture-of-poverty theorists link to their theory. What they do argue is that this behavior is situationally deter-

[9] Lewis, *La Vida,* p. xiv.

[10] Walter B. Miller, "Lower-Class Culture as a Generating Milieu of Gang Delinquency," *Journal of Social Issues,* 15 (1958), 5-19. See also, David A. Schulz, *Coming Up Black* (Englewood Cliffs, N.J.: Prentice-Hall, Inc., 1969).

mined. As one sociologist observes, "People respond to the situations—and opportunities—available to them and change their behavior accordingly."[11]

Several empirical studies, using a variety of methods, support the conclusion that the poor share the values and aspirations of the larger society and that their behavior patterns result from an inability to realize those aspirations.[12] Insecurity, a sense of failure, and a loss of self-esteem haunt those unable to improve their material lot in life. Those whose lack of education and job skills confine them to low-paying or irregular employment sense that their wages measure not only the worth of their labor to employers but their worth as persons. They do not like to talk about their work. Even those who have a skill and a trade but do manual labor may feel dissatisfied. Elliot Liebow records a conversation with Tally, a cement finisher. Tally explains why he would like to change stations with another man, even though the other man makes less money:

> It's not the money. [Pause] It's position, I guess. He's got position. When he finish school he gonna be a supervisor. People respect him . . . Thinking about people with position and education gives me a feeling right here [pressing his fingers into the pit of his stomach].[13]

Many of the jobs held by the poor are dead-end jobs, offering little chance for advancement or learning new skills.

> The busboy or dishwasher in a restaurant is not on a job track which, if negotiated skillfully, leads to chef or manager of the restaurant. The busboy or dishwasher who works hard becomes, simply, a hard-working busboy or dishwasher.[14]

No wonder, then, that the commitment to the job is tenuous. Why should it be otherwise? The present-time orientation described in the culture-of-poverty literature is not a lack of concern with the future but a set of disappointed and frustrated feelings born of reading a future that is all too clearly dismal.

Failure in the work world gives rise to a series of predictable responses to family, friends, and life in general. Males earning low wages

[11] Herbert Gans, "Culture and Class in the Study of Poverty," in *On Understanding Poverty,* ed. Daniel P. Moynihan (New York: Basic Books, 1969), p. 206.

[12] Liebow, *Tally's Corner;* Leonard Goodwin, *Do the Poor Want to Work?* (Washington, D.C.: The Brookings Institution, 1972); Lee Rainwater, "The Problem of Lower-Class Culture and Poverty-War Strategy," in *On Understanding Poverty,* Moynihan, pp. 229-59; and *Washington Inner City Poverty Survey,* prepared for the Subcommittee on Employment, Manpower, and Poverty of the Committee on Labor and Public Welfare, United States Senate (Washington, D.C.: Government Printing Office, 1968), pp. 113-21.

[13] See Liebow, *Tally's Corner,* pp. 21-22.

[14] Ibid., p. 63.

and working in low-prestige jobs cope with their failure (that is, failure in terms of conventional standards) by adopting what Liebow calls "shadow values," antimarriage sentiments, and exploitive attitudes toward others (especially females) as a way of hedging, of protecting the sense of self-esteem from failure. But undergirding the shadow values are the conventional standards. The "street-corner" male, Liebow argues, "wants to be publicly, legally married, to support a family and to be head of it, because this is what it is to be a man in our society, whether one lives in a room near the carry-out or in an elegant house in the suburbs."[15]

Far from being callous and unfeeling exploiters of others, the street-corner men observed by Liebow showed a genuine desire to build personal and intimate relationships with others, relationships based on love, friendship, and familial responsibility. That they often failed in these efforts was not from lack of trying, but from trying too hard and pinning too many hopes on relationships that, in an atmosphere of want and failure, are bound to be strained to the breaking point. Surrounding all these efforts is that key failure in the job market. *Early failures and disappointments breed a pattern of retreat and defeat.* Liebow observed of the men on "Tally's corner":

> Convinced of their inadequacies, not only do they not seek out those few better-paying jobs which test their resources, but they actively avoid them, gravitating in a mass to the menial, routine jobs which offer no challenge—and therefore pose no threat—to the already diminished images they have of themselves.[16]

A strong case can be made for the view that behavior traits identified by culture-of-poverty proponents reflect not a separate set of values but a series of adaptations and ego-protecting devices through which economic failure is coped with. To those whose self-esteem is not in question, this behavior pattern may appear to be impulsive and irresponsible, but for those who have tried to look at poverty from the inside out, such behavior is readily understood—and it is understood precisely because it occurs in the shadow of the standards and values of a predominantly middle-class society.

The observers who label this alternative standard the "culture-of-poverty" believe that, once started, it is self-perpetuating even in the face of new and broadened opportunities. Others believe that it is not a genuine culture and that it is maintained only by the lack of opportunity and by the experience of failure. If opportunities were truly broadened, the alternative standard would fade away. Certainly, they argue, experiences of success would do much to change the outlook of the lower class.

[15] Ibid., p. 210. See also Rainwater, "The Lower-Class Culture and Poverty-War Strategy," pp. 237-39.

[16] Ibid., p. 54.

The critics of the culture-of-poverty theory do not suggest that there are no cultural advantages and disadvantages. Clearly some home and community environments are more psychologically supportive than others; some are more intellectually stimulating than others; and perhaps most important of all, some are more conducive to upward mobility than others. Yet, the critics make a convincing case that cultural disadvantages cannot be changed without first making a fundamental change in the pattern of economic opportunities.

POVERTY AND RESTRICTED OPPORTUNITY

While we do not ascribe economic failure to a permanent and ingrained set of lower-class aspirations, goals, and values, we do think that certain disadvantages of a low-income life tend to perpetuate themselves. Reduced chances for a healthy and job-ready body, lack of information, restricted educational opportunities, a lack of access to decent jobs and other economic opportunities—these all-too-common problems make some poverty permanent. In this section we will focus on two related forces that tend to perpetuate economic disadvantage: discrimination and the "dual labor market."

Discrimination

Though much progress has undoubtedly been made under equal opportunity legislation and affirmative action plans, racial and sex discrimination stand as substantial barriers to reducing poverty. Past practices and past attitudes have held many people back from better pay and from more prestigious jobs. But more than that, past discrimination has marked the feelings and attitudes of minorities, undermining their self-confidence and damaging their psychological well-being.

Some of the income "costs" attributable to discrimination rest with the educational system rather than with the job market, but job and pay discrimination themselves have been very substantial factors. In an earlier time, employers made no secret of the fact that they paid dual wage rates. For example, in the 1920s a New York manufacturer placed the following advertisement: "White Workers $24; Colored Workers $20."[17] Although such discrimination is no longer permitted, its consequences are not easily eliminated and blacks still have lower incomes than whites, on the average. The reasons for this gap are debated, but differences in employment rates are surely a key factor.[18]

[17] Quoted in Schiller, *Poverty and Discrimination,* p. 149.

[18] Otis Dudley Duncan, "Inheritance of Poverty or Inheritance of Race," in *On Understanding Poverty,* Moynihan, p. 108.

A look at income data also sheds some light on the feminization of poverty. In 1975, the college-educated woman earned a median income of $11,400 compared to $18,450 for the college-educated man. High-school-educated men outearned high-school-educated women $13,500 to $7,800. To be sure, some of the male-female difference can be attributed to career interruptions for females due to motherhood, but even women who have worked full time since leaving school earn only 75 percent as much as men. As with race, there is an irreducible income gap that can be attributed only to discrimination.

The "Dual Labor Market"

The "dual labor market" ties in with the factor of discrimination. According to some observers, the poor and nonpoor participate in different labor markets. The nonpoor work in a primary market consisting of the better-paying and preferred jobs, which carry with them such benefits as employee rights, job security, and advancement possibilities. By contrast, the poor are confined to a secondary market consisting of low-paying, unsteady, and undesirable jobs characterized by frequent layoffs and discharges, no advancement possibilities, and scant worker rights. Because these jobs are unattractive, voluntary turnover is high. Instead of movement into established positions, there is a great deal of shuttling around from one unattractive job to another. The term "dual labor market" suggests what is the fact, that the two markets are somewhat independent of one another. More jobs in the primary market do not necessarily benefit those in the secondary labor market. Social barriers prevent many potential workers—women, racial minorities, young people, and the poor generally—from competing in the primary market. More than economic factors, the social unacceptability of these groups has been a barrier to their placement in the primary labor market. Race, sex, and shared social beliefs may weigh more heavily than the presence or absence of job-applicable skills in the initial placement of people. Since in many occupations on-the-job training and socialization are more vital to job performance than preentry training, education and formal credentials may serve more as indicators of social acceptability than of job-related skill.

THE WELFARE SYSTEM

Today's welfare programs have severe critics on the left and on the right: too much, too little; too demeaning, too indulgent; too trusting, too bureaucratic; the criticisms run on. Attacking welfare policies is one political exercise that almost everyone engages in.

Welfare policy readily reveals American biases about the poor. In one study comparing welfare policies in the United States, Britain, France, West Germany, and Canada, the United States ranked lowest in social security expenditure as a percentage of gross national product.[19] The United States, moreover, was the last country to introduce such social services as old-age pensions, unemployment insurance, and medical services. Officials are heavily influenced by our tradition of privatism and by beliefs that private enterprise is more efficient than government and that government is inherently wasteful. In short, the American tradition holds that government should have limited responsibilities, especially in the area of social policy. While the popular belief is that welfare recipients are generously supported by taxpayers, the truth is that we provide only a minimal welfare system in a somewhat grudging fashion.

Welfare Myths

Debates over welfare policy are clouded by myth. Perhaps the greatest myth is that welfare recipients are lazy, shiftless, and able-bodied and could get jobs and earn a decent living if they tried. The fact is that of more than 11 million people who get welfare benefits, 8 million are children. Most of the rest are their mothers. According to a Rand Corporation study of welfare recipients in California, 65 percent of the welfare mothers have children under age 6. Nationwide, only 150,000 of the 11 million welfare recipients are men.

How much truth is there in the notion that people on welfare do not want to work? A careful study by Leonard Goodwin of the Brookings Institution demonstrates that people on welfare *do* want to work. Goodwin compared welfare and nonwelfare mothers, welfare and nonwelfare fathers, and welfare and nonwelfare sons. In each instance, the welfare poor and the nonwelfare people had remarkably similar attitudes about the value and importance of work. Goodwin concluded that the ways in which the poor differ from the affluent can be attributed to their different experiences of success in the world.[20]

An even more telling refutation to the myth is the number of poor people who do work. As pointed out earlier, more than half of the heads of poor families are now working. A third work full time! The problem is that a full-time job at the federal minimum wage for a year would leave a family of four well below the Social Security Administration's official poverty line.

Another myth is that cheating is rampant. Considered judgments set the cheating figure at a low rate. The dean of the School of Social Work at

[19] Anthony King, "Ideas, Institutions and the Policies of Governments: a Comparative Analysis," Parts I and II, *British Journal of Political Science* 3 (1973), 291-313, 409-23. That finding was reaffirmed and elaborated in a recent study by Alfred Kahn and Sheila Kamerman of Columbia University's School of Social Work. See *Washington Post*, January 25, 1984.

[20] Goodwin, *Do the Poor Want To Work?* especially pp. 112-18.

Columbia University, for one, estimates that 5 to 10 percent of the people on welfare may be receiving payments for which they are not eligible but that probably half of those are due to administrative error. A Massachusetts study, matching recipients with bank accounts, found that fewer than 1 percent had more assets than the law allowed (*Washington Post*, October 9, 1982). Others estimate a higher figure for cheating, but the experts agree that "cheating among welfare recipients is probably less prevalent than cheating by income-tax payers or lying on expense accounts."[21] Welfare cheating, like income-tax cheating, could be virtually eliminated, but such an effort would be very costly and would invade the privacy of citizens. Sometimes it has been suggested that the government would be better advised to round up absent fathers and make them support their families. In 1976, however, New York City spent $18 million to collect less than $6 million in child-support payments from parents who had absconded.

Another myth is that the poor spend their money on unessential goods. In fact, the poor spend a greater proportion of their income on necessities (about 88 percent of their expenditures are on food, clothing, transportation, shelter, and medical care) than do people with higher incomes.

A final myth is that poor blacks leave states like Georgia, Alabama, and Mississippi, where benefits are low, for places like New York and Detroit because of the greater welfare benefits. A Census Bureau study found that southern blacks who migrated to northern cities were less likely to be on welfare than blacks who had been born in those cities. Employment and earning opportunities seem to be the primary motivation for moving to the cities.

Unfortunately, welfare policy over the years has been influenced more by the myths than by the realities. The result has been a melange of policies that have failed to deal successfully with many of the problems of poverty.

Antipoverty Strategies and the Welfare Program

There are several categories of governmental programs that deal with poverty. One classification scheme lists five kinds of governmental assistance.[22]

1. *Cash transfers* include social security and various public assistance programs that pay cash directly to individuals.

[21] David E. Rosenbaum, "Officials Are Up Against the Myths of Welfare," *New York Times*, May 22, 1977, p. E3.

[22] Plotnick and Skidmore, *Progress Against Poverty*.

2. *In-kind transfers,* such as rent supplements and food stamps, give the poor a particular commodity that policy makers think is important, instead of money directly.
3. *Direct services* such as the legal services programs developed in OEO.
4. *Human resources programs* such as manpower training and the College Work-Study Program are part of the develop-your-way-out-of-poverty approach.
5. *Community participation and development,* such as the Community Action Program of the 1960s give the poor the chance to define their own goals.

Underlying the various categories of antipoverty programs are two broad strategies. One is to provide the poor with a greater income so that they can go into the marketplace and buy the goods and services they need and want. The income provided can be straight monetary assistance, which can be spent for any purpose, *or* it can be a cash benefit tied to a particular purpose, as in the case of rent certificates and education vouchers.

The second approach is the services strategy. Services themselves fall into various categories. Some, such as public-housing or day-care programs, are of direct benefit to poor people, reducing their housing costs or providing child care so parents can work. Others, intended to equip the poor to face the problems of the world better, are of indirect assistance. Job training, counseling and social services casework, planned parenthood advice, consumer training, and adult education are just a few of the examples.

In recent years, the services approach has been severely criticized. First of all, it involves a public bureaucracy and all of the disadvantages of bureaucratically run programs. Second, when services instead of income are provided, the poor have fewer alternatives; they are limited to using the government program or doing without. Third, many of the indirect services strike the poor as paternalistically inspired—as keeping the poor in tutelage. Fourth, some services are based on faulty assumptions, as when the poor are trained for jobs that don't exist.

In attempting to assure the poor an adequate income, commensurate with their own needs and with the needs of the larger society, the government has tried and continues to try a little of everything. One policy issue, then is how shall we shift the emphasis—toward straight income guarantees, toward more in-kind transfers, or toward greater service? Public-assistance programs pose the issue most sharply.

Public Assistance

There are numerous public-assistance programs: Supplemental Security Income (aid to the aged, blind, and disabled), Aid to Families with Dependent Children (AFDC), and General Assistance (emergency aid for people not covered by other programs). In addition, income maintenance includes such social insurance programs as Social Security, Unemployment

Compensation, and Workmen's Compensation. We will center our discussion on AFDC because that is the program most people think of when the word "welfare" is used, and because it is the most controversial and widely criticized of all the public-assistance programs.

AFDC came into being as part of the Social Security Act of 1935. Originally, the federal government paid half of a state's costs; now it pays up to 83 percent. Benefits are limited to families with children lacking parental support due to death, continued absence, physical or mental incapacity, and in some states, the father's unemployment. Children must be under eighteen (or eighteen to twenty-one and in school).

The fifty states make their own determinations of the amount of money needed by families with dependent children. Monthly needs are calculated on the basis of a family of four (one adult, with three children). Eighteen states pay the figure that they determine as the need, but the other thirty-two states make reductions from these basic figures. For example, AFDC payments vary from an average of $157 per month for a one-parent family in three of eight southern states to $345 per month in the five Great Lake states. Within these two groups the extremes are $96 per month in Mississippi and $462 per month in Michigan.

The amount of state discretion is enormous. For example, in the 1960s, AFDC was amended to include families whose heads are unemployed. State participation, however, is discretionary, and only twenty-eight states participate in this unemployed-fathers program. While the program's intent was to keep poor families together, the failure of twenty-two states to participate negates its intent in a large part of the nation. States also determine who is eligible for AFDC benefits and how much earnings recipients can deduct in calculating the gross income figure that determines the level of benefit.

The federal share of each state's AFDC costs varies with the state's per capita income. The thirteen states with the highest levels of per capita income receive the minimum federal percentage of 50 percent. States with lower per capita incomes receive higher percentages of assistance; the federal government, for example, pays 79 percent of Mississippi's AFDC costs.

City governments are also affected by the widespread disparities in the program. Some localities have significant welfare responsibilities, while others have none. About half the states administer welfare themselves; there is no local administrative responsibility. In the other states, local units (sometimes cities, sometimes counties) are charged with administering welfare programs. In these states, city governments typically share the costs with the state. Again, there is considerable variation in the local share because each state makes its own determination. The local share might be a quarter or higher of the total welfare costs, or it might be 5 percent, or it might be nothing at all—depending on the state. For example, Baltimore is required to pay a relatively small share of welfare costs (less than 10 percent) but San Francisco is required to pay a much larger share (about 25 percent). New York's requirement is even higher; thus, that city's welfare obligations make a significant drain on its resources.

Over the years, AFDC has been changed frequently but never radically. The 1962 amendment to AFDC permitted the federal government to pay a three-quarters share of the salaries of public-assistance caseworkers engaged in giving services to individual clients (previously, the federal share had been 50 percent). The assumption behind this cash incentive was that problems of economic dependency could be alleviated by more and better social casework. The goals were small caseloads for the workers and many services for the clients. The services concept was and is somewhat fuzzy, however. State-provided services included everything from prenatal care to planning for a mother's future to help in child care to help with legal problems.

Several years of experience with the services strategy did nothing to reduce the welfare rolls. Indeed, the number of AFDC recipients rose dramatically during the 1960s. In 1967, Congress passed the Work Incentive Program (WIN), which requires "appropriate" welfare recipients to participate in WIN (job-training program) or face the loss of welfare payments. Who is "appropriate"? Unemployed fathers are the first priority. Teen-age children in AFDC families who are not in school and welfare mothers with no preschool children are other high-priority categories. The assumption is that physically able welfare recipients can be trained and/or educated and can move into the labor force.

WELFARE REFORM

Criticisms of the AFDC program are rampant. One target is cost, which increased tremendously in recent years. AFDC payment costs rose especially fast (260 percent) in the 1960s decade. Another closely related criticism is the jump in the number of AFDC recipients. There were many reasons for the increase; the major point, however, is that an increased number of welfare recipients indicates that we are not solving the basic problems involved.

High administrative costs also come in for attack. By one estimate, the administrative costs total 18.5 percent of the benefits paid (the comparable figure for Social Security is 3 percent),[23] most of it spent for eligibility determination, very little for counseling and other social services. Though the pattern varies with the state, as much as 75 percent of staff time is spent on eligibility determination.

[23] Williamson et al., *Strategies Against Poverty in America,* p. 49.

The state regulations surrounding welfare are both numerous and harsh. Families face restrictions not only on income they can earn but on property, insurance, and other assets. Since most restrictions are state imposed, they vary from area to area. In Georgia, welfare recipients cannot own a car less than four years old. In Maryland, total assets including not only money but also insurance and equity in a car are limited to $1000, while in Arkansas their car can't be worth more than $300. Some states limit the amount of equity in a house that welfare recipients can have. In Alabama that amount is $2,500. Regulations are quite detailed. Minnesota allows life insurance up to $500 in cash value. Whether intended or not, the effect of many regulations is to discourage ownership and thrift, traits that the average citizen would want to encourage among the poor. A divorced or widowed woman with small children may, if she owns a house and a car, be ineligible for aid, even though she has no income. To become eligible, she would have to sell her house and car and spend that money. Some restrictions are national. Recent proposals call for restricted opportunities to share living quarters with the extended family.

AFDC has been criticized because of the social stigma attached to being a welfare recipient. In this regard, it is worth noting the changes in clientele since the program began in the 1930s. Then, more than 30 percent of the recipient families were headed by widows. Today, less than 6 percent are headed by widows; in most cases, the father is absent because of desertion, divorce, or separation, or because the father and mother were never married. For most Americans, widows are viewed as deserving poor, who should receive society's largesse. But with widows now making up such a small portion of today's AFDC heads of household, welfare recipients are now viewed as undeserving, as loose women who are rewarded by society for fooling around. One U.S. senator referred to them as "brood mares." Yet most serious analysts of the welfare system believe that such thinking confuses cause and effect. They argue that the AFDC program contributes to family instability and even encourages desertion, since in twenty-two states (as we noted earlier) a family with an unemployed father is not eligible for the program.

AFDC has also been criticized because it discourages employment among recipients. Money earned from a part-time job, for example, reduces assistance. Perhaps the most tragic criticism of the system is that many needy people are not included; it covers only those persons who fall into selected categories. As a consequence, some working families have even less income than those on AFDC. The program has also been attacked because it encourages long-term dependency on public support. The argument that we are creating future generations with a welfare mentality is disturbing but in fact most recipients are short-term clients.

Finally, there are two basic criticisms. First, benefit levels are simply not adequate to provide a decent standard of living. Even after recipients are paid, they remain poor. Second, and this criticism was noted earlier but is worth reiterating: there is tremendous inequity because of the variation in benefits among the states. While there are differences in the cost of living, there is no satisfactory reason for the wide disparities in the program.

Work Reform: the Untried Alternative

Underlying the problem of income assistance is another, even more complicated, problem—the job market itself. The analysis of welfare policy cannot go very far without raising questions about the nature of low-income jobs. Unemployment is one problem. But beyond that is the ticklish question of the secondary labor market—the question of who shall do society's "dirty" work. Sociologist Herbert Gans has observed that proposals to provide income guarantees are surrounded by a fear "that the people who do the underpaid and dirty work in our society will walk off their jobs and leave these functions unfilled."[24] Welfare reform, then, is intertwined with the issue of work. While many welfare recipients themselves are unemployable, the dependent family comes about, in part, because of the nature of the job market. Some families are abandoned because the father in them cannot get jobs that are steady and not demeaning and pay a living wage. Income sufficiency, *family stability*, and even social health itself depend greatly upon the availability of good jobs. Research has shown, for example, that social pathology in the ghetto is more highly correlated with the proportion of unskilled workers in an area than with unemployment.[25] And psychologist Kenneth Clark put the blame squarely on the "menial, low-income jobs held by most ghetto residents."[26]

One of the dilemmas welfare reformers always confront is the issue of where to set the benefit level. If the benefit level is low, some family needs will go unmet. But, if the benefit level is high, then people may leave the secondary labor market because the jobs are so unattractive. Income supplements for low-wage earners are, of course, one way of upgrading "dirty" work, but they are also government subsidies of low-paying employers. Supplements might provide employers with a disincentive for wage increases. There are other aspects to the problem too. Many jobs offer no vacation time, no retirement plan, nor any other fringe benefits. Indeed, the benefits of some jobs are so few that, because of medicaid and other services, welfare recipients are eligible for, a given family may be better off

[24] Herbert J. Gans, "Income Grants and 'Dirty Work,' " *The Public Interest,* no. 6 (Winter 1967), p. 110.

[25] Ibid., p. 111.

[26] Clark, *Dark Ghetto,* p. 34.

on welfare than with a salaried income. (Less rigid categories of eligibility would ease that problem, however.)

Particularly with reform moving more and more in the direction of requirements for welfare recipients (even the mothers of school-age children) to go into the job market, the nature of job opportunities is a matter of urgent concern. With persistently high unemployment rates, there is a tendency to view the problem as solely one of the availability of jobs. But real success in making a large proportion of the society economically self-sufficient depends upon making jobs not only available but also more attractive. So far, even generous-minded welfare reformers have gone no further than proposing income supplements for the working poor. But what about advancement or on-the-job training opportunities? What, too, about those jobs that offer no fringe benefits? What about the idea of a system of family allowances that applies to wage earners? Sociologist Nathan Glazer argues that such a plan "would reflect family needs in the same way that take-home pay is now affected by numbers of dependents through the withholding of income tax." He adds:

> The aim would be not only to provide assistance to those with larger families, but to give value and meaning to work, because it is through work that this assistance comes.[27]

Glazer makes the interesting argument that in this country we have a dual labor market *and* a triple system of support. The three forms of support consist of

1. the good job—one in the primary labor market;
2. the poor job with no benefits—a job in the secondary market; and
3. welfare, a form of maintenance with a low cash income but more benefits than the secondary labor market provides.

Welfare decision makers operate under substantial pressure to nudge people into the secondary labor market (that is, into doing "dirty" work) by making welfare unattractive. A by-product of this system is that some people, even those who cannot enter the labor market, are punished by low payments, extensive regulation, and demeaning requirements such as work-registration procedures. Instead of more extensive regulation of welfare recipients, Glazer suggests the alternative strategy of making poor jobs more attractive. We think it is an idea well worth pursuing.

[27] Nathan Glazer, "Reform Work, Not Welfare," *The Public Interest,* no. 40 (Summer 1975), p. 8.

CONCLUSION

Poverty remains a controversial issue. The poor continue to be thought of as childlike and irresponsible—in need of regulation and guidance. Consequently, there is widespread fear that money given to the poor would be squandered on nonessential items and that children in particular would suffer.

Such devices as rent certificates and food stamps bypass that problem—they give the poor the means to buy in the private market but restrict their purchases to the subsidized items. There is resistance to extending that idea, but attacks on welfare bureaucracy remain politically popular. Fundamental reform remains difficult, however, because there is no consensus on what changes to make. Further, welfare is interrelated with other problems.

Welfare aid, from the early English Poor Law down to the present, is closely linked with work incentives. The fear runs deep that the poor would rather receive governmental assistance than work. In some ways, this fear is unjustified. Most of the poor do want to work, and above all, they want to be self-supporting. On the other hand, so long as the jobs available pay low wages, provide few fringe benefits, offer no advancement, and carry low status, this fear is not entirely unfounded. Yet, few welfare reformers attack the problem by designing a more attractive labor market. That would be even more difficult than restructuring the welfare program. The dilemma decision makers have encountered is one of trying to provide needy families with adequate income assistance but at a level that does not compete with low-paying jobs. Some policy makers have thus become interested in formulas for supplementing the wages of those who earn meager incomes. Such income supplements would not remove all of the barriers to a decent and respectable economic position, but they would be a start.

SUGGESTED READINGS

EHRENREICH, BARBARA, and FRANCES FOX PIVEN. "The Feminization of Poverty." *Dissent* (Spring 1984), 162-170.

GOODWIN, LEONARD. *Do the Poor Want to Work?* Washington, D.C.: Brookings Institution, 1972.

______. *Causes and Cures of Welfare*. Lexington, MA: Lexington Books, 1983.

HARRINGTON, MICHAEL. *The New American Poverty*. New York: Holt, Rinehart and Winston, 1984.

KREFETZ, SHARON PERLMAN. *Welfare Policy Making and City Politics*. New York: Praeger Publishers, 1976.

LEWIS, OSCAR. *La Vida*. New York: Random House, 1965.

LIEBOW, ELLIOT. *Tally's Corner*. Boston: Little, Brown & Co., 1967.

MOYNIHAN, DANIEL P., ed. *On Understanding Poverty*. New York: Basic Books, 1969.

PATTERSON, JAMES T. *America's Struggle Against Poverty, 1900-1980*. Cambridge, MA: Harvard University Press, 1981.

ROSSI, PETER H., and WALTER WILLIAMS, eds. *Evaluating Social Programs*. New York: Seminar Press, 1972.

SCHULZ, DAVID A. *Coming Up Black*. Englewood Cliffs, N.J.: Prentice-Hall, 1969.

SCHWARZ, JOHN E. *America's Hidden Success: A Reassessment of Twenty Years of Public Policy*. New York: Norton, 1984.

SHEEHAN, SUSAN. *A Welfare Mother*. New York: New American Library, Mentor Books, 1977.

VALENTINE, CHARLES A. *Culture and Poverty*. Chicago: University of Chicago Press, 1968.

WAXMAN, CHAIM I. *The Stigma of Poverty*. New York: Pergamon Press, 1983.

chapter 16

Urban Transportation Policy: Politics and Technology

Transportation policy means many different things to different people. From the viewpoint of an official in the Department of Transportation, it may mean a continuing search for the elusive "balanced" transportation concept. For an officer of the American Automobile Association, transportation policy means seeing to it that highways and roads keep on getting the largest share of federal, state, and local government funds available for transportation improvements. For the owner of a business in a declining downtown neighborhood, transportation policy may mean traffic engineering and improved public transportation that will revitalize the area and help business to pick up. The users of public transportation have quite different perspectives. For them, transportation policy is likely to come through not as a policy but as a confusing mix of incompatible bureaucratic statements, activities, and behaviors that have resulted in high fares, poor service, decrepit equipment, and a belief that no one really cares about the public transportation consumer.

The fact that each of these perspectives is at least partly correct highlights the confusing nature of transportation policy in the United States today. The conflicts among them help to explain the low estate of public transportation—in attractiveness, efficiency, and level of use. Public transportation is caught up in the controversies and crises over service delivery that beset the rest of urban America. Beyond that, the transportation field has its own unique mixture of interests, actors, issues and problems that make it a fascinating and complex case study. In this chapter, we will be using the issue of public transportation—both the making of policy and the delivery of services—to illustrate many of the themes we have already developed.

First, we will sketch the sequence of events that have brought about the crisis in urban transportation. Then, we will try to describe some of the mind-sets—in particular the heavy reliance on technology fostered by federal policy—that have dominated efforts to revitalize public transportation. Next, we will offer a case study in citizen participation, which will suggest that the poor are as powerless as ever when they oppose the combined forces of technical experts and public officials. Finally, we suggest some ways to improve urban public transportation.

SOME PERSPECTIVES ON URBAN PUBLIC TRANSPORTATION

For most metropolitan dwellers, enjoying the benefits of urban transportation services is a simple matter of walking out of their suburban homes, getting into their automobiles, and driving where they want to go with minimal delay caused by congestion. Yet, in the past several years, the realization has grown that transportation in the contemporary metropolis must be more than auto-mobility.

President Kennedy's transportation message to Congress in 1962, calling for a system of good urban transportation, balanced between the use of private automobiles and modern mass transportation, signaled a rebirth of public transportation after a half century of decline. As diagnoses were made of civil disorders in the mid-1960s, one conclusion was that the lack of mobility for inner-city residents—especially their isolation from the new job market on the surburban ring—was an important cause of discontent. Out of these and other concerns came the passage of federal and state legislation designed to improve public transportation.

One obvious villain in the piece was the love affair between the suburb and the automobile. Though the discovery that the two had caused significant changes in urban development and life styles was made in the 1960s, the process had been going on since the 1920s. The percentage of central-city residents working in the central business district (CBD) and using public transportation to get to work fell from 66 percent in 1900 to 30 percent in 1960 and 22 percent in 1970. By 1960, only 15 percent of suburb-to-city commuters used public transportation, and by 1970 the number had declined to 11 percent.

Conventional wisdom places the entire blame for the decline of public transportation on the automobile. But as transportation engineers, planners, and public officials have known for years, and as the general public is beginning to understand, there is no simple cause-and-effect relationship between auto usage and the sorry state of public transportation. Like so many other urban problems, the ones affecting public transportation spring from an overwhelmingly complex array of decisions and nondecisions. Each of a host of policy choices and personal choices has played its part—land-use plans or the lack of them, residential and employment location, views on the good life, economic subsidies to some forms of transportation and not others, the failure to assign to each mode of transportation its full social and economic costs, the preference for a suburban life style, as well as the preference for the private automobile over public transportation.

Suburbanization is the main proximate cause of the malaise of public transportation. Its dispersed residential patterns, employment sites, and travel patterns make it almost impossible for traditional fixed-route, fixed-schedule, downtown-oriented public transportation systems to compete with the private automobile. Fifty years ago when the most common journey to work was a fairly short trip from a central-city neighborhood to a central business district (CBD) location, the bulk of all such trips were made on public transportation. Today CBD-oriented trips make up an ever smaller fraction of area travel; and suburb-to-suburb travel and central-city-to-suburb travel make up an ever larger proportion.

Transportation and communication technologies now make it possible to stretch the distances between residence, work, school, recreation, shopping, medical services, and other activities to a degree not even remotely possible at the turn of the century. What this means is that traditional CBD-oriented public transportation is no longer geared to take people where they want to go.

Urban population dispersion is so powerful a force that transportation systems can only adapt; they cannot reverse the trend. As the transportation systems focused on downtown become less important, patronage on these systems declines, and the demand for more and better roads on which to travel in an automobile increases. If one accepts the premise that transportation of any kind is never an end in itself but merely a means for achieving some greater goal, then the argument for shaping metropolitan development to suit the capabilities of mass transit does not stand up very well. A more realistic and achievable goal is to reshape public transportation to serve societal, community, and individual goals.

Not only is this approach more politically and socially desirable, it has the added advantage of applying measures other than simple economic efficiency to decisions about critical urban services. Even though urban public transportation is a means to an end—to get to and from home, work, school, medical services, recreation, and so on—we tend to judge it as though it were an end in itself. Therefore, we use as yardsticks of transportation effectiveness a narrowly conceived cost-benefit analysis—the number of riders carried per miles traveled and the number of riders that can be carried in a given travel corridor per hour of travel time.

Many of the recent studies and demonstration projects clearly show that the benefits of public transportation are external to the transportation systems; they flow to society. How can you measure in direct short-term dollars the worth of public transportation that brings inner-city unemployed to suburban job sites? On what budget line do you credit the role of public transportation in saving the aesthetic quality of an urban area? Whose profit-and-loss statement credits revitalizing a central business district? How easy is it to trace the energy conserved through mass transit? This does not mean that we should treat public transportation as only a social good and not be concerned with its costs or efficiency, but it does mean that public transportation must be viewed as a public service and not as a profit-making venture. Were economic efficiency to be the sole criterion, public transportation in most areas could not survive a comparison with the automobile. Yet it cannot be abandoned without serious social consequences.

For public transportation, as for most issues, public policy in the United States is the product of incremental decision making: new policies or solutions tend to be minor variations on what is already being done. In any case, nobody is going to scuttle a road network that has been built over more than a century. So any new system of mass transportation, be it buses, rapid rail transit, or some of the more exotic personal rapid transit technologies, must fit into an existing transportation system in which there is already a big investment. What we need to do is develop transportation in a way that melds—economically, socially, politically, and technologically—with what already exists. And that is not an impossible objective.

A NATIONAL TRANSPORTATION POLICY?

One problem that proponents of mass transportation cite repeatedly is the absence, at the federal level, of any comprehensive, coherent statement as to just what our national posture toward urban mass transit is or ought to be. A favorite topic of people who are interested in mass transportation systems is the piecemeal approach that the federal government has taken. If only, they note with frustration, urban public transportation were blessed with the singularity of purpose and the budget that put a man on the moon. However, if advocates of a national urban transportation policy are seeking a simple, relatively fixed statement or set of decisions that will once and for all define the goals and objectives of urban transportation, then they are bound to be disappointed. That is not going to happen.

Observers agree, then, that the federal approach to mass transportation has been piecemeal, an amalgam of approaches that attempt to respond to a given set of pressures or crises that often work at cross-purposes with each other. Decisions are made, action is undertaken, money is spent, rail systems are built, and freeways get constructed without anyone's determining exactly what the purpose of an urban transportation system ought to be. The federal urban transportation effort consists of a long and expensive series of programs—the Interstate Highway System; federal research, development, demonstration, and technical studies; and grants to build experimental personal transit systems. The net effect is not a policy but a set of compartmentalized policies developed at different times, at various levels of public responsibility, by different interests and actors, concerned with different issues and outcomes, interested in different modes of travel, and administered by different techniques.

One of the first statements of policy on urban transportation came with the passage of the Transportation Act of 1940, which called for the improvement and development of all modes of transportation—including rail, highway, and water. This concept of "balanced transportation" has become the much-sought-after but elusive solution to our current transportation woes. Perhaps the most important piece of transportation legislation ever enacted was the Federal Highway Act of 1956. The most visible part of that act is the Interstate Highway System of almost 40,000 miles that criss-crosses the United States and has made automobile travel safe, swift, and convenient. From a policy perspective, the most significant feature of that act was the creation of the Highway Trust Fund, which earmarks revenues from taxes on the sale of gasoline, tires, and auto parts and supplies for the construction and improvement of the interstate network. As a result, the highway lobby, with funds ever available, can pursue its aims without having to worry about how new highways will be paid for. No other public-works project in the history of the United States has been given such special financial treatment.

While there is no similar "money tree" for public and mass transit, backers of the nation's public transportation systems have succeeded in getting federal and state dollars allocated to public transportation. What began as a relatively modest program in 1961 to prevent private bus and rail operators from going out of business grew to the point where former President Carter's last budget, for fiscal 1982, called for some $3.75 billion to be spent on all transit, with $1.11 billion to be spent on operating subsidies. However, President Reagan's budgets have initiated cuts and called for the elimination of all operating subsidies by 1985.

There is no doubt that public transportation receives less federal funds than do highways, but public transportation enjoyed great success in getting favorable legislation passed and significant sums appropriated during the 1970s. A major breakthrough occurred when the Highway Act of 1973 was passed. That legislation made $3 billion available for transit aid in addition to the $3.1 billion that had been authorized under the Urban Mass Transportation Assistance Act of 1970. In addition to, and perhaps more importantly than the money provided, the 1973 legislation allows the Highway Trust Fund dollars to be used for public transportation purposes. Given the symbolic importance and the historic sanctity of the Highway Trust Fund, making it available for mass transportation purposes proved to be a relatively easy process. By 1973, the pro-transit lobby had become influential. In mid-1973, as funds for the highway system were running out, pro-highway forces found that the transit lobby was stronger than they had anticipated; thus they would have to compromise if any highway funds were to be approved by Congress that year.

As important as opening up the Highway Trust Fund was from a symbolic perspective, perhaps the long-term importance of the legislation is that it gives local governments more independence in determining the kind of transportation system that they want for their communities. Historically, the federal government made highway and not mass transit funds available to local communities. With the passage of the 1973 legislation, local governments could now choose between highways and other transportation improvements all funded out of the Highway Trust Fund.

After successfully cracking open the Highway Trust Fund, there was one other major item on the transit lobby's shopping list; operating subsidies. With the federal government covering 80 percent of the cost of acquiring capital equipment and two-thirds of the cost of research and demonstration projects, the next major item was to get Washington to assist in covering the huge deficits that were being experienced in the day-to-day operations of public transportation systems. While costs vary from city to city, daily operating costs, which are primarily personnel costs, make up approximately 80 percent of a transit system's operating budget. As transit employees negotiated better and better contracts, as oil prices tripled the costs of diesel fuel, as new buses got poorer mileage due to federal safety and handicapped-accessibility requirements, and as transit systems found that they were unable to increase fares to keep pace with increasing costs, operating deficits skyrocketed. The Urban Mass Transportation Assistance Act of 1974 provided a program of federal operating aid based on population and population density to all urbanized areas in the United States. Local officials could decide whether to use the federal money for capital improvements, in which case the federal share was 80 percent of cost, or operating aid, in which case federal aid was 50 percent of cost.

While transit interests will argue that urban areas are finally getting their fair share of federal transportation money, it must be pointed out that even with the billions spent on mass transportation in the 1970s, less than 3 percent of all daily trips in the United States are made by public transportation. The 3 percent includes journey to work trips, by far the largest single generator of all public transportation travel. If work trips were excluded from the calculation, public transportation in the United States would provide less than 1 percent of all the daily travel of U.S. citizens.

Even with federal money available, the future of mass transportation remains clouded. Most people believe that public transportation on a bus or an aging commuter rail car is not particularly dependable, comfortable, or attractive. As likely as not, buses or trains will come late, if they come at all; they may be crowded, forcing some people to stand for all or part of their journey; seating is uncomfortable and not very spacious; and in general, public transportation is to be avoided if at all possible.

In the language of the economists, public transportation is an "inferior good," which people abandon as soon as it is possible for them to do so. People willingly wait several weeks to get new cars in the colors of their choice with the options that they most desire. They enthusiastically flock to the expressways at an average of 1.3 passengers per automobile. They patiently waited in gasoline lines for up to three hours or paid blackmarket prices to get gasoline during the Arab oil embargo of 1973. They regularly endure commuter traffic problems. But they are unwilling to walk two blocks to a bus stop, transfer to another vehicle to complete their journey, or accept any of the other inconveniences associated with using mass transportation. Because of the American love affair with the automobile, public policy makers have assumed that everyone who wants or needs a car has access to one, and policy decisions have been made that are consistent with that assumption. The consequence of this assumption is that, for most Americans in most cities, there is no real choice between public and private transportation. The corollary is that some proportion of our metropolitan population is trapped by a lack of mobility. Yet urban travel in this country is auto and highway dominated and in all likelihood will remain that way for years to come.

TECHNOLOGY

If we have the technological capacity to deliver whatever we need—and the consensus is that we do—then why is it we cannot point to a single example in this country of a properly balanced system of private and public urban transportation? Technologists blame "politics." Others point an accusing finger at the technologists and charge them with forgetting that it is real people that transportation systems are to serve. There can be no doubt that most recent efforts to improve public transportation have sought to apply glamorous technologies even though there is strong evidence that political, social, economic, and other people-oriented issues are more important than hardware in determining the relative success of a transportation system. Certainly the federal government has tilted the process toward technological solutions. In public transportation, as in many other spheres, the federal government has research and development money to influence the choices of state and local government. And the disbursement of federal dollars has been heavily slanted toward hardware, with the two largest chunks of federal money tagged for capital grants and technical-studies programs.

Local governments have found that federal dollars are available only for certain purposes, generally for new buses and rail transit vehicles, and only very limited funds for experiments in service improvement that do not focus on hardware and technology. Until the passage of the National Mass Transportation Assistance Act of 1974, no funds were available for operating deficits. In sum, by its choice of what to subsidize, the federal government has actually encouraged local governments to take a hardware approach to the solution of their problems while ignoring the social aspects of the problem.

The space program had its impact, too. The "discovery" of the problems of mass transportation coincided with the nation's efforts to put a man on the moon. The belief that technology, especially aerospace technology, could solve the nation's transportation problems reached its logical conclusion during the 1973 debates in Congress over opening up the Highway Trust Fund for rail rapid-transit investment. During those debates, a peculiar coalition of mass transit advocates, environmental interests, and aerospace interests persuaded Congress to allow some highway funds to be diverted for mass transportation. As space exploration lost its preeminence among the nation's priorities, aerospace firms were looking for ways to stay alive. Their performance record in providing mass transit hardware has been anything but enviable, however. The fact is that technology cannot be transferred directly from aerospace, or from anything else, to mass transportation. The problems of mass transportation are unique, and they call for unique solutions. Nevertheless, the notion that there can be a quick technical fix to mobility problems remains with us.

The Urban Mass Transportation Administration (UMTA), the federal agency currently in charge of spending federal money, is still enamored of the rapid-transit systems with their complex and sophisticated technology. In many instances, new technologies seem to be chosen for their wave-of-the-future aura rather than for everyday usefulness. A minor but interesting illustration of this mentality is the choice of speedometers for the Atlanta and San Francisco rapid-transit systems. Instead of simple speedometers, like the ones used on every passenger car and bus, the new systems have direct-digital readout instruments. While such instruments are certainly more advanced than traditional ones, they are also more complex, expensive, and prone to failure. Ironically, they are installed on vehicles that are operated automatically from a central computer and have human attendants on board only as observers and to be able to take over in emergencies.

BART and METRO, Two Cases in Point

The rail rapid-transit systems built in San Francisco (BART) and Washington, D.C. (METRO) are classic examples of transportation planning's fascination with technology and the resulting limitations that such fascination can bring. BART's planners were not content to simply try and provide a way that was better than buses or private cars to get to work in San Francisco. BART, its early proponents said, is to be "more than a rapid-transit system. It is the partial embodiment of a bold concept for a better way of urban living." Similar claims were made in Washington, D.C. for the METRO system whose original costs were projected at $2.1 billion and will easily top $6 billion if the full 100-mile system is built. When judged by the huckster-like projections made for it, BART has been a dismal failure. It serves only about 2 percent of all trips made within the three county transit district and only 5 percent of all rush-hour trips. It carries about half of the 285,000 daily patrons originally estimated, at fares 475 percent higher than projected.[1] At least half of BART's riders had been bus riders. BART's planners thought that if commuters were provided a high quality, attractive, fast mass-transit system, they would willingly leave their cars at home and ride the train. But BART has had virtually no impact on reducing automobile congestion nor have there been any discernible changes attributable to BART in the auto-using habits of the people of the Bay region.

BART's difficulties can be attributed to three basic problems, one of which is easy to fix, one will take longer, and one problem is virtually insoluble. The easiest problem to fix is the mechanical and electronic. As equipment becomes more reliable so that BART trains run on time and people can depend on them, patronage may improve. Similarly, if and when feeder buses and parking lots in the suburbs are developed to the point where they enhance access to BART, some bus and car users will likely become BART riders. But at this point, there is really no way of knowing when these changes will take place, nor how many people will give up cars and buses for the train.

The intermediate problem, and one that all transit planners face, is how to break up the love affair between the American and his or her car. Despite all of the shortcomings and expense, Americans still would prefer to drive to work in their own cars than travel in any other way. Even in the 1970s, gasoline lines and large increases in gasoline prices caused few

[1] Melvin M. Webber, "The BART Experience—What Have We Learned?" *The Public Interest*, No. 45, Fa-1 (1976), p. 104.

Americans to leave their cars at home and ride the bus or train. Now, of course, it must be noted that many commuters have no choices. They live in cities, or more likely suburban areas, in which there is no public or mass transportation. But even in those cities and metropolitan areas where there are good bus systems or commuter-rail or rapid-rail systems, people still prefer to drive their cars. A Gallup poll taken in 1980 showed that if gasoline reached $2.00 per gallon, half of the auto commuters said they would still drive to work. We must note that even these estimates of potential public transportation usage are probably too high. Gasoline prices are already at the $3.00 per gallon mark in Japan, West Germany, and other industrially advanced countries, and auto usage is still considerable (though less than in the United States). Rather than switch to public transportation where it is possible to do so, more people are likely to park or sell the gas-guzzler and replace it with a gas-sipper. High gasoline prices and the memory of gasoline lines have caused some people to leave the car at home and use mass transportation. But, it is unlikely that gasoline costs alone will be the catalyst to cause people to start swarming to BART and its related systems.

As one die-hard auto commuter observed:

> We drive because we really want the freedom to move about at will—Alone.
>
> We fundamentally choose wheels for the same reason Greta Garbo chose sunglasses. Ve vant to be alone.
>
> We prefer private hassles to the public ones, and the illusion of control to the feeling of being controlled. But more than anything else, the automobile is our isolation booth, our own piece of solitary confinement . . .
>
> Mass transportation is for people, yes; but I'm afraid that the pollution on four wheels is for a person. Until they turn subways into isolation booths, or separate us with magnetic field suits, I think most of us will choose to go on paying through the hose—for a mobile room of our own.[2]

The third BART problem, and the one that is not susceptible to solution, is its basic design. The values it maximizes are those that commuters and potential transit riders value least, while the values it minimizes are those that commuters value most. BART's designers decided that what car commuters wanted most were high speed, comfort, ambience, and a downtown destination. Thus, the system was designed to maximize those goals. It maximized them by designing an aesthetically pleasing system, by running trains frequently enough so that waiting time at a station is relatively short, and by operating trains that are capable of reaching seventy miles per hour between station stops. But high speed requires that stations be placed relatively far apart. A long distance between stations means that

[2] Ellen Goodman, "Solitude and the Solo Commuter," *The Washington Post*, April 10, 1978, p. A-23.

relatively few people can walk to a station; thus a network of feeder buses and parking lots are required if people are to get to BART. Given the dependance of BART on buses and cars to get people to the trains, it is surprising to discover that virtually no serious thought was given to establishing a feeder-bus network or building sufficient parking lots in the suburbs. In essence, BART planners conceptualized the system as one that was independent of its surrounding environment. Thus, many people simply find BART hard to get to. One study of the Bay Area found that 50 percent of those people who did not use BART but who lived near the system and worked in San Francisco, Oakland, or Berkeley did not do so because it was "impossible" for them to get to work on the system. While BART treats its patrons rather well once they get to a station or on a train, ridership would be higher if the system were easier to get to and if its route structure were more extensive.

In Washington, D.C., only part of the proposed one hundred miles of the METRO system is completed and operating, and delays in opening additional sections have been common. While not experiencing the technical problems of BART, METRO too has had more than its share of operating and mechanical problems. At one point, the escalating costs of METRO construction prompted the Washington Center for Metropolitan Studies to call for halting construction when the lines within the city and close-by suburbs were completed. Instead of building high-cost rail lines into the suburbs where population and employment densities did not warrant such expensive transit, express bus service could be developed and provided at far less cost.[3] Whatever the objective merits of that proposal, various transportation officials remain committed to the entire rail system.

On the plus side, METRO has been quite successful in its ability to attract riders. Daily ridership has reached approximately 250,000. While a considerable portion of those riders are commuters, METRO is also increasingly popular as an intracity transportation mode. Federal workers can get from one part of town to another as they attend to interoffice matters; business managers can go from their offices to their favorite restaurants via METRO; and Washington's ever-present tourists have added a ride on METRO to the list of things to do in the nation's capital. As a result, while METRO is providing many rides per day, like BART it has had no dramatic impact on traffic congestion. There is realistically no way of knowing to what extent METRO will cause people to leave their cars at home and take the train until the suburban lines are operating and the full regional system is in place.

METRO supporters point out that their system is quite different from BART. While BART has thirty-four stations spaced over a seventy-one-

[3] Henry Bain, *New Directions for METRO, Lessons from the BART Experience* (Washington, D.C.: The Washington Center for Metropolitan Studies, 1976).

mile system averaging 2.1 miles per station, METRO will have eighty-seven stations over its one hundred-mile length if the entire system is built. Obviously, with stations less than 1.2 miles apart, access to the system should be much better in Washington than in San Francisco. In San Francisco there was little serious planning of feeder-bus lines or sufficient parking lots, while in Washington both METRO and the bus system are part of the same region-wide transit authority, thus making inter-modal coordination more likely. Finally, METRO supporters point out that since the area of the national capital is much larger than that of San Francisco and has more intense traffic problems, METRO makes much more sense than does BART.

Despite the fact that it is possible to provide equivalent transportation at far lower capital and operating costs than either BART or METRO, those systems have been built. As one critic of BART has said:

> But in the long run, say in fifty years, when the bonds will have been retired, when everyone will regard BART as just another built-in feature of the region, rather like Golden Gate Parks, perhaps no one will question whether BART should have been either built or abandoned. It will then be regarded as a handy thing to have, a valuable facilitator of trips that would not otherwise be made by the elderly and the young, a blessing that enriches the quality of Bay Area life. And who will gainsay then the wisdom of having built a white elephant today?[4]

Downtown People Movers

As the costs and political acceptability of the BART-METRO-type rail systems become increasingly difficult to justify, other transit modes are increasingly favored. Our societal fascination with technology and expensive toys and gadgets has led several metropolitan areas to plan and begin to build "downtown-people-mover" (DPM) systems. Basically, a DPM is a small, elevated rail system designed to move people to and through a downtown area. The cars carry between thirty-five and sixty people and are automatically controlled via a central computer. Los Angeles, Miami, and Detroit are moving ahead on such systems while Cleveland, Houston, and St. Paul have rejected the idea.

Since DPM's traverse the downtown area, their construction costs exceed the per-mile construction costs of BART-METRO-type systems and can even be higher than the per-mile construction costs of urban freeways. In Los Angeles, for example, a three mile DPM would cost $175 million (at 1981 prices), or almost $60 million per mile. Befitting a project with almost $60 million per-mile costs, the Los Angeles DPM project has its share of

[4] Melvin Webber, "The BART Experience—What Have We Learned?" in Alan Altshuler ed. *Current Issues in Transportation Policy* (Lexington, Ma.: Lexington Books, 1979), p. 132.

critics. One opponent has referred to the system as a "Computerized Toonerville Trolley," and has suggested that "with stations less than four blocks apart, a healthy frog probably could jump the distance from station to station and get there just as fast."[5] The Miami system is estimated to cost $83 million for a 3.7-mile system while Detroit plans a two-to-three-mile system at a cost of $75 to $100 million.

Obviously, such systems are not designed to be the primary public transportation mode in an area. Miami planners, for example, see the DPM as the "final jewel" in the area's building and revitalization program. Their DPM would pick up as many as 40,000 people a day from the 20.5-mile, $795 million rapid-rail system currently under construction. The DPM would then transport these people throughout the downtown area. Advocates of Detroit's DPM hope that it will be the beginning of a public transportation network that will ultimately include rail transit, express bus lanes, cable cars to Windsor, Canada, and maybe even hydrofoil service on the Detroit River.[6]

Whether or not such projects will be built, and if built will be successful, is pure speculation at this time. The experience of BART should warn us that patronage estimates of up to 72,000 riders per day in Los Angeles, 52,400 in Detroit, and 40,000 per day in Miami are guesswork. While the technology is reasonably well-developed, the only places in the country where DPM type systems are in operation are in airports. These systems were part of the original design and building of the airports, not grafted on to an already existing structure.

As in other transportation undertakings, whether or not DPM's are cost-effective and will carry the number of people projected is probably of less importance than whether or not such projects are politically acceptable. While the Carter administration committed more than $1.5 billion to rail-transit projects during 1980, President Reagan's plans call for cutting mass-transit spending, eliminating operating subsidies, and eliminating demonstration grants for DPM systems.

Light Rails (LRV's)

One of the newest ideas in rail transit is really one of the oldest—trolley cars. In today's lexicon, trolley cars are Light Rail Vehicles (LRV's), or Light Rail Transit (LRT's). Trolleys, or street cars, are technically different from LRV's because while the vehicle is the same, an electrically powered, steel-wheeled vehicle, LRV's operate on exclusive rights-of-way while trolley and streetcars must share a right-of-way with other vehicles. In Europe LRV's do both, and the sixteen mile system that opened in San

[5] *The New York Times*, December 14, 1980, p. 14.

[6] "DPM Update: A Mixed Bag," *Mass Transit*, Vol. 6, No. 5 (May 1979), p. 11.

Diego in 1981 operates on fourteen miles of exclusive right-of-way and two miles of downtown streets.

In the United States, nine LRV systems are currently in operation with eight systems under construction, in the planning stages, or being seriously discussed. For comparative purposes, there are thirty-three such systems operating in West Germany alone.

Unlike their BART-METRO and DPM counterparts, contemporary LRV systems don't involve high levels of technological sophistication. The San Diego system, nicknamed the "Tijuana Trolley" because it stops at San Ysidro, just across the border from Tijuana, Mexico, has no computers nor any other kind of electronic aid. Each train consists of two cars operated by a driver. Other cities that are up-grading their existing systems or are planning new LRV systems seem to be following the same pattern—basic rail transit with a minimum of gadgetry and computers, technology that adds to the cost and increases the likelihood of malfunction. San Diego has carried simplification so far that they have adopted the European honor-fare system rather than install expensive fare booths and turnstyles. In doing so, San Diego officials noted that the Chicago Transit Authority spends upwards of 15 percent of its budget on fare collection, while the District of Columbia's METRO has been plagued since its opening by automatic fare collections and fare-card dispensing equipment that often fails to work properly.

The San Diego "Tijuana Trolley" has attracted attention from throughout the country for several reasons.[7] It was built without any federal funds, a feat virtually unheard of in today's transit world. In addition, it was built on time (thirty months) and on budget ($86 million). The reasons for San Diego's success are partially luck and partially good management and political skills. In 1974, California State Senator James Mills of San Diego was successful in getting voters to approve a measure to permit diverting some state gasoline-tax money from highways into rail and other fixed guideway systems. He then got the California legislature to pass a bill allowing a Metropolitan Transit Development Board to be created in San Diego, and allocate the gasoline-tax funds for the Board's use. The legislation specified that if the tax funds were not used within five years, they would lose them. This move was undertaken by Mills to prevent San Diego from getting involved in protracted negotiations with the federal government over possible federal funding of the project.

The luck occurred in 1976 when heavy rain washed out sections of the 105 mile San Diego and Arizona Eastern Railroad's tracks. Southern Pacific, the parent company, petitioned to abandon the line and San Diego bought the line for $18.1 million instead of the $80 million that the railroad

[7] *Chicago Tribune*, October 12, 1980, p. 14 and *The Wall Street Journal*, January 19, 1981, p. 19.

wanted. San Diego's transit board chairperson, Maureen O'Connor referred to the purchase as "the steal of the century."

DOS AND DON'TS OF DESIGN AND BUILDING

What is it about the design and building of systems like BART and METRO that seems to guarantee high costs, low patronage, and dashed hopes? In any public-works undertaking as complex as a mass-transit system it should not be too surprising that Murphy's Law (if anything can go wrong, it will) tends to rule the day. From the time that the first traffic engineer, city councilperson, frustrated auto commuter, group of CBD business people, chamber of commerce, or city-beautiful people get the idea that the ideal solution to a city's troubles is to build a system of rapid transportation to the day that the first rider boards a vehicle, thousands of decisions will have been made affecting all manner of individuals, groups, and interests. The planning and design process will be one of the most complicated undertakings ever engaged in by human beings.

From a purely abstract and theoretical standpoint, the design and building of transportation systems is not especially complex. On the basis of user preferences, local officials are supposed to make the decisions about the nature and frequency of service that they would like for a given cost, and the engineers and planners are charged with implementing those decisions. Reality, though, is different. This simplistic model assumes that all interested individuals and actors possess the same amount and quality of information, share the same goals and values, desire the same outcomes. Nothing could be further from the truth. Any good traffic engineer or transportation planner can tell a client what levels of patronage are necessary to make highways, express buses, or rail systems profitable. Consider the following:

1. It is a fairly widely accepted transportation-planning principle that travel demand approximating twenty-five thousand people per hour in a given travel corridor must be present before rail transit can even come close to meeting operating expenses. But only in New York City and Chicago is traffic anywhere near that figure. Why then have San Francisco, Baltimore, Washington, D.C., and Atlanta embarked on massive rail-building programs when they do not have the travel demands necessary to support such systems?
2. Any good transportation planner can tell a client that the higher the densities of homes and workplaces, the easier it is to design inexpensive, high-quality mass transportation systems. Suburbs with homes and work-places scattered over metropolitan areas that stretch for hundreds of square miles, in no way meet this test of workability.
3. Any good transportation planner can tell a client about the short-comings of any particular mode of travel. Highways, buses, and rail systems all do some things very well and others badly.

Automobiles are an excellent choice in low-density areas, for example, to move an individual from a suburban housing development to a suburban industrial park. Automobiles perform very poorly in high-density areas such as the CBDs of large cities. Yet, it seems, clients of urban transportation planners either do not know such simple facts or ignore them. Each mode of travel has its proponents and detractors; each is promoted as a panacea or panned as an evil. In reality, no simple solution exists. The issue is complex, especially because many nontransportation considerations come into play, including the following:

1. Consumers want to be able to select any travel mode at any time of the day and get the same results. They naively assume that the best system of transportation is one that enables them to travel the way they want to, where they want to, when they want to.
2. City officials and downtown business interests, concerned about the outflow of dollars and people to the suburbs, may take a narrow view of public transportation, focusing on it as the key to CBD revitalization. Their dream is that mass transit will bring hordes of affluent commuters and shoppers into the CBD and thereby enhance property values there.
3. Transportation planners and engineers have not been free of narrow-gauge vision either. For decades, these professionals have said that their work was entirely apolitical, that their plans and designs were technically sound, and that it was up to public officials and decision makers to choose from among existing alternatives. They assumed, incorrectly, that elected officials had some unique ability to determine the public interest. Public officials assumed, also incorrectly, that the technical superiority of one system over another made the choice of mode a clear-cut, noncontroversial decision.

Since then transportation specialists have learned a lot about pinpointing how and why people choose certain travel modes over others. Some general principles that apply to mass transit are emerging:

1. Experimenting with different fare structures will not affect ridership a great deal. While it is possible to increase ridership by lowering fares, it is hard to divert large numbers of auto users to public transportation by means of fare changes.
2. Use of public transportation is more responsive to qualitative changes, such as decreases in travel times, than to decreases in fares.
3. Improved vehicle speed is overrated as a way to attract more users. Ridership is more sensitive to changes in how people funnel in and out of the system than to changes in vehicle speed. What makes the automobile attractive to millions of people are its door-to-door, no wait, no-transfer characteristics. Yet in the new rail systems in the country, people have to travel from their homes to a transit station on a bus or by private car, wait for a transit vehicle, travel at high speeds and in relative comfort for fifteen or twenty minutes, and then probably transfer to another line, incurring another wait, then walk, take a bus, or a taxi to their place of employment. The process forces people to sacrifice the values they want most.

4. High speed may make good public relations copy ("This system will be able to whisk travelers downtown comfortably at speeds of over seventy miles per hour.") but it causes other problems that designers have not yet solved. The higher the vehicle speed the farther apart stations must be placed, so as to achieve high speeds. The farther apart the stations are, the harder it is for possible riders to gain access to the system. Hence system planners must provide an elaborate feeder-bus network in order to bring riders to the train stations.

The inescapable conclusion is that numerous critical choices made by professional and public decision makers virtually foredoomed the new rapid rail systems to relatively small riderships. Plans were laid that were inconsistent with our best knowledge of why people, given a choice, use private and not public transportation. In designing and building the three new rapid rail systems, they did little to provide the linkages and support facilities that would improve the chances of success of their decisions. To be successful, new systems have to fit into and be compatible with existing patterns of private and public transportation. Yet the three systems mentioned here were not planned as additions to ongoing systems, but as if they would be the dominant mode of travel for decades to come. It would have been far better to adapt to the existing patterns of travel than to assume that rapid rail transit would revolutionize urban transportation.

CITIZEN PARTICIPATION IN TRANSPORTATION PLANNING

So far, though we have mentioned many interests and actors involved in transportation planning, we have not considered the role of the citizen. It could be argued that one important reason for the unfortunate state of public transportation service is the failure to involve the ordinary citizen in the planning process. Citizens have had little chance to say how they want services improved.

There is nothing new about that. Rarely have individual citizens or groups of citizens had much voice in the design, delivery, or evaluation of urban public services. It is also true, of course, that people do not become much interested in public issues, including transportation issues, unless they perceive that some particular project will have a direct effect on their daily lives. Those who do participate are generally the affluent, better educated, and more influential.

One of the features of postreform politics is the participation of more and different kinds of people in planning processes of all kinds, and there is reason to believe that the demand for participatory rights will not wither away. In the case of urban transportation, the central question is not whether but how such participation might best be realized. The long-range nature of planning for transportation, with its inherent technical and engineering complexity, works against effective involvement by the average citizen. Unlike such services as education, where many citizens perceive a real stake in the outcome of decisions, citizen interest in areas like transportation tends to be aroused too late—after plans are already drawn and decisions made about the location of a new freeway or bus line, or whether and where to build a new rapid transit line. While a citizen group may advise and agitate for the placement of a transit line in a particular location, there may be sound economic and engineering reasons for placing that line in a different location. But it is difficult for a citizens' group to see and respond to all of the competing objectives and technical considerations. It is harder still for the lay person to know when such reasons are valid and when they are being used as a smoke screen for debatable value choices.

In order to improve the quality and quantity of citizen participation in transportation decisions a number of steps need to be taken, none of them easy or cheap. Initially, someone must decide which citizens will participate in any given issue. If the premise is that those who pay the most will get to participate most, then the poor and minority groups will be left out. If, on the other hand, those who will benefit from the improved services get the major voice, then who is to speak for those taxpayers who will pay the bills but may not benefit directly?

Consider this example. If the deletion of bus service to certain suburban areas is proposed, which groups of citizens ought to be involved in making that decision? Only the suburban residents, whose local government funds the service? Then we will never hear from the inner-city residents who may be using that service as a way of obtaining access to suburban jobs—or *would* use it if schedules were adjusted to fit their needs. On the other hand, opening the floodgates to all affected groups does not necessarily improve on the quality of the advice presented. It may just lead to stalemate. If there is no clear single message from citizens, those who are used to making such decisions then feel free to choose whatever course of action best suits their own purposes.

Ironically, it is the professionals rather than elected officials who hold the key to involving citizens in highly technical areas. At a minimum, the professionals need to develop a set of relatively simple models for the average citizen to be able to understand and respond to. It certainly does little good for a group of transportation professionals to loudly proclaim its commitment to active citizen participation if they then expect those citizens to respond to alternatives couched in the latest professional language and jargon. Citizens have a right and need to know about such things as costs, frequency of service, and the effect on property taxes of several different courses of action. What they do not need, and what they cannot deal with, are recommendations and alternatives displayed in such technical terms as "modal-split analysis" and "gravity flow models."

An implicit assumption in our discussion is that average citizens do have something substantive to contribute to the transportation decision-making process. With citizen confidence and trust in government low, certainly it can be argued that opening up the system is healthy for the body politic. Any move that builds citizens' confidence that government and its decision makers are open and responsive to the needs of the people is desirable. Certainly the experiences with BART and METRO suggest that attempts to probe consumer attitudes before construction would have paid off for those systems. The most critical role for the citizen may be to bring government back constantly to a focus on people, on human needs. Without an effective citizen voice, government is prone to behave as if it were a business whose sole task is to show a profit. Nothing could illustrate the point better than the experience of an organization in Shaw-Cardozo, an inner-city neighborhood in the nation's capital. This group tried to keep transit service for their area in the final plans for METRO,[8] but they proved to be no match for the combined forces of transportation professionals and public officials.

The neighborhood, populated mainly by blacks and low-income people, fell victim to the profit-and-loss sheet before the new METRO subway was even funded. The Columbia Heights branch line that was to serve the neighborhood was eliminated on the grounds that it would be the weakest link in the subway system, in terms of peak-hour patronage.

The residents of the area initiated a three-pronged attack on the plan to eliminate the Columbia Heights line. They attacked the planning assumptions that the line was uneconomical, they challenged the basic planning analysis that recommended the elimination of the line, and they pleaded with the decision makers against isolating central-city residents from jobs and other opportunities lest another Watts-type situation be created. In documenting their case, supporters of the Columbia Heights line pointed to a study done by the National Capital Transit Authority (NCTA) showing that in low-income areas, 88 percent of all travelers would use transit where travel times between auto and rail were equal. Beyond that, they pointed to another conclusion of the study that showed that even when auto travel was six times faster than rail transit, 76 percent of the low-income group would still use the subway.

To further support their case, they pointed to a poll taken by the neighborhood business community, in which 74 percent of those polled said they would use the Columbia Heights line at least five times a week and only five percent said that they would never use the subway. According to supporters of the line, the evidence cast significant doubt on the validity of

[8] The case material is drawn from William J. Murin, *Mass Transit Policy Planning* (Lexington, Mass.: Lexington Books, 1971).

the NCTA's claim that the line would not generate sufficient patronage to be economically justifiable and that the area residents already received adequate transportation from the existing bus lines.

The position of the Columbia Heights groups can best be summarized by the following testimony by Chauncey Thomas of CHANGE (Columbia Heights Association for Growth and Environment) Inc.:

> Traditionally, the use of public funds for a transportation system has been justified on the grounds that mass transit benefits blue-collared groups who otherwise could not afford transportation to employment or shopping centers. This is especially valid in this area, where racial segregation in housing prohibits many workers from living near their jobs. The decision to drop the Columbia Heights line . . . is surely an attempt to misuse funds by suggesting a subway to benefit white suburbanites who can afford other means of transportation while leaving blue-collar Negroes and Spanish residents of upper Cardozo to the mercy of inadequate, inconvenient, and expensive bus service.[9]

Richard Severo, *Washington Post* columnist, put all the arguments together in delivering a blast at the plan to eliminate the Columbia Heights line. His column noted:

> If the poor people who live in rundown areas of center-city Washington are waiting for a subway system to whisk them to jobs downtown or in suburbia, someone ought to tell them that the wait may be a long one. For the bitter truth of the matter is, there is nothing planned for them in the immediate future. Later on, maybe, but not now. . . . Some of the people connected with the National Capital Transportation Agency are known to feel that they never could have got Congress to go along with the subway system if they had insisted that initial digging start where it is needed most—in predominately Negro areas of Washington. . . .
>
> No matter what happens, Washington remains impressively ingenious in its ability to avoid serving the people who need services the most. . . . The subway which was originally designed to serve the urban poor of the District is to be diverted . . . to serve the commuters of the suburban metropolitan area. . . .
>
> This will be the only subway in history to serve the classes instead of the masses.[10]

During congressional hearings on the proposed changes, subway system officials referred often to the congressional mandate that the system pay for itself out of the fare box. The modified plan, without the Columbia Heights line, easily passed both houses of Congress.

This episode points up a number of realities in the mass-transportation planning process and the effectiveness of citizen involvement in that

[9] U.S. Senate, committee on the District of Columbia, *Amend the National Capital Transportation Act of 1965, Hearings before the Committee on the District of Columbia on S. 2094 and H.R. 11395*, 90th Congress, 1st Session, 1967, p. 56.

[10] Richard Severo, "Potomac Watch," *Washington Post*, March 15, 1967.

process. As presented by planners and officials, the Columbia Heights issue was one of eliminating an uneconomic part of the system in order to provide more highly utilized and more profitable service on the rest of the system. It is technically correct to say that the Columbia Heights line was probably uneconomic in cost-benefit terms, but the arguments used by the Columbia Heights people to try to save their subway line are significant. They wanted a transit system that would serve people in need of greater mobility.

Typically, neighborhood mobilization came only in reaction—as a defense against a known threat. And predictably the defense was too little and too late. At no time during the preliminary planning and early hearings on the proposed system had Columbia Heights residents provided positive pressure on planners and officials to keep their subway line. Could residents of the area have prevented the change (or would it even have been proposed) had they been white and middle class? The answer is not entirely clear.

In any case, given the requirement that METRO pay for itself out of the fare box, transportation planners and Columbia Heights residents operated on radically different premises. The neighborhood appeal was based mainly on "need" and "discontent," arguments not likely to be persuasive—given the cost-orientations of the system planners.

This and other case studies make it possible to suggest some generalized comments about the difficulties encountered in trying to achieve a meaningful level of citizen participation in the planning process:

1. As a rule, only a few of the most vocal and active citizens become involved, and there is no way of knowing whether their views are truly representative of the entire community.
2. Most local involvement tends to be a reaction to decisions already reached by the professionals and decision makers and comes at or near the conclusion of a study; such citizen involvement has less of a chance of success than if it had occurred throughout the process.
3. The usual techniques for eliciting citizen views, such as general public hearings, tend to provide only for random local comment that will probably not be incorporated into the decision-making process. Middle-class residents sometimes are able to overcome this problem but poorer residents are not.

Citizen participation in the urban planning process is likely to remain haphazard and ad hoc until we develop better ways to help citizens share in setting goals.

THE URBAN TRANSPORTATION PROBLEM AND POSSIBLE SOLUTIONS

The transportation policy that exists today is a patchwork of more than three decades of decisions that reflect the biases and values of those who made them. The net effect has been to favor the movement of automobiles over the movement of people and goods, with the result that citizens must provide their own means of transportation in most situations. For the average American family with at least one, and usually two, automobiles at its disposal, such planning has few negative effects. But to base urban transportation policy on the assumption that everyone owns a car is to inflict hardship on those who do not. Twenty percent of all American households and one-third of households in the central city do not own automobiles. They desperately need an alternative to the private automobile. Even automobile commuters do not lead an easy life. Fighting morning and evening rush-hour traffic, they probably spend more time going to and from work than they would have forty years ago. Automobile owners and nonowners face different situations, however. Planners and policy makers focus their attention on trying to solve the technical problems of moving and parking automobiles. In setting these priorities, they are simply reflecting the dominant attitudes of a middle-class society.

Even though there is now some unease about the energy shortage, the nation still seems to believe that it has the ability to move more and more commuters from more and more decentralized locations to more and more decentralized destinations more quickly, comfortably, and economically than was the case several decades ago. As a society, we have difficulty in understanding why the people and technology that put us on the moon cannot take us downtown. The new mass transit we *have* produced reflects an undue faith in space-age solutions to people problems.

Our transportation decision making, even disposed as it is to favor the middle-class suburbanite, has not come to terms with the overriding fact of contemporary urban life—the increasing decentralization of both homes and workplaces. Even the exotic technologies, ranging from people movers to personalized rapid transit systems, all require fairly dense origins and destinations to enable them to achieve their inherent capabilities. For the affluent who have private automobiles, we need a process for working our way toward a road system and system of mass transportation that will acknowledge the suburbanization of America. For the millions of Americans who do not have a car—because they are too young, too old, too poor, or too handicapped to drive or because they prefer to have an alternative to the private automobile—our policy makers need to consider how to distribute the benefits of urban mobility to those who do not now enjoy them.

If we had such a redesigned policy, what might urban transportation look like in the future? It is a temptation to begin by identifying the characteristics of an idealized mass transportation system and then modifying those characteristics to suit a particular metropolitan area. But such an approach can lead to frustration. No system will ever fully live up to the theoretical possibilities. Political, social, economic, aesthetic, and physical limits will always intervene. Furthermore, planning ideal systems can be harmful; when the crunch of reality comes, the powerless often lose out entirely. More modest goals very often produce greater benefits. Our example of the Columbia Heights line of Washington's METRO shows what can happen to a neighborhood when its transportation needs do not meet the criteria of profitability and economic efficiency.

It *is* possible, however, to suggest not an ideal but a set of essential characteristics for any transportation system:

1. It must provide good service to all, but not necessarily collectively. The system must be capable of serving the travel needs of each individual regardless of whether travel needs are CBD to suburb, suburb to CBD, suburb to suburb, or intracity.
2. It must give its users cheap, quick, comfortable, convenient, dependable, and safe transportation.
3. It must be able to fit into the societal goals as desired by citizens and public officials and not impose its own goals.
4. It must confront all users of all modes with the economic costs that result from their personal choices.
5. It must be energy efficient.
6. It must meet whatever aesthetic goals the community demands of it.
7. It must be diverse: the travel needs of a heterogeneous population cannot be adequately served by only one mode of transportation.

A caveat is in order. Transportation, even when designed to meet social goals, cannot be a cure-all for social problems. Consider the problem of inner-city unemployment. In the wake of the disorders in the 1960s, the federal government funded over a dozen experimental or demonstration projects creating a transportation link between central-city residences and suburban job opportunities, at a cost of over five million dollars. The results, however, were generally disappointing.

The evaluation of one project that linked the Watts area of Los Angeles with large industrial plants out near the Los Angeles International Airport revealed two problems.[11] First, jobs did not materialize in the expected numbers. Some observers felt that racial discrimination was a factor. Others argued that it is common practice in auto-oriented cities like Los Angeles not to hire people who do not have regular access to an automobile because of the likelihood of chronic absenteeism and lateness

[11] "Summary of Progress, Report No. 107 for California Transportation Employment Project," June 25, 1968, mimeographed.

for work. In addition, the airport was only one employment site. The extreme scattering of employment sites throughout the Los Angeles area made the automobile, not a fixed-route bus, the only practical means of getting to many jobs. Second, bus riders displayed no long-term commitment to public transportation. A majority of the riders of the experimental bus line acknowledged that the bus provided opportunities they would otherwise not have had, but almost all of the riders interviewed said that they would ride the bus only until they had saved enough money to buy a car and then they would drive to work.

Another project, in St. Louis, also involved bus routes to an outlying industrial area. When the project began, there were thirteen round trips daily to the industrial complex, but when the project came to an end twenty months later, only two such round trips were still being made. Evaluators concluded that personal problems, not the unavailability of transportation, had the greatest effect on the employment rates of low-income people.[12] Certainly, expanded bus routing alone is not going to reverse the economic position of the poor.

The experimental projects tell us quite clearly that the relationship between employment and transportation is much more complex than generally assumed. Transportation is only a small part of the unemployment problem faced by the central-city poor. For central-city residents to take advantage of a possible suburban job, much more is needed than a simple city-to-suburban transportation link. Job possibilities must be in the right place at the right time, and they must be tied to a set of opportunities and skills that make sense to central-city residents.

Just as fixed transportation lines and permanent schedules do not seem to meet the needs of middle-income workers, they do not seem to meet the employment-related transportation needs of the poor. Any policy that relies upon public transportation as a way of improving the employment prospects of the poor must include flexible routes and schedules so as to be compatible with decentralized urban residential patterns and suburban jobs. In fact, one researcher has noted that the costs of providing such flexible public transportation are so high and the potential patronage so low that it would be cheaper to buy luxury automobiles and give them away free to low-income central-city bus riders than it would be to operate and maintain a subsidized city-to-suburb bus system.[13]

Is this the kind of radical proposal we ought to be taking seriously? Whatever the political, social, economic, and ethical repercussions, it would give the transportation-disadvantaged a degree of access to *all* urban activities that they do not now possess. While a subsidized bus system might

[12] J. M. Goering and E. M. Kalachek, "Transportation and People: Public Transportation and Black Unemployment," *Society* 10 (July/August 1974), 39–42.

[13] Vincent L. Marando, "Metropolitanism, Transportation, and Employment for the Central City Poor," *Urban Affairs Quarterly* 10 (December 1974), 166.

be able to provide an adequate home-to-work travel link, it does little to get people to school, shopping, medical services, recreation, and other urban amenities that the more mobile portion of the metropolitan population takes for granted. But providing free or publicly subsidized automobiles for the poor not only violates the American ethic about working for what one has, it goes against other important interests—those concerned about energy conservation, those who want to preserve the aesthetics of an urban area, and those who want to decrease air and noise pollution by getting automobiles off the already congested roadways. All in all, despite the American attachment to the private automobile, there is little public support for direct subsidization of its use by the poor.

We would thus caution that any simplistic solution to the problem of transportation services carries the danger of imposing on society a range of unintended and undesirable consequences. Our present auto-oriented system has imposed great personal, social, and economic hardships on those individuals who do not have access to an automobile. Future decisions could do the same. Take, for example, the often suggested banning of the private automobile in the CBD. Numerous observers of the transportation scene have suggested that one way of improving the attractiveness and economic efficiency of mass transportation is to prohibit private autos from entering the downtown portions of major cities during rush hours or even throughout the day. While some cities have successfully experimented with reserved lanes for buses or closing off certain streets to the private automobile during specific hours of the day, the full-blown version of the proposal to prohibit cars in the downtown area has never been implemented—perhaps fortunately so, given the ramifications of such a decision. Unless citizens were provided with a transit system that was a reliable alternative, they would not benefit from the ban. No American city has such a transit system now, and no city is likely to be able to afford the costs of supplying the extra buses, rail cars, and the like for such a system. Even if a city could, it would be unlikely to do so for fear it would undermine its own tax base. Prohibiting the use of private cars in the downtown area might very well lead to a further decline of the CBD, as people chose to shop, go to restaurants, locate office buildings, etc. in places where the automobile has free access.

Other proposals that would tend to give mass transportation a competitive advantage over the auto also have their negative side effects. Transportation economists and others have suggested that such devices as peak-hour pricing, higher tolls or parking charges, and freeway taxes would probably encourage people to abandon auto travel for public transportation. Again, such policies could work only if mass transportation were a realistic and viable alternative to the automobile. In most cities even for the rush-hour journey to work, traditional public transportation just does not present consumers with the convenience alternatives they most desire.

Any proposal to charge auto users for bringing their automobiles into the city in the morning would inevitably cause some businesses to seek new locations, thus placing those citizens who must depend on public transportation to get to work at a disadvantage.

Beyond all these considerations, of course, is a political fact of life. To implement any policy that would tax auto users would require a conscious, visible decision by elected officials. There are not many who would jeopardize their reelection chances by going on record in favor of such a policy.

Throughout this chapter, we have described many public policies and transportation services that *do not* work. We have also discussed several proposals for change that in our judgment *will not* work. We are brought now to the question of whether there are practical and realistic changes that would help.

The most essential change is one of the managerial and marketing attitudes of transit system managers. There has been little real effort to manage or market mass transportation in ways that will make it attractive to the consumer. Along with service improvements must go a new believable identity to convince citizens that public transportation can give them the service they want and that such service is an essential part of the package of urban services that a city makes available to its citizens. All too often, mass transportation systems have the image of being dirty, dingy, and totally unattractive. In addition, bus and rail systems are likely to have the lowest priority among all urban services and be the first to have subsidy or other financial support reduced when a city finds itself in budget difficulty. In sum, transportation operators need to develop policies, service, and public relations measures that assure the citizenry that they have a right to expect, and can count on, quality public transportation at a reasonable cost. Only when such assurances are provided will people begin to feel that they can depend on public transportation, and only then will they begin to consider it as a viable alternative to the use of the private automobile.

As for service improvement, all available evidence indicates that improved service can increase mass transit ridership. Again, a caveat must be issued. Seldom will the increased ridership offset the extra costs of service improvement, especially if certain groups of citizens are to be given reduced fares. Special fares for students, senior citizens, the handicapped, and the poor put more people on the transit vehicles, but they do little to improve the financial picture of the system. For most cities, the easiest, and perhaps the most effective, way to improve urban transportation is to rely more on the existing freeway system to move buses and other transit vehicles. This idea could significantly improve the quality of mass transportation in nearly every American city at very low cost. All it would entail is a limited outlay for some instrumentation, some modification in the design of freeway ramps, and a policy decision to give public transit vehicles priority access to freeways during peak travel hours.

Bus transportation is the only form of public transportation available for most American cities. Buses also use the road system so elaborately developed for the automobile (and truck). Given these two realities, many observers believe that efforts to improve public transportation should zero in on ways to improve bus service. Below is a shopping list of possibilities, all of which meet the tests of technical feasibility. The social, political, and economic viability need to be determined on a city-by-city basis.

ROUTES

1. Lay out direct routes, without regard to political boundaries, to places where people live, work, shop, and play.
2. Provide express service throughout the day between high-density parts of the city and its suburbs.
3. Have transit vehicles make use of freeways, parkways, and other highways.
4. Offer frequent crosstown and intersuburban sevice at key points.

SPEED

5. Create traffic patterns and priorities so that buses can move quickly even in rush hours.

FARES

6. Allow no fare increases, at least until service is excellent.
7. Establish twenty-five-cent off-peak fare for all, city and suburb.
8. Offer weekly passes, group rates, weekend family plans, and other special encouragements.
9. Charge peak or premium fares only during rush hours and then only in the direction most heavily used (inbound in the morning, outbound in the evening).

CONVENIENCE

10. Assure seats for all even if it means running more than one bus on some heavily traveled routes.
11. Build bus shelters at all major stops.
12. Use radio control and visual inspection to assure that schedules are adhered to.
13. Assure taxi service and police protection at major bus stops.
14. Advertise bus service aggressively in places where nonriders will see the ads.[14]

One significant change in attitude, on the part of citizens and officials alike, would be to stop expecting public transportation to be a profit-making venture. Other basic urban services—police and fire protection, garbage collection, education, parks and recreation, municipal health programs—are accepted as necessary and desirable aspects of contempo-

[14] "Excerpt: Transit for the '70's" *The American County* 37 (October 1972), 34.

rary urban life. They are not expected to show a profit at the end of the fiscal year. Why treat public transportation differently? Even if transit service itself and the management and marketing of that service are upgraded and the overall image of urban public transportation is improved, some level of subsidy will be necessary, whoever operates the service. And that subsidy will be higher as the transportation system is asked to serve more social goals.

Since the power of federal dollars controlled by the Urban Mass Transportation Administration (UMTA) is so great, a major policy shift in its approach to public transportation is needed. UMTA's highest priority ought to be reserved for the most flexible systems of public transportation, and for most cities at present that means some form of transportation operating on freeways. Systems that can change and react to changing places of employment and residence in the quickest, cheapest, easiest manner should get priority over fixed-rail systems. In addition, transit systems that serve neighborhoods of low-income, unemployed, carless people ought to be given priority over systems that serve more affluent areas.

There are no simple, easy solutions to the problems facing urban transportation in the United States. Whatever solutions are ultimately proposed and adopted will certainly have to meet the test of technical feasibility; more important, they will have to be politically and socially acceptable. The latter requirement is the more difficult one to meet, and the one that transportation planners and public officals have tended to ignore over the past several decades. Only when political and social conditions are considered on a par with technical problems will the future of public transportation be brighter than it is currently. And only when public officials recognize the importance of addressing the political and social implications of their decisions will public transportation approach the levels of acceptability needed to give all citizens of America's urban areas the mobility they need.

SUGGESTED READINGS

DeSalvo, Joseph S., ed. *Perspectives on Regional Transportation Planning*. Lexington, Mass.: Lexington Books, 1973.

Hamer, Andrew Marshall. *The Selling of Rail Rapid Transit*. Lexington, Mass.: Lexington Books, 1976.

Kendrick, Frank J. "Urban Transportation Planning: Politics, Planning, and People." *Policy Sciences Journal* 3 (Summer 1975), 375-87.

Meyer, John R., and Jose A. Gomez-Ibanez. *Autos, Transit, and Cities*. Cambridge, MA: Harvard University Press, 1981.

Muller, Herbert J. *The Children of Frankenstein. A Primer on Modern Technology and Human Values*. Bloomington: Indiana University Press, 1970.

Murin, William J. *Mass Transit Policy Planning*. Lexington, Mass.: Lexington Books, 1971.

Whitt, J. Allen. *Urban Elites and Mass Transportation*. Princeton, NJ: Princeton University Press, 1982.

Winner, Langdon. *Autonomous Technology*. Cambridge, MA: MIT Press, 1977.

chapter 17

Economic and Community Development

To some observers, land is what urban politics is mainly about. Land is directly related to economic activities and therefore to the capacity to raise revenue. Land use is also a means for controlling social access and therefore for defending and promoting various life styles. Because of local government's strong involvement in land-use questions, economic and community development are a major focus of controversy.

In this chapter we will first discuss the general importance of land-use policies in local politics. We will then follow with an analysis of major issues in development policy. After that we will turn to the federal government's role and the question of block grants.

THE DYNAMICS OF URBAN LAND USE

Considering that everyone "knows" that America is an urbanized nation, it is surprising how much land in our urban areas is undeveloped. For example, only about one-third of the land in the Boston metropolitan area is developed; much is forest, wasteland, or meadow. This situation is not unique to Boston. The question, however, is under what circumstances land is developable. Developers say that a site must be "ripe": located well in relation to jobs, transportation, and other private and public facilities, so that it can be developed and marketed at reasonable costs. And, of course, land has to be properly zoned. Land that meets these tests is very scarce.

This scarcity, plus the private ownership of land that is characteristic in the United States and the growth that has been the political and economic hallmark of American urban communities, has created a situation of intense competition among spatial areas in metropolitan areas. Individuals, companies, and government jurisdictions are engaged in a constant struggle to enhance the land-use potential of their property. It is important to remember, however, that although government programs provide incentives for land developers, the vast majority of development and redevelopment is private. There is little public ownership of land in our cities. One study indicates, for instance, that, in a five-year period, public authorities in the United States built between 1.4 and 5.6 percent of dwelling units, while British figures ranged from 53.3 to 73.4 percent.[1]

Why do Americans shy away from public-sector control of land, especially of residential development? Economics is one obvious answer. There's big money to be made and lost. A desire for homogeneity is another. Americans want to live in a community with other people of similar life styles. Related to this desire is one for privatism—a term that encompasses not just a wish for privacy but an insistence on being in a position to choose one's neighbors, at home and at play. Some have linked this passion for privatism to political withdrawal in the suburbs. But let a land-use plan threaten pocketbook or privacy and a political battle will ensue that knows no boundaries. To many, the public sector smacks of inadequate facilities and the influx of undesirables. Our point here is that land-use controversies are not rooted just in economics; sometimes they stem from preferences about life style.

Citizens may treasure the private ownership of land and what is built on it for their own reasons. Local governments take a keen interest because the property tax accounts for the greatest portion of locally raised public revenue in the United States. So land use is central to the fiscal situation of local governments, and urban governments often try to follow policies they think will enhance their property-tax base.

Zoning

A community's property-tax base depends, to some degree, upon its zoning policies. Zoning—one of the many state powers delegated to the local level—is a restriction on private property, imposed by the local government, that requires land use to conform to certain specified uses—

[1] Anthony King, "Ideas, Institutions and the Policies of Governments: A Comparative Analysis, Parts I and II," *British Journal of Political Science* 3 (1973), 301.

single-family houses, high-rise apartments, light industrial use, commercial development, and the like.

Despite the fact that planners have for years criticized the use of zoning, it remains the most important power a local government has for managing land use. It is a power that has been used mainly to promote and preserve single-family residential neighborhoods. The greatest controversies over zoning arise when a neighborhood of single-family homes is threatened by a commercial development, a high-rise apartment, or some other "undesirable" use.

The competitive economic pressures of urbanization in metropolitan areas have generally resulted in demands for rezoning from lower to higher residential densities and from residential to business. Some communities have tried to avoid the effects of urbanization by zoning substantial parts of their land area into large-lot categories. For example, some Philadelphia suburbs have rezoned much of their land area from commercial and small-lot residential to four-acre residential minimums. Generally speaking, in making zoning decisions, local governments have been sympathetic to private developers when the latter have been pitted against citizens' groups. Not so, when the proposed change involved public housing. Then, the citizens' groups have generally been able to prevail.

The pattern of suburban opposition to low-cost housing is not restricted to the United States. A study of Stockholm, Sweden, illustrates the universality of the point.[2] When the government built low-income housing in Stockholm's suburbs, the reaction of suburban Socialist politicians was the same angry opposition that we hear from Democrats and Republicans in suburban areas in this country. Class and income are important considerations; we want the poor out of sight. Communities fear that they will become a "magnet for the poor." In addition there is a question of costs. Affluent citizens pay their own way in local taxes and often upgrade their property. As income goes down, homeownership rates go down also. So, too, does the ability to upgrade property. And a substantial poverty population implies additional public expenses for education and other services. Suburban communities reason that low-income housing can mean higher taxes.

Zoning is linked with many urban ills, not just the tendency to create class-homogenous communities. In recent years, some observers have even suggested that zoning should be abolished. They argue that zoning is responsible for inflated housing costs, dull and monotonous housing developments, urban sprawl and energy waste, unnecessary bureaucracy, excessive regulation, and graft. Their most telling criticism is that zoning has discriminated against the less affluent in our society.

[2] Thomas J. Anton, *Governing Greater Stockholm* (Berkeley: University of California Press, 1975).

Bernard Siegan has outlined succinctly how zoning has discriminated against the poor and minorities.[3] He observes that the best way to lower the cost of housing is to increase the supply. Zoning does the reverse, and those with the least money are hardest hit. Affluent and rural communities erect zoning barriers to exclude apartments, town houses, and inexpensive homes such as mobile homes. Zoning also raises housing costs in indirect ways—through requirements, for instance, that developers must provide recreation facilities. Again, these practices hurt lower-income people the most. If zoning prevents construction of new homes or apartments, it restricts supply and increases prices, thereby squeezing nonaffluent people out of the market. Finally, Siegan notes that zoning prohibitions prevent the construction of stores and shops close to homes and apartments, thus hurting poorer families who have no car. The criticisms are serious enough to raise questions about the place of zoning in the future of American cities.

It is instructive to contrast the American urban experience with the Third World urban experience, in which growth is concentrated in squatter communities—on the suburban fringe. Some urbanists have argued that these communities have a very important function. If housing is cheap, the rural immigrants have money available for other necessities. Ultimately, people upgrade their housing as they get a foothold in their new setting. While the United States is unlikely to move in this direction, these models of urban growth in the Third World do indicate that the poor need not be confined to central cities.

MAJOR POLICY ISSUES

Over the years, urban governments have based land policies on the idea that land should be used at its "highest and best use." In practice, this means its most economically productive use. Thus cities have often been inattentive to other concerns. Residential stability and the conservation of housing stock were ignored as cities built expressways, located convention centers and stadiums close in, provided land for office buildings and hotels, encouraged the expansion of universities and medical institutions, and constructed a variety of public facilities. City actions, however, are in part a response to federal policy. Federal grants and regulations encourage city action along certain paths. Equally important, cities are part of a national economy. They respond to trends in that economy. Thus, there are a number of issues of national importance that shape development in urban communities. Let us start with a look at the housing issue.

[3] Bernard H. Siegan, *Other People's Property* (Lexington, MA: Lexington Books, 1976), esp. pp. 37-60.

HOUSING.

For the affluent, America's housing supply is among the best in the world. Through tax deductions, the federal government subsidizes homeownership, and it does so in a way that increases the subsidy as income goes up and as housing becomes more costly. Under the nation's tax law, the renter receives no subsidy, the family that owns a modest home receives a modest subsidy, and the well-to-do owners of expensive homes receive a large subsidy. It is a system that promotes building for homeowners rather than renters and encourages the building of luxury housing rather than inexpensive housing. It reinforces the biases of zoning law, with the result that there is a severe shortage of housing for low-income people. Moreover, trends in financing suggest that rental housing, in particular, faces diminished production.[4]

While there is a supply of public housing, it comes nowhere near need. Local jurisdictions are reluctant to build public housing for fear of adding to their poverty problem. Neighborhoods resist low-income housing for fear it will transform the character of the community. Federal funds for constructing new public housing have diminished. Consequently most jurisdictions have long waiting lists, and the vast majority of nonaffluent families are dependent upon the private market. The government accounts for only about 2 percent of the housing supply.

Theoretically, the housing market in the United States works on the basis of a filtering or trickle-down process. When a neighborhood is new, housing is good and higher-income people live there. Over the years, the income of residents may improve still further, and they may seek better and newer housing as the neighborhood grows older. Typically, then, the first occupants move out and poorer families move in. But, the demolition of housing for development, gentrification in some areas, disinvestment and deterioration in other areas, racial steering by realtors and other practices that encourage segregation, and the conversion of rental housing to condominiums have all contributed to a diminished supply of standard housing available to the poor.

It is for the lowest fifth of the population in income that the housing problem is acute.[5] In this income category, half of those who own their homes live in substandard dwellings. Among renters, nearly three-quarters live in substandard housing. This does not, of course, include the problem of homeless individuals.

Many low-income families simply cannot afford standard housing. A quarter of those who rent already spend more than 40 percent of their

[4]Anthony Downs, *Rental Housing in the 1980s* (Washington, D.C.: Brookings Institution, 1983).

[5]Ibid.

income on housing, and two-thirds spend more than 25 percent on housing. Since many families are priced out of the market for standard housing, one possible solution to the problem is to supplement the income of poor families through a system of housing allowances or vouchers. Just as food stamps increase the purchasing power of the poor in the grocery market, housing vouchers could increase their capacity to afford standard housing.

Ideally, housing allowances would enable poor families to move into standard housing and do so without concentrating the poor in any one location. Experiments with the program have, however, not had entirely encouraging results.[6] The neediest—the very poor, the elderly, and minorities—were least likely to use the program. Many were reluctant to move out of substandard housing for a variety of reasons. Some were tied to their existing neighborhoods, and did not want the social dislocation of moving. Others faced racial discrimination. And many were unable to locate standard housing to move to—even with added purchasing power. Few of the very poor could afford to pay moving expenses. Where the program was used, it had little dispersing effect. Racial discrimination was a factor; and one community, Saginaw, Michigan, was dropped from participation in the experiment because its suburbs, fearing the immigration of blacks, would not cooperate.

The housing-allowance program turned up no evidence of an inflationary impact on housing costs but also no evidence of a stimulus effect on housing production. What the experiment did suggest is a trade-off that works against any dramatic improvement in housing conditions. When the experiment emphasized rigorous criteria of standard housing, then participation dropped off because it was very difficult for the nonaffluent to find standard rental housing that was affordable even with the help of allowances. When loose criteria were used to determine what housing was eligible, participation increased. But in this latter instance, the program was mainly an income supplement because it brought about little improvement in the quality of housing the poor lived in.[7] Apparently the private market is so heavily oriented toward homeownership for the affluent that moderate amounts of assistance to the poor have little impact.

NEIGHBORHOOD CONSERVATION AND REVITALIZATION.

While public policy has been largely unconcerned with residential stability, the people who live in urban neighborhoods are themselves keenly interested in the issue. Over the past few decades, numerous community organi-

[6] Raymond J. Struyk and Marc Bendick, Jr., eds *Housing Vouchers for the Poor* (Washington, D.C.: Urban Institute Press, 1981).

[7] See the exchange: Chester Hartman, "Housing Allowances: A Critical Look," *Journal of Urban Affairs* vol. 5 (Winter 1983), 41-55; Philip Abrams, "Another Look at Housing Allowances: A Response to Chester Hartman," *Journal of Urban Affairs* vol. 5 (Spring 1983), 151-18; and Chester Hartman, "Rejoinder to 'Another Look at Housing Allowances,'" *Journal of Urban Affairs* vol. 5 (Spring 1983), 159-70.

zations have been formed to protest against various kinds of displacement. Although many of these efforts failed and some organizations have faltered, cities now seldom engage in the massive clearance projects that characterized urban renewal and expressway construction in the 1950s and 1960s. Smaller, spot clearances for specific projects still occur, and neighborhood groups remain keenly interested in investment patterns.

Neighborhood residents have become aware of how their communities can be affected by others. Steering efforts by realtors can undercut efforts to achieve racial stability. Decisions by absentee landlords to abandon or disinvest in an area have a devastating effect, especially if accompanied by such practices as "arson for profit."[8] Financial institutions have long been criticized for the practice of "redlining"—privately designating areas in which loans would not be made.

The opposite of "redlining," speculative reinvestment in an area, can also bring about neighborhood change. If speculators or affluent "pioneers" in an area are able to attract large numbers of new buyers and investors, then housing values will escalate and some long-time residents may be priced out of the market. The replacement of the nonaffluent with affluent residents is a process called "gentrification," though many prefer the more neutral-sounding term, "neighborhood reinvestment."[9]

Is there any pattern to these processes of disinvestment and reinvestment? Apparently there is. A detailed study found that abandonment occurs principally in black and Puerto Rican neighborhoods in older industrial cities of the northeast and midwest.[10] But these are also cities experiencing some reinvestment. Neighborhoods are bearing the social costs of economic transformation.[11]

While older cities, especially in the snowbelt, continue to experience a net outmigration, their changing economic function and population characteristics reflect a shift from industrialism to post-industrialism. Reinvestment reflects this change. It is more characteristic of larger cities than of smaller cities. In one study, nearly three-fourths of the cities over 500,000 had significant neighborhood reinvestment, but only one-third of the central cities under 100,000 had such reinvestment.[12]

[8] Kevin Krajick, "The Arson Epidemic," *Police Magazine* (July 1979), 4-18.

[9] See, Michael H. Schill and Richard P. Nathan, *Revitalizing America's Cities: Neighborhood Reinvestment and Displacement* (Albany: State University of New York Press, 1983); Shirley B. Laska and Daphne Spain, eds. *Back to the City: Issues in Neighborhood Renovation* (New York: Pergamon Press, 1980); Deborah Auger, "The Politics of Revitalization in Gentrifying Neighborhoods," *APA Journal* 45 (October 1979), 515-22; and Michael H. Lang, *Gentrification Amid Urban Decline* (Cambridge, MA: Ballinger, 1982).

[10] George Sternlieb and others, "Housing Abandonment in the Urban Core," *Journal of the American Institute of Planners* 40 (September 1974), 321-32.

[11] Susan S. Fainstein, and others, *Restructuring the City* (New York: Longman, 1983).

[12] Laska and Spain, *Back to the City*, p. 7. See also Harvey Marshall and Bonnie L. Lewis, "Back to the City: An Analysis of Trends in the Sixties and Seventies, *Journal of Urban Affairs* 4 (Winter 1982), 19-32.

As one might guess from the size factor, reinvestment corresponds to the economic function of the city; it is greatest in those cities with central business districts containing large concentrations of administrative activity—corporate and government headquarters, with supporting service activities. The inmigration to neighborhoods close to these business districts also reflect economic change; those moving in are visible participants in post-industrialism—white-collar professionals and managers. They are affluent and are often singles or young marrieds with no children. As such, they may be less interested in schools than in the shopping and entertainment opportunities the city can offer.

Against this background of dislocation and transformation, many cities have witnessed an upsurge in neighborhood political activity. Some cities have created advisory councils to deal with such matters as zoning and budget priorities. In several cities, neighborhood groups have displayed evidence of growing power at the ballot box. Some have been a vital part of winning coalitions in city elections. The 1983 election in Boston, for example, saw the successful mayoral candidate, Raymond Flynn, run on a platform oriented toward neighborhoods. Flynn made a number of pointed criticisms of his predecessor for emphasizing the central business district to the neglect of neighborhoods.

Urban neighborhoods are, of course, not homogeneous. Many of the most politically active are characterized by class and racial diversity.[13] Homeowners and renters may be on opposite sides in some issues. Unity within a neighborhood is not an automatic occurrence. Similarly, unity among neighborhoods may also be elusive. They compete with one another over spending priorities and over such questions as who will bear the dislocation costs of a new traffic artery. While they may come together in a city-wide alliance for some purposes, inter-neighborhood cooperation is sure to be tenuous.

ECONOMIC DEVELOPMENT

A central concern in all cities is economic development. The need for jobs and for a local tax base puts this issue high on everyone's agenda. With the exception of some residential suburbs able to count on neighboring jurisdictions for employment opportunities, there is general agreement that local governments should be promoting economic growth. Agreement, however, is on the principle, not on the operational realities of actually achieving economic development. The reality is always a mixed blessing with losers as well as gainers.

[13] Matthew A. Crenson, *Neighborhood Politics* (Cambridge, MA: Harvard University Press, 1983).

City officials make economic development policy in response to the changing character of the urban economy. Federal policy and national trends constitute the basic forces; cities can only accommodate to or modify these forces in a limited way. The general pattern is for jobs and people to move out of the city and locate in low-density settlement patterns. Retail business has followed people. Advanced technology and communication makes this trend toward deconcentration possible. Affluence enables large numbers of people to afford low-density living, and fragmented local government facilitates class and racial segregation in residential patterns. Federal policy has abetted and encouraged this trend. Tax policy encourages spending on new homes and new plants, rather than on conservation and long use of the old. Transportation policy encourages economic and residential dispersion.

Almost all cities have responded to these centrifugal forces by promoting revitalization of the central business district as a place for office buildings, professional services, and tourist and convention attractions. This transformation to the post-industrial city has come about through active partnership between government and business. For its part, local government has used the power of eminent domain to obtain and clear land, made land available at written-down prices, provided tax abatements, and built a variety of supporting facilities. Expressway construction provided links between the central core and outlying suburbs. And mass transit represents an effort to use public transportation as a way of maintaining the central business district as a hub of activity.

Although central business district transformation and revitalization have been widely supported, they are policies that have engendered recurring opposition. Massive clearance is no longer politically feasible. But other challenges have also risen. In Washington, D.C., merchants have formed a Downtown Retail Merchants Association to contest some of the city's development plans and fight for what they describe as the "survival of small retailers."[14] In Boston, Mayor Kevin White declined to seek a fifth term, partly because there was doubt that he could be reelected. His program of economic transformation left many city residents skeptical that they had benefitted.[15] A study of Cleveland turned up the fact that 70 percent of the jobs in the central business distict are held by people who are not city residents.[16]

In most localities there is little analysis of the benefits and costs of economic development. As a result, local governments tend to be uncritical in responding to business demands for assistance.[17] Some writers are con-

[14] *Washington Post,* November 1, 1983. See also the issue of December 9, 1983.

[15] *Boston Globe,* May 28, 1983.

[16] Katharine L. Bradbury, Anthony Downs, and Keneth A. Small, *Urban Decline and the Future of American Cities,* (Washington, D.C.: Brookings Institution, 1982), p. 282.

[17] Lynn Bachelor, "Reindustrialization in Detroit: Capital Mobility and Corporate Influence," *Journal of Urban Affairs* 4 (Summer 1982), 35-36.

vinced that local governments give away far more than is necessary in tax abatements, subsidized loans, and written-down land.[18] In general, investment decisions are little affected by such practices.[19] Consequently, cities and other local governments find themselves making extensive concessions to business without being sure how much they benefit or whether such concessions are really essential. As a *Washington Post* editorial observed, many officials are unsophisticated about corporate finances and are too short-tenured to learn such matters while in office. Consequently they don't realize that most investment decisions are based on factors over which local officials have no control.[20]

Some of the most publicized cases of business pressure involve professional sports. One New York official observed, "There would be no professional sports without public subsidies."[21] Having lost franchises to New Jersey's Meadowlands, New York City agreed to a $50 million property tax break for Madison Square Garden to keep the Knicks and Rangers from leaving. Many facilities are built and operated by governments at considerable loss. Louisiana floated bonds to build the Superdome in New Orleans and continues to spend $5 million per year to keep it going. Convention centers are another money-losing development that cities venture into. Buffalo's new $22 million dollar center hosted only four events in 1982 and lost $400,000. Washington, D.C., presumably a much more attractive convention site, also faced the prospect of losing money on its new facility. Although attracting two hundred events in its first year, it spent $5 in operating costs for every $1 taken in, and had a $7.2 million shortfall.[22]

The mobility of capital investment enhances business power in numerous ways. Kellogg threatened to move its headquarters from Battle Creek unless the city and Battle Creek Township consolidated. They did.[23] In Yonkers, New York, Otis Elevator took advantage of a $14 million urban renewal grant in building a new factory, which the company then declined to use but sought to rent out at a profit for itself.[24] In Monroe County, New York, several large firms, including Eastman Kodak Company and Xerox Corporation, simply refused to pay pollution-inspection fees.[25]

[18] Bryan D. Jones, Lynn W. Bachelor, and Richard Wang, "Rebuilding the Urban Tax Base." Paper prepared for delivery at the Annual Meeting of the Midwest Political Science Association (Cincinnati, Ohio: April 16-18, 1981.)

[19] Bradbury, Downs, and Small, *Urban Decline and the Future of American Cities.*

[20] *The Washington Post,* December 8, 1983.

[21] Quoted in ibid., January 25, 1984.

[22] Ibid., December 30, 1983.

[23] Lyke Thompson, "The Politics of Economic Development," *Urban Resources* 1 (Summer 1983), 33-40.

[24] *The Washington Post,* May 15, 1983.

[25] *Rochester Democrat and Chronicle,* May 1, 1983.

Business investment practices themselves have become a growing national issue. Litigation involving Amoco Fabrics Company, a subsidiary of Standard Oil Company, turned up evidence that a number of companies refused to locate plants in localities in which blacks exceed 30 percent of the population.[26]

Business is, of course, also averse to locating plants in areas in which labor unions are strong. In California, an Oakland-based community coalition, the Plant Closure Project, worked with the United Electrical, Radio and Machine Workers Union to challenge a plant relocation from Redwood City to Vacaville, California. A suit was brought under a California law prohibiting the use of tax money to "raid" jobs from other communities—Vacaville offered tax-exempt financing to build a new plant just as the union contract was expiring at the Redwood City plant. Efforts to work out an agreement have involved provisions to assure Latino workers the opportunity to move and retain their jobs. The company president has nevertheless asserted a right to select his own employees with no special favors to long-term employees. Further, he described the union as "intransigent" and indicated he intended to reopen in the new location without the union.[27]

Because almost all economic development efforts involve a variety of subsidies to business, the issue of one jurisdiction "raiding" another is sure to become more intense, and perhaps lead to additional legislation on the European model. Partisan politics at the national level is also involved. Jersey City, New Jersey, has received a $40 million Urban Development Action Grant from the federal government in support of a project located across the river from Manhattan. New York City's Deputy Mayor Kenneth Lipper has challenged the grant on the grounds that it is illegal for such federal grants to promote the location of industry from one distressed area to another. New Jersey Governor Thomas Kean, a Republican heading President Reagan's 1984 reelection campaign in New Jersey, responded: "I don't think Mr. Lipper will be successful in blocking the grant because my connections in Washington are very good with the present administration."[28]

It is perhaps worth noting that in contrast with Governor Kean of New Jersey, New York's governor, Mario Cuomo, is a Democrat, elected in 1982 in an anti-Reagan campaign. There is reason to think, then, that the Reagan administration would not be inclined to take a pro-New York stance in this dispute over the use of federal money to attract investment from one jurisdiction to another.

[26] *The New York Times*, February 15, 1983. For further evidence of a business disinclination to invest in areas with a large black population, see Bradbury, Downs, and Small, *Urban Decline and the Future of American Cities*.

[27] *The Washington Post*, January 30, 1984.

[28] Ibid., December 26, 1983.

The use of tax-exempt bonds to promote development has also become an issue on the grounds that these bonds are undercutting federal revenue at an astronomical rate. A U.S. Treasury Department estimate set the revenue loss from these bonds at $600 million per year. Over their life time, the tax-exempt bonds issued in a single year would amount to a loss of $4 billion.[29] The bonds, however, are strongly supported by state and local officials as well as by business interests because the revenue loss is by the federal government, not by state and local governments.

An advertisement by Mobil Corporation stated that ". . . government's responsibility is to provide the economic climate in which business can prosper."[30] Economic development programs operate on that premise. But some observers are now asking if what is good for business is necessarily good for the public. Government has now shouldered a significant share of the costs and risks of economic growth, but it appears that some segments of the population benefit from these development activities while others do not. As with housing subsidies under the federal tax law, the affluent fare better than the non-affluent. Investments seem to stimulate white-collar more than blue-collar employment, and there is evidence of business investments being steered away from concentrations of minority population and union sentiment. Further, there is the issue of tax-exempt bonds and various forms of tax abatement reducing public revenue at a time when government budgets at all levels are being squeezed. Local government officials often feel that they have no choice but to compete with one another for business favor, but there is no convincing evidence that this competition leaves everyone better off. America's tradition of privatism has provided no obstacles to public-private partnership in economic development, but it has perhaps been a barrier to a more critical analysis of benefits and costs.

THE FEDERAL ROLE IN COMMUNITY DEVELOPMENT

With local governments inadequately prepared to evaluate the consequences of various economic development strategies but nevertheless feeling compelled to engage in economic competition, the involvement of the federal government in development policy is a substantial issue. Yet, at a time when local governments are faced with difficult decisions, the federal government has opted for an even less direct involvement in community development policy than it has had in the past. Officially, federal policy dates back only to the Housing Act of 1949, which established the urban renewal program, but the national government has always played a

[29] Ibid., October 22, 1983.

[30] Ibid., September 6, 1982.

part, generally indirect—providing money and encouraging planning and coordination, but for the most part, expecting local governments to solve their own social and economic problems.

Consider first the urban renewal program. Under it, the federal government paid two-thirds of the cost to a local government when it bought and cleared land and sold it to a developer. This payment amounted to a huge subsidy for private developers, who were able to buy choice urban land for a discount price. The program was originally intended as a housing program, but urban renewal legislation was amended so that project areas could include nonresidential areas and uses. The major concerns of the program became the renewal of downtown business areas and the upgrading of central-city tax bases instead of the provision of housing units for the poor. Over the years, urban renewal was successful in rebuilding downtown areas and providing land for new public facilities such as hospitals, colleges, and civic centers. These benefits, however, were achieved at great social cost, as poor people were dislocated and viable urban neighborhoods were destroyed.

Recent federal efforts in these areas are centered in the Community Development Block Grant Program, which was created by the Housing and Community Development Act of 1974. This program replaced such old programs as Model Cities; urban renewal; grants for water and sewer projects, open space, urban beautification, historic preservation, and neighborhood facilities; and loans for public facilities and housing rehabilitation.

The block-grant approach used in community development contrasts sharply with the categorical-grant approach used in transportation policy. Like revenue sharing, community development block grants give localities more flexibility. For example, a city can obtain a single block grant to be used for a number of purposes instead of applying for separate, specific projects in all of these areas. The ability to set priorities at the local level is further enhanced by the elimination of local matching-share requirements. Another parallel to revenue sharing is the simplification of administrative requirements. There is only one application and review process for these programs instead of several.

Problems with Block Grants

Community development block grants have come under attack on two grounds: inequities in the formulas for distributing money *to* cities and *within* cities, and the failure to promote broader social objectives, such as citizen participation and the dispersal of low-income housing. In many respects, these are typical criticisms of the federal government's involvement in planning and community development.

In discussing community development block grants, the question of *where* aid should go is of paramount importance. Should money go to the neediest communities, those with the most poor and the oldest housing stock? Should money be distributed on a population basis? Or should there be rewards for the cities with the most political influence? As originally passed in 1974, the community development block grants formula took into account population, overcrowded housing, and the extent of poverty, the last item weighted twice. At first, the formula seemed excellent because objective criteria replaced grantsmanship and political deals. The problem, however, was that many of the oldest and largest central cities, located in the frostbelt states of the East and Midwest would lose substantial amounts of money, while the sunbelt cities with growing populations would be rewarded. In the face of much criticism, revised aid formulas were proposed, and the 1977 renewal of the program took into account physical deterioration, aged housing stock, and population losses, in determining grants. This plan benefits older cities in the East and Midwest to a greater extent than the initial formula did.

The formula *within* cities presents another kind of problem. There is no guarantee that community development block grants will be spent on problems related to poverty and low-income housing. The legislation originally required communities only to give "maximum feasible priority" to activities that benefit low- or moderate-income families and that help prevent or eliminate slums or blight. Subsequently guidelines were introduced to require cities to spend 75 percent of their money in low- or moderate-income areas, but these guidelines have now been modified to require only 51 percent. A city could easily spend its community development block grants on building a new stadium, a convention center or some other project to enhance the central business district while totally neglecting the needs of the poverty population. There is another danger, too. City hall can be faced with so many demands from community groups that it might approve hundreds of different small projects. Every neighborhood might get a piece of the action, but nothing of consequence would be accomplished in dealing with urban problems. Thus, problems have not ended even though community development block grants are given directly to local governments.

Community development block grants, like other urban programs passed since the mid-1960s, have very lax citizen-participation provisions. In effect, federal legislation has taken power away from the community groups and neighborhood activists of the 1960s, and returned it to city halls. Citizen-participation provisions now require only that citizens be informed, public hearings held, and citizens provided with an adequate opportunity to participate in developing applications. And even this last requirement has now been eased. Aside from broader notions of informing the public and allowing citizen input, the vital components of citizen participation, such as technical assistance and reimbursement for the costs of participation, which were instituted in the 1960s, have now largely been eliminated.

The targeting of block grant money—that is, requirements that a large portion of it be spent to benefit low and moderate income families—has emerged as a partisan issue. At this writing, the Reagan administration has proposed a rule that eliminates any numerical requirement for aiding the nonaffluent. House Democrats have responded by successfully promoting a legislative requirement for localities to show that they are spending at least half of their community development block grant money on the needy. What seems likely is not a final resolution of the issue, but a continuing partisan conflict, with Democrats in favor of targeting funds for the needy and Republicans opposed.

CONCLUSION

Control of development is still a local function in the United States, although many pressures faced by local governments are national and even global in scope. Because local governments are responsible for budgets and planning in their jurisidictions, and are generally responsible for the state of the local economy, they are caught up in economic competition with one another. They compete for economic growth and for affluent citizens. In order to attract business, local governments may hold back on taxing businesses. They generally levy low taxes on business and provide numerous incentives. In so doing, local governments fail to raise the amounts of revenues they might if competition among localities were not so sharp. Indeed, it is ironic that the fiscal crisis of our cities is always viewed as an expenditures problem, when it is equally an income problem.

In concluding this chapter, we must again emphasize that most planning and community development decisions are made privately. When the federal government is involved, it is generally true that the incentives are weak and indirect in relation to the problems that are tackled. Moreover, the trend in federal programs has been toward greater and greater reliance on private business. Leveraging, that is the use of public money to subsidize private investment, goes back at least as far as the urban renewal program; but it has become more extensive in recent years. It is the central principle, for example, in Urban Development Action Grants.

In comparing urban development policies in the United States with those of other nations, we can see that the United States is rather extreme in terms of the amount of power it gives local governments over land use and the amount of influence exercised by private interests. Local governments in this country plan for, build, and operate major facilities. The nation also accords the private sector a major role in planning and community development. The prevailing view has been that the public sector does not perform very well and therefore the public-sector role should be minimal. But as urbanist Brian Berry points out, another argument can be made:

> The poor performance of the public sector in . . . the United States is . . . a function both of the free-enterprise ideology and the fragmented governments which the ideology maintains, together with *fiscal systems that allocate tasks without resources* to city governments.[31]

Given the poor performance of our local governments in planning and community development, we might think about the federal government's having a more extensive role. At the very least, we should consider adopting a national policy of urban growth that would limit some of the economic competition among local governments. What we have now is a policy that began with the urban renewal legislation of 1949 and continued with the community development legislation encouraging local governments to compete with one another as they pursue their individual economic well-being. At no point have national policy makers shown how federal aid will enable local governments to solve such problems as energy supply and labor costs, much less how they can balance their economic development efforts with protection of the environment and care for the poor. Curiously, the disappointments of the 1960s gave rise to no official efforts to set national goals by which community development or other programs could be evaluated. Quite to the contrary, the federal government has simply provided local governments with some financial aid and washed its hands of any responsibility for program failures. As a nation, we proceed as if the community development activities of thousands of localities will somehow be guided by a benevolent invisible hand to produce a better quality of urban life. But, as we survey the urban condition, the evidence of such guidance is scarce indeed.

SUGGESTED READINGS

ALPEROVITZ, GAR and JEFF FAUX, *Rebuilding America*. New York: Pantheon Books, 1984.

ANTON, THOMAS. *Governing Greater Stockholm*. Berkeley: University of California Press, 1975.

BACHELOR, LYNN. "Reindustrialization in Detroit: Capital Mobility and Corporate Influence." *Journal of Urban Affairs*. Vol. 4 (Summer 1982), 35-50.

BLUESTONE, BARRY and BENNETT HARRISON. *The Deindustrialization of America: Plant Closings, Community Abandonment, and the Dismantling of Basic Industry*. New York: Basic Books, 1982.

CRENSON, MATTHEW A. *Neighborhood Politics*. Cambridge, MA: Harvard University Press, 1983.

[31] Brian J. L. Berry, *The Human Consequences of Urbanization* (New York: St. Martin's Press, 1973), pp. 166-67, emphasis added.

Cunningham, James V. and Milton Kotler. *Building Neighborhood Organizations.* Notre Dame, IN: University of Notre Dame Press, 1983.

Danielson, Michael and Jameson Doig. *New York: The Politics of Urban Regional Development.* Berkeley: University of California Press, 1982.

Fainstein, Susan S., and others. *Restructuring the City: The Political Economy of Urban Redevelopment.* New York: Longman, 1983.

Friedland, Roger. *Power and Crisis in the City.* New York: Schocken Books, 1983.

Hallman, Howard. *Neighborhoods: Their Place in Urban Life.* Beverly Hills, CA: Sage, 1984.

Hanson, Royce, ed. *Rethinking Urban Policy: Urban Development in an Advanced Economy.* Washington, D.C.: National Academy Press, 1983.

Harloe, Michael, ed. *Captive Cities: Studies in the Political Economy of Cities and Regions.* London: John Wiley & Sons, 1977.

Hartman, Chester, ed. *America's Housing Crisis.* Boston: Routledge & Kegan Paul, 1983.

Heidenheimer, Arnold, Hugh Heclo, and Carolyn Adams. *Comparative Public Policy: The Politics of Social Choice in Europe and America.* 2nd ed. New York: St. Martin's Press, 1983.

Henig, Jeffrey R. *Neighborhood Mobilization.* New Brunswick, NJ: Rutgers University Press, 1982.

Mollenkopf, John H. *The Contested City.* Princeton: Princeton University Press, 1983.

Molotch, Harvey. "The City as a Growth Machine: Toward a Political Economy of Place." *American Journal of Sociology* 82 (September 1976), 309-32.

O'Brien, David J. *Neighborhood Organization and Interest-Group Processes.* Princeton: Princeton University Press, 1975.

Raines, John C., Lenora E. Berson, and David Gracie, eds. *Community and Capital in Conflict: Plant Closings and Job Loss.* Philadelphia: Temple University Press, 1982.

Siegan, Bernard H. *Land Use Without Zoning.* Lexington, Mass: D.C. Heath, Lexington Books, 1972.

______. *Other People's Property.* Lexington, Mass.: D.C. Heath, Lexington Books, 1976.

Smith, Michael P., ed. *Cities in Transformation.* Beverly Hills, CA: Sage Publications, 1984.

Stone, Clarence N. *Economic Growth and Neighborhood Discontent.* Chapel Hill: University of North Carolina Press, 1976.

chapter 18

Police Behavior in the Urban Community

The police evoke contrasting images, ranging from the highly favorable and even heroic to the hated and feared. To some they are "crime busters," a thin line protecting civilization against a violent and lawless element. Others see them as arrogant, hostile, and heavy-handed—more concerned about their own power and well-being than about the laws they are supposed to enforce. Of course, police behavior itself is varied. It differs from community to community, from individual police officer to individual police officer, and above all, from situation to situation. Yet what the sharply contrasting images signals is not so much diversity in behavior as the fact that police conduct has become an emotionally charged issue.

Police behavior is a major political question, and the police themselves, through unionization and increased involvement in local elections, have become important political actors. On the ideological right, they have vocal allies. Several groups have voiced their strong support of the police while attacking the critics of police conduct. Minority groups and civil libertarians as well as national study commissions have, on the other hand, made some pointed attacks on police practices.

Despite these pockets of criticism, citizens generally give their local police a favorable performance rating. Even minorities, who have been the most critical of police behavior, are more approving than not; and their criticisms include complaints about too little policing as well as complaints about excesses of police power. At the same time that most Americans "support their local police," their feelings are mixed and changeable. All of us worry about abuses of power, and police power is certainly of a kind that evokes concern. Moreover, corruption scandals surface often enough to cause some disquietude about the integrity of police conduct.

Then, too, we surround the police with contradictory expectations. We want them to be fair and impartial but also to be friendly and not too strict. The boundaries of proper conduct are not drawn very clearly. The business proprietor does not want a police shakedown but is not averse to rendering favors for a little extra protection. Ours is a society that gives strong verbal backing to law and morality, but it is also a society in which law breaking is widespread and conduct falls far short of the morality we legislate. Because the police work in constant view of hypocrisy, double standards, and other human failings, they are cynical.

As police conduct has become a matter of public concern, the police have reacted strongly. They have assumed the stance of a beleaguered minority. To understand why police conduct has become an emotion-charged issue, among both the citizenry and the police themselves, we need to know something about police work and the influences on police bahavior.

CRIME

To the average citizen, police duties are simple—to apprehend law-breakers and prevent crime. The reality of police work is much different. One study showed that only 16 percent of all police calls were crime related.[1] Police responses ranged from answering questions about sonic booms to mediating family disputes to providing emergency first aid. Yet, it is the crime-related activity that provides the critical events in the life of a policeman and that makes police behavior a major political issue. Let us look first at crime and its relationship to police activities. Then we will examine the nature of police work more closely.

Crime comes in many forms, but most types of crime receive relatively little public attention. White-collar crime, for example, involves billions of dollars a year in tax evasion, embezzlement, price fixing, stock frauds, and other forms of swindling and consumer fraud. In dollar amounts, these forms of crime overshadow all others. Former Attorney General Ramsey Clark has observed that bank embezzlements, that is, known and reported bank embezzlements, cost ten times more than bank robberies each year.

[1] Thomas E. Bercal, "Calls for Police Assistance," in *Police in Urban Society*, ed. Harlan Hahn (Beverly Hills, Calif.: Sage Publications, 1970), p. 268.

And, he adds, "one corporate price-fixing conspiracy criminally converted more money each year it continued than all of the hundreds of thousands of burglaries, larcenies, or thefts in the entire nation during those same years."[2] Yet there is no hue and cry over white-collar crimes. Moreover, the penalties for such crimes are consistently light.

Public concern centers on a small number of high-fear crimes—homicide, forcible rape, aggravated assault, robbery, and burglary. A presidential commission concluded that the "prevalence of the two crimes of burglary and robbery is a significant, if not a major, reason for America's alarm about crime."[3] And, indeed, in one national survey well over half the people reported worrying about burglary or robbery. Among females, even those who had never been a victim, more than three-fourths were worried. In this same survey, a third of the total national sample indicated that they felt unsafe about walking alone at night in their own neighborhoods (and they felt safer in their own neighborhoods than in other neighborhoods).[4]

As the "law and order" issue emerged isn the 1960s, concern was not restricted to crimes of violence. It included a wide variety of acts of impropriety in public places. A survey of Boston homeowners found, for example, that people worried not only about crime and violence but also about public immorality, disorderly youth, delinquency, racial tension, and improper behavior in public places.[5] These findings are in some ways startling. Concerns about crime and disorder have proved not to be confined to a few well-to-do political conservatives but to be pervasive concerns, especially prevalent among the poor and elderly. Indeed, for many people these worries have overshadowed more traditional urban problems such as jobs, housing, pollution, and transportation. On reflection, the findings prove less surprising. The old and the poor are the most frequent victims of such crimes as robbery and burglary. Also, they are the most likely to live in older and changing neighborhoods, the places where standards of "proper" behavior in public places are in greatest transition.

With public concern over crime and disorder running at a high level, many people clamor for tighter controls on the criminal element. But who are the criminal element? In contrast to what most people believe about criminality, students of criminal behavior generally reject the idea that there is a distinct criminal class. Though relatively few people are arrested, most people at one time or another have committed acts for which they

[2] Ramsey Clark, *Crime in America* (New York: Simon and Schuster, 1970), p. 38. See also, Edgar May, "White Collar Crime," *Police Magazine* (March 1980), pp. 27-35.

[3] President's Commission on Law Enforcement and Administration of Justice, *The Challenge of Crime in a Free Society* (Washington, D.C.: Government Printing Office, 1967), p. 4.

[4] Ibid., pp. 50-51.

[5] James Q. Wilson, *Thinking about Crime* (New York: Random House, Vintage Books, 1975), p. 25.

could have received prison sentences. There is, however, a distinct age and class structure related to various categories of crime.[6] While the majority of offenders arrested on all counts are white, male, and over twenty-four years old, arrest rates for specific crimes show quite a varied pattern. Motor vehicle theft is greatest among those under eighteen. Willful homicide is greatest for those over twenty-five. White-collar crimes, as the label indicates, are committed mostly by people of high status and in responsible positions. Crimes of violence are most frequently committed by persons of low status and income. Burglary and larceny arrest rates are highest for those under eighteen; robbery arrests are highest for those eighteen to twenty-four years old. But most of the people arrested for such varied offenses as embezzlement, fraud, crimes against the family, gambling, drunkenness, and vagrancy are twenty-five and over. Even though the differences have diminished some in recent years, males are arrested much more frequently than females. Many more whites than blacks are arrested each year, but the arrest *rates* are higher for blacks on many offenses. Racial differences in arrest rates, like sex differences, have diminished somewhat in recent years; and, of course, racial differences in arrest rates are heavily intertwined with class differences. When whites and blacks living under similar socioeconomic conditions are compared, differences in arrest rates become very small.

While criminal acts are committed by all segments of the population, the police are not equally concerned with all types of criminal activity. The police deal mainly with what is sometimes called street crime, that is, the high-fear crimes plus breaches of the peace. Police arrests and other exercises of policy authority thus do not fall with equal weight on all types of criminality. They fall heaviest on those who commit street crimes—on the young, non-affluent, male, and minority members of the population. Publicity, too, focuses on high-fear crimes and their perpetrators, thus reinforcing stereotypes about criminality—stereotypes often shared by the police.

THE NATURE OF POLICE WORK

Crime, as we have seen, is committed by all classes, but middle-class crime is dealt with mainly by civil authorities. The police concentrate on lower-class crime. Noncrime police activities have a similar class orientation. When the affluent face emergencies, they use private resources and facilities to cope. The poor call the police. Thus those who come to the police for help are not a random sample of the whole population. They are mostly the poor, the down and out, and the desperate. Whether the work be that of render-

[6] The findings reported here are based mainly on *The Challenge of Crime in a Free Society*, pp. 147-57.

ing emergency assistance, aiding a victim of a crime, reestablishing public order, questioning a witness, or making a criminal arrest, the policeman deals largely with a lower-class clientele. Consequently, police frustrations and police misconduct are more likely to be visited upon the lower classes than upon other elements of the population.

In looking at the nature of police work—how the police go about their work and what they do—we will concentrate on three factors: (1) the use of individual discretion, (2) the maintenance of authority, and (3) work in a bureaucratic setting. These factors provide the on-the-job pressures and experiences that do so much to shape police behavior.

Unlike the drama and excitement in the lives of television police, real police perform work that is largely routine, often boring, and frequently involving much paper work and report writing. But the testing ground for a policeman is the occasion when he or (increasingly) she must use judgment about how to handle a problem. Although police life is often dull, it can also be dangerous. If a suspect reaches for a pocket, is it an innocent action or a move to draw a weapon? The need to be on guard against potential threats to personal safety is an ever-present element in police work. How much force should be used, and when? These are difficult questions. Even if no danger is involved, a moment's hesitation can enable a numbers runner or a junkie to destroy incriminating evidence.

Law enforcement itself is an endless web of judgments. Should a disorderly drunk be locked up or taken home to his wife? When is a rowdy group of teenagers engaged in behavior serious enough to warrant arrest for disorderly conduct? What about a family or neighborhood fight—when should the police officer simply try to mediate and restore order, and when should he or she threaten an arrest? Particularly in circumstances where community standards are at variance with the letter of the law, how stringently should antivice laws be enforced? Most observers agree that the police underenforce the law. Some infractions are ignored completely, and others are dealt with by restoring order and perhaps issuing a warning. The heart of police work is discretion—when and to what extent to enforce the law; when, how, and to what extent to assert authority. Since the police do not, indeed cannot, arrest all of the offenders they encounter, they must use judgment. Police departments, James Q. Wilson has observed, are somewhat unique organizations in that "discretion increases as one moves down the hierarchy."[7]

If judgment is one key element in the police work experience, then another equally important element is authority. The authority that police exercise is ultimately coercive. No matter how many cats they get down out of trees, small kids and old people they help across the street, lost drivers

[7] James Q. Wilson, *Varieties of Police Behavior* (Cambridge, Mass.: Harvard University Press, 1968), p. 7.

they give directions to, babies they deliver in patrol cars on the way to the hospital, or injured people they give first aid to, the police badge is still a symbol of the coercive authority of the state. The blunt reality is that the police have the legal power to deprive an individual of her or his liberty. Since few people are totally innocent under the law, most citizens are at least a little apprehensive in the presence of police authority.

Police assert their authority in conditions of uncertain compliance. Resistance to arrest is the extreme case. A more frequent problem for the police officer is that of gaining control of an unsettled situation. In a sense, the police officer must establish a legitimate right to intervene. When called upon, the police are often thrown into an adversary situation. Their authority may be recognized but still resisted and almost certainly resented by some. They can use force, but the use of force may escalate conflict rather than contain it. Often, they are involved in a situation only because other methods of social control have broken down. They are the last resort in restoring a breach of the peace. They have the threat of force; and the coercive authority of the state, as symbolized by the uniform, badge, nightstick, and gun, lies behind them. But the real key to their success lies in an ability to act in an authoritative manner. One participant-observer of police conduct offered the following assessment:

> [The patrolman] must learn how to establish and express his authority by cajoling, requesting, threatening, "bullshitting them," as patrolmen say, to avoid using force. He must learn to use his body to express with his whole self the authority represented by the appearance he presents; he must learn to use it as a weapon when the occasion demands. He must learn when to mobilize his physical resources and when to let them slumber, allowing his legal power to act for him. In all of his actions he must learn to acquire a quickness, resolution, and decisiveness that urge him forward when others withdraw. He must accept and welcome the fact that, as a policeman, he must be in control of the situation lest it be in control of him.[8]

Police operate in uncertain and even dangerous circumstances and therefore have a strong investment in maintaining authority. Understandably, they expect deference and, in fact, feel threatened by any show of disrespect or other lack of deference. They tend to act tough—to avoid at almost any cost a loss of face. Indeed, the police ideology holds that

> the officer who ignores challenges from citizens loses the respect of the citizenry and makes it difficult for other officers to work in the precinct. No challenge to authority, therefore, can go unmet until there is acquiescence to it. The [informal] police code prohibits "backing down."[9]

[8] Jonathan Rubinstein, *City Police* (New York: Farrar, Straus and Giroux, 1973), p. 274.

[9] Albert J. Reiss, Jr., *The Police and the Public* (New Haven: Yale University Press, 1971), p. 150.

Police "excesses," especially the excessive use of force, occur mainly when the police feel that citizens are disrespectful. One author reminds us that police use of physical force is not the only way that nondeferential citizens can be "punished." The policeman can use an "insulting tone, talk down to someone, adopt a familiarity that is unwanted. . . ."[10] And while the police can be ordered to avoid doing these things, they will either disregard the order or stay out of some situations. The patrolman and the police administrator alike face a dilemma. There is no polite way to order someone around, but an uncivil tone or derisive manner will almost certainly generate resentment. On the other hand, impolite words and tones are preferable to the use of force. The patrolman on the beat wants the full, unrestricted repertoire of techniques for asserting control.

A third important element of the policeman's work world is the bureaucratic setting. Police work in a strictly hierarchical or command structure. Discipline and obedience have long been hallmarks of police organization. Even though the patrolman on the beat operates away from the watchful eye of headquarters much of the time, there is still a definite chain of command, and the policeman's duties are defined by that command structure. Rewards in the form of good assignments or promotion are controlled by superiors.

At the same time that police work in a bureaucratic setting, they do not conform rigidly to bureaucratic patterns. By tradition, police work is a craft. The police officer on the job learns more from other police officers than from official manuals, orders, or formal training courses. Further, police officers learn to have confidence in their own judgment and ability to handle situations. They therefore regard departmental regulations with great skepticism. If they feel a need for guidance, they look to their co-workers more than to the rules set forth by their superiors. They even expect their superiors to fit rules and procedures to the situation; they do not expect their superiors to insist that the rules and procedures be followed without regard to the particular circumstance. Moreover rank-and-file members of a police department are not without counterpressures they can exert on their superiors.

Today, however, there are opposing forces at work. On the one side there is the craft tradition of individual independence and loyalty to co-workers. On the other side, modern technology and the bureaucratic impulse encourage strict hierarchical control. Police on patrol are kept in touch with a dispatcher. They are expected to call in periodically and give their exact location, and they are subject to spot checks. Police in New York are now expected to fill out a log book and have it verified by a field commander. Report writing constitutes a large portion of their duty. And

[10] Rubinstein, *City Police*, p. 324. On the problem of coercive power, see the brilliant study by William K. Muir, *Police: Street-corner Politicians* (Chicago: University of Chicago Press, 1977).

with modern techniques of data processing, they are increasingly subject to performance standards based on quantitative measures.

THE POLICE PERSONALITY

Is there a police personality? Obviously many kinds of people enter police work, and behavior varies from place to place and individual to individual. But are there certain regularities of conduct and outlook that occur with great frequency? Most observers think there are. To be sure, the policeman in the wealthy suburb probably differs both in background and on-the-job pressures from the patrolman in the inner city. And, no doubt, as more women and minority members enter law-enforcement work, the police occupation is undergoing some significant changes. Nevertheless, we can identify some recurring observations among those who have studied police behavior.

Characteristics widely attributed to the police include the following: cynicism, punitiveness, repressiveness, conventionalism, excessive concern with masculinity, political conservatism, prejudice against minorities and other lower-status persons, secretiveness and a high degree of in-group solidarity, alienation, resentfulness, and militancy. Let us look more closely at some of these traits, first to see more precisely what they are, and then to see how they might come into being.

Police cynicism has many targets. First of all, police have a pessimistic view of human nature. Their work, after all, involves crime, disorder, vice, violence, people fighting with one another, people cheating and stealing from one another, people who are hostile and who are interacting mainly on the basis of ill will. The late Chief William Parker of the Los Angeles Police Department, an influential member of the police profession, frequently made predictions that this civilization would destroy itself. In a study of the Chicago police, nearly half agreed with the statement that "most people obey laws simply from fear of being caught."[11]

Police are also cynical about public support for law enforcement. A New York policeman, in accusing the public of complacency and even complicity, argued, "It's getting to the point where mugging is becoming acceptable as a way of life."[12] In a thirteen-city study done for the National Commission on Civil Disorders, researchers found that police at the precinct level perceived their greatest problem, by far, to be lack of public

[11]James Q. Wilson, "Police Morale, Reform and Citizen Respect: The Chicago Case," in *The Police*, ed. David J. Bordua (New York: John Wiley & Sons, 1967), p. 147.

[12]Quoted in Nicholas Alex, *New York Cops Talk Back* (New York: John Wiley & Sons, 1976), p. 131.

support.[13] Time and time again, researchers have found that people generally do support their local police; at least they express a favorable attitude toward their local police. Yet the police themselves feel that they operate in an unfriendly and uncooperative environment.

Finally, police in many large cities are cynical about the running of their departments. They feel that there is a large amount of political interference with police administration. And very large percentages believe that promotions and other rewards are given on the basis of favoritism. Even after a reform superintendent was put in office, a large majority of the Chicago police felt that duty assignments in their department were not handled fairly.[14] In a study of New York police, a third of those queried thought that special assignments depended on "whom you know, not on merit."[15]

Disillusionment sets in early for many police officers. They come out of the police academy already torn between the ideals of the profession and advice about the necessity to deal with the world pragmatically. As one writer explains:

> The rookie begins with faith in the system. He tries to follow the book of rules and regulations. Then, he discovers that many cases have repercussions of which the book seems wholly ignorant. He is chastized by his colleagues for being naive enough to follow the book. Gradually he learns to neglect the formal rules and norms and turns elsewhere for direction. Individual interpretation replaces the formal authoritative dictum of the official book and the young policeman is an easy prey to cynicism.[16]

New police officers are inducted into a number of rituals—from taking unauthorized breaks to, in some cases, various forms of corruption. They learn that the way to get ahead in the department is to have a "rabbi," that is, an influential person in the hierarchy who will promote their careers. They may also learn about "contracts," that is about the need to repay favors, and about various reciprocal obligations and arrangements. Much of their record keeping involves widespread collusion and deception.

Cynicism, especially about human behavior, is associated with a tendency to be punitive and repressive. We have already seen that police work encourages a strong concern for asserting and maintaining authority. The police officers may also "learn" that the people they deal with "only understand force." The old timers warn the young recruits, "You gotta be tough, kid, or you'll never last."[17] Police also display a number of other traits associated with authoritarianism. Traditionally, they have displayed exces-

[13] Peter H. Rossi, Richard A. Berk, and Bettye E. Eidson, *The Roots of Urban Discontent* (New York: John Wiley & Sons, 1974), p. 117.

[14] Wilson, "Police Morale," p. 145.

[15] Arthur Niederhoffer, *Behind the Shield* (New York: Doubleday, Anchor Books, 1967), p. 228.

[16] Ibid., pp. 52-53.

[17] Ibid., p. 56.

sive concerns about masculinity and have been particularly hostile toward homosexuals. They are poltically quite conservative, and sometimes support radical right groups. A study of Memphis police, for example, found that police in that city had "warm" feelings toward a wide variety of groups on the right, groups as varied as the American Legion, the National Guard, conservatives, Republicans, the Ku Klux Klan, and the military.[18] Police also adhere strongly to conventional middle-class values.

Police are quite likely to stereotype various racial, ethnic, and class groups. They are markedly unsympathetic to blacks, the poor in general, welfare recipients in particular, and other underdog groups. Numerous studies have documented the negative feelings that white police have about blacks. They tend to embrace the stereotypes of blacks as lazy, violence prone, and irresponsible. Thus in the 1960s they attributed civil disorder to failings in the black community itself—disrespect for law, broken families, and agitation. They gave little credence to poverty, discrimination, and frustration as causes. In fact, they believed that blacks had achieved equality and, if anything, had come to be favored. As for themselves, white police in the ghetto believe that they are surrounded by an indifferent and even hostile people. The National Advisory Commission on Civil Disorders study of thirteen cities showed that only a third of the police believed that most blacks were "on their side." Over half believed that most adolescents in the ghetto regarded the police "as enemies."[19] Black police officers are, as onc would predict, more sympathetic to the plight of blacks generally; but they, like their white counterparts, see relatively little ghetto support for the police.

For their part, blacks have, in fact, looked less favorably on the police than whites have. Post-riot surveys in the 1960s showed ghetto residents to be critical of police conduct. And in a national opinion survey, blacks were less likely than whites to say that the police were doing an excellent job and more likely than whites to say that the police were doing a poor job. On the question of police honesty, 63 percent of the whites said "almost all" were honest, but only 30 percent of the nonwhites agreed with that view. And whereas only 1 percent of the whites said that "almost all" police were corrupt, 10 percent of the nonwhites agreed with that position.[20] Blacks are also critical of the police for providing too little protection and for responding too slowly to police calls.

Given the high level of tension between blacks and the police and given the negative feelings of white police officers toward blacks, one would guess that the police would be more harsh with blacks than with

[18] Alan Edward Bent, *The Politics of Law Enforcement* (Lexington, Mass.: D.C. Heath, Lexington Books, 1974), p. 99.

[19] National Advisory Commission on Civil Disorders, *Supplemental Studies* (Washington, D.C.: Government Printing Office, 1969), pp. 108-14.

[20] The President's Commission on Law Enforcement and the Administration of Justice, *The Challenge of Crime in a Free Society*, p. 99.

whites, committing more acts of brutality against blacks and directing uncivil remarks disproportionately against blacks. Such is not the case, however. One student of police conduct found that "although more than three-fourths of all white police officers made prejudiced statements about Negroes, in actual encounters the police did not treat Negroes uncivilly more often than they did whites."[21] In fact, this student found that both black and white police officers were more likely to use undue force against members of ther *own* race. Arrest decisions offer the same pattern. In comparable circumstances, the police have not been found to be more inclined to arrest blacks than whites.[22]

Though some police chiefs make efforts to promote good public relations and increase police-community communications, the police in their role tend to be introverted and secretive. One chief had a weekly radio program called "Buzz the Fuzz," in which he answered all calls from the public.[23] However, many police officers are reluctant to talk with outsiders about police work. Some departments even have an official policy against the discussion of police business with civilians. Socially, too, individual police officers shy away from civilian contacts. Police officers tend to be friends with other police officers. They belong to police fraternal organizations and attend their social functions with notable frequency. The social pattern comes about partly because civilians often are uneasy in the presence of even off-duty policemen.

Along with their isolation, police tend toward a high degree of solidarity. Generally they are not critical of one another, especially in public. A survey in New York City revealed that two-thirds of the patrol officers agreed with the statement that the "police department is really a large brotherhood in which each patrolman does his best to help all other patrolmen."[24] The feelings of fraternal loyalty should not be exaggerated. Racial, ethnic, and other tensions are often divisive forces within police departments. But as soon as there is outside criticism, the police unite.

Solidarity has a practical foundation. Police work is dangerous, and the danger tends to draw the members together. No crime is more diligently pursued than the killing of a police officer. And any police officer in trouble, regardless of race, color, or creed, can count on immediate and full help from fellow officers. Because of the danger inherent in their work, the police genuinely attach a high value to teamwork. In many circumstances they must rely on one another for protection. And the teamwork and mutual protection must come automatically and instantaneously—there may be no time for deliberation.

[21] Reiss, *The Police and the Public*, p. 147.

[22] Donald J. Black and Albert J. Reiss, Jr., "Police Control of Juveniles," *American Sociological Review* 35 (February 1970), 63-77. See also Jerome Skolnick, *Justice Without Trial* (New York: John Wiley & Sons, 1966), pp. 83-86.

[23] Bent, *Politics of Law Enforcement*, p. 60.

[24] Hahn, "A Profile of Urban Police," p. 19.

Police solidarity runs vertically up and down the command structure as well as horizontally among detectives and those on patrol. Consequently, a police department is hard to control from outside. It is almost invulnerable to ordinary forms of executive or civilian control. Some forms of misconduct are widely accepted among the police, and such actions as the unjustified firing of a weapon are infrequently punished. A Police Foundation report, for instance, found that police officers who fired their revolvers without justification were rarely subject to strong disciplinary measures. The report concluded, "Apparent violations of both the letter and the spirit of department policies have been condoned either by outright justification or by extremely mild discipline."[25]

Several liberal mayors have run into insurmountable resistance in trying to redirect the behavior of recalcitrant police departments. Carl Stokes, who called his inability to reform the Cleveland Police Department "my greatest frustration and my greatest failure."[26] recounts an experience from his second and final term as mayor. Stokes was strongly opposed to police carrying private weapons and was shocked to learn that his commissioner of public safety had authorized the police to carry weapons not issued by the department. When Stokes sent a memorandum to his commissioner instructing him to reverse the authorization, the commissioner responded:

> Mr. Mayor, I have to confess my being unable to carry through an instruction of yours. I received this memo. There are some very practical things in life sometimes that one has to face. Whatever I tell those police, whether I tell them to carry these weapons or not to carry them, they are going to carry them anyway. So since they are carrying them anyway, why don't we show our cooperation with them.[27]

After other disagreements on topics ranging from the use of dumdum bullets to the location of police headquarters, the public safety commissioner resigned, charging in his letter of resignation; ". . . I am not receiving from you and your administration the support my programs require. And the enemies of law enforcement continue to receive support and comfort from you and your administration."[28] Stokes subsequently chose not to run for reelection; the opposition of the police and their political allies was a key factor in his decision. Like others before and after him, Stokes was often unable to get his orders carried out; and by asserting his leadership against police resistance he generated costly political opposition. Few officeholders are willing to push their leadership to the point where they will be labeled enemies of law enforcement. Those who do, and

[25] *The Washington Post,* May 17, 1977.

[26] Carl B. Stokes, *Promises of Power* (New York: Simon and Schuster, 1973), p. 171.

[27] Quoted in ibid., p. 196.

[28] Ibid., p. 200.

engender oppostion, seldom enjoy long tenure. Stokes was in office four years.

Not just in Cleveland but in many places, police hostility has many targets: elected officials, the news media, black leaders and other spokespersons for minorities, judges, and the public in general. The police often see themselves as pawns in a political game over which they have no control. They attack "the hypocrisy of the whole liberal movement" and attribute their anger and frustration to a "soft, permissive, over-legalized society."[29] The courts are a particular target of police resentment; judges are accused of being unconcerned with true justice—turning dangerous criminals loose, enforcing unrealistic standards, ignoring the practicalities of law enforcement, and even disregarding the law itself. The police feel totally misunderstood. A New York policeman complained:

> You cry police brutality without knowing what is happening. You talk about crime in the streets but you tolerate courts giving criminals a slap on the wrist. You don't know what a cop is for or what he should do.[30]

When the police corruption scandal broke in New York in 1970, members of the force reacted by blaming almost everyone but themselves. They accused the news media, for example, of singling them out and thereby undermining respect for law enforcement.

Police have responded to their frustration and alienation by becoming more militant politically and by unionization. Both responses are viewed as methods for defending themselves in a hostile and threatening environment. Though police strikes were for a long time taboo, police now engage in job actions with increasing frequency. They may not call it a strike, but refer instead to a sick-in, blue flu, or a show of dissatisfaction. Whatever the label, police are no longer reluctant to use such action to further their interests.

ROOTS OF POLICE BEHAVIOR

If there is, as most observers argue, a distinctive pattern of police behavior, how and why does this behavior come about? Are particular personality types attracted to police work, or do the pressures of the job shape and largely determine the attitudes and conduct of the police? Social scientists have long been interested in a personality type known as the authoritarian personality. It is associated with such traits as a concern with power and toughness, racial and ethnic prejudice, a tendency to stereotype, a low

[29] Alex, *New York Cops Talk Back*, p. 131.

[30] Quoted in Nicholas Alex, *Black in Blue* (New York: Appleton-Century-Crofts, 1969), p. 11.

tolerance of ambiguity (that is, a tendency to see things in strict good-and-evil terms), cynicism, aggressiveness, conventionalism, and support of extremist politics. Since those are traits displayed by the police to varying degrees, one could easily speculate that police work does indeed attract authoritarian types. On the other hand, the pressures of the job are very intense, intense enough to have a strong shaping effect by themselves.

Police work traditionally has been attractive mainly to working-class males. Undoubtedly, police behavior reflects this recruiting base. Police language is crude, and police banter is filled with ethnic and racial stereotypes, in part because working-class talk is crude and filled with stereotypes. Despite their role in upholding the standards of the nation, the police have never been the "goody-goody two-shoes" of the nation. Sociologist Jerome Skolnick explains:

> The policeman's culture is that of the masculine workingman. It is of the docks, the barracks, the ballfield—Joe DiMaggio was a helluva good "wop" centerfielder, not an athlete of Italian "extraction," and similarly the black man is a "nigger," not a member of an "underprivileged minority."[31]

In their work style the police also reflect a working-class manner. An overriding concern with maintaining self respect, a macho style (that is, a preoccupation with proving one's masculinity), not being "shown up," not being "taken in," and "not taking any crap," all of these are recurring concerns of working-class men. Moreover, the police are not sticklers for the rules. Quite to the contrary, they are at best casual about them and often outright contemptuous of them. They like the direct approach in action and language. Skolnick attributes this, in part, to the constant pressure of physical danger—an ever-present reminder to stick to the basics. He compares the police officer to the combat soldier: "Like the dogface, he is irritated by most manifestations of what he terms 'chicken shit'—an inclusive abstraction encompassing minor organizational rules, legal technicalities, and embellished descriptions."[32]

The working-class subculture contains some authoritarian traits and certainly is not conducive to a high level of middle-class-defined civility. But working-class authoritarianism, if that is an apt phrase, is quite different from an authoritarian personality. Training and other inducements can change working-class manners, or new patterns of recruitment—such as bringing in college graduates—can eliminate such manners from the beginning. But an authoritarian personality is a different matter. The behavior pattern is presumably based on some deep-seated need—an inner-felt compulsion to see the world and react to it in a certain way. Such a personality-based behavior is not so easily changed, and most police

[31] Skolnick, *Justice Without Trial*, p. 82.

[32] Ibid.

departments of any size, as a matter of standard practice now, conduct psychological tests to weed out the psychologically unfit.

There is, in fact, no substantial evidence that police work attracts authoritarian personalties. Quite to the contrary, police recruits generally appear to be psychologically sound and competent persons, little different from the larger population of which they are a part. Far from showing any great concern with power or the opportunity to do battle with the forces of evil, most police recruits are concerned mainly with getting a steady job that carries a good pension. They do show a tendency to be active, energetic, and aggressive. There is a certain restlessness that needs an outlet. Few recruits to the police force are seeking a desk job. Instead, they are looking "for action and opportunity for muscular activity."[33] That, however, is not evidence of authoritarian traits.

Among scholars there is a growing consensus that police behavior comes more from the pressure of the work situation than from the inner dynamics of personality. Surrounded by danger, beset by a high degree of uncertainty about the proper role of the police, and plagued by conditions conducive to cynicism, police work has always given rise to a certain amount of authoritarianism. In recent years, as the pace of social change has accelerated, the police occupation has come under tremendous pressure to modify its traditional character. However, this pressure has intensified police anxiety (and perhaps thereby heightened some authoritarian tendencies). Infused with new uncertainty, police behavior is often defensive. In an occupation long filled by members who, first and foremost, were seeking economic security, the prospects of fundamental change have been deeply disturbing. Under the circumstances, political militancy and a new found penchant for union affiliation should not be surprising.

Contemporary police behavior thus has both a traditional basis and a basis in newly emerging trends. Let us first look at some of the traditional pressures on police. Then we can consider some of the new pressures.

Police by the very nature of their work are taught to be suspicious and distrustful, to expect the worst, and to be on guard. It is no wonder that they view the world in a cynical way. They are led to conclude, as did Napoleon's minister of police many years ago, that the world is composed of "scoundrels, hypocrites, and imbeciles,"[34] They also fall easily into the pattern of stereotyping. They are taught to look for the unusual, and their need for making instantaneous decisions leads them into shorthand techniques for identifying dangerous or suspicious behavior. They learn to look for what one observer has termed "symbolic assailants"—"persons

[33] Jesse Rubin, "Police Identity and the Police Role," in *The Police and the Community*, ed. Robert F. Steadman (Baltimore: Johns Hopkins Press, 1972), p. 20; see also Niederhoffer, *Behind the Shield*, pp. 109-60, esp. p. 159.

[34] Niederhoffer, *Behind the Shield*, p. 99.

who use gesture, language, and attire that the policeman has come to recognize as a prelude to violence."[35]

As we have already seen, authority is central to police performance. The police are specialists in force, in coercive authority; and like all specialists, they attach great importance to their specialty. Despite the fact that they spend much time in service activities and in peace-keeping roles (such as mediating family disputes), their training *and their occupational images* center on the crime-fighting and force-using aspects of their work. They often are not trained in service work or family intervention, and indeed, they tend to look down on such work. In police work there are, as one writer points out, "no built-in rewards for good performance as a peace keeper." Further, "Police officers believe that citizens have little regard for their performance in the area of peace-keeping and community service."[36] By contrast:

> . . . the apprehension and conviction of the felon is, for the policeman, the essence of police work. It is the source of prestige both within and without police circles. It has career implications and it is a major source of justification for the existence of the police before a critical and often hostile public. . . .[37]

Thus, community service work with a predominantly lower-class clientele is not a source of satisfaction but a source of frustration. Police have few incentives to develop and value skills other than their coercive ones. Some are contemptuous of human-relations training. One police officer said of Miami's cultural awareness program:

> It was a joke. We sat around with a couple of shrinkheads who told us that the Haitians were oppressed people. Well, I don't give a damn. What the hell does that have to do with me? They still aren't welcome in my house.[38]

In dealing with crime-related matters, police are under conflicting pressures. First of all, in the police academy they may be taught the finer points of due process,the need for a high level of civility, and the virtues of restraint in the use of coercive authority; but the actual work experience and the advice of veteran officers run in a different direction. Police officers are judged by their arrest records, and any new police officer who seems reluctant to make an arrest or assert authority is needled by the veterans. Thus, the formal expectations of the larger society—that legal

[35] Skolnick, *Justice Without Trial*, p. 45.

[36] Rubin, "Police Identity and the Police Role," p. 26.

[37] William A. Westley, "Violence and the Police," *American Journal of Sociology* 59 (August 1953), 35.

[38] Quoted in, Philip B. Taft, Jr., "Policing the New Immigrant Ghettos," *Police Magazine* 5 (July 1982), 18.

procedures will be followed closely, that citizens are due a presumption of innocence because the wielders of coercive authority may make mistakes and wrongfully deprive someone of liberty, and that citizens will be treated with respect—are not in tune with the actual operating code of the police. Instead, the police function on the basis of a "crime control" model, one in which the emphasis is not on due process but on effective and efficient administration of criminal law. It is a model, sociologist Skolnick points out, that stresses "social control over individual justice."[39] The actual model of operation is based on the perceived need to apprehend and convict a large number of criminal offenders. No matter what others might say about due process, police believe that their effectiveness is measured by their performance as agents of social control. Criminal justice practices (such as stringent rules on questioning suspects and on obtaining evidence, easy pretrial release, and heavy reliance on probation) are seen by the police as illogical interferences with the work they are supposed to do. When the police are criticized for not preventing crime at the same time that judicial restraints on their operations are being increased, their frustrations are multiplied. As Skolnick observes, the police believe that they are required to work in an environment "filled with extraneous and . . . needless restrictions."[40] They ask, if the aims of the community are to prevent crime, why are criminals permitted to manipulate the system to their own advantage and evade punishment?

In recent years as judicial standards of due process have risen and as citizen complaints, especially minority complaints, about police brutality have increased, police have become embittered because the public, as they see it, has become less supportive of the conditions needed for effective job performance. They see themselves as experts who are not allowed to practice their trade as they best know how. They do not see themselves as experts with formal training but as practitioners of a craft; sensible persons who have a realistic understanding of the world and sound, practical ideas about how to carry out their duties. Skolnick maintains that the policeman looks on crime control with the "*administrative bias of the craftsman.*" He adds:

> . . . the policeman tends to emphasize his own expertness and specialized abilities to make judgments about the measures to be applied to apprehend "criminals," as well as the ability to estimate accurately the guilt or innocence of suspects. He sees himself as a craftsman, at his best, a master of his trade. As such, he feels he ought to be free to employ the techniques of his trade, and that the *system* ought to provide regulations contributing to his freedom to improvise, rather than constricting it.[41]

[39] Skolnick, *Justice Without Trial*, p. 182.

[40] Ibid., p. 202.

[41] Ibid., p. 196.

The police, as they have operated traditionally, thus give little weight to abstract principles like due process. They have operated more on the basis of practical experience and individual judgment. They have been inclined to think that they knew who the criminals were and needed only to be left free to deal with them in the most effective way.

One response to the shortcomings in police conduct, indeed the favored response of top-level police administrators, is to call for police professionalism. The term *professionalism* is a difficult one to define. It means different things to different people. Almost always, it is linked with a high level of formal training. In the case of the police, there is growing interest among officials in a college degree as a preemployment educational requirement, and there is also interest in more extensive in-service training programs. Yet many of the veteran officers are skeptical of these trends and perhaps even feel threatened by them.

At the same time that more rigous formal credentials are being talked about, police departments are also under pressure to recruit more women and minorities—in some instances adopting more flexible recruitment criteria to do so. And some police officers feel that their status is threatened by a perceived lowering of occupational standards. Many view the two-moves—professionalism and more open recruitment—as contradictory.[42] They resent what they see as official hypocrisy. Such feelings feed the belief that police administration is politically motivated, and officers react with heightened disillusionment.

In reality, police professionalism has meant more than simply greater formal training. It has also meant more centralized managerial control—a practice very much at odds with classical ideas of professionalism and also at odds with the craft ideals of the police. Thus recent trends in police administration call for more rules, more reports, more internal controls, routinization of procedures, less individual discretion, centrally controlled deployment, and tighter discipline. In the view of some, the police department is, and should be, strictly a "command" organization; and in order to assure impartiality and predictability, its quasi-military character should be strengthened at the hand of the craft traditions of the police. Obviously, those who were recruited into the police with the craft image in mind decry the trend. As one observer points out, the craft view of the police calls for a job free of fixed routine and depicts the individual police officer as a "free, independent, active, masculine, autonomous man."[43]

Everywhere the police look they see conflicting pressures, opposing pressures on their departments, and conflict between their own ideals and the trends at work in their occupational environment.

[42] On the reaction of police departments to affirmative action requirements, see Marc R. Levinson, "Affirmative Action: Is It Just a Numbers Game?" *Police Magazine* 5 (March 1982), 8-27.

[43] Alex, *New York Cops Talk Back*, p. 54.

The intense cross pressures of the postreform period have made the police not less authoritarian but rather more defensive about their authority. The cross pressures undoubtedly have increased cynicism. Instead of modifying their behavior in the direction sought by their critics, the police have become more isolated. And they have also resented and resisted tighter managerial direction. Their alienation and militancy, at least at their current levels, are not long-standing traits of police behavior. They are traits that have emerged in recent years. Some observers talk about "the siege mentality" of the police. As we have seen, police are no longer reluctant to engage in strikes or other job actions. Moreover, in some departments their alienation has apparently lowered performance. Reflecting on the Liberty City Riot in Miami, one police officer explained how patrol officers had reacted to the combined circumstances of heightened departmental emphasis on good human relations *and* significant budget cuts. He said, "My honest opinion is that this riot is the last thing the men needed; they had already stopped working before the riot came about."[44]

Sometimes police officers feel that what they do makes no difference. Add to that a concern about their actions being subjected to departmental scrutiny and discipline, and the result is almost sure to be minimal patrolling.

If we look again at police traits such as cynicism, authoritarianism, and alienation, we see that these traits do not come from a single cause but from many sources. Their work experience and their socialization into the craft give the police some authoritarian traits. And these traits probably are reinforced by the stresses and strains of an occupation that contains the seeds of both danger and controversy. The nature of their work, and the immediate expectations surrounding it, have lent themselves to neither a liberal-professional role model nor a disciplined, command-following role model. As we look at the police in transition, as we consider the possible impact of new recruitment patterns, and as we entertain reservations about traditional methods of police work, we would do well to remember Jerome Skolnick's caution issued at the end of his now classic study of policing. He warns us that while personality and social background are significant, police behavior is explained more by the nature of the work assignment than it is by the individual characteristics of police officers.[45]

Police departments, like many other organizations, don't respond well to demands for change. Security-minded and suspicious of outsiders, the typical police officer does not welcome the chance to respond to social change. In many cities, immigrants from Latin America and Asia bring, literally, alien customs and non-English languages into their contacts with

[44] Quoted in John Katzenbach, "Overwhelmed in Miami," *Police Magazine* 3 (September 1980), p. 11.

[45] Skolnick, *Justice Without Trial*, p. 270.

the police. Communication, so vital to police work, is weak at best. While some departments have made efforts to encourage language training, diversify recruitment, and institute special procedures, these often fall short. Police officers sometimes resent the strange ways of new immigrants and blame the immigrants for not learning and knowing English. They may respond by being hostile and aggressive, but probably more often they simply steer clear of involvement. Many immigrant and minority communities may suffer more from underpolicing than overpolicing.[46]

CONCLUSION

For many years, the police were fairly well satisfied with their position. Most policemen chose their occupation as one that afforded a high degree of economic security. Although police work was never a prestigious line of work, it was especially attractive to young men from working-class backgrounds without a college degree. It was work that was regarded as socially useful and had a positive image. Moreover, individual police officers could look upon themselves as independent, active, and autonomous persons. Two things have changed the traditional place of the police. First, the relatively unhampered use of authority—from the dispensing of "curbstone justice" to the somewhat uninhibited use of search, seizure, and interrogation methods—has now been challenged legally and politically. Second, and related to the first, police administrators and other public officials have shown a growing interest in the professionalization of the police—professionalization meaning such changes as college degrees,[47] more formal training of all kinds, and tighter standards of police conduct. In addition, affirmative action requirements have altered recruitment practices. Often the rank-and-file in police departments and sometimes top officials have reacted defensively to these changes and have, in many cases, come to see themselves as put upon.

Despite the large amount of controversy surrounding police practices, we know little about the impact of various methods of law enforcement. It has not been shown, for instance, that "old-fashioned" policing is any more effective than new and more restricted methods of law enforcement. In fact, it is not even clear that more policing is better than less policing. One study failed to show that increased patrolling had a deterrent effect on crime. To be sure, a total absence of police would almost certainly encourage crime. Massive patrolling, especially on foot or in a confined

[46] Taft, "Policing the New Immigrant Ghettos," p. 26. See also, Robert Fogelson, "From Resentment to Confrontation," *Political Science Quarterly*, 83 (June 1968), 217-247.

[47] A recent estimate puts the number of police officers with college degrees at 10 percent. Probably well more than half now have some college. See Philip B. Taft, Jr., "College Education for Police: The Dream and the Reality," *Police Magazine* 4 (November 1981), 10.

space like a subway car, would almsot certainly reduce crime (as well as be prohibitively expensive). In between those extremes, we are not so sure.[48] But the prominent issues have not been the quantity of policing so much as the quality of it.

We can identify four problem areas:

1. corruption;
2. inefficiency caused by goldbricking and failure to perform required duties;
3. brutality, especially the use of force beyond what is required for self-defense; and
4. the use of policing methods out of line with the preferences of a substantial part of the community being policed.

Because the police exercise coercive authority, the list is one of potentially very serious problems. Some problems, such as corruption, are endemic to police work but are not unmanageable in themselves. Other problems—low morale and lackadaisical performance of duties, for instance—may be especially acute now because police work is in transition; once the transition is completed, then morale may rise to its former level. But what about the problems of brutality and inappropriate standards? How should police discretion be handled? Can new and more stringent rules do the job?[49]

There are no magic formulas. Civilian review boards, aside from not being effective, have not proved politically viable. They heighten police anxiety. The police become defensive and, particularly if there are overtones of racial conflict, they may (as in New York City) be able to mobilize the support of a substantial segment of the white population. Because city dwellers are greatly concerned about order and safety, many tend to give unquestioning support to the police. The police are, thus, not subject to the same kind of political control that many other public agencies are.

Like civilian review boards, community control (at least in the sense of direct control by a neighborhood) generates strong resistance. But some of the objectives sought by community control advocates may be achieved in more subtle ways. New recruiting efforts, especially those bringing in minority members, may pay good dividends in police-community relations. Given the nature of their work, police officers need the ability to "read" and understand the communities they serve in. They need good rapport with the neighborhoods they patrol. They need to know the "language" and the style of life. For these reasons, even those white police officers who have misgivings about extraordinary efforts to recruit blacks admit that black officers understand black culture in a way that white officers cannot.

[48] Wilson, *Thinking about Crime*, pp. 89-108.

[49] See the debate over deadly-force rules discussed by Bruce Cory, "The New Politics of Deadly Force," *Police Magazine* 4 (March 1981), 6-22.

And white police officers also admit that black police officers are not less tough. Yet, as one white police office explained, the "black cops are listened to more than I was."[50] With new immigrant groups in many cities, the case for diversified recruitment becomes increasingly clear, even to old-fashioned police administrators.[51]

Another way to improve police-community relations is to restructure the organization of police work. The retention of small departments where they exist and administrative decentralization in large ones can serve to improve police-community contact. A number of researchers in various communities, led by Elinor Ostrom, have found that citizen satisfaction is higher with small police departments (and that costs are higher in large departments).[52] Some police departments have sought better police-neighborhood relations by introducing forms of administrative decentralization known variously as the community service model, team policing, and the neighborhood police team. There is some evidence that the approach is more effective in solving crimes.[53] Certainly there are recurring concerns that police departments are becoming remote from the communities they serve. "The motorized cruiser mentality" is a source of misunderstanding and may lead both to a greater use of force (without being more effective as a crime deterrent) and greater community resentment about the use of force.

Despite the experimentation with decentralization and the favorable findings on small departments, the opposing trends may be stronger. Much of the police establishment—top-level police administrators and academicians in criminal justice programs—favor large departments, uniformity and professionalization, and more formal and centralized kinds of managerial control. They would, of course, run the large and centralized departments and place their students in them. The effectiveness of the professionalized and centralized approach is unproven. Its shortcomings are in evidence in places like New York City, with its dispirited police force. It can be argued that professionalizing police administration, by attuning administrators to their national professional associations, has made them more remote from the communities they serve. "Reforming" police work has certainly made it more bureaucratic, but the urge to resort to the old methods of "reform" is still a potent force.

[50] Quoted in Alex, *New York Cops Talk Back*, p. 147. See also Bruce Cory, "Minority Police: Tramping through a Racial Minefield," *Police Magazine* 2 (March 1979), 4-14.

[51] For example, see the interview with Los Angeles Chief of Police Daryl Gates, in "Spotlight," *National Centurion* (October 1983), esp. pp. 52-3.

[52] Elinor Ostrom and Gordon P. Whitaker, "Do We Really Want to Consolidate Urban Police Forces?" *Public Admimistration Review* 33 (September/October 1973), 423-33; and Elinor Ostrom and Roger B. Parks, "Suburban Police Departments: Too Many and Too Small?" in *Urbanization of the Suburbs*, ed. L. H. Masotti and J. K. Hadden (Beverly Hills, Calif.: Sage, 1973), pp. 367-402.

[53] See Wilson, *Thinking about Crime*, pp. 100-160.

Yet, "reform" has demonstrated no strong capacity to check police excesses and, by its very nature, the reform style calls for a uniform—not a diversified—approach to policing. But even beyond that, the imposition of reform methods (especially formal and centralized kinds of managerial control) seems to weld a police department into a monolith—a relatively homogeneous group committed to and united by a fixed set of norms and values—largely immune to conventional external controls.

Some observers believe that police power can be checked only if police departments become less monolithic. The recruitment of women and minorities may have a healthy diversifying effect. Perhaps, too, the recruitment of more college-educated police will encourage diversity. Other suggestions call for the recruitment of more civilians into police work and the use of lateral entry to infuse police administration with a broader perspective. However, unless new recruitment practices are accompanied by some form of decentralization, police (especially at the patrol level) may remain unreceptive to norms and values from the civilian community. Moreoever, efforts to achieve diversity are not painless. Some of the police-community conflict of the past has now been transformed into intergroup conflict within police departments, especially over hiring and promotion policies.

In large communities with large departments, direct citizen pressure may have little observable impact on police behavior. Though change can be introduced by installing new officials with different attitudes at the top of the command structure, even this approach has limited effect. New procedures tend to lose their reform thrust as they are implemented.[54] Still, if change is to occur, it may have to come from inside the police occupation itself. Direct efforts at external control have had limited success so far. On the other hand, studies of citizen satisfaction with small and decentralized departments offer some indications that tacit or indirect control is quite effective. While there are common tendencies in police behavior, there are enough variations in law-enforcement style to suggest that police behavior is not immune to community pressures. If those pressures are exerted in a relatively consistent manner, as in smaller and more homogeneous jurisdictions, police behavior and citizen preference can apparently be brought into line with one another.

SUGGESTED READINGS

ALEX, NICHOLAS. *Black in Blue.* New York: Appleton-Century-Crofts, 1969.

BENT, ALAN EDWARD. *The Politics of Law Enforcement.* Lexington, Mass: D.C. Heath and Co., Lexington Books, 1974.

[54] Ronald Kahn, "Urban Reform and Police Accountability in New York City: 1950-74," in *Urban Problems and Public Policy*, ed. Robert L. Lineberry and Louis H. Masotti (Lexington, Mass.: D.C. Heath, Lexington Books, 1975), pp. 107-27.

BROWN, MICHAEL K. *Working the Street.* New York: Russell Sage Foundation, 1981.
DALEY, ROBERT. *Prince of the City.* Boston: Houghton Mifflin, 1978.
FOGELSON, ROBERT M. *Big-City Police.* Cambridge, Mass: Harvard University Press, 1977.
GOLDSMITH, JACK, and SHARON S. GOLDSMITH, eds. *The Police Community.* Pacific Palisades, Calif.: Palisades Publishers, 1974.
HEINZ, ANNE M., HERBERT JACOB, and ROBERT L. LINEBERRY, eds. *Crime in City Politics.* New York: Longman, 1983.
JURIS, HERVEY A. and PETER FEUILLE. *Police Unionism.* Lexington, MA: Lexington Books, 1973.
KAHN, RONALD. "Urban Reform and Police Accountability in New York City: 1950-74," in *Urban Problems and Public Policy,* ed. Robert L. Lineberry and Louis H. Masotti. Lexington, Mass.: D.C. Health, Lexington Books, 1975.
LEINEN, STEPHEN H. *Black Police, White Society.* New York: New York University Press, 1984.
MUIR, WILLIAM K. *Police: Streetcorner Politicians.* Chicago: University of Chicago Press, 1977.
RUBINSTEIN, JONATHAN. *City Police.* New Y ork: Farrar, Straus, and Giroux, 1973.
SHERMAN, LAWRENCE W. *Police Corruption.* New York: Anchor Books, 1974.
SKOLNICK, JEROME. *Justice Without Trial.* New York: John Wiley & Sons, 1966.

chapter 19

Educational Policy and Politics

By any count, education is a major policy arena. In the American belief system, education is both a channel for individual upward mobility and a guarantor of collective well-being. We Americans have prided ourselves on our system of "common" schools, through which education is universally available.

Forty million students are enrolled in public elementary and secondary schools. Sixty million people—considerably more than a quarter of the total national population—are enrolled in some type of school, kindergarten through college. There are more than two million public school teachers, and well over three million public school employees of all categories. In 1981, public school expenditures totaled more than one hundred billion dollars. Despite years of consolidation, the nation still has more than fifteen thousand school districts. School budgets are a major item of local expenditure, and where school district lines coincide with city or county jurisdictional lines, education is often the largest single item in the local government budget. In some suburban jurisdictions, more than half of the budget goes to schools.

About evenly divided between those headed by elected boards and those headed by appointed boards, the nation's school systems are a major locus of citizen involvement. Although voter participation in school board elections and school bond referendums is frequently low, turnout can and sometimes does increase dramatically when citizens are aroused. One California district moved from a 17-to a 37-to a 67 percent turnout in succeeding elections, when faced with the prospects of school desegregation.[1] Thus an initial low turnout came to exceed the usual rate of voting in presidential elections. High participation, whether in elections or school board hearings, is rarely sustained. But the potential for wider popular involvement is always there. Schools are never far from popular consciousness; their impact is too direct to move far away from public concern. Citizen interest has an earlier outlet when school boards are elected, but appointed boards are far from immune to waves of popular sentiment.

Even without dramatic election issues, many parents are involved in a variety of school activities. And a number of pressure groups make continuing efforts to influence educational policy. While citizen apathy is certainly not absent from the politics of education, citizens are more involved in schools than in most areas of governmental activity. Building or closing schools, curriculum philosophies, modes of ability grouping, stringency of discipline, student rights, the range and caliber of extracurricular activities, censorship, religion in the schools, creationism versus evolution in biology classes, sex education, level of expenditure and taxation, forms of testing, collective bargaining, employment practices, administrative accountability, the treatment of women, bilingual education, schooling for the handicapped, and policy on racial grouping illustrate the range of issues attracting citizen interest.

We will not try to cover all or even most of these issues in this chapter. Particular issues, after all, are surface activities on a largely entrenched set of arrangements. Schools don't easily change these arrangements. Their procedures are based on long experience with recurring problems. Further, the alliances and tacit agreements between school officials and various community interests are not easily renegotiated. The costs and risks of political reorganization are substantial. Besides, few opponents of things as they are have the resources and the staying power to work out an alternative set of arrangements and put them in place. Most outbreaks of opposition can be managed by making token concessions or by simply outwaiting the protestors.[2]

Yet, school systems never face static situations. Some communities grow and must accommodate an expanding student body. Others have declining school-age populations. The demography of race and nationality in any given community is subject to change. Moreover, local school systems are increasingly caught up in forces beyond their borders. State and

[1] Lillian B. Rubin, *Busing and Backlash* (Berkeley: University of California Press, 1972).

[2] Cf. Michael Lipsky, *Protest in City Politics* (Chicago: Rand McNally, 1970).

federal requirements are now major components of school life.[3] The disestablishment of racial segregation, mandates to provide education for the handicapped, competency testing for students and faculty, graduation and curriculum requirements, and gender equity are among the major obligations now imposed on local school systems by higher levels of government. And these are obligations backed by powerful sanctions—legally enforced orders, the withholding of funds, and court-appointed Masters serve notice that local officials are not free to operate on their own.

Less than half of school funds are raised by local jurisdictions, hence school systems are weakly situated to resist demands from above. Moreover, local school districts are legal creations of state governments and have no constitutional standing by which they could resist state mandates. Dealing with the federal government is also a one-sided legal contest. Because the federal Constitution is the supreme law of the land, judges applying constitutional requirements can be backed by federal force if necessary, and on occasion, they have been.

Some legally imposed changes have been quite abrupt. After a period of "deliberate speed," many southern school districts were brought abruptly into the era of genuine desegregation. Other changes are gradual but no less important for that reason. For example, the very role of education in national life is undergoing a major transformation as industrial society gives way to post-industrialism. Formal knowledge, verbal skills, and the ability to analyze and use bodies of quantitative data have gained an importance far greater than they enjoyed even in the first half of the twentieth century. To a considerable extent we have become a "credential society," in which educational credentials are the key to one's position in the social and economic order. Consequently, many parents are preoccupied with the educational advantages they can confer on their children; these advantages are the "property" they seek to pass on to their heirs. As a result, educational institutions inevitably become the objects of an open political struggle. In the words of one observer, "whoever controls the gateways to affluence and social position exercises power. . . ."[4] Education has become such a gateway.

Education is thus an arena in which the full force of postreform politics is in evidence. In this chapter, we begin with the transition to a postreform politics of education and a consideration of the degree to which school sytems are autonomous. Then we take up two major policy questions: the experience with school desegregation and the debate over approaches to teaching and curriculum. We conclude with an examination of the forces contributing to the bureaucratization of educational practice.

[3] J. Myron Atkin, "The Government in the Classroom," *Daedalus* 109 (Summer 1980), 85-97; and Frederick M. Wirt and Michael W. Kirst, *Schools in Conflict* (Berkeley: McCutchan, 1982).

[4] Charles E. Silberman, *Crisis in the Classroom* New York: Random House, 1970), p. 69.

THE TRANSITION TO A POSTREFORM POLITICS OF EDUCATION

In the earliest days of educational politics, school systems were numerous, small, and thoroughly controlled by lay leaders in the local community. Communities monitored teacher conduct closely inside and outside the classroom. Hiring and dismissal, most matters of curriculum, and guidelines for discipline were not regarded as subjects of professional expertise, but rather as questions of practice properly controlled by representatives of the community. One historian observed: "Teachers knew to whom they were accountable: the school trustees who hired them, the parents and other taxpayers, the children whose respect—and perhaps even affection—they needed to win."[5] Order in the classroom has always been tenuous, and principals and teachers were accountable in detail for their performance. In one Oregon community, a principal was put on probation when he lost a fight with a student—clearly principals were not supposed to lose in the struggle for order.[6]

In the cities during the 19th century, schools were subordinate to ward-based politics. Large elected boards and decentralized forms of control were dominant forces. Neighborhood leaders controlled school employment and determined matters of curriculum, including the teaching and use of non-English languages.[7]

Beginning in the nineteenth century and extending throughout the first half of the twentieth century, education reformers sought to consolidate school districts and centralize executive control in the hands of a professional education administrator, the school superintendent. State control of teacher certification served to institute professional credentials for faculty, and this process was linked with the struggle to end patronage politics. In alliance with business interests and the educated middle class, education reformers succeeded in decreasing the size of school boards to today's typical small board of five to seven members. Ward representation gave way to at-large election, or in many cases, to an appointed board. Terms of office were staggered so that not all members could be replaced in any given election. Where city school boards were appointed by the mayor, reformers often succeeded in persuading elected executives to use nominating panels dominated by members of the civic elite.[8] Fairly early in the twentieth century, city school boards already consisted mainly of busi-

[5] David B. Tyack, *The One Best System* (Cambridge, MA: Harvard University Press, 1974), pp. 18-19.

[6] Ibid., p. 19.

[7] On the history of urban school practices, see ibid.; and Joseph M. Cronin, *The Control of Urban Schools* (New York: The Free Press, 1973).

[8] Cronin, *The Control of Urban Schools*, pp. 160-61.

ness and professional men.[9] Concerned that parochial, backward-looking, and particularistic concerns would impede the quest for the best and most modern education practices, reformers successfully promoted the idea of centralizing school administration in the hands of professionally-trained school superintendents. In a close parallel with the city manager system, school board members, elected or appointed, were expected to leave all "details" of school administration to the superintendent.

Schools are much too vital in the life of a community for the aura of nonpartisan expertise to prevail completely, but at mid-twentieth century the rhetoric of keeping politics out of the schools was a substantial factor in educational practice. In many ways, schools seemed to be highly autonomous. The stage was set for a revolt against self-directing bureaucracies and a challenge to professional expertise.[10] It came in the 1960s. Much of the community-control controversy centered on the schools.[11] The question of school performance, particularly in educating lower-class and minority students became a major item on the public agenda. Schools came in for close scrutiny, and a myriad of demands from community groups, elected officials, and policy entrepreneurs pushed aside the once-formidable claims to professional autonomy. Long restive under centralized administrative control, teachers embraced unionization at an accelerating pace.[12] Unionization and nonpolitical expertise do not make a very creditable combination. Hence there is no going back to the reform style of education politics. Quite the contrary, the myth of community consensus behind the one best system is now thoroughly shattered. Schools, as one observer notes, have become "magnets for dissension."[13] Further, federal and state, especially state, involvement in education policy is now relatively uninhibited. The notion that education is strictly a local matter has now faded, as has the idea that only education officials should speak on educational policy.

[9] George S. Counts, *The Social Composition of Boards of Education* (New York: Arno Press and The New York Times, reprint edition, 1969), p. 52.

[10] See, for example, the view of education politics presented by David Rogers, *110 Livingston Street* (New York: Random House, 1968).

[11] Norman I. Fainstein and Susan S. Fainstein, *Urban Political Movements* (Englewood Cliffs, NJ: Prentice-Hall, 1974); and Marilyn Gittell, *Local Control in Education* (New York: Praeger Publishers, 1972).

[12] For a general discussion of public employee unionization, see Sterling D. Spero and John M. Capozzola, *The Urban Community and Its Unionized Bureaucracies* (New York: Dunellen Publishing Co., 1973). For the rise of teacher union power in Chicago, see William J. Grimshaw, *Union Rule in the Schools* (Lexington, MA: Lexington Books, 1979); on New York City, see Philip Taft, *United They Teach* (Los Angeles: Nash Publishing, 1974); and Marilyn Gittell, "Education: The Decentralization-Community Control Controversy," in *Race and Politics in New York City*, ed. Jewel Bellush and Stephen M. David (New York: Praeger Publishers, 1971), pp. 134-63.

[13] Diane Ravitch, *The Troubled Crusade* (New York: Basic Books, 1983), p. xii.

BUREAUCRACY, AUTONOMY, AND CHANGE

How much have the schools themselves changed? Are they different today from a generation ago? These are not questions that can be answered precisely. Certainly there is evidence of some change.[14] And neo-conservatives in particular argue that these changes have substantially altered the role of authority in the public schools, leaving both administrators and teachers in a weakened position to pursue the purposes of education. In their view, romantic notions about childhood and human development led to unwise practices such as open and unstructured education.[15] Purpose was lost, and discipine weakened. Other changes also undercut the autonomy and authority of education professionals. State and federal regulations heighten the vulnerability of schools to pressure groups. Significant social change has also occurred. One author describes earlier times this way:

> In the 1940s, few teachers belonged to a union; strikes were uncommon; administrators were powerful within their school building or their district in hiring, promoting, and assigning teachers. Though their pay was low, teachers had more education than did the parents of their students and commanded the respect that went with the authority they wielded. Teaching attracted a number of gifted women, for whom other career opportunities were limited. In some communities, there were substantial restrictions placed on teachers' behavior. . . .[16]

Higher levels of education among the lay public, expanded job opportunities for women (making them less dependent on teaching as a career option), and at least for a time, a greater tendency to display anti-authority attitudes all combined to weaken the deference paid to school administrators and to teachers as well.

Bureaucracy

Yet, with all of these societal changes, the basic structure of school systems is unchanged. The problem of order and discipline may have intensified, but order maintenance has always been and remains a central concern of school officials. Consider the basic elements of the situation. Schools are, first of all, formal organizations. They have limited resources but are mandated to pursue purposes to which the mass of students have

[14] A highly useful treatment of this issue is Mary Haywood Metz, *Classrooms and Corridors* (Berkeley: University of California Press, 1978). However, this is a study of an atypical community in California, and may therefore accentuate the impact of change.

[15] See, esp., Ravitch, *The Troubled Crusade.*

[16] Ibid., p. 323.

weak or undeveloped commitments. Students are not there as voluntary participants but as a consequence of compulsory attendance laws and parental direction. School staff are few in proportion to the student body, making instruction and order maintenance a matter of mass control with limited resources. If order breaks down in a publicly visible manner, the breakdown has direct consequenes for the professional reputations of the staff. Generally there is an unspoken agreement among the staff that "keeping the lid on" is top priority.

Rules hierarchically enforced are an efficient means for guiding a mass of people, and in many institutions including schools, these rules reflect the priority on order maintenance. Indeed one study of public schools reported that teachers receive reprimands and advice more often regarding order maintenance than regarding the academic performance of students.[17] Certainly school rules are pervasively concerned with order and with the inculcation of routines. This concern dates well back into the history of public education.[18] Recounting a classroom recitation of the 1890s, one observer explained that students were expected "to stand on the line, perfectly motionless, their bodies erect, their knees and feet together." The teacher was quoted as saying: "How can you learn anything with your knees and toes out of order?"[19]

This concern with order has enjoyed and continues to enjoy public support. In a national survey, nearly two-thirds of the parents of high school students agreed with the statement that "maintaining discipline is more important than student self-inquiry."[20]

Desegregation and the placing of other demands on educational institutions at a time when school authority was being questioned did strain the established system of order maintenance. Modifications did occur, though not in the same way in all systems. In many places, rules eased and discipline became more lax. Decreased requirements and a greater variety of electives placed fewer academic demands on students.[21] Schools almost certainly became more permissive, but they did not become nonbureaucratic. Nor did they, in most cases, actually embrace open and unstructured schooling—more fragmented and less demanding, yes, but not open and unstructured. Even many of the specially funded innovations in open education were either superficially tried or deliberately ignored.[22] Predictably, concern with order maintenance has risen, and rhetoric and practice have swung back toward greater discipline and more uniform

[17] Silberman, *Crisis in the Classroom*, p. 144. See also James Herndon, *The Way It Spozed to Be* (New York: Simon and Schuster, 1968).

[18] Tyack, *The One Best System*, pp. 42-43.

[19] Ibid., pp. 55-56.

[20] Silberman, *Crisis in the Classroom*, p. 145.

[21] See Metz, *Classrooms and Corridors*, pp. 245-46.

[22] David P. Weikart and Bernard A. Banet, "Planned Variation from the Perspective of a Model Sponsor," *Policy Analysis* 1 (Summer 1975), 485-510.

requirements. Given the task schools perform and the limited resources at their disposal, that swing was to be expected.

Rules to maintain order and uniform requirements work best with a homogeneous student body, but few school systems have ever enjoyed that luxury. Of course, unless desegregation plans enter as a complicating factor, class homogeneous neighborhoods do simplify somewhat the demands on school systems. Even so, education administrators long ago devised testing and placement as means for grouping students in order to facilitate mass instruction.[23] As a consequence, schools have gravitated toward serving as institutions that sort and certify students, not as institutions that transform students. Confronted with complaints about the low academic performance of students, a Boston school official unapologetically placed the blame elsewhere: "We do not have inferior schools; we have been getting an inferior type of student."[24] Obviously there are some schools in which genuine teaching occurs, and education is highly effective even for those with "inferior" backgrounds.[25] But sorting and labeling are the easiest paths for schools to travel.

Autonomy

Before tackling the question of whether the schools of today are less autonomous than schools in the reform era, we should give some thought to the nature of administrative autonomy. Schools, after all, are under the day-to-day direction of professional managers. These managers are full-time and rise to top positions as they advance *within* a career in school administration. School-board members, by contrast, are part-time and often serve no more than one or two terms of office. Education administrators are legally subordinate, but they enjoy the advantage of comprehensive knowledge and full occupation with school affairs. Administrators are the masters of operational details and the beneficiaries of professional networks. Given their limited involvement, school-board members necessarily have only general knowledge of school affairs. Non-school-board community leaders, pressure group representatives, parents and other citizens are even more disadvantaged informationally than are school-board members.

A detailed study of eleven school systems revealed that education administrators tend to dominate school board deliberations. Administrators set the agenda, make their preferences known, and their recommendations are accepted about 99 percent of the time.[26] At the same time, it is important

[23] Tyack, *The One Best System*, pp. 182-98.

[24] Quoted in ibid., p. 282.

[25] See, for example, Silberman, *Crisis in the Classroom*, pp. 95-112.

[26] Harvey J. Tucker and L. Harmon Zeigler, *Professionals Versus the Public* (New York: Longman, 1980), p. 155.

to remember that recommendations by administrators are, on occasion, rejected. And superintendents out of line with the educational ideologies of their boards may be and are dismissed. It is not unusual for a change in political control of the school board to be followed by the firing of the superintendent. Success in dominating the school-board agenda may, then, be as much a testament to the political perceptiveness of administrators as to their power. Perhaps their most acutely needed skill lies in anticipating what is acceptable. As we have seen, school practices, such as the concern with order and discipline, are often strongly supported by public sentiment. And, though responsiveness is a complex phenomenon, school agendas do in fact seem to be responsive to public concerns, especially the concerns of community elites.[27] Responsiveness, however, is not necessarily an admirable trait. It depends on what one is responsive to. Throughout much of their history, public schools have been quite accommodating to racial discrimination, where that accorded with prevailing sentiment.

Examined closely, administrative dominance of school-board agendas is something of a paper tiger. It consists largely of control over routine and housekeeping affairs. On broad questions of policy, school administrators are very dependent upon the alliances they make and maintain in the community.[28] Studies of school desegregation, for example, have found that school boards, not superintendents, set the tone for policy decisions.[29]

The history of public education indicates that school administrators have long believed that they should adapt schools "to the existing social structure."[30] While responsiveness may sometimes take the form of appearance rather than substance, it seems clear that school administrators operate with an understanding that they must maintain a base of political support. This is easier if they can insulate the details of administration from outside interference (and this is one reason for the concern "to keep the lid on"). But few school administrators are inclined to pursue policy goals that lack a base of support in the community.

What changed in the 1960s with the emergence of postreform politics was not so much a loss of political autonomy—the autonomy was always based on an accommodation with community interests—as an end to political quiescence by minorities and others who had not been well served by institutions of public education. The appearance of community consensus

[27] Ibid., p. 226.

[28] See, for example, Rubin, *Busing and Backlash.* For a more general discussion, see the analysis of "the vulnerable superintendent" by Larry Cuban, *Urban School Chiefs Under Fire* (Chicago: University of Chicago Press, 1976), pp. 111-39.

[29] Robert L. Crain, *The Politics of School Desegregation* (Chicago: Aldine Publishing Co., 1968). See also Harrell Rodgers and Charles Bullock, *Law and Social Change* (New York: McGraw-Hill, 1972).

[30] Tyack, *The One Best System*, p. 188. See also Ravitch, *The Troubled Crusade*, p. 55.

was shattered, and school administrators faced a turbulent and conflict-ridden political environment. Particularly once the issue of race surfaced, accommodation to the social structure became more difficult because the social structure itself was in transition. Accommodation was no less necessary, but achieving stable understandings became impossible in many communities. Because stability had characterized school-community relations in the previous era, the situation was starkly different.

David Kirp characterized the end of the reform period in northern California this way:

> When racial concerns were first aired by Bay Area civil rights groups in the late 1950s, the several school districts held a shared and quite conventional understanding of the mission of public education. Humane progressivism had largely vanished. Gone, for the most part, was the child-centered school that Dewey had urged, gone too was the very idea that schools might reshape the social order. The task of the schools, it was felt, was to provide a differentiated education that matched the varied abilities of a heterogeneous population. The most able were given rigorous preparation for college, and the rest were offered vocational training or a terminal "general education" program. Differentiation reached into the primary schools, which often were rigidly tracked. The fact that it was professionals' children who received the advanced education while poor children were assigned to the non-college preparatory classes was taken for granted, if noticed at all. . . .[31]

It was this set of arrangements and the cast of mind accompanying it that the civil-rights movement sought to change and, with the aid of court decisions as well as state and national programs, did modify. For school administrators, the emergence of the issue of race meant an uncertain and unpredictable political environment. The question was never one of school autonomy—yes or no. The question was: On what terms would schools adapt to their political environment? The school desegregation issue altered these terms. Let us then turn to some major education issues, starting with desegregation.

ISSUES IN EDUCATION

Desegregation

To comprehend the school desegregation issue, one must start with the understanding that education is not just an individually consumed service, one that happens to be provided by government. It is fundamentally different from water supply or garbage collection. Education is a social good, in every sense of that term. In education, it matters with whom one

[31] David L. Kirp, *Just Schools* (Berkeley: University of California Press, 1982), p. 255.

associates and how. Both formal instruction and the informal process through which one forms attitudes and makes social attachments are shaped by the character and composition of one's learning cohorts. Education, one writer states, "is inherently communal."[32] School officials and parents alike have long recognized that grouping students is fundamental in the education process. How, then, shall it be done? Once the Supreme Court struck down the Jim Crow system of segregated public education as "inherently unequal," the issue of school attendance zones and even within-school grouping moved to the forefront of the debate over educational policy.

There are three interrelated questions that pervade the desegregation controversy: What is constitutionally required? What is socially desirable? And what is politically feasible? The answer to none of these questions is crystal clear. Certainly there is much debate about each.

Constitutionally prohibited segregation is based on Court interpretation of the Fourteenth Amendment guarantee that all citizens must be afforded "equal protection of the laws." In one interpretation, this requires that no action of the state can be based on race or color. In a more sophisticated interpretation, the Court is obliged to recognize that in a race-conscious society many actions have racial consequences and the people who take these actions often realize that their actions have such consequences. The recognition may be tacit and therefore not part of the formal deliberations in official decision-making processes. In this more sophisticated interpretation of the fit between law and society, what is constitutionally forbidden is any governmentally-sanctioned action that is antagonistic to a racial or ethnic minority.[33] The federal courts have in practice followed an intermediate interpretation, emphasizing the overt intent to discriminate but recognizing the need to prescribe racially-based remedies to disestablish legally-prohibited segregation.

Prohibited actions include not only the dual system of schools operated in the south but any practice intended to maintain racially identifiable schools. Among the specific actions covered by this prohibition are the gerrymandering of attendance districts, the manipulation of feeder patterns, faculty assignments, and failure to relieve overcrowding by not reassigning students of one race to less crowded schools in which students of another race are predominant.[34]

[32] Lance Liebman, "Constitutional Values and Public Education," in *Race and Schooling in the City*, ed. Adam Yarmolinsky, Lance Liebman, and Corinne S. Schelling (Cambridge, MA: Harvard University Press, 1981), p. 265.

[33] William L. Taylor, "*Brown* in Perspective," in *Effective School Desegregation*, ed. Willis D. Hawley (Beverley Hills, CA: Sage Publications, 1981), pp. 15-31.

[34] Gary Orfield, *Must We Bus?* (Washington, D.C.: Brookings Institution, 1978), pp. 15-24. See also J. Michael Ross and John Leubsdorf, *"I Respectfully Disagree with the Judge's Order": The Boston School Desegregation Controversy* (Washington, D.C.: University Press of America, 1981), pp. 155-57.

The complicating factor is, of course, that residential areas are largely segregated by race and class. Personal preference, racial steering by realtors, zoning laws, and various forms of social pressure contribute to the development and maintenance of homogeneous neighborhoods. Further, the relationship between school and residential area is not one way.[35] The character of each shapes the other. The composition of a neighborhood affects the reputation of the schools in it, and the reputation of a school affects housing prices and therefore the composition of the neighborhood. The picture is further complicated by the fact that blacks and Latinos, the principal minorities, are *on the average* less well-off economically than the white majority. Homogeneously priced housing, a practice encouraged by all levels of government, is itself a barrier to residential integration. Moreover, majority and minority groups differ in the form of residential integration they prefer. According to some estimates, blacks feel most comfortable with a fifty-fifty mix, but whites prefer predominance. Hence there is no spontaneous point of residential stability.

Given the tendency for public and private actions over which school boards have little control to produce racially concentrated and economically homogeneous neighborhoods, school officials have to do little to end up with de facto segregation. The courts have, however, ruled that de facto segregation itself is not constitutionally prohibited. Further the Supreme Court has ruled that the presence of racially concentrated school districts does not necessitate the moving of students across school district lines. City-suburban school integration, for example, is not required. Further, in school districts such as Atlanta's composed mostly of minority students, the courts have recognized the ineffectiveness of racial balance formulas and have allowed other measures, such as enhanced black participation in school administration, to be adopted.[36]

Viewed as a set of aggregate statistics, the problem of desegregation appears manageable. About a fourth of the national public school enrollment consists of racial and recent-immigrant minorities; 16 percent are black, 8 percent Latino, and less than 2 percent Asian. Many of these minority students come from middle-class backgrounds. In the Washington, D.C., metropolitan area, for example, the median level of education for the parents of Asian students is higher than the median level of education for the parents of white-majority students.

In reality, the problem is less manageable than the overall statistics suggest. The tendency for minorities to be concentrated in older urban and

[35] Gary Orfield, *Toward a Strategy for Urban Integration* (New York: The Ford Foundation, 1981).

[36] Barbara L. Jackson, "Urban School Desegregation from a Black Perspective," in *Race and Schooling in the City*, ed. Yarmolinsky and others, pp. 204-16. In this same volume, see also the essay by Charles V. Willie, "The Demographic Basis of Urban Educational Reform," pp. 126-35.

suburban areas, the class barriers that areas raise through zoning and related practices, and the social and economic forces at work in the housing market, generally, all serve to perpetuate a pattern of racial concentration and to make racially indentifiable schools a significant feature of American education.

Is it socially desirable to have racially balanced schools? In the abstract the answer is, of course, "Yes." And most Americans of all races support that view—in the abstract. The question of racial balance is, however, not an abstract one, and it is intertwined with the issue of class-integrated schools, about which there is probably less agreement as an abstract principle. Concrete proposals not only generate public opposition, they also have very complicated social consequences. Busing to achieve racial balance may, for example, hinder parental involvement in school affairs (that is the argument against one-way busing). And elaborate schemes to avoid racial concentration may themselves send the subliminal signal that predominantly black or Latino schools are undesirable because they are predominantly black or Latino. Stereotyped views about minorities may be reinforced rather than countered. The question of racial balance is thus not an easy one to address.

We could start by asking if racial balance is to be regarded as an end in itself or as a means to other objectives. Those who regard the "common school" as the heart of American democratic practice are likely to say that a genuinely democratic community requires racially integrated schools. Racial balance, one might argue, is too important symbolically to be sacrificed. Yet, symbolism in race relations is multifaceted. There are all black schools that are highly effective educational institutions, and in a pluralistic society that too is a condition worthy of wide recognition.

The issue is complicated on instrumental grounds too. If we ask what are the consequences of desegregation on the academic performances and the social attitudes of students, the case for mandatory racial balancing is uncompelling. Consider the actual experience with desegregation. "White flight" has been a significant problem; a number of school systems have resegregated in that they have become preponderantly black (or black and Latino) and therefore racially imbalanced. Racial-balance plans are most likely to remain stable where blacks and other minorities are a relatively small proportion of the school population (under 30 percent is a figure cited by some), or where the school district is large and comprehensive enough and private schools scarce enough to make "flight" highly inconvenient.[37] Not only is racial balance hard to maintain, its immediate consequences are of uncertain value. Most studies have shown that, on balance, the academic performance of black and white students is little affected by

[37] David J. Armor, "White Flight and the Future of School Desegregation," in *School Desegregation*, ed. Walter J. Stephan and Joe R. Feagin (New York: Plenum Press, 1980), pp. 187-226; Christine H. Rossell and Willis D. Hawley, "Understanding White Flight and Doing Something About It," in *Effective School Desegregation*, ed. Hawley, pp. 157-84.

the desegregation experience. While there is some evidence that racially mixed classrooms are academically beneficial to black students if the experience begins in kindergarten or the early primary grades, the evidence is not overwhelming.[38] Interracial contact also has an uncertain effect on attitude formation, and attendance at a racially mixed school, in itself, does little to promote positive interracial feelings. From a benefit-cost perspective, pro forma desegregation—that is, the mere numerical mixing of the races in public schools—offers little. One analyst made this observation:

> As implemented to date, racial mixing in schools has rarely harmed majority-group children. Minority-group children have gained in some respects, but may have suffered in others. Whether for children of either race the benefits outweigh possible harm seems to depend on how desegregation is accomplished in schools—on the leadership given by the principal, on a teaching staff that is unbiased and trained in ways of handling diversity in the classroom, on the cultural pluralism of the curriculum, and —above all—on equality of status for each racial group within the school.[39]

Another writer observes: "Desegregation is in trouble." He adds: "in trouble not in the Courts, but in the schools themselves."[40] To be effective and achieve socially desirable results, school desegregation must be seen as more than symbolic. Substantial attention needs to be directed to the question of how it can be achieved, not just in the formal sense of racial balance, but also as part of the operational reality of the school experience. Successful integration involves a great deal more than the devising of racially balanced attendance zones. The goal, after all, is compliance with the spirit of the constitutional guarantee of equal protection, not compliance with the letter of a specific formula.

It is helpful to remember that desegregation, even as a symbolic achievement, is not an end in itself, but a means to a larger goal of building a sense of democratic community. The mix of students within a school building is, as one author put it, "an opportunity, not a cure."[41]

There are a number of analyses of the schoolhouse and classroom experience with desegregation, and few find that schools make constructive use of their opportunities to promote racial understanding, reassure parents, and enhance the academic performance of minority students.[42]

[38] Nancy H. St. John, "The Effects of School Desegregation on Children: A New Look at the Evidence," in *Race and Schooling in the City*, ed. Yarmolinsky, pp. 84-103; and Robert L. Crain and Rita E. Mahard, "Minority Achievement: Policy Implications of Research," in *Effective School Desegregation*, ed. Hawley, pp. 55-84.

[39] St. John, "The Effects of School Desegregation on Children," p. 99.

[40] Robert E. Slavin, "Cooperative Learning and Desegregation," in *Effective School Desegregation*, ed. Hawley, p. 225.

[41] Ibid.

[42] Among the useful and thought-provoking analysis of "dos" and "don'ts" in desegregating schools are the following: James E. Crowfoot and Mark A. Chesler, "Implementing 'Attractive Ideas': Problems and Prospects," pp. 265-95; Willis D. Hawley, "Equity and Quality

Tracking and other sorting and labeling devices are rampant. Numerically desegregated *schools* often contain racially concentrated schemes of student grouping. Tracking and special education classes serve not only to segregate students in many instances, but they reinforce labeling tendencies and tendencies to treat minority students, in particular, with self-fulfilling expectations of failure.[43] While schools have a tendency to standardize tasks and employ a single mode of instruction, the standardization is adapted and applied through systems of ability grouping. Those labeled with low ability, whether by track or racial stereotyping or a combination of the two, receive differential treatment. Teachers make a "downward adjustment of expectations" often mixed with "an attitude of condescension."[44] Interaction with students and modes of discussion differ. Classes perceived as having less ability have their work evaluated less frequently, and the evaluations given are more negative in tone.[45] Or consider the matter of race. According to one report, in classes with a predominance of black students more time was spent on discipline and other nonacademic matters (50-80 percent) than was the case in white classrooms (30 percent).[46] Yet disciplinary pressures as well as performance expectations were less for lower track classes with predominantly minority enrollments.[47]

Tracking and labeling are perhaps the most damaging practices. But the general tendency to emphasize individual competition and individual differences in accomplishment work against more positive racial attitudes. Alternative practices are possible, and have achieved considerable success in pilot programs.[48] Significantly, team sports and the associations that grow out of them have more positive attitudinal consequences than do classroom contacts. After all, the conventional classroom interaction is largely competitive, and interaction is quite formal and therefore socially shallow. While

---

in Education: Characteristics of Effective Desegregated Schools," pp. 297-307; and Slavin, "Cooperative Learning and Desegregation," pp. 225-44, all in Hawley, ed. *Effective School Desegregation*; Elizabeth G. Cohen, "Design and Redesign of the Desegregated School," pp. 251-80; Jane R. Mercer, and others, "Building Multiethnic Schools," pp. 281-307; Norman Miller, "Making School Desegregation Work," pp. 309-48; and Arthur L. Stinchcombe and D. Garth Taylor, "On Democracy and School Integration," pp. 157-86, all in Stephan and Feagin, eds. *School Desegregation*; Willis D. Hawley, "Increasing the Effectiveness of School Desegregation," pp. 45-63; and Nancy H. St. John, "The Effects of School Desegregation on Children," pp. 84-103, both in Yarmolinsky, and others, eds. *Race and Schooling in the City.*

[43] See, for example, Walter E. Schafer and Carol Olexa, *Tracking and Opportunity* (Scranton: Chandler Publishing Co., 1971); Eleanor Burke Leacock, *Teaching and Learning in City Schools* (New York: Basic Books, 1969); H.B. Gerard and N. Miller, eds. *School Desegregation* (New York: Plenum Press, 1975; and John Ogbu, *The Next Generation* (New York: Academic Press, 1974).

[44] Metz, *Classrooms and Corridors*, pp. 104-5.

[45] Silberman, *Crisis in the Classroom*, pp. 88-89.

[46] Ravitch, *The Troubled Crusade*, p. 152.

[47] Metz, *Classrooms and Corridors*, 105-7.

[48] See, in particular, Cohen, "Design and Redesign of the Desegregated School"; and Slavin, "Cooperative Learning and Desegregation.

sports are competitive, the competition is between teams. Group activities, such as team sports, afford opportunities for considerable social interaction.

Finally, we turn to the question of political feasibility. It is closely intertwined with the issue of social benefits and success in building a democratic community. Racial balance, civil-rights attorney Derrick Bell has argued, faces formidable opposition. It is not opposition to the principle but to the costs and complications that accompany its pursuit. Concrete problems cannot be ignored, but Bell maintains, some proponents of desegregation "take the position that racial balance is necessary even if expensive, disruptive, educationally nonproductive, and temporary." Not one to mince words, Bell, a black attorney, adds that a "once despised and still subordinated racial minority is not likely to succeed with that argument."[49] Courts have shown themselves to be sensitive to the political consideration of developing support, and elected officials at all levels are sure to remain responsive to popular sentiment on matters as emotion-laden as school-attendance practices. Although it is tempting to say that the principle of racial balance is right and that we should proceed regardless of the consequences, that view ignores the wisdom of government-by-consent. The necessity of winning consent forces us to look at concrete experiences and to ask what is right in practice, not just what is right in the abstract.

Staff attitudes and behavior crucially affect the desegregation experience. Formal instruction in human relations appears much less important than overcoming faculty atomization (in most schools teachers are generally lone operators) and changing the conditions of interaction among faculty and between faculty and administration. Mutual support in these interactions, of course, depends on recruiting and retaining a racially diverse and supportive staff.[50] Finally, there is wide agreement that involvement of parents at the classroom level contributes to effective desegregation.

Desegregation turns out *not* to be simply a matter of compliance with a rule or a racial-balance guideline. If it is to be effective and socially constructive, it requires significant modification in the procedures followed in many schools. For understandable reasons, schools have strong bureaucratic tendencies. But if bureaucratization is allowed to take the form of atomization of faculty and students, extensive reliance on impersonal control through rules and routines, and above all, processing students through on the basis of ability-labeling, then bureaucratization will undercut any social benefits that could come from desegregation.

Derrick Bell suggests that we shift the focus from arithmetic racial balance to effective education. But that strategy is fraught with danger too, if it simply means "leave the schools alone." Close attention needs to be given

[49] Derrick Bell, "Civil Rights Commitment and the Challenge of Changing Conditions in Urban School Cases," in Yarmolinsky and others, eds. *Race and Schooling in the City*, p. 200.

[50] Hawley, "Equity and Quality in Education."

to what goes on inside all schools, no matter what racial composition they have. And it is also the case that racial integration is itself a positive value, and there are many steps from financial incentives for integrated housing to magnet schools and small classes that could increase public acceptance of racially integrated schools.[51]

Liberal versus Conservative Approaches to Education

Desegregation is by no means the only policy controversy surrounding public education. Both educators and parents differ over approaches to teaching and curriculum. Within education circles, the debate is sometimes framed as progressive education versus "back to the basics", or as child-centered versus subject-centered.[52] More broadly the debate is sometimes depicted as liberal versus conservative.

Liberals are those who presumably take the broadest view of education, what it is and how it can best be promoted. Their concerns are with the whole child, and they see education as consisting not only of the development of cognitive skills, but also of developing a broad capacity to understand and cope with modern life. They are more inclined, for example, to see instruction in such sensitive topics as sex education as a proper school activity. Liberals are also more likely to see proper nutrition and good mental health as complements to formal instruction in the provision of educational opportunity. Much more so than conservatives, liberals see education as properly concerned with honing critical abilities. For liberals, one purpose of an education is to raise fundamental issues about society and how it operates. Their concern is with the individual's ability to make reasonable and informed choices, attentive to the full range of human experience. Curriculum, for them, is thus somewhat open ended.

Conservatives are associated with the view that education consists largely of passing on a traditional body of knowledge. They also tend to place more emphasis on discipline and respect for established authority, and they are less inclined to raise fundamental questions about "the American way." Conservatives see education as a narrowly defined activity; they look less favorably on a broad range of school services. And they prefer that schools stay mostly with traditional subjects taught in a traditional teacher-centered way.

[51] Rossell and Hawley, "Understanding White Flight and Doing Something About It"; Stinchcombe and Taylor, "On Democracy and School Integration"; and Miller, "Making School Desegregation Work."

[52] For extended examinations of the debate over approaches to education, see Lawrence A. Cremin, *The Transformation of the School* (New York: Alfred A. Knopf, 1961); Ravitch, *The Troubled Crusade*; Deborah Meier, "'Getting Tough' in the Schools," *Dissent* (Winter 1984), pp. 61-70; and the exchange between Ravitch and Meier, "A Debate on Education," *Dissent* (Spring 1984), pp. 223-29.

Three issues weave through the various debates over approaches to education:

1. The purpose of schooling—instruction of the intellect versus developing the whole child
2. Attitude formation—especially the question of teaching respect for authority versus nurturing the natural curiosity and creativity with which, many believe, children come to school[53]
3. The nature of the cognitive task itself—passing along a body of knowledge from one generation to the next versus developing a capacity within students to formulate their own questions and pursue their own answers

In considering the political controversy surrounding these issues, several cautions are in order. The first of these is that most people do not fall neatly into one camp or the other. Many people hold positions that fall toward the middle of the spectrum on one or more of the continuing issues, or they are ambivalent about many of the questions. Some take the view that "it depends"—what is appropriate for math may not be appropriate for a lab science, or what is appropriate for social studies may not be appropriate for foreign language instruction. Thoughts about appropriate approaches to education also vary according to the level of schooling in question. What is appropriate for kindergarten might not be for the upper elementary grades or for secondary schools.[54] Further, many teachers would argue that the aptness of an approach varies even with the individual student.

Another caution to keep in mind is that rhetoric differs much more sharply than practice.[55] Conservatives tend to see liberals as romantic and unrealistic. Liberals counter with a tendency to see conservatives as harsh and repressive. But most teachers appear to take a mixed position,[56] and in actual practice they tend somewhat toward the conservative position. That is, they treat education primarily as a matter of transmitting a body of knowledge, and they emphasize order and discipline. After all, a genuinely progressive and child-centered approach makes much greater demands on a teacher's time and ability. And most teachers are faced with large numbers of students, heavy demands on their time, and expectations that order will be maintained. Cost-cutting pressures give additional impetus to conservative practices. While these pressures vary from time-to-time and

[53] Rubin, *Busing and Backlash*, p. 53.

[54] Ravitch, *The Troubled Crusade*, pp. 245-48.

[55] Metz, *Classrooms and Corridors*, is particularly attentive to the question of why practice is more constrained than rhetoric, and why the constraints operate mostly in a conservative direction.

[56] Ravitch, *The Troubled Crusade*, p. 256.

place-to-place, they are never absent. Schools are always institutions with large demands and scarce resources.

Moreover, the teaching process is such that classroom teachers enjoy significant autonomy.[57] Their actions cannot be tightly programmed and closely controlled. Their attitudes matter, and they tend to be conventional about both teaching methods and the purposes of education. Efforts made in the 1960s and 1970s to promote widespread innovation came to little. Although curriculums were opened up and requirements decreased, classroom practices underwent no transformation. Educators have a penchant for the rhetoric of innovation,[58] but the barriers to actual innovation are substantial.[59] In commenting on the failure of curriculum reforms in the social sciences to bear much fruit, education historian Diane Ravitch, observes that: " . . . the curriculum reformers misunderstood the needs of classroom teachers." She explains that teachers, social science teachers in particular, "are primarily concerned with managing their classroom and teaching students good citizenship."[60] Ravitch maintains that teachers felt no urgency about changing what they had been doing. Quite the contrary, they believed that the conventional approach not only fit their values and beliefs but those of their communities as well.[61]

What, then, is at issue in controversies over teaching? Citizens, we should remember, do differ in their views about education, and they differ over the values they want reinforced in the schools. Traditionally, school conflict has been associated with a cleavage between a less-educated-and-nonaffluent working class or marginal middle class on the one side and a more-educated-and-affluent upper middle class on the other side.[62] As a presumably more provincial group, the parents of modest background have been more favorable to conventional educational practices and a narrow view of the education function. They have favored lower expenditures and less experimentation in curriculum. Sex education, school psychologists, sensitivity training, top-heavy administration, human relations courses and other departures from the three Rs, foreign language for elementary school students, lax discipline, and social studies courses that questioned

[57] But most observers credit school principals with a capacity to control the educational character of their schools. See, for example, Silberman, *Crisis in the Classroom*, pp. 98-112.

[58] John Pincus, "Incentives for Innovation in the Public Schools," *Review of Educational Research* 44 (Winter 1974), 113-44.

[59] Ravitch, *The Troubled Crusade*, p. 265; and Weikart and Banet, "Planned Variation from the Perspective of a Model Sponsor."

[60] Ravitch, *The Troubled Crusade*, p. 263.

[61] Ibid. See also, Harmon Zeigler and Wayne Peak, "The Political Functions of the Educational System," *Sociology of Education* 43 (Spring 1970), 129-42.

[62] See, for example, Herbert Gans, *The Levittowners* (New York: Random House, 1967); Keith Goldhammer and Frank Farner, *The Jackson County Story* (Eugene, OR: Center for the Advanced Study of Educational Administration, 1964); Everett C. Ladd, Jr., *Ideology in America* (New York: W.W. Norton & Co., 1972); and Rubin, *Busing and Backlash*.

rather than reinforced patriotism and other conservative social values have been among the specific targets of their opposition. Upper-middle-class groups have often been on the opposite side in these controversies. Sociologist Lillian Rubin has linked this kind of political cleavage over education to differences in occupational experience.[63] She argues that upper-middle-class parents work in professional positions that require a large amount of independent thought and initiative—positions that reward innovativeness. Those less educated, by contrast, hold positions in which they are expected to be submissive to organizational authority and follow orders. A rebellious spirit can undercut job security, and job security is one of their topmost concerns.

As appealing and plausible as this explanation is of conflict in education, it does not fit all circumstances. On close examination, it appears the conflict over education grows out of considerations more complex than occupationally-based perspectives. To cite a concrete case, in Montgomery County, Maryland (a suburb of Washington, D.C.) a liberal-conservative split over education has little to do with social class.[64] Both factions are led by and draw support from the affluent and educated middle class. While the present factions grew out of reactions to a school desegregation plan, the conflict is much broader. Liberals favored and conservatives initially opposed creating a position for a student member of the school board. And when conservatives gained a majority of the school board in 1978, they instituted county-wide examinations and mandated homework, as well as tightening disciplinary standards on such matters as class attendance. They used their budgetary control to decrease funding for auxiliary services and concentrated attention on basic academic instruction. In anticipation of the theme sounded by the Gardiner Commission at the national level, they insisted that school resources be devoted to promoting academic excellence.[65]

At issue is not just a matter of different tastes in educational practice. Rather, there are searching questions about the kind of education appropriate for post-industrial society. There is a sense that from the individual to the nation-as-a-whole we live in a competitive world, and those who fall behind in cognitive skills will lose. But how does one prepare for the post-industrial world? Is it best done by focusing on standard academic instruction and not being diverted into extraneous inquiries and activities? If fundamental academic instruction is the key, is that best achieved by seeking the kind of knowledge transmission that can be monitored through

[63] Rubin, *Busing and Backlash*, p. 54.

[64] For a fuller account, see Clarence N. Stone, "Conflict in the Emerging Post-Industrial Community." Paper given at the Annual Meeting of the American Political Science Association (Denver, Colorado: September 2-5, 1982).

[65] The National Commission on Excellence in Education, *A Nation at Risk: The Imperative for Educational Reform* (Washington, D.C.: U.S. Government Printing Office, 1983).

standardized exams? Or is skill in open inquiry more appropriate for a world in which knowledge is expanding, and innovation is a central feature?[66]

What about the fit between home and school? As upper-middle-class parents become more keenly concerned about conferring a competitive advantage on their children, they may be less inclined to see scarce school resources used to educate "the whole child" and to lessen the handicaps of children who come from educationally unenriched backgrounds. Such parents may press hard for schools to continue and even refine the practices through which the academically gifted are identified early and pushed ahead at an accelerated pace.[67] After all, schools have long experience in sorting and labeling students.

A question should also be raised about individual achievement, social well-being, and the role of public schools. Are there *public* purposes to be fulfilled by schools? Do they have a responsibility to teach us about social interdependence in modern life? If so, how can this best be done—as an academic exercise or as a concrete experience? Or consider another question: Does the common welfare rest mainly on the superior achievements of a few or does it rest more on the educational attainments of the vast majority? If it rests more on the latter, how can quality education be achieved on a mass basis? That is the recurring question in American public education, and that question confronts us now with great urgency.

CONCLUSION

Education is no longer regarded as a local matter. National and state policy makers as well as national and state pressure groups are very much part of the political environment of education. Further, the very terms in which education is debated now transcend the local community. A recent national commission stated: "Learning is the indispensable investment required for success in the information age we are entering."[68] Along with noting that international standing generally but economic position particularly are affected by "knowledge, learning, information, and skilled intelligence," the commission reported that "the educational foundations of our society are presently being eroded by a rising tide of mediocrity. . . . "[69] The recommendations of the commission included more extensive course requirements, especially in math, science, and other basic academic sub-

[66] See Daniel Bell, *The Coming of Post-Industrial Society* (New York: Basic Books, 1973), pp. 167-265; and Peter F. Drucker, *Technology, Management and Society* (New York: Harper & Row, 1977), p. 168-77.

[67] See the comments by Meier, "'Getting Tough' in the Schools," p. 64.

[68] National Commission on Excellence in Education, *A Nation at Risk*, p. 7.

[69] Ibid., pp. 5, 7.

jects; more rigorous and measurable academic standards; more time in schools and more homework outside the school day; and competency testing for teacher accreditation. These recommendations do not point in a new direction so much as they reinforce actions already taken by a number of state and local school authorities in the past several years. Will these actions contribute to a reinvigorated system of American education? Probably not, though they address significant problem areas.

The commission's recommendations not only reinforce specific actions, they also reinforce a general tendency—a tendency toward greater bureaucratization of the American educational system.[70] The effort in education is increasingly surrounded by formal mandates, elaborate reporting requirements, and quantitative measures of performance. These might be appropriate responses to technical and precisely understood problems. They are not appropriate responses to education.

The educational enterprise does not lend itself easily to close managerial control. Goals and methods that are intellectually connected in analyses made at distant command posts are much more loosely connected in the concrete experiences of those directly engaged in the teaching activity itself. Attempts to manage closely activities not suited for such control lead to posturing, ritualistic activity, and more than isolated instances of outright deception.[71] What, after all, are schools being told? "Look good and don't cause problems." "Show good results, appear not to neglect any worthy goal, and minimize requests for resources." Such unrealistic commands produce a dual system: an external side in which appearance is what counts and an internal set of coping arrangements.[72]

We should keep in mind what it is that schools must cope with today. First, they must "process" highly diverse students, including those with various handicaps and those with special education needs. Even among those not in need of special education programs, students begin their formal education at different starting points. Second, they are faced with multiple goals and public expectations, at least some of which are not amenable to explicit definition and quantitative measurements. And, at the operational level, the pursuit of some goals conflicts with the pursuit of others.

Third, their traditional practices of accommodating residential segregation and engaging in further sorting and labeling within schools are under attack. These practices, it is widely argued, are damaging to some

[70] A particularly incisive analysis of this phenomenon is Arthur E. Wise, *Legislated Learning: The Bureaucratization of the Classroom* (Berkeley: University of California Press, 1979).

[71] Clarence N. Stone, "Efficiency Versus Social Learning: A Reconsideration of the Implementation Problem." *Policy Studies Review* (February 1985).

[72] Michael Lipsky, *Street-Level Bureaucracy* (New York: Russell Sage Foundation, 1980); Victor A. Thompson, *Modern Organization* (New York: Alfred A. Knopf, 1961), pp. 138-51; and Richard A. Weatherly, *Reforming Special Education* (Cambridge, MA: MIT Press, 1979).

students. Certainly they are practices that perpetuate inequalities, and they may even intensify inequalities. In addition, they are practices that run counter to one of the objectives of a democratic society—the promotion of intergroup understanding and the building of social solidarity. For shortcomings on this count, schools continue to receive criticism.

In other words, we are variously asking schools to provide high quality and multifaceted services to all, to increase equality and to keep costs down. We are asking this impossible performance while increasing pressures on teachers and administrators and we are doing so at a time when salary competition for the best personnel, particularly in the math and science area, is becoming keener. Women are no longer confined largely to teaching careers. Meanwhile state and federal authorities rely more and more on such devices as formulas for equalizing expenditures for education among schools, racial balance within schools (but not necessarily classrooms), more elaborate course requirements, and more extensive use of standardized tests. The result, predictably, is greater bureaucratization. One principal complained of an "almost fanatic concern for accountability" that "results in a blizzard of the most complex reporting forms imaginable."[73] Coping devices abound, and schools engage in such practices as the use of special-education classes as a covert form of tracking and racial grouping.

There are no easy solutions to the problems faced by schools. Locally-run schools accommodated only too well to class and racial biases in the local community. But federal and state pressures to counter these and other shortcomings brought about new problems. Efforts at reform have served only to bureaucratize further a set of institutions that were already highly bureaucratic. What is missing is a means by which federal and state aspirations can be transmitted to local school systems in such a way as to lessen rather than add to the bureaucratic overlay on public school education.

SUGGESTED READINGS

BUELL, EMMETT H., JR. *School Desegregation and Defended Neighborhoods*. Lexington, MA: Lexington Books, 1982.

BULLOCK, CHARLES S. III, and HARRELL R. RODGERS, JR. "Coercion to Compliance: Southern School Districts and School Desegregation Guidelines." *Journal of Politics* 38 (November 1976), 987-1011.

CLARK, REGINALD. *Family Life and School Achievement*. Chicago: University of Chicago Press, 1983.

GARBARINO, JAMES, and C. ELLIOTT ASP. *Successful Schools and Competent Students*. Lexington, MA: Lexington Books, 1981.

GITTELL, MARILYN. *Limits to Citizen Participation*. Beverly Hills, CA: Sage Publications, 1980.

[73] William C. French, "Local Control Under Attack," in *Government in the Classroom*, ed. Mary Frase Williams (New York: The Academy of Political Science, 1979), p. 9.

HAWLEY, WILLIS D., ed. *Effective School Desegregation: Equity, Quality, and Feasibility*. Beverly Hills, CA: Sage Publications, 1981.

HERNDON, JAMES. *The Way It Spozed to Be*. New York: Simon and Schuster, 1968.

HOCHSCHILD, JENNIFER L. *The New American Dilemma: Liberal Democracy and School Desegregation*. New Haven: Yale University Press, 1984.

KIRP, DAVID L. *Just Schools*. Berkeley: University of California Press, 1982.

MEIER, DEBORAH. "'Getting Tough' in the Schools." *Dissent* (Winter 1984), 61-70.

METZ, MARY HAYWOOD. *Classrooms and Corridors: The Crisis of Authority in Desegregated Secondary Schools*. Berkeley: University of California Press, 1978.

MORGAN, EDWARD P. "Two Paradigms of Urban Educational Policy." *Polity* 15 (Fall 1982), 48-71.

MURPHY, JEROME T., and DAVID K. COHEN. "Accountability in Education—the Michigan Experience." *The Public Interest* No. 36 (Summer 1974), 53-81.

ORFIELD, GARY. *Toward a Strategy for Urban Integration: Lessons in School and Housing Policy from Twelve Cities*. New York: The Ford Foundation, 1981.

PETERSON, PAUL E. *School Politics Chicago Style*. Chicago: University of Chicago Press, 1976.

RADIN, BERYL. *Implementation, Change, and the Federal Bureaucracy: School Desegregation Policy in HEW (1964-1968)*. New York: Teachers College Press, 1977.

ROSSELL, CHRISTINE H. "Magnet Schools as a Desegregation Tool: The Importance of Contextual Factors in Explaining Their Success." *Urban Education* 14 (October 1979), 303-20.

RUBIN, LILLIAN B. *Busing and Blacklash: White Against White in an Urban School District*. Berkeley: University of California Press, 1972.

TUCKER, HARVEY J., and L. HARMON ZEIGLER. *Professionals Versus the Public: Attitudes, Communication, and Response in School Districts*. New York: Longman, 1980.

WEATHERLY, RICHARD A. *Reforming Special Education: Policy Implementation from State Level to Street Level*. Cambridge, MA: MIT Press, 1979.

WILLIE, CHARLES V., and SUSAN L. GREENBLATT. *Community Politics and Educational Change*. New York: Longman, 1981.

WIRT, FREDERICK M., and MICHAEL W. KIRST. *Schools in Conflict: The Politics of Education*. Berkeley: McCutchan, 1982.

WISE, ARTHUR E. *Legislated Learning: The Bureaucratization of the American Classroom*. Berkeley: University of California Press, 1979.

chapter 20

Client-Serving Bureaucracies

Now that we have looked at some major areas of policy, we can consider the mechanisms through which policy is carried out. Most programs involve a major role for public bureaucracy. Hence, if we want to know how responsive polices are to various segments of the urban public, we must examine the behavior of client-serving agencies. This we do in the present chapter.

There are other issues as well. Public bureaucracies operate without detailed direction from elected officials. Now that traditional and highly personal forms of electoral politics have largely faded, the administrators of urban services do not face extensive case-by-case interventions from elected officials. To be sure, some intervention occurs on an individual basis, even in cities with a long reform tradition. And organized citizen groups can be a formidable force, capable of delaying and sometines reversing specific decision. Yet, most policies are administered most of the time through general rules. It is the nature of bureaucracy to operate through such rules and to apply them without much attention to individual circumstances. That is what makes bureaucracy "efficient." They treat cases, not on the basis of their unique features, but on the basis of common categories. To be sure, bureaucracies are staffed by people, whose subjective preferences creep in. But for the most part, bureaucracies are organized around performing tasks with limited resources. They follow set routines, and officials encourage this form of predictability in order to facilitate coordination. In the following chapter, we look at these bureaucratic decision rules and how they relate to questions of equity. Who benefits from these rules? The succeeding chapter takes up still another question about bureaucratic performance: the issue of whether contracting out service activities to private firms makes a difference.

Public bureaucracies play such a pervasive role in modern government that it is easy to see them as enormously powerful. They make most of the concrete decisions about the allocation of benefits, and they enjoy considerable operational autonomy. Are they, then, powerful? The answer is yes. But that can be a misleading answer. Bureaucracies are in many ways passive political actors. They have much inertia. They react to client demands and make do with limited resources. To be sure, there are policy entrepreneurs who pursue aggressive tactics, but most service-providing agencies are not guided by such program activity.

Agency officials exist in a treacherous political world, and most proceed with caution. They seek to stabilize their relations with the larger world. Their competition with one another is limited. They cultivate the image of acting on the basis of technical criteria. They lean toward performance measures based on volume of cases processed. They put forward their rules as rational and impartial. Yet these various measures through which bureaucracies strive for autonomy and seek to avoid external intervention are products of a political environment. Public bureaucracies show little inclination to engage in behavior that invites prolonged conflict. Few knowingly take actions that invite attack from powerful groups. For the most part public bureaucracies are a conservative force.

Technical decision making and the autonomy it brings about are thus not to be seen as nonpolitical. These are stances taken in order to come to terms with a political environment. Moreover, bureaucratic autonomy does not amount to being a dominant power. Instead, autonomy represents an accommodation achieved with a dangerous political world. The authority of public agencies is by no means inconsequential, but it is more often used to come to terms with than to challenge private centers of power. In considering the place of bureaucracies in urban policy and politics, let us begin with client-serving agencies.

One of the major frustrations of modern life is bureaucracy. For many of us, the word "bureaucracy" conjures up images of unfeeling, pettyminded employees sitting in dull offices shuffling papers, refusing to deal with people or clients on a humane basis, making as few decisions as possible and basing the ones they do make on a narrow and unimaginative interpretation of rules and regulations. Also, for most of us, bureaucracy is a handy label for all that is wrong with current society and the large impersonal organizations we are forced to deal with.

Though large, impersonal organizations are an integral part of all of modern society, we ascribe most of their failings to public bureaucracies—forgetting that private bureaucracies, such as department stores or car dealerships or medical insurance corporations, can be equally dehumanizing and exasperating. Thus, although private-sector bureaucracies are not without inefficiency, red tape, and delay, those characteristics bother us more when they appear in the public sector.

THE CHARACTERISTICS OF BUREAUCRACY

Much has been written about large-scale organizations, but it is the German sociologist Max Weber who is generally credited with first describing and defining the phenomenon of bureaucracy.[1] Weber used the word "bureaucracy" to describe any modern, rational form of organization possessing the traits of hierarchy, specialization, and impersonality.

Even though bureaucracy is a universal phenomenon, bureaucracies are not homogeneous in their philosophy or outlook. The United States Department of Defense and a city department of recreation are both bureaucracies and therefore share many characteristics, but no one will seriously claim that they are organizational twins.

Despite the efforts of many writers to develop new descriptions of bureaucratic organizations most of their ideas can be traced to Weber's writings. Bureaucracy is nothing more or less than a way to organize large groups of people in order to accomplish a task. Whether that task is providing national defense, building automobiles, picking up garbage, or converting pagans, bureaucratic concepts are involved. Weber's model of organization—his "ideal type"—includes the following characteristics:

1. Fixed and official jurisdiction
2. Hierarchy (the organization looks like a pyramid)
3. Recruitment and promotion based on expertise and skill not on family connection, wealth, influence, or the like
4. Use of rules and regulations
5. Development of a career system
6. Impersonal relationships between and among staff members and in dealing with their clientele

Weber also argued that bureaucracy, as represented by his ideal type, has an inherent autonomy that places it beyond ordinary control. Within its sphere of action, Weber maintained, "the power position of a fully developed bureaucracy is always overtowering." He added that the elected

[1] H.H. Gerth and C. Wright Mills, eds., *From Max Weber: Essays in Sociology* (New York: Oxford University Press, 1946), pp. 196-204.

executive, legislative body, or any other external political entity is at a severe disadvantage: "The 'political master' finds himself in the position of the 'dilettante' who stands opposite the 'expert.' . . ."[2] Weber's own feelings about bureaucracy were mixed. He saw it as an efficient and in some ways preferable form of organization. But he also viewed bureaucratic power with concern and described the process whereby bureaucracies tried to protect their power position by "keeping their knowledge and intentions secret."[3]

Subunits within bureaucracies behave toward the larger organization in much the same way that bureaucracies behave toward the larger society. They too seek autonomy and the maintenance of a monopoly on their bodies of expertise. Thus there is an unresolved tension within bureaucracies—a tension between the principle of hierarchy and the principle of specialization. The new executive trying to bring about a change in policy confronts a mass of expertise and professional pride that resists control from the top or from the outside. Executives are not powerless to promote change, but neither can they bring about change simply by decreeing a new policy.

There are other real-life weaknesses in Weber's characterization of bureaucracy. He viewed bureaucracy as a formal structure and so it is, but in actual operation every formal organization develops within it an informal organization—a set of relationships based on convenience, friendship, shared interests and experiences, skill-group solidarity, and many other factors. Some agencies have a great deal of internal politicking because there are competing factions and rival cliques. Decisions are made, alliances are formed, and resources are allocated as much through this informal network as through formal channels. And as we saw in the police chapter, actual operating procedure may be quite different from formally defined procedure. Informal goals and unofficial norms grow up, and, as in the case of the "police code," on-the-job actions may derive more from unofficial norms than from the formal rules of the organization.

Weber also failed to treat the political environment of public bureaucracies. In a democratic system, public opinion is a significant force. Pressure groups also are a substantial presence. Indeed, a vital part of any agency's operation is the effort to develop ties with groups that can serve as political allies. Similarly agencies try to forestall opposition; they want no powerful or aroused enemies.

An aspect of the political environment is the evolution of clientele-oriented bureaucracies. Ideally, of course, an agency serves the entire citizenry in some way. Realistically, agencies provide subsidies, protection, and other services to a particular segment of the public. This clientele and

[2] Ibid., p. 232.

[3] Ibid., p. 233.

the agency develop ties of mutual support and protection. The pattern was first evident at the federal level. Beginning in the middle of the nineteenth century, the federal government created a series of departments and agencies giving formal recognition and support to various economic and other interests—the Department of Agriculture for farmers, Commerce for business, Labor for labor, and so on.

At the federal level, there is often no ambiguity about who the clientele is—and the clientele is clearly dominant in its sphere of interest. The Department of Commerce, for example, represents and serves business, not consumer, interests. That is why there is demand for a separate consumer protection agency—to give consumers an advocate.

As attention is shifted from the federal to the local level, the agency-clientele tie becomes less clear. There is more ambiguity about who the clientele is, or the clientele may not be dominant in its sphere of interest. Public-health agencies, for example, serve a loosely defined clientele; some programs are for the general public, others for the poor. And public-health agencies are also constrained by a desire to appease private practitioners. Public-health planning thus skirts those issues that might impinge on the practice of private physicians.

Welfare agencies serve a clearly defined clientele, but it is a politically weak clientele. If costs go up, taxpayers fret and fume. If maids or other service workers in the secondary labor market become scarce, then employers cast a suspicious eye toward the welfare system. Welfare administrators thus are mindful of groups other than their clients, and in fact, are notorious for discouraging clients from seeking help. Two researchers described a typical procedure in a small town:

> A woman with two young children, who is separated from her husband, asks about [Aid for Dependent Children]. No application is taken, but she is advised to try to get back a job she had and to file suit against her husband for support. She says she will return but does not. . . .[4]

Police protection provides a different problem. Who is the clientele—the person arrested, the family whose quarrel is mediated, or the business firm whose property is protected? In some communities, police officers receive free meals, gratuities, discounts, and numerous other favors from people seeking special protection. The clientele may emerge from these special relationships rather than from objective conditions of need. Similar problems surround housing-code enforcement—is the clientele the slum dweller or the owner of substandard housing?

From these examples, we can see that urban agencies serving mainly the poor have a special dilemma. Not only are their clients—that is, the

[4]Quoted in Frances Fox Piven and Richard A. Cloward, *Regulating the Poor: The Functions of Public Welfare* (New York: Random House, Pantheon Books, 1971), p. 153.

"natural" allies of the agency—politically weak, but there are other concerned interests with competing claims that are politically strong. Thus, those agencies with the poor as a primary clientele face a treacherous environment. Overall, urban agencies need to be seen as more than Weberian bureaucracies. They are that, but they are also creatures of the urban political environment. Both their bureaucratic traits and their political milieu shape their behavior.

THE BUREAUCRACY PROBLEM

The bureaucracy problem is, in reality, not a single problem but multiple problems. And as James Q. Wilson has cautioned us, the amelioration of one bureaucracy problem may aggravate another.[5] A strong concern for proper expenditure of money and strict financial accounting can, for example, make operations less flexible and even less efficient. Similarly, there is a difficult balancing act between the need for fair and uniform treatment on the one hand and the need for quick and compassionate responses to individual cases of hardship on the other hand.

In this chapter we will attempt to deal mainly with those factors involving agency-client relations. We will not zero in on such problems as fiscal integrity and cost effectiveness, but will center our attention on the questions of how and why urban agencies sometimes fail to provide their clients with the services they want and need in a way that is fully commensurate with the dictates of human dignity.

When we talk about public-service bureaucracies, it is important neither to exaggerate nor to underestimate the scope of the problem. A popular stereotype of government bureaucracy is that of total incompetence—a bumbling and wasteful enterprise that leads nowhere and accomplishes little. Yet government has run a highly successful space effort, built an elaborate highway system, solved a number of health and sanitation problems, provided educational facilities for a baby-boom population come of school age, and through social security and related programs done much to eliminate poverty among the old. Moreover, during World War II, the government mobilized a massive war effort. Even in areas like public safety, education, and welfare—areas where criticism has been sharpest—some places have had excellent services, and overall performance is probably better than it ever was in the past. Yet dissatisfaction is great. Why?

One reason is that our expectations have risen. Past accomplishments are taken for granted, and we want to see new goals reached. Another reason is that we have gotten more sophisticated about our expectations.

[5] James Q. Wilson, "The Bureaucracy Problem," *The Public Interest*, no. 6 (Winter 1967), pp. 3-9.

Once we thought that school systems were doing a good job if they could provide safe and adequate facilities run by people who had professional credentials. Now we want evidence that the formal education experience does in fact endow students with a high level of knowledge and skill. Our expectations have risen in another way. We have also come to expect public services to work well for all segments of society. It is not enough that some children be well educated, that some people get good health care, or that some neighborhoods are relatively safe; we expect that services will be available and effective for all. That is a standard neither expected of nor achieved by agencies in earlier times. Even in the boss era with all of the activities of the political machines, service efforts did not reach everyone. That is one reason why the reform movement could gather support.

Today, the problem is not that government can do nothing well or that services are ineffective. As former Secretary of Housing and Urban Development Robert Wood, said:

> The real difficulty is that public agencies often achieve goals and carry out objectives that political observers or the public have come to feel are out-of-date, inadequate in scope, or plain wrong. (Alternatively, we feel the objectives are in fact set internally by the public organizations themselves; hence they are self-serving, not serving us.)[6]

It took concern with the poverty issue in the 1960s to reveal fully that there was a service-delivery problem. Once uncovered, the problem proved not to be restricted to services for the poor, but it is certainly a problem that is most acute for the less-affluent segments of society. After all, if the public schools perform badly, the well-to-do can send their children to private schools. And if the system of public safety is only partially adequate, those who can afford extra protection will buy it. The prosperous can pick and choose, using some public services but not others or using a public service up to a point and then meeting the balance of their needs with services bought in the private sector. But the nonaffluent have few alternatives and little opportunity to supplement. They sink or swim with public services as they are.

There are three hardships that can confront the clients of urban service agencies:

1. Agencies may be slow to modify practices and meet the changing needs of clients. For instance, in the 1960s the Oakland library system neglected to develop a collection on the civil-rights movement despite the timeliness of the topic and the growing minority population in the city.[7]

[6] Robert C. Wood, "When Government Works," *The Public Interest* no. 18 (Winter 1970), p. 40.

[7] Frank S. Levy, and others. *Urban Outcomes.* (Berkeley, CA: University of California Press, 1974), pp. 195-200.

2. Agencies may serve only a select, and often the least needy, portion of their potential clientele—a practice known as "creaming." Administrators of employment programs, for example, have been accused of selecting applicants with the best skills and qualifications to make their programs look successful.
3. Agencies may treat their clients in a superficial and thoughtless manner, and in the worst cases they may subject them to long waits, curt and abusive behavior, and restrict their freedom through elaborate rules and regulations. Welfare agencies frequently exemplify these abuses. One writer cited the example of an AFDC mother trying to get assistance to move to a different apartment. On her fourth trip to the welfare office, she was so outraged by the insulting remarks of the welfare workers that she tore up the forms and left without completing the necessary parperwork.[8]

With these potential problems in mind, let us turn to some possible explanations for anticlient behavior by public-service bureaucracies.

SOURCES OF ANTICLIENT BEHAVIOR

As with most social phenomena, there are many ways of explaining anticlient behavior. And they are *not* mutually exclusive. We will concentrate on three:

1. The personal predispositions and cultural biases of service-providing bureaucrats and professionals
2. The inner dynamics of large-scale organization, that is, the bureaucratic structure itself
3. The external constraints on agencies

Personal Predispositions and Cultural Biases

A recurring theme of the 1960s was the middle-class bias of persons providing services to the poor. Schools provided young inner-city children from backgrounds of poverty with reading material that related primarily to life among the affluent of suburbia. Personality and I.Q. tests contained culture-bound items that meant little to children from a Spanish-language background. Teaching techniques or mental health practices that worked among the upper middle class were tried, and failed, among the lower class. White police officers had difficulty understanding the street-corner life of black youth. The list could run on. The problem was, and perhaps still is, real; but it is surmountable. Protests by clients, new recruitment practices, and all-out efforts to respond to cultural variations could and did

[8]This incident is recounted by Susan Sheehan, "Profiles: A Welfare Mother," *New Yorker*, September 29, 1975, pp. 77-78.

have some impact. But the problem proved to be more deep-seated than cultural bias.

Some observers have suggested that there is a problem inherent in the pattern of recruitment into public-service agencies. Some of them, for instance welfare agencies, provide relatively good beginning pay and substantial job security but little opportunity for advancement. The persons attracted to such jobs, it is argued, are likely to be unimaginative, methodical, and cautious—more concerned about protecting their own positions than they are in promoting the well-being of clients. One welfare commissioner described his hiring experience as one of employing middle-aged men "washed out of the economic system," not the kind of people likely to offer bold and client-oriented leadership.[9] Other studies have shown welfare and related agencies to be staffed, at the lower levels, with young people who have no long-term career interest in their work, individuals often without college degrees. They work a few years in welfare and eventually move to other careers. Though the teaching profession has undergone significant changes, the prevailing view of teaching was once that of a fallback occupation–as something to do if other opportunities did not open up or as a career that married women could move in and out of as family demands allowed. Police work, we saw earlier, has been attractive mainly on grounds of economic security for those from working-class backgrounds.

With the recruitment pattern and motivation problem in mind, some observers have strongly urged professionalization of various public-service occupations—teaching, social work, and policing among others. People with career aspirations within an occupation, trained to a high level of skill and imbued with a professional commitment to the ideal of service, it is argued, will bring a large amount of dedication and imagination to their work. And it is true that welfare workers with college degrees and social work training do appear to be more client oriented than those who are not. Professional training frees workers from some of the negative stereotypes of the poor and gives them a better understanding of the social and economic barriers faced by those below the poverty line.

Yet professionalism is a two-edged sword. It can increase understanding and strengthen the service ideal, but it can also divert staff members from some client problems. Professionals are career and self-development oriented. Well-educated teachers want to teach the brightest and most-intellectually able students, not ordinary or slow students. Hospitals with research and teaching connections want medically interesting patients, not patients with ordinary ailments and injuries. An analysis of the "blindness system" (that is, the network of agencies serving the blind)

[9]Quoted in Edgar May, *The Wasted Americans* (New York: Harper & Row, 1964), pp. 105-6.

found that professionalism led to a concentration on "worthy" clients, those who could respond to assistance by moving toward becoming independent and self-sufficient. But those, like the elderly, who could not move toward self-sufficiency were given relatively little attention though they desperately needed help.[10]

Middle-class bias, it turns out, is a complex phenomenon. The poor and the middle class often have the same basic set of values. Still, there are cultural and style-of-life differences, most evident perhaps when clients are a foreign-language or ethnic minority. Communications across cultural boundaries in human-service programs can be difficult. Beyond that, middle-class bias is sometimes a label attached to what is really a conflict between the wants and convenience of professionals and the wants and needs of clients. Sometimes it is a matter of professionals wanting to give in-depth treatment to a few "worthy" clients while clients may be mainly interested in ordinary physical and material assistance. For example, the elderly blind do not need vocational retraining, but they may need help getting to the grocery market or the doctor's office.

Sometimes middle-class bias is the pop-knows-best paternalism of the expert dealing with the lay person. Sometimes it is a matter of professionals wanting conventional nine-to-five hours in a pleasant and convenient location whereas clients need unconventional hours, nights and weekends, in neighborhoods that are neither attractive nor convenient to middle-class professionals.

Still, when all of the aspects of middle-class bias are considered, we have only scratched the surface of agency-client relations. Almost everyone who has done research on such urban service agencies as schools, health departments, and welfare offices agrees that there are a large number of imaginative, dedicated, and sensitive people in these agencies. While many of these employees may be concerned about economic security, such concerns are not incompatible with people-oriented attitudes. Moreover, it is significant that the frustration level among some public servants is very high. They complain loud and long about paper work, red tape, inappropriate rules and regulations, and the general inflexibility of bureaucratic organizations. Turnover in some occupations is extremely high. In some welfare departments and public-health nursing units, it runs close to 50 percent per year. Those who stay may do so because they become hardened to the bureaucratic setting. If that is the case, then we need to turn to the inner dynamics of bureaucracies. The key factor in the bureaucratic personality may be the bureaucratic structure itself.

[10] Donald A. Schon, "The Blindness System," *The Public Interest*, no. 18, (Winter 1970), pp. 25-38.

Bureaucratic Structure

Recruitment patterns are only one factor in the overall development of bureaucratic behavior. Probably far more important are the everyday pressures that come from working in a large-scale organization. Specialization and the necessity for coordinating specialists breed certain modes of conduct that we associate with the bureaucratic personality.

First of all, specialization encourages impersonality and routinization. Public-service professionals and bureaucrats do not aid the whole person. Services are fragmented. A public-health nurse is trained and authorized to deal only with health problems, not with the many factors that can contribute to health problems. A public-housing manager collects rent and manages housing, and is neither trained nor rewarded for tackling such things as family-relations or employment problems.

Specialization increases the need for coordination; the greater the specialization, the greater the need for coordination. And in a large-scale organization, this coordination can come only through a heavy reliance on formal rules and set procedures. The keys to organizational efficiency are precision and reliability—organizational needs that set in motion an unrelenting pressure for employees to be "methodical, prudent, and disciplined."[11] In fact, when these needs are especially strong, they produce not only an atmosphere of rule following but also a tendency toward overconformity. In some bureaucracies, the first law of survival is that you never get in trouble for following rules; trouble comes when you make an exception and the exception creates a problem. In general, people in large-scale organizations tend to be preoccupied with productivity and administrative efficiency. These preoccupations confine workers to their areas of specialization and encourage them to devise routine procedures for handling a large number of clients.

Exceptions, because they are short-lived, demonstrate the strength of the generalization. An innovative manpower agency, strongly oriented toward finding genuinely attractive jobs for the poor, was pressured to put trainees in less-desirable positions.[12] Why? Vacancies could be found more easily, more people could be placed, and costs-per-job placement could be reduced. Ignored was the fact that job turnover was high in low-paying, undesirable jobs. The innovative program did not survive.

Another characteristic of large-scale organization is rule-bound activity. Rules and written guidelines are omnipresent. Some employees tie their careers to mastery of the rules. Others use rules as a protective

[11] Robert K. Merton, "Bureaucratic Structure and Personality," *Social Forces* 18 (May 1940), 562.

[12] Stephen A. Waldhorn, "The Role of Neighborhood Government in Postcategorical Programs," in *Restructuring the Federal System,* ed. Joseph D. Sneed and Stephen A. Waldhorn (New York: Crane, Russak & Company, Inc., 1975), pp. 149-51.

device—any time they are asked to do anything extraordinary or even inconvenient, they fall back on a rule as the unanswerable excuse for not acting. Still others use rules as a weapon, to gain a bargaining advantage or to punish an enemy. Because rules and regulations are such an important part of organizational life, they become an inseparable part of the job itself. When rules and regulations are applied to clients, employees feel a need to justify what is so integral to the job itself. They begin to see regulation as something to "protect" clients, "for their own good," not as something that is punitive.[13]

To be sure, organizations differ. Some are more rule oriented than others. A study comparing the welfare departments in Baltimore and San Francisco found that Baltimore workers were lenient while San Francisco's bureaucrats rigidly followed the rules.[14] Service delivery to clients varied because of the differing agency heads (San Francisco's top administrator came from a background of business administration and accounting, Baltimore's from a professional social work background) operating in different political environments (San Francisco's administrator was closely guided by the Social Services Commission while Baltimore's administrator was given considerable support and autonomy by the mayor).

Within organizations, individuals also differ. Some are risk takers, more concerned with finding and taking advantage of new opportunities than they are with protecting some existing position. The long-run propensity of organizations, however, seems to be toward more rules and a higher proportion of people who are cautious and rule oriented. Yet if it is true that the change oriented tend to be driven out by a climate of rigidity and routinization, it is still not entirely clear why that is the case. If one examines the feelings and attitudes of employees in public-service bureaucracies, it becomes apparent that there is massive disenchantment with rules and regulations. In some agencies they are widely disregarded. In welfare agencies, for example, there is substantial evidence that workers become less rule oriented with the passage of time. They become cynical about regulations and simply adopt the view that in order to help clients it is necessary to learn to manipulate the rules or ignore them altogether. Caseworkers "work the system" to obtain extra benefits for clients, sometimes in open disregard of the rules and objectives of their departments. Some workers condone cheating. One remarked, "Welfare grants haven't kept up with inflation in recent years, so a lot of the cheating today is justified."[15] In some cases, "secret" (that is, unreported) jobs

[13] W. Richard Scott, "Professional Employees in a Bureaucratic Structure: Social Work," in *The Semi-Professions and Their Organization*, ed. Amitai Etzioni (New York: Free Press, 1969), pp. 119-22.

[14] Sharon Perlman Krefetz, *Welfare Policy Making and City Politics* (New York: Praeger Publishers, 1976).

[15] Quoted in Sheehan, "Profiles: A Welfare Mother," p. 59.

are tolerated because a welfare worker feels that poor families need all the income they can scrape up.

If, as this pattern suggests, the bureaucratic personality turns out to be only a sometime thing, then we need to look elsewhere for contributing factors to anticlient behavior. Large-scale organization clearly does give rise to some pathologies, but such factors as specialization and overconformity seem to explain only a part of the gap between client expectations and agency performance. Let us then turn to external constraints on public agencies.

External Constraints

We have already suggested that agencies serving the poor work in a particularly treacherous political environment. Even those agencies that do not work mainly or exclusively with the poor face substantial cross-pressures. While politically generated difficulties vary from community to community and agency to agency, there are recurring patterns. Most public-service bureaucracies confront two persistent problems: inadequate resources and contradictory or ambiguous expectations about their roles.[16] In this section we will focus on these two general problems and how they affect agency operations.

Running a public agency is not like running a business. For most businesses, the more customers the better. In contrast, most public-service agencies are primarily concerned with controlling costs for the larger community and for the agency itself. In most communities the successful welfare administrator is not the one who serves the most clients but the one who adds the least to the local government's tax bill. While it is true that most agencies seek to increase their budgets, each tries to preserve as much of that budget as possible for internal purposes. They therefore want clients who can be assisted easily and who show quick results. Job-training programs thus are aimed at those who can be brought into the job market quickly, not at those who are in greatest need of training. Aid to the blind is geared to "those who can be trained to leave the blindness system quickly, thereby maximizing turnover rates and minimizing costs to the blindness system."[17] Those who have multiple handicaps or those who, like the elderly, cannot be rehabilitated out of the system and need continuing assistance tend to be neglected—they consume too many resources and fail to provide good public relations copy. Social agencies like to tout their successes in bringing clients to self-sufficiency; they don't talk much about the people who need help year after year, without end.

"Creaming," that is concentrating on the easy-to-help clients, can thus be seen as a product of an uncertain political environment and a

[16] Much of this section draws on Michael Lipsky, *Street-Level Bureaucracy* (New York: Russell Sage Foundation, 1980).

[17] Schon, "The Blindness System," p. 32.

desire to conserve resources. Similarly, agencies develop procedures to ration their services. Some things cannot be done because there is not the staff or the wherewithal to do it. But long lines, inconvenient locations, routine or superficial or even brusque treatment, delays, waiting lists that never seem to shorten, and other such practices also serve to discourage clients and reduce the demand for agency services. Agency leaders sometimes have difficult decisions to make: if they ask for more money to serve more people, they increase the visibility of the agency and heighten the chance that it will be attacked by its enemies. Public-housing authorities have therefore not been aggressive in expanding their facilities. New site locations mean more controversy. More facilities mean more anxiety among real estate interests and more likelihood of their opposition.

Even with a rent assistance program, administrators are unaggressive. The director of the District of Columbia Department of Housing and Community Development admitted publicly that his agency made it hard for city residents to apply for aid. Offices receiving applications were open for only three hours a day, from one to four in the afternoon—hardly a convenience for the working poor. The director justified the agency's policy by maintaining that it was useless to receive a large number of applications because the city had federal money to assist only two-hundred families. No mention was made of the possibility of using a large number of applications as an arguing point for a larger program of assistance.

Often circumstances do not encourage program administrators to be aggressive. Service-providing professionals rarely enjoy a clear mandate. Seemingly simple charges, such as teaching children, turn out to be very complex. Not only are there competing academic goals but there is the issue of how much attention to give to academic skills versus how much emphasis to place on social development and interpersonal skills. And schools have a tendency to become custodial because one of their unstated but inviolable goals is to maintain order. As we have already seen, the police, too, are subject to contradictory expectations. For some agencies, the conflicting expectations flow from different sources. For example, welfare clients want more tangible assistance while taxpayers' groups want no giveaways. Or clients object to investigations of their personal lives and to highly personal questions, but taxpayers want tight controls against welfare cheating. As a consequence, regulations tend to be quite extensive, but caseworkers, who are in close touch with clients, ignore regulations on a widespread basis. Counseling tends to be very general; caseworkers stay away from sensitive issues such as social life and home care. With the added factor of heavy caseloads, "discretion" is principally exercised as noninvolvement.[18]

[18] Joel F. Handler and Ellen Jane Hollingsworth, *The "Deserving Poor"* (New York: Academic Press, 1971), p. 203.

If the welfare worker looks to the general public, there are only vague guidelines about how to operate. As those vague guidelines are applied in actual practice they serve only to highlight contradictory expectations. Help the poor, but not enough to make them dependent. Be lenient and understanding, but don't allow cheating. Help everyone who is needy, but don't increase the number of welfare recipients. Aid those who are neediest or most hopeless, but show results in moving people to self-sufficiency. Provide quick assistance, but maintain a low error rate. Many of the inconsistencies and absurd practices in welfare and other bureaucracies occur not because bureaucracies are inherently capricious but because they are subject to contradictory expectations. If some of their actions are anticlient, it is in part because they are subject to anticlient pressures.[19]

CONCLUSION

Employees come into public-service agencies with mixed expectations. They want a stable and secure future, but they also want work that is interesting and challenging. And, those who go into social agencies often have a strong people orientation—that is, they want to be helpful to others. Moreover, unlike the police, those who go into social agencies are likely to be politically liberal and have a sympathetic view of the client groups with which they work.

We might, therefore, expect such employees in their work with clients to be generous, concerned, innovative—always striving for a higher level of service. And with many individuals, that is the case. Yet in the aggregate, they are cautious and unimaginative. Rather than working to improve the service-delivery system, they acquiesce to things as they are. Sometimes they use their discretion to maneuver around and even disregard the rules. Even so, the overall tendency is toward routine and somewhat superficial interaction with clients.

While genuine innovators are rare, public-service professionals are typically dissatisfied with the status quo. Younger employees especially often appear frustrated. And many leave for other career opportunities. For those who stay, there is much stress and strain. Under the circumstances, tensions between agencies and their clients are to be expected. When frictions develop, public-service professionals are unlikely to blame themselves. They see themselves in the heroic role, doing a good job under adverse circumstances. They turn blame outwards. Sometimes they stereotype clients as apathetic or childlike and therefore blame them if

[19] See Michael Lipsky, "Bureaucratic Disentitlement in Social Welfare Programs," *Social Service Review* (March 1984), 3-27.

programs do not work. Sometimes they blame society or cultural disadvantage, thus relieving themselves of responsibility for unsolved problems. Often, they become cynical and feel that little can be done. As a result, they may take a Band-Aid approach—dealing with immediate problems on an ad hoc basis. Or they may simply concentrate on furthering their own careers because the helping relationship is so unsatisfying. And as we saw earlier, in some cases an agency staff may concentrate on those client problems that are interesting personally or rewarding professionally.

There is some basis in fact, then, for the popular view of public-service bureaucrats as callous and indifferent. But there is also much that this view misses. Work in a service-providing agency takes place in a complex field of forces. Modifications of that field can unleash some of the potential for more client-oriented services. Several possibilities need to be explored. One is to consider various ways of deprofessionalizing public-service provision. Frequently, clients want material or physical assistance, often of a very ordinary kind, but that is a kind of aid that highly trained professionals resist giving. A second possibility is to reduce the scale of organization. Instead of everything being done within one huge organization, many service activities could be devolved to small organizations. Professionalism and large-scale organization both have a way of heightening concern with such matters as rank, status, and authority. Small organizations are more informal and perhaps less inclined to generate status anxieties and other nonclient-related concerns. In a later chapter, we turn to another alternative—contracting out. It shows how simple-sounding answers may turn out to be very complex. For now, let us consider some issues of equity and equality.

SUGGESTED READINGS

EDELMAN, MURRAY. *Political Language: Words That Succeed and Policies That Fail.* New York: Academic Press, 1977.

ERMER, VIRGINIA, and JOHN H. STRANGE, eds. *Blacks and Bureaucracy: Readings in the Problems and Politics of Change.* New York: Thomas Y. Crowell, 1972.

GOODSELL, CHARLES T. *The Case for Bureaucracy.* Chatham, NJ: Chatham House, 1983.

———, ed. *The Public Encounter: Where State and Citizen Meet.* Bloomington: Indiana University Press, 1981.

HUMMEL, RALPH P. *The Bureaucratic Experience,* 2nd ed. New York: St. Martin's Press, 1982.

JOFFE, CAROLE E. *Friendly Intruders: Childcare Professionals and Family Life.* Berkeley; University of California Press, 1977.

LEVY, FRANK S., ARNOLD J. MELTSNER, and AARON WILDAVSKY. *Urban Outcomes: Schools, Streets, and Libraries.* Berkeley: University of California Press, 1974.

LIPSKY, MICHAEL. *Street-Level Bureaucracy.* New York: Russell Sage Foundation, 1980.

MILLER, S. M., PAMELA ROBY, and ALWINE A. DE VOS VAN STEENWIJK. "Creaming the Poor." *Trans-action* 7 (June 1970), 39-45.

PALUMBO, DENNIS AND ELAINE SHARP. "Process Versus Impact Evaluation of Community Corrections." In *The Practice of Policy Evaluation,* ed. David Nachmias. New York: St. Martin's Press, 1980, pp. 288-304.

PIVEN, FRANCES FOX, and RICHARD A. CLOWARD. *Regulating the Poor: The Functions of Public Welfare*. New York: Random House, Pantheon Books, 1971.

PROTTAS, JEFFREY M. *People-Processing*. Lexington, MA: Lexington Books, 1979.

SMITH, DENNIS. *Report from Engine Co. 82*. New York: Simon and Schuster, Pocket Books, 1972.

WARREN, ROLAND L., STEPHEN M. ROSE, and ANN F. BERGUNDER. *The Structure of Urban Reform*. Lexington, MA: Lexington Books, 1974.

chapter 21

Dissatisfaction with Public Services: Issues of Equity and Equality

Client-serving agencies, the previous chapter suggested, often engage in behavior not responsive to the needs of clients, especially of lower-class clients. Does this mean that services are delivered in an inequitable fashion? Are urban bureaucracies able to circumvent constitutional requirements of equality under the law? Is there systematic discrimination against the lower class in service delivery? There are no simple answers to these questions.

First, in opinion surveys lower class and minority respondents express more dissatisfaction with urban services.[1] Yet evidence of intentional discrimination is sparse. The central concern in most agencies seems to be that of how to perform their main tasks with limited resources. They must cope not only with limited money and too few workers but with limited information as well. Agencies have neither the time nor the capacity to find out about each individual service-receiving unit and treat it as a unique case. Instead, agencies develop routines, and, in doing so, they devise rules by which they allocate their resources and determine service priorities. These decision rules largely determine which individual or area receives what

[1] David M. Jones," The Urban Service Delivery Literature: A Critique." Paper prepared for delivery at the Annual Convention of the Western Social Science Association (Denver, Colorado: April 22-24, 1983).

kind of service benefits.[2] Sometimes these rules are written, but often they are nothing more than unwritten practices passed on by word-of-mouth.

In many respects these decision rules are based on technical considerations—how to perform a task efficiently. Some are based on criteria derived from professional associations. Some are simply guidelines for coping with the pressures of a heavy workload; emergency rooms, for example, take life-threatening cases first.[3] As one study concludes, these decision rules "are embedded deep within the structure of the organization and exist to regulate the repetitive tasks that the organization is required to perform."[4] If they have a political purpose, it may be to ward off individual or group demands for special considerations.[5] After all, the long struggle between reform forces and traditional practices involved an effort by reformers to substitute professional and technical criteria for favoritism. Decision rules stamped with the label of impartiality can be used to forestall outside intervention and promote agency autonomy: "They are a way of controlling a potentially threatening environment, especially if rule-governed behavior is regarded as legitimate by citizens."[6]

Of course, one needs to be cautious about generalizing. Communities differ, and even within a given community, political environments may vary from one agency to another. There are findings about the capacity of organized groups to intervene and gain concessions,[7] and access to the dominant political organization can make a difference in who is favored.[8] Moreover, electoral support for the mayor may bring rewards in the form of greater services.[9] Decision rules can take into account partisan and factional considerations.

For the most part, however, distributional consequences appear to be largely unintended. No one sits down and calculates who is to receive what

[2] Among the major discussions of bureaucratic decision rules are: Bryan D. Jones in association with Saadia Greenberg and Joseph Drew, *Service Delivery in the City* (New York: Longman, 1980); Kenneth R. Mladenka and Kim Q. Hill, "The Distribution of Benefits in an Urban Environment," *Urban Affairs Quarterly*, Vol. 13 (September, 1977), 73-94; Robert L. Lineberry, *Equality and Urban Policy* (Beverly Hills, CA: Sage Publications, 1977); and Pietro S. Nivola, "Distributing a Municipal Service," *Journal of Politics*, Vol. 40 (February 1978), 59-81.

[3] Jeffrey M. Prottas, *People-Processing* (Lexington, MA: Lexington Books, 1979), p. 75.

[4] Jones with Greenberg and Drew, *Service Delivery in the City*, p. 230.

[5] Ibid., p. 239.

[6] Ibid., p. 241.

[7] Levy and others, *Urban Outcomes*, pp. 130-34, 157-59; and Richard C. Rich, "Distribution of Services," in *Urban Policy Making*, ed. Dale Rogers Marshall (Beverly Hills, CA: Sage Publications, 1979), p. 248.

[8] Bryan D. Jones, "Party and Bureaucracy," *American Political Science Review*, Vol. 75 (September 1981), 688-700; and David Koehler and Margaret Wrightson, "Inequality in the Delivery of Urban Services: A Reconsideration of the Chicago Parks." Paper prepared for delivery at the Annual Meeting of the American Political Science Association (Chicago, IL: September 1-4, 1983).

[9] Frederic N. Bolotin and David L. Cingranelli, "Equity and Urban Policy: The Underclass Hypothesis Revisited," *Journal of Politics*, Vol. 45 (February 1983), 209-19.

precise benefits. Distributional consequences are "resultants," and do not represent conscious preferences among groups. One set of authors explains this indifference toward policy outcomes in this way:

> The decision makers of today began their careers when public service meant doing an efficient job of handling the business that came to them. If they were asked why they did not seek equality of results, they could rightly say that it was not their business to remake society. They never had a mandate from the electorate or their administrative superiors to alter outcomes in favor of selected social groups. If some people use cars more than others or like to go to libraries, that is the way of the world; when income patterns and reading habits change, . . . rules will favor new users as much as they did the old. These rules are fair for those citizens fortunate enough to make use of them.[10]

Administrative decision makers thus take a very restricted view. They pay little heed to whether their actions reinforce or modify an existing inequality. Decision rules are evaluated mainly in terms of efficiency criteria—how well they serve in accomplishing a given task with limited resources.[11] Little attention is given to the question of whether that is the most appropriate task. Engineers want to use streets to carry the most cars at the fastest speed; they don't ask about how well transportation facilities serve to reduce unemployment. Librarians want their book collections to have a high circulation; they may not ask about how their selection preferences fail to widen the reading public.[12] Indeed most public agencies are quite unaggressive about expanding their clientele reach. They seem content to limit organizational activity and to serve those who seek out established services.[13] Instead of pursuing change, bureaucratic decision makers seem content to follow the path of least resistance and concentrate on tasks that offer results with minimum resistance. Housing-code enforcers, for example, tend not to concentrate on large slum holders because such property holders are legally adept enough to evade quick compliance through the courts.[14] One study refers to a pattern called "the more, the more." It explains: "New library acquisition funds go to those who already read. Roads go only where the cars already are. Experienced teachers transfer to the well-to-do schools."[15] This is the path of least resistance and minimum bother. It offers results without struggle and controversy.

[10] Levy and others, *Urban Outcomes*, p. 246.

[11] Jones with Greenberg and Drew, *Service Delivery in the City*, p. 230. See also Clarence N. Stone and Robert Stoker, "Employee Inefficacy in Selected Client Serving Bureaucracies," *Journal of Urban Affairs*, Vol. 6 (Summer 1984), 5-18.

[12] See Levy and others, *Urban Outcomes*.

[13] Ibid., pp. 227-36. See also, Nivola, "Distributing a Municipal Service."

[14] Pietro S. Nivola, "Whom Regulators Regulate: Observations from an Urban Code Enforcement Program," in *Selected Papers from the 1981 Annual Meeting of the Council of University Institutes for Urban Affairs*, pp. 35-48.

[15] Levy and others, *Urban Outcomes*, p. 224.

The various findings on urban services thus suggest that distributional consequences reflect no overt effort to favor the well-off and shortchange the poor. Nevertheless, the unintended consequences of pursuing efficiency (without asking, "efficiency for what?"), following the road to quick and easy results, and not rocking the boat can eventuate in a pattern of class bias.[16] But the situation is more complicated than that. Not all studies find a class bias in the distribution of urban services. Some characterize distributional effects as "unpatterned."[17] Certainly they are complex. Still, distributional effects may, perhaps, best be described as conditional.[18] After all, some programs are intended to be compensatory and provide special assistance to those most in need. And some patterns of unequal distribution, whether intended or not, have been challenged and changed.[19]

TOWARD UNDERSTANDING CITIZEN DISSATISFACTION

Before returning to the question of why lower-class and minority populations are less satisfied with urban services, it might be useful to review available findings.

1. There are some class inequalities in facilities,[20] but probably more often this is not the case.

[16] See especially, ibid., p. 246.

[17] Lineberry, *Equality and Urban Policy*. For a strong critique of this characterization, see David M. Jones, "The Urban Service Delivery Literature "; Bolotin and Cingranelli, "Equity and Urban Policy"; Koehler and Wrightson, "Inequality in the Delivery of Urban Services"; and David L. Cingranelli, "Race, Politics and Elites," *American Journal of Political Science*, Vol. 25 (November 1981), 664-92.

[18] See Koehler and Wrightson, "Inequality in the Delivery of Urban Services," and John Boyle and David Jacobs, "The Intra-City Distribution of Services," *American Political Science Review*, Vol. 76 (June 1982), 371-79.

[19] See Jones, "The Urban Service Delivery Literature."

[20] Note the argument in ibid. about change over time. The reader should be mindful of the fact that significant inequalities in facilities have been found by several observers. Especially was this the case before minority and lower-strata groups were politically activated in the postreform era. Several studies, for example, found inequalities in school resources and facilities: Patricia Cayo Sexton, *Education and Income* (New York: Viking Press, 1961; Jesse Burkhead, Thomas G. Fox, and John W. Holland, *Input and Output in Large-City High Schools* (Syracuse: Syracuse University Press, 1967); and Martin T. Katzman, *The Political Economy of Urban Schools* (Cambridge, MA: Harvard University Press, 1971). It should also be noted that the controversial Coleman report did find disparities in school facilities by race, but also found these disparities between schools to be weaker statistically in accounting for differences in test scores than disparities between schools in socioeconomic background of students—see James S. Coleman and others, *Equality of Educational Opportunity* (Washington, D.C.: U.S. Government Printing Office, 1966).

2. When facilities are equal, there may still be inequalities in upkeep and in the quality of the services provided.[21]
3. While most decision rules are based on internal task-performance considerations, there are cases of political intervention by organized and influential groups.[22] Political alliances sometimes matter in direct ways.
4. Some decisions reflect efforts to promote economic development and retain affluent taxpayers.[23]
5. Some decision rules reflect preferences for avoiding work with a lower-class clientele.[24]
6. Some decision rules based ostensibly on professional and technical criteria reinforce inequities in distributions—resulting in a pattern of "the more, the more."
7. However, some programs are deliberately compensatory, especially in the area of education. These are often based on state and federal directives, and sometimes they are resisted by local communities.[25]
8. Some decision rules ration scarce resources by concentrating on those with the greatest need.[26]
9. Occasionally decision rules based on racial prejudice (property tax assessment in San Antonio[27]) or employee-negotiated benefits (teacher-union contracts in New York City that reduce student load in compensatory education classes[28]) work to the distributional advantage of the lower strata.

Then, too, there is the matter of the importance of the decision. Some are not small and routine, and therefore assume greater visibility and greater importance in the eyes of those affected. The location of freeways primarily through lower-class neighborhoods, for example, may overshadow impartiality in the allocation of library facilities.[29]

Since the overall pattern of service distributions is mixed, is there a basis on which "have nots" might feel that they do not receive an equitable share of urban services? First, taking into account such hard to measure

[21] Koehler and Wrightson, "Inequality in the Delivery of Urban Services."

[22] In addition to note 7 above, see Koehler and Wrightson, "Inequality in the Delivery of Urban Services"; Cingranelli, "Race, Politics and Elites"; and Bolotin and Cingranelli, "Equity and Urban Policy." For a broad conception of political influence, see Peter F. Nardulli and Jeffrey M. Stonecash, *Politics, Professionalism, and Urban Services* (Cambridge, MA: Oelgeschlager, Gunn and Hain, Publishers, 1981).

[23] Levy and others, *Urban Outcomes*; and Boyle and Jacobs, "The Intra-City Distribution of Services."

[24] Levy and others, *Urban Outcomes*; and Prottas, *People-Processing*.

[25] John F. Hughes and Anne O. Hughes, *Equal Education* (Bloomington: Indiana University Press, 1972); and Paul Berman and Milbrey McLaughlin, "Implementation of Educational Innovation," *Educational Forum*, Vol. 40 (March 1976), 345-70.

[26] Nivola, "Distributing a Municipal Service."

[27] Lineberry, *Equality and Urban Policy*.

[28] Sara L. Silbiger, "Collective Bargaining and the Distribution of Benefits," in Dale Rogers Marshall, ed. *Urban Policy Making* (Beverly Hills, CA: Sage Publications, 1979), pp. 261-79.

[29] See Lineberry, *Equality and Urban Policy*, p. 173.

considerations as the quality of service and the attitudes of service providers, one might reasonably conclude that there is in fact considerable inequality. Moreover, it is important to take context into consideration.[30] For example, if the task is largely impersonal or the pressures of the situation too demanding to allow for discretionary behavior, then probably equality is the norm. But if the task is highly personal and there is opportunity for discretionary behavior, inequality may well be the prevalent pattern. Significantly, emergency-room staff seem not to discriminate racially in cases involving severe injuries but do so with less serious cases.[31] The latter may shape the patient's perception more strongly than the former.

Context is important in other ways as well. Much inequality in service delivery has nothing to do with decision rules. It is inequality based on differences *between jurisdictions*.[32] Expenditures on education, for example, vary with the wealth and class composition of the school district.

Perceived inequality may also be based partly on different patterns of client treatment *between types of agencies*. If agencies primarily serving the poor—agencies providing welfare assistance, for example—have long waiting lines and many forms to fill out, their practices may feed a feeling of inequality. This is particularly the case if agencies such as public libraries, for example, that serve a mainly middle-class clientele follow different practices. Consider another example. If bus service on which the poor are especially dependent deteriorates, while new expressways serving car owners are built on a large scale, then there is a class bias in service provision. And those disadvantaged are keenly aware of the bias.

Further, dissatisfaction with public services is based to some extent on the fact that publicly-funded services often do not match what can be bought privately.[33] If the poor are dependent on health care in public clinics and hospitals, and if the quality of care differs between public and private facilities, then those who receive inferior care are likely to be dissatisfied. They perceive inequality in access to services, and that perception may override details about the combination of mechanisms through which the inequality occurs.

Similarly, some inequalities in service-provision come about through the superior ability of affluent neighborhoods to supplement public efforts and enhance service quality. PTA's raise money for books and additional equipment. Nonpoor communities provide resources for recreation pro-

[30] See Kenneth R. Greene, "The Impact of Agency and Individual Decision Rules on the Delivery of Urban Services." Paper prepared for delivery at the Annual Meeting of the Midwest Political Science Association (Chicago: April 1979); and Nardulli and Stonecash, *Politics, Professionalism, and Urban Services*.

[31] Lipsky, *Street-level Bureaucracy*, p. 109. See also Prottas, *People-Processing*, pp. 77-79.

[32] Richard C. Rich, "Distribution of Services," in Marshall, ed. *Urban Policy Making*, pp. 242-5.

[33] Lineberry, *Equality and Urban Policy*, pp. 174-5.

grams. Or, to take a different kind of example, affluent families or large property holders may purchase the protection of private security to supplement local police service. Differences in the total service received may then be quite marked even when public expenditures are uniform from neighborhood-to-neighborhood.

Finally, we might also take note of unequal capacities to modify or evade the impact of decision rules. If school integration and compensatory education efforts cause people to be dissatisfied, not every one need remain so. Those who can afford to pursue choices and who face no discrimination in the market place can either engage in "flight" to another jurisdiction or place their children in private schools. The writ of public authority is quite limited, and many people evade its impact. To cite another example, enforcement of housing codes is always restricted by the possibility that the offending property owner, perhaps having already reaped a substantial tax write-off from depreciation, will abandon susbstandard property rather than fix it up. Thus, the inequality that the lower class feels may not be based on uneven enforcement of housing codes so much as on the uniform weakness of such codes as a means to improved housing for the poor.[34] Citizens are not equally dependent on the protection of housing codes. Those who are dependent feel the weakness of these codes more sharply than those who are not dependent.

ISSUES OF EQUITY

Though important, bureaucratic decision rules by which services are distributed turn out to be only a part of the overall picture. For some people, the key issue is one of results—what are the consequences of a service delivery effort? Dissatisfaction and perceptions of inequality cannot be eliminated merely by providing public service on some seemingly equal basis. Some so-called impartial rules—basing library appropriations on book circulation, for example—are so passive as to reinforce existing inequalities. It is no easy matter to come up with fair rules. After all, people differ in their conceptions of equity. Those who are successful and highly productive may see little wrong with the distributional consequence labeled, "the more, the more." To them, it may be fair that those who pay more taxes, sponsor more employment opportunities, and bring more prestige to the community should receive more. A rule of what we might call supply-side equity—"reward the productive"—can be defended on the ground that benefits will trickle down to everyone. And it might be further argued that such a distribution formula will motivate the less productive to become more productive.

[34] Nivola, "Distributing a Municipal Service," pp. 77-78.

However, because not everyone starts with the same resources and opportunities to be productive, those who are disadvantaged may well prefer a different rule of equity. They want to see opportunities and abilities to produce equalized. Equal public expenditures on education, for example, do not necessarily yield equal results. Those with the most direct needs or the most severe handicaps can make a case that equity requires equalizing their positions, otherwise life's competition is unfair. Some start the race far behind others. Moreover, the bond of social solidarity requires concern for the needy and the less advantaged.[35] This effort to equalize productive capacities might be called "compensatory equity."

Supply-side versus compensatory equity is an ideological contest that has come to surround many service-providing agencies. Treated as a matter of competing formulas for service benefits, service-delivery controversy tends to heighten group conflict. It is part of the postreform era, but the heightened group conflict does not necessarily work to the political advantage of "have nots." Those of middle means often want to distance themselves politically from the needy. To them, equity may mean practices that correspond to the formal equality of the law—equal benefits to everyone, regardless of station in life or productive capacity. Forced to choose, the middle class may favor supply-side over compensatory equity, or they may become disenchanted with the authority of government. One set of authors concluded that these doctrinal disputes "compromise other values such as equal treatment of all citizens, and by doing so they undermine the legitimacy of political institutions . . . ."[36] Thus, they suggest that both supply-side and compensatory arguments need to be weighed against other considerations.

CONCLUSION

In conclusion, we can see that most inequalities in urban services do not *originate* in bureaucratic decision rules. It may be possible to modify these rules in order to lessen the extent to which they reinforce inequalities. But any substantial decrease in the inequalities of urban life will have to be based on something more far-reaching than the way in which public bureaucracies seek to routinize their performance of service-delivery tasks. In looking at bureaucratic behavior and how it might be changed, it is probably more useful to think of this behavior as reflecting than as causing inequality.

[35] William J. Goode, "The Protection of the Inept," *American Sociological Review*, Vol. 32 (February 1967), 5-19.

[36] Levy and othrs, *Urban Outcomes*, p. 259.

We turn now to another perspective on public bureaucracy. Is there a case to be made for minimizing the role of public bureaucracy through contracting out service activities to private firms?

SUGGESTED READINGS

ANTUNES, GEORGE and JOHN PLUMLEE. "The Distribution of an Urban Public Service." *Urban Affairs Quarterly*, Vol. 12 (March 1977), 313- 32.

BOLOTIN, FREDRIC N. and DAVID L. CINGRANELLI. "Equity and Urban Policy: The Underclass Hypothesis Revisited." *Journal of Politics*, Vol. 45 (February 1983), 209-219.

BOYLE, JOHN and DAVID JACOBS. "The Intra-City Distribution of Services." *American Political Science Review*, Vol. 76 (June 1982), 371-79.

CINGRANELLI, DAVID L. "Race, Politics and Elites: Testing Alternative Models of Municipal Service Distribution." *American Journal of Political Science*, Vol. 25 (November 1981), 664-92.

JONES, BRYAN D. "Party and Bureaucracy: The Influence of Intermediary Groups on Urban Service Delivery." *American Political Science Review*, Vol. 75 (September 1981), 688- 700.

———, in association with SAADIA GREENBERG and JOSEPH DREW. *Service Delivery in the City*. New York: Longman, 1980.

LEVY, FRANK, ARNOLD MELTSNER, and AARON WILDAVSKY. *Urban Outcomes*. Berkeley: University of California Press, 1974.

LINEBERRY, ROBERT L. *Equality and Urban Policy*. Beverly Hills, CA: Sage Publications, 1977.

MLADENKA, KENNETH R. "The Urban Bureaucracy and the Chicago Political Machine." *American Political Science Review*, Vol. 74 (December 1980), 991-8.

MLADENKA, KENNETH R. "Citizen Demands and Urban Services." *American Journal of Political Science*, Vol. 25 (November 1981), 693-714.

MLADENKA, KENNETH R. and KIM Q. HILL. "The Distribution of Urban Police Services." *Journal of Politics*, Vol. 40 (February 1978), 112-33.

NARDULLI, PETER F. and JEFFREY M. STONECASH. *Politics, Professionalism, and Urban Services*. Cambridge, MA: Oelgeschlager, Gunn and Hain, Publishers, 1981.

NIVOLA, PIETRO. *The Urban Service Problem*. Lexington, MA: Lexington Books, 1979

RICH, RICHARD C. ed. *Analyzing Urban Service Distributions*. Lexington, MA: Lexington Books, 1982.

RICH, RICHARD C. ed. *The Politics of Urban Public Services*. Lexington, MA: Lexington Books,

———, *The Politics of Urban Public Services*. Lexington, MA: Lexington Books, 1982.

STONE, CLARENCE N. and ROBERT STOKER. "Employee Inefficacy in Selected Client Serving Bureaucracies." *Journal of Urban Affairs*, Vol. 6 (Summer 1984), 5-18.

chapter 22

A Postscript on Alternatives to Public Bureaucracies: Delivering Governmental Services via the Private Sector, the Alternative of Contracting Out

If client-serving bureaucracies, staffed by street-level bureaucrats, are not delivering services in accord with citizen expectations, different organizations, delivering services in a different manner, might well take over the job. While alternative service-delivery modes are common in some program areas, most notably garbage removal, they are virtually unknown in other areas. Before we discuss alternatives which differ from city employees delivering services as part of a city-owned monopoly, it seems useful to review the process of public-sector service delivery in general.

In most communities, services provided by local government are delivered by employees of the city. Law enforcement and safety are provided by police officers, fire protection and extinguishing by a fire department, street repairs by employees of the street department, library services by librarians who are city employees, and so on. While the services are different and while the people are different, they do share certain characteristics. To the general public they are all bureaucrats, and in our culture bureaucrats and bureaucracies are presumed to be non-productive. Thus, whatever substantive problems bureaucratic service delivery causes, those problems are compounded by the presumption that bureaucracies are inefficient, unfeeling, and uncaring. In addition, most service-providing agencies are monopolies, and according to dominant economic theory, monopolies are inefficient because they face no competition.[1] The presence of competition encourages organizations to provide goods and services in an efficient manner or else risk losing business to more efficient firms. Monopolies face no competition; efficiency is not required as a condition of survival, thus, other values can be served. In many cases, the other values are those of administrative ease, career advancement, and the personal goals of the workers of the monopoly. Thus, public services provided by the public sector are said to be inefficient because they are provided by monopolies without the discipline of a competitive market system.

Hard on the heels of the dissatisfaction with the way some public sector bureaucracies were delivering services, came Proposition 13 in California and the resulting concern with delivering governmental services in a more efficient manner. It was only natural, given the privatist traditions so common in the United States, that attention was turned to private sector alternatives for the delivery of public services.

An anti-public sector ethos, dissatisfaction with client-serving bureaucracies, and fiscal dilemmas brought on by recession, taxpayers in tax-cutting moods, and Reagan-styled government have combined to create the possibility that local government services might be delivered by other than employees of local government. In the not too distant past, it was generally accepted that public services would be performed by public employees funded by tax dollars. That assumption no longer necessarily holds.

In deciding how to deliver services, local governments have numerous possible options. If the service is an optional one and not mandated by state or federal governments, the local government can choose not to provide it at all. While municipalities operate tennis courts, golf courses, zoos, museums, and so on, they do not have to. In the case of optional services, citizens or groups of citizens may acquire the service by contracting with a private provider for it or by providing the service themselves. Citizens may band together to deliver the service using volunteers. A

[1] Albert O. Hirschman, *Exit, Voice and Loyalty: Responses to Decline in Firms, Organizations and States* (Cambridge, Mass: Howard University Press, 1970).

second way of providing services is the traditional way—municipal personnel using municipally-owned equipment.

Governments can enter into contracts with other governments to provide certain services. Currently, the state of Wisconsin contracts with Minnesota to provide prison space for some of Wisconsin's criminals. Such agreements are common in the United States. About two-thirds of the municipalities in the United States have formal or informal agreements for the provision of services to their citizens by other governments.

The most famous example of this approach is known as the "Lakewood Plan" in Los Angeles, California. Municipalities enter into contracts with Los Angeles County to buy services at a level of quality that they want. Savas shows that

> In 1981 the city of Lakewood, in Los Angeles County, was purchasing 41 different services from the county; 76 other cities also purchased election services from the county, and other county services being marketed included animal regulation; emergency ambulance service; enforcement of health ordinances; engineering services; fire and police protection; library; sewer maintenance; park maintenance; recreation services; assessment and collection of taxes; hospitalization of city prisoners; personnel staff services such as recruitment, examination, and certification; prosecution; building inspection; weed abatement; school fire-safety officers; mobile-home and trailer-park inspection; milk inspection; rodent control; mental health services; tree trimming; bridge maintenance; preparation and installation of street signs; street sweeping; traffic-signal maintenance; traffic striping and marking; traffic-law enforcement; business license issuing and enforcement; and crossing guards.[2]

Yet another way is to use *vouchers*. Vouchers are designed to encourage the use of particular services or goods, usually by a particular group of people. The most widely used form of vouchers is the food stamp program. Eligible individuals are supplied with food stamps that they use in grocery stores. It is assumed that the food-stamp user has an incentive to comparision shop and purchase wisely because her or his money will then go further. While vouchers have generally been used to subsidize food, housing, and medical services for poor people, they have also been used for certain cultural activities such as the theater, and have been proposed for such services as museums, transportation, and zoos.[3]

The last alternative we will deal with is government contracting with private companies to provide services. The justification for the private contracting of government services is based in part on the belief that such services can be more economically performed by a private sector firm. A

[2] E.S. Savas, *Privatizing the Public Sector* (Chatham, N.J.: Chatham House Publishers, 1982), p. 60.

[3] Gary Bridge, "Citizen Choice in Public Service: Voucher Systems," in E.S. Savas ed. *Alternatives for Delivering Public Services* (Boulder, Colo.: Westview Press, 1977).

1973 survey of 2,375 cities revealed that sixty-six services were being contracted for with private providers.

This list is only the beginning, for as Savas observes:

> . . . even this list is not complete; custodial services for government buildings and grounds are also obtained through this arrangement, as are lunchroom operations in schools and government office buildings; demolition work; operation of auditoriums and convention centers; tree pruning, tree removal, planting, grass mowing, lawn and golf course maintenance, weed abatement, and other horticultural services; traffic signal maintenance; towing away of illegally parked and abandoned autos; processing parking tickets; traffic striping and marking; parking lot operations; bus shelters; school bus transportation; vehicle maintenance; street sweeping, leaf collection; maintenance of communication equipment, key punching, and data processing services; test scoring; laundry services; secretarial and clerical work; water meter maintenance; and management consulting. Such social services as day care, foster home care, group home care, adoption, institutional care, rehabilitative services, family counseling, child protection, homemaker services, and legal aid for improverished defendants are obtained by state and local government contracts with private firms and non profit institutions.[4]

More recent data show that only a very small percentage of municipalities contract out any services. For those services that are contracted out, most fall into what might be called "professional services" or "housekeeping," rather than services which are directly consumed by citizens. There is one noticeable exception to this pattern. Solid waste (garbage) collection is the only citizen-received service that is commonly contracted out.

In the drive to make government more efficient and more businesslike by transferring service to private providers, a great deal of misinformation is exchanged that passes for hard facts and truth. To our knowledge, there is no body of empirical evidence to support the claim that the private provision of services is more efficient, effective, or humane than the public provision of those same services. In a perfectly rational world, a delivery structure would be chosen because it maximizes or realizes certain goals established by citizens and government officials. In the real world, cost efficiencies appear to be the primary reasons why organizational arrangements, other than city departments, are chosen to provide a particular service.

Cultural anthropologists and sociologists have long told us that we Americans (like other people) tend to be ethnocentric. That means that we tend to see things American as superior to things that are non-American. We often, then, equate non-American with un-American. Campaigns to buy American-made products, especially automobiles, are especially illustrative.

[4] Savas, *Privatizing*, p. 62.

TABLE 22-1 The Number of Cities Using Private Firms to Supply Municipal Services Under Contract

SERVICE	NUMBER OF CITIES CONTRACTING WITH PRIVATE FIRMS
Refuse collection	339
Street lighting	309
Electricity supply	258
Engineering services	253
Legal services	187
Ambulance services	169
Solid waste disposal	143
Utility billing	104
Animal control	99
Planning	92
Water supply	84
Mapping	74
Water distribution system	67
Payroll	65
Street construction and maintenance	63
Hospitals	57
Special transportation services	49
Cemeteries	47
Microfilm services	47
Nursing services	34
Assessing	31
Public relations	30
Bridge construction and maintenance	25
Industrial development	24
Tax collection	24
Mental health	22
Sewage disposal	21
Management service for publicly-owned transit	18
Electrical and plumbing inspection	17
Libraries	17
Zoning and subdivision control	16
Sewer lines	14
Treasury functions	14
All fire services	13
Mosquito control	12
Museums	12
General development	10
Alcoholic rehabilitation	9
Records maintenance	9
Election administration	8
Police communications	8

TABLE 22-1 The Number of Cities Using Private Firms to Supply Municipal Services Under Contract *(Continued)*

SERVICE	NUMBER OF CITIES CONTRACTING WITH PRIVATE FIRMS
Building and mechanical inspection	7
Fire communications	7
Housing	7
Recreational facilities	7
Personnel services	6
Urban renewal	6
Crime laboratory	5
Irrigation	5
Parks	5
Traffic control	5
Water pollution abatement	5
All public health services	4
Juvenilie delinquency program	4
Licensing	4
Soil conversion	4
Civil defense communications	2
Fire prevention	2
Noise abatement	2
Patrol services	2
Registration of voters	2
Training of firemen	2
Air pollution abatement	1
Jails and detention homes	1
Welfare	1

NOTE: Based on responses of 2,375 cities to a mail survey in 1973.

SOURCE: Derived from the CHALLENGE OF LOCAL GOVERNMENTAL REORGANIZATION, Vol. 3, appendix table 3.A (Washington, D.C.: U.S. Government Printing Office, Advisory Commission on Intergovernmental Relations, Feb. 1974).

Since we tend to be culture-bound, it is useful to look at the examples of other societies to see if there is anything that we can possibly learn from them. For example, a survey of twenty-two California city managers revealed that the only way building inspection should be provided is by a city department. But in France, all building-inspection functions, except for fire safety, have been turned over to private industry. Under French law, builders are liable for damages associated with the durability or quality of their buildings. French insurance companies hire building inspectors to determine if insured buildings are safe. French citizens are protected by the desire of the insurance industry to minimize damage claims. In Denmark, the Falck Company provides fire protection and rescue services to half of the country. The company employs almost five thousand people full- and part-time, and owns in excess of one thousand five hundred fire trucks and ambulances. It even has boats and an airplane for specialized medical emergencies. Some 271 of the 279 municipalities in Denmark contract with Falck for one-or-more services. The company provides ambulance service to 98 percent of Denmark and it provides fire services to 62 percent of the municipalities.

In Switzerland, more than thirty villages and township officials have contracted with Securitas, a private security firm for foot and car security patrols, building security checks and other police-type activities. There are numerous other examples that could be cited throughout Europe and Japan, the country that leads the world in contracting for the delivery of public services. Even though there are numerous examples of successful contracting in Europe, a note of caution is in order. European observers cite many of the same problems with contracting as are mentioned in the United States; namely that undercapitalized firms provide poor services, companies with political ties get padded contracts resulting in increased costs to taxpayers, and the potential for widespread corruption is present. Europeans believe that such problems can be overcome by proper management practices, clear specification of service levels, limited-term contracts, competitive bidding, and an investigation of the financial strength of contractors.

Despite strong popular belief, there is no real evidence to show whether the public or private sector is more successful in holding down the costs of service delivery. There is, however, evidence that a monopoly, be it public or private, is subject to abuse. It is difficult if not impossible to try and guarantee accountability and responsiveness under monopoly conditions. Dominant economic theory argues that monopolies are inefficient and that the solution to monopolies is competition. Data from several studies indicate that public provision of services can be as cost-efficient as pri-

TABLE 22-2 Classification of Services Contracted

FREQUENCY (in percent)	PROFESSIONAL	HOUSEKEEPING	DIRECT CITIZEN DELIVERY
50 or more	Architectural services Engineering services	Street construction Building repair	
33 to 49	Legal counsel	Equipment maintenance Building maintenance	Solid waste collection
15 to 32	Land use planning	Vehicle maintenance Administrative support Food service, employees Street maintenance	Ambulance services Elderly care Child-day care Halfway houses
5 to 11		First aid, employees Police communications	Elderly, recreation Leaf collection General public, recreation

SOURCE: "Contracting Out for Public Services," *Minnesota Cities*, V. 65 (June 1980), p. 9.

vate provision of those same services so long as conditions of competition exist. Service costs tend to increase and quality decrease as conditions of monopoly develop. If this is correct, we can tentatively conclude that if conditions of competition can be created, whether the provider is the public or private sector is more or less irrelevant from a cost standpoint. But even this conclusion must be issued with a caveat. While economic theory asserts the advantages of competition over monopoly, and experiments in St. Paul and Kansas City show that public-sector providers can provide garbage collection services at about the same cost as private providers, there are virtually no serious attempts by local governments to use competition as a cost-control tool in service delivery. Therefore, our practical knowledge of the actual effectiveness of creating competition to maintain quality while decreasing the cost of public services is extremely limited. The only service area in which we have relatively good information is that of garbage collection and we would caution against generalizing the findings from those studies to other policy areas with different policy characteristics. Nor do we know the extent to which competition is possible in the provision of certain public services. It just may turn out that many cities are not large enough to attract bids from enough qualified service providers for competition to exist. Then the city is forced to choose between a private monopoly provider or a public monopoly provider.

With this warning then, let us examine some of the alleged advantages of the private delivery of public services. The advantages are summarized in Table 22-3.

As for the first advantage, as we have already indicated, data are limited and the results of several studies are mixed. In some instances, costs are reduced while in others there are no cost differences, and in still others, costs increase. And even where costs do change, it is not entirely clear if cost savings are due to improved managment efficiencies or if the services being delivered are different in quality from what they were before the change.

TABLE 22-3 Advantages of the Private Delivery of Public Services[5]

May cost less or provide better performance
Provides specialized skills
Limits the growth of government
Avoids large initial costs
Permits greater flexibility in adjusting program size
Provides a yardstick for comparison
Promotes increased objectivity
Produces better management
Produces better management information

[5] Donald Fisk, Herbert Kiesling, Thomas Muller, *Private Provision of Public Services: An Overview* (Washington, D.C.: The Urban Institute, May 1978), pp. 6-7.

For smaller jurisdictions or for services that are used rather infrequently, contracting may make specialized skills or services available at lower cost than if a municipality had to provide them for itself. It may be true that the size of government can be limited by using contractors, but the limits are in personnel, not in total government spending. Contracting simply shifts costs from one budget line to another. And to the extent that extensive contracting requires hiring contract compliance people, inspectors, monitors, and so on, contracting may actually result in increased costs. It is often argued that municipal officials feel that contracting gives them more flexibility in adjusting program size by being able to terminate contracts more easily than they can lay off municipal workers. Again the evidence of the validity of this assertion is quite limited. It may well turn out that cities pay for this convenience. A city might get a better cost for a service if it enters into a long-term contract with a private provider than if it negotiates a contract annually.

Where services are comparable, such as building maintenance, vehicle repair, and others, contracting may provide a yardstick for comparison. But it is not necessary to contract to achieve comparison. Some services are comparable regardless of who performs them. Vehicle and building maintenance are performed in the public and private sector and comparable cost figures can easily be obtained without actually entering into a contract for services.

As for the rest of the assumptions there is simply not enough evidence available for us to conclude whether or not they have any basis in reality. E.S. Savas, the individual best known for popularizing the issues of public versus private delivery of services, has concluded: "with few exceptions, little rigorous research has been done to evaluate and compare public and private provision of services."[6] He does point out that where there have been rigorous studies, private provision has been shown to be superior to public provision of services. While his conclusion is probably true from an *efficiency* standpoint, we are hesitant to accept it because the studies really do not attempt to measure service *effectiveness* or *equity* to any large degree. Another problem with the Savas conclusion is that many of the services were not typically provided by local governments. Among his examples include the provision of airline service, postal service, nursing homes, health insurance administration, family planning, social services, forestry in Germany, and weather forecasting.

Having examined the alleged advantages of contracting, it is now time to look at the other side—the disadvantages. Table 22-4 provides a summary list.

The simplest answer to these charges is probably the best and most accurate. It all depends. Depending upon how examples are chosen and data presented, one can present a picture of contracting as inefficient and

[6]Savas, *Privatizing*, p. 116.

TABLE 22-4 Disadvantages of the Private Delivery of Public Services[7]

May cost more
May result in poorer service for citizens
Increases the chances for corruption
Raises the possibility that contractor may not complete operations
Displaces public employees and is opposed by unions
Problems in drawing up adequate contracts
May be restricted by law
May cause problems in enforcing public policy
Fails to guarantee competition for contracts
Reduces flexibility to respond to change
Provices less control over final services
May interfere with tradition
Requires close monitoring

corrupt or honest and cost-effective. The opponents of contracting argue that far from being a potential money-saving device, contracting is a major source of governmental corruption, financial waste, and ineffiency. They argue that some of the worst political scandals in recent years can be attributed to contracting and that the more that government officials deal with the business community, the more the taxpayer suffers. They also argue that any saving and service improvements are likely to be temporary as the contractor tries to look good on the first contract, drive out competition, and then get the locality to commit itself to a long-term monopoly situation. At that point, cost overruns occur, service deteriorates, corruption emerges and citizens suffer. Opponents of contracting point out that when Boston started providing its own street-light maintenance rather than contracting for it, the city saved $867,000 in the first year of the program.[8]

At this point in the evolution of the public provision-private provision debate, much heat but little light exists on the subject. We agree with Savas when he says, "the issue of which arrangement is best should properly be addressed as an empirical question, not an ideological or emotional one."[9] We also agree with his observation that "the relevant criteria to use in comparing arrangements are efficiency, effectiveness, and equity."[10] Unfortunately our analysis reveals that only efficiency as measured in dollars tends to be looked at when a decision to move from public provision to private provision is made.

In this fiscally constrained era of government finance, the cost argument is a wholly natural and reasonable one. But if the opponents of

[7] Fisk, *Private Provision*, pp. 7-8.

[8] See for example, John D. Hanrahan, *Government for Sale: Contracting Out: The New Patronage* (Washington, D.C.: ASFCME, 1977).

[9] Savas, *Privatizing*, p. 92.

[10] Ibid.

contracting are correct, then short-term cost advantages may be realized at the expense of long-term service effectiveness and equity.

Despite the fact that evidence to prove one position or another is generally lacking, there are some conclusions that can be drawn about the type of services likely to be contracted. Evidence indicates that newer rather than older service, infrequent rather than frequent, unique rather than common, services with clear output indicators, services with relatively simple technologies where productivity improvements can be realized, and services using unskilled or semi-skilled labor are all more likely to be contracted rather than their opposites. Services with few production function uncertainties are prime candidates for contracting. This type of service permits tightly written contracts and contractor performance monitoring on the basis of predetermined standards. While there are subjective elements in all services (for example what is a *clean* street), the ability to define service quality is an important consideration in determining the contractability of a service. In this context, tangible services, such as solid waste collection, water supply, street paving and maintenance, ambulance services, and transportation have performance standards and output that are relatively easily determined. Thus, we would conclude that they are obvious candidates for contracting out. Services of an intangible nature, especially where there is difficulty in determining acceptable output standards are less likely to be contracted.

CONCLUSION

The delivery of public services and the management of the public sector will not necessarily be improved by a wholesale transfer of government functions to the private sector. Under carefully controlled conditions, costs and benefits may favor one delivery system over another. As we have previously indicated, there is little hard data on the whole issue. Our conclusion is that despite the claims made by both sides, the basis for a contracting decision is essentially subjective and shrouded in much myth and assumption. Local governments do not have the time, staff, or money to devote to a comprehensive analysis and evaluation of alternate means of providing services. For those governments, in the absence of a crisis, the status quo is likely to be the most feasible alternative. There is little information on the real versus anticipated benefits of contracting. What we know is sketchy, anecdotal, and not without methodological shortcoming. Only for solid waste collection can we conclude with some confidence that contracting is less costly than direct service provision by local government. Even here we do not know the relative magnitude of the cost savings and whether or not the savings are significant enough to have a real impact on a municipality's fiscal situation.

As if all this was not enough to discourage contracting, the possibility may well exist that a municipality may not have the legal authority under state law or a collective bargaining agreement to unilaterally decide that it wants to contract a service currently provided by municipal workers. In 1968, Milwaukee, Wisconsin, decided that contracting for garbage collection would be more efficient than providing it by city workers. A contract was signed with a private firm and 260 sanitation employees were laid off. The employees' union took the city to court claiming that their contract prohibited the firing of employees with civil-service status. The court ruled in favor of the union, and the city found itself back in the garbage business two months after it had switched to contracting.

SUGGESTED READINGS

AYRES, DOUGLAS W. "Municipal Interface in the Third Sector: A Negative View." *Public Administration Review* 35 (September/October 1975), 459-463.

BENDICK, MARC. "Privatization of Public Services: Recent Experience." In *Public-Private Partnership: New Opportunities for Meeting Social Needs*. eds. Harvey Brooks, et al. (Cambridge, MA: Ballinger, 1984, pp. 153-171.

BRUDNEY, JEFFREY L. "Coproduction: The Potential for Responsiveness and Effectiveness in the Delivery of Urban Services." *Urban Interest* 4 (Spring 1982), 87-94.

DE HOOG, RUTH HOOGLAND. *Contracting Out for Human Services*. Albany: State University at New York Press, 1984.

DIMOND, PAUL R., CONSTANCE CHAMBERLAIN, and WAYNE HILLYARD. *A Dilemma of Local Government: Discrimination in the Provision of Public Services*. Lexington, MA: D.C. Heath, 1978.

FERRIS, JAMES M. "Coprovision: Citizen Time and Money Donations in Public Service Provision." *Public Administration Review* 44 (July/August 1984), 324-333.

FLORESTANO, PATRICIA S. and STEPHEN B. GORDON. "Public *vs.* Private: Small Government Contracting with the Private Sector." *Public Administration Review* 40 (January/February, 1980), 29-34.

FLORESTANO, PATRICIA S. and STEPHEN B. GORDON, "A Survey of City and County Use of Private Contracting." *Urban Interest* 3 (Spring 1981),

GOODSELL, CHARLES T. *The Case for Bureaucracy*. Chatham, NJ: Chatham House, 1983.

HATRY, HARRY P. *A Review of Private Approaches for Delivery of Public Services*. Washington, DC: Urban Institute, 1983.

LEVINE, CHARLES. "Citizenship and Service Delivery: The Promise of Coproduction." *Public Administration Review* 44 (March 1984-Special Issue), 178-187.

MARLIN, JOHN T., ed. contracting Municipal Services, *A Guide for Purchasing from the Private Sector*. New York: Ronald press, 1984.

PASCAL, ANTHONY H. "User Charges, Contracting Out, and Privatization in an Era of Change." *Urban Interest* 3 (Spring 1981), 6-12.

Passing the Bucks: The Contracting Out of Public Services. Washington, DC: American Federation of State, County, and Municipal Employees, 1983.

RICH, RICHARD C., ed. *The Politics of Urban Public Services*. Lexington, Mass.: Lexington Books, 1982.

SAVAS, E.S. *Privatizing the Public Sector*. Chatham, New Jersey: Chatham House Publishers, 1982.

STIPAK, BRIAN. "Citizen Satisfaction with Urban Services: Potential Misuse as a Performance Indicator." *Public Administration Review* 39 (January/February, 1979), 46-52.

STRAUSSMAN, JEFFREY D. "More Bang for Fewer Bucks? Or How Local Governments Can

Rediscover the Potentials (and Pitfalls) of the Market." *Public Administration Review* 41 January/February, 1981), 150-158.

SUNDQUIST, JAMES L. "Privatization: No Panacea for What Ails Government." In *Public-Private Partnership: New Opportunities for Meeting Social Needs*. Harvey Brooks et al, eds. Cambridge, MA Ballinger, 1984, pp. 303-318.

SUSSKIND, LAWRENCE et al. *Learning from Citizen Action and Citizen Participation in Western Europe*. New York: Plenum Press, 1983.

WHITAKER, GORDON P. "Coproduction: Citizen Participation in Service Delivery." *Public Administration Review* 40 (May/June, 1980), 240-246.

chapter 23

Closing Thoughts

Throughout this book we have talked about the interplay of the public and the private. Urban politics does not exist in a vacuum. The character of urban politics reflects the larger social and economic system of which it is a part. As society has gotten more complex, urban politics has changed. Big organization has become a central factor. Most policy coalitions revolve around large-scale enterprises, profit and nonprofit. The economy iself is less and less organized around local units. National and international firms make the key decisions, and they do so with little regard for local consequences. They, after all, are playing on a much larger scale. As the economy has increased in scale, local officials have become increasingly responsive to the mobility of business investment. The policies that cities pursue are shaped by the economic and organizational constraints surrounding elected officials, and the administrative practices urban agencies engage in are shaped by the social environment and inter-organizational arrangements in which they operate.

Given the interrelatedness of public and private life, we can look anew at how and what we might change. We have suggested that improved governmental and managerial techniques are likely to alter little. Many of the limitations on governmental capacity lie in the private sector. Self-reform in the public sector is not enough.

Past experience should be useful. The municipal reform movement provides one overridingly important lesson. Because it was concerned mainly with the technical complexity of modern life, that movement promoted institutions and procedures that ignored the pervasively political character of government. "Good government" reform thus produced some mistaken notions and unwise practices—and a turbulent postreform period brought that lesson home and taught us something about diversity, representation, and conflict management. The social-reform efforts of the 1960s, especially the War on Poverty, provided other lessons. Underestimating the complexity of the problem, antipoverty warriors waged a two-front battle—one against "cultural disadvantage" and the other against bureaucratic inertia. But they made no direct assault on the inequalities of income and opportunity, which undergird the cultural disadvantages of the poor and encourage unresponsiveness among the agencies that serve them. As a consequence, the nation is still struggling with the problems of poverty and inequality.

Although complexity enhances the role of the technical expert, it presents more than a series of technical problems. It also presents a political challenge. And, although complexity has helped undercut some traditional forms of deference and authority, it has not increased popular control. For the public to exert control, it needs information and a capacity to engage in sustained action. Consequently, complexity works against control by a mass public. It tilts power from the unorganized to the organized, and among those organized, from those who act through small organizations to those who act through large organizations. The problem of democracy thus becomes one of scale, of how to match public control with large organizational scale. Urban politics is thus not a separate and autonomous sphere of "grass-roots" democracy. It is instead an arena that reveals the interconnectedness of modern life. Let us now turn to some closing thoughts on this theme.

Modern urban governments face a dilemma. On the one hand, modernity itself involves complexity and interdependence. Complexity calls for technical expertise, and interdependence calls for some form of comprehensive (that is, centralized) planning in order to take all of the interdependencies into account. Urban governments, on the other hand, are democratic, and as a practical matter, democracy is not easily reconciled with technical expertise and centralized planning.

Other problems complicate the dilemma. Neighborhoods have unequal resources; local governments themselves have unequal resources; states and even regions of the country have unequal resources. How are fiscal imbalances to be lessened? Clearly that can be done most effectively through the national government. How are urban programs to be administered? The larger, the more far-reaching, and the more complex the administrative arrangement, the harder it is to operate—suggesting that decentralized administration or reliance on the market is more workable. Clearly, urban service programs cannot be administered out of Washington.

A number of questions thus confront urban students. What role should the national government play? How is technical expertise to be reconciled with democratic practice? On what scale shall urban service delivery be organized? These, we think, are some of the key issues for urban communities today. In order to suggest some tentative and partial answers to these questions, we need to consider first that elusive concept, the public interest. Then, we need to take one final look at the issue of power.

POVERTY, ECONOMIC GROWTH, AND THE PUBLIC INTEREST

The contrast between reform and postreform politics poses very well the problem in defining and realizing the public interest. The reformers, with their unitary conception, had a concern for the generalized well-being of the community, which they thought had to be protected against the greed of self-serving individuals and against the narrow demands of various ethnic and neighborhood groups. In the postreform period, we see with the sophistication of hindsight that there are as many public interests as there are publics. If there is an overall public interest, it must lie in processes like the maintenance of social peace *and* a guarantee that all share in the life of the larger community. There are difficulties with both conceptions of the public interest. The reformers assumed that the urban community is relatively homogeneous in its service needs and wants, but, in fact, some groups, such as the poor, have special needs and wants, and they cannot meet them in the private market. In the postreform era, we have also discovered that even with all-out competition and open conflict, some interests never get taken care of—not only those of the poor but also some diffuse and loosely-organized interests that might be lumped together under the label, "quality of life."

What we suggest is that urban policy and politics be guided by two complementary conceptions of the public interest. Attention should be given to both and to those factors that may undermine either. First, there are a set of substantive ideals that mark a humane and civilized community:

1. Ample opportunity for individual development
2. A culturally-rich life
3. A clean environment
4. A poverty-free population in the sense that everyone has his or her basic needs met and also has at least a few of the amenities of modern life

5. Tolerant intergroup relations and an inclusive sense of community
6. Integrity in financial and other transactions of government

These are grand ideals that are hard to realize and get agreement on in practice, but that is what politics in the best sense is about.

Second, there is a procedural ideal of political equality and openness through which urban politics might approach something like the pluralists' notion of mutual accommodation—all groups, even those with a low income, would be able to get some of the things that they cared most about; and they would feel that the political system was open and responsive enough to make that possible.

Both the substantive and the procedural conceptions of the public interest are idealistic—that is, they are ideals that the nation may approach to some degree but never attain in full. For that reason, there is some tendency to dismiss them altogether. Certainly in our own review of urban policy and politics, we have offered little ground for optimism. Ideals that are compatible in the abstract conflict in practice. Moreover, ardent reformers and proponents of high ideals, once in office, fall sway to the pressures of office and the pursuit of self-interests. Given the socioeconomic diversity of modern life, conflict is inescapable, and scarce resources almost assure that there will be many losers in the competition for what is available. Yet despite harsh realities, we see grounds for hope and a fresh promise for a better-governed urban community.

We think there are lessons to be learned from our review of urban policy, politics, and bureaucracy. To cite our most important example, we think that President Johnson's War on Poverty was a mistake, but a useful one. At the time, the Community Action and related programs made good sense. The poor were powerless and politically uninvolved in the programs that bore directly on their lives. Local government programs to aid the poor, such as welfare and urban renewal, often worked hardships instead of providing help. General service programs, such as transportation, education, and law enforcement, seemed insensitive to the poor. Why not get the poor involved and give them the access and the clout to make urban bureaucracies more responsive? What we learned, however, is that it is difficult to organize the poor and keep them organized; and even when organized, they often lost. The poor in coalition came out second best. The poor in confrontation were outlasted and outmaneuvered.

Why did we have so little success in empowering the poor? One answer is to trot out the culture-of-poverty argument again. Aside from its what's-the-use pessimism, the difficulty with that answer is that in many instances the poor did become active and involved *and still lost.* They lost because they encountered so much resistance among the very people who were supposed to be responsive to active and discontented groups—local officials.

Local officials are not an inherently hard-hearted group. Why, then, was it a mistake to wage war on poverty through local government, as was the case under the Johnson program? Because, we think, local jurisdictions had, and still have, other and more pressing issues on their agendas. The evidence lies in the behavior of local officials, elected and appointed. Federal programs and federal monies, whether under categorical grants, block grants, or revenue sharing, have seldom given the poor high priority even when that was the clear legislative intent behind them. Local governments seem to have an inexorable tendency to move in the direction of three interlocked goals: the promotion of economic growth and favorable business climate, an appeal to and accommodation of affluent residents, and discouragement of and nonaccommodation of the poor. This is not to say that these goals are immune to political pressures. They are not, and communities differ in the vigor with which they pursue them. Communities also differ in the priority they attach to each of the three. Still, there is a clear pattern of movement by most communities most of the time in the direction of the three interlocked goals.

Local governments are subject to two basic sets of pressures: political and economic. Political pressures dictate that officials be responsive to voters who are or can be mobilized *and* who can stay mobilized so that they constitute a deliverable vote at election time. That is a principal reason public employee unions have become a force.

Economic pressures are different. They work on local governments in much the same way that they work on business enterprises—confronting them with the ever-present problem of maximizing revenue and of balancing expenditures with revenue. What happens, then, is that local governments apply a double standard to the various segments of their citizenry. They see middle- and upper-income groups as an economic boon and treat assistance to them as a benefit to the whole community. In other words, aiding the well-off is in the public interest. If the economic plight of the community is severe, officials will see policy accommodations to the well-off as something that is necessary for the survival of the government in which they hold office. From this economic perspective, assistance to the poor is a charity—something that one does out of compassion or political expediency so long as it is not carried too far and certainly so long as it does not strain the government's revenue capacity. In this view, a pragmatist does not confuse aid to the poor with the public interest.

The poor suffer political as well as economic liabilities; service agencies see them as unteachable, unreachable, and a drain on their resources. The culture-of-poverty and other kindred ideas about the poor are widely shared, putting the poor at a disadvantage as a political ally. And concerted efforts to increase voter turnout among the poor are regarded with great suspicion—indeed, among the Community Action efforts that generated very strong opposition were a few scattered attempts to increase voter registration in poverty neighborhoods. The poor, then, do not find it easy to overcome their economic weakness with their political strength. They even face the dilemma that where their numbers are greatest and their potential political strength is at a maximum, local government is likely to have the most tenuous economic situation and for that reason resist policy accommodations to the poor.

How, then, are the poor viewed, especially when they are numerous? In the eyes of many officials, the poor suffer the following liabilities:

1. There is a limited need for the cheap and unskilled labor they offer.
2. They do not vote in large numbers, and if they did, it would upset established political leins.
3. Their service demands exceed their revenue production—consequently they represent a revenue deficit.
4. Their problems are hard to solve and they are not a sought-after clientele by service agencies.
5. Their presence has a contagious effect, driving out the affluent and attracting more poor.

Local governments, for their part, are financially constrained; they have a limited tax base, limited borrowing power, and a restricted right to levy new taxes. They exist in economic competition, one metropolitan region with another and, within metropolitan regions, one jurisdiction with another. They are in open competition for enterprises that will add to the property tax and wage base, without adding unduly to the service costs. They are in covert competition to avoid accommodating the poor.

In the days of machine politics, the poor were a needed source of votes deliverable through an organized network of personal relationships. For today's local political leaders, they are an impersonal category with more minuses than pluses. The political weakness of the poor is both cause and effect. Their apathy and nonparticipation give them an even smaller share of the benefits of public action than would be the case if they were politically active and involved. On the other hand, their apathy and nonparticipation are born of frustration and disappointment. The 1960s taught them again, and should have taught all of us for a first time, that protest and political activity do not necessarily yield substantial results. The poor are apathetic and uninvolved because they encounter such strong resistance that the payoff from political activity is not worthwhile. That is inevitable in a local-government setting characterized by the idea that the public interest consists of maximizing the community's revenue-producing capacity and minimizing its service costs. That underlying idea tends to crowd out aid for the poor or any other idealistic notion of the public interest. We conclude, that the problem is not that the poor are unorganized, apathetic, or politically weak, but that these conditions are symptoms. The basic problem is that the logic of the urban situation runs against fostering the interests of the poor and other non-economic-growth publics. In the case of the poor, it is not that they lack influence because they are apathetic; they are apathetic because they lack influence—and they lack influence because their presence is an economic threat to the local community.

New forms of federal aid, intergovernmental restructuring, metropolitan consolidation, local government reorganization, and other such steps will have little impact until the problems of poverty and fiscal imbalance are addressed. And we think that fiscal imbalance cannot be addressed successfully without also addressing poverty. We think further that these problems can be addressed best by the national government. It should attack the problem of inadequate income by a combined attempt to improve work opportunities and raise income floors. As the extremes of poverty are eliminated, fiscal imbalances should become less severe. Even so, some will remain. Those can be attacked by seeking to promote a more even pattern of national economic growth. Fiscal imbalances can also be attacked directly by revenue-sharing and block grant formulas that assure more aid to those jurisdictions with a needy population and a limited tax base. In short, there should be a fiscal counterbalance for local governments from the national government for having a lower-income population. That should at least serve as a disincentive to local governments in adopting covert policies of driving out the poor.

If all three things were accomplished—the extremes of individual poverty eliminated, economic growth somewhat evened out among all regions of the country, and fiscal imbalances substantially decreased—then there would at least be a basis on which the more idealistic versions of the public interest might be addressed. If local governments were freed from the necessity of an economic-growth mentality, then they could pursue multiple objectives and serve many interests.

The problem of unequal economic opportunity is more, however, than a problem of uneven economic development. It is also a question of how to make even a growing economy more inclusive. How do we offer all segments of society a partnership in the economic life of the nation? In a technically complex society, only highly specialized capacities and credentials are valued. Some forms of work are not much valued or sought after. Those activities that do not fit into the large network of technical processes are largely unrewarded and may fall into neglect. They become part of the secondary labor market—dead-end jobs filled by people who do day-work or simply hold a succession of short-term positions on a ladder to nowhere.

Ironically, as society becomes more interdependent, some people and their work capacities come to be treated as unwanted and outmoded surplus. It is unlikely that individual communities operating alone can reorient our approach to the labor force, but any national solution must, of course, be able to work at the community level.

If we had a more inclusive work force and less inequality in income, some of our present conflicts would be less intense. Supply-side versus compensatory equity is bound to be divisive. As far back as Aristotle, political thinkers have realized that a large middle class is a stabilizing force. In our own country, Thomas Jefferson believed that the firmest foundation for democracy was a populace of small property holders—which he thought most attainable in an agrarian, not an urban society. Political stability and the quality of political life may well depend upon our finding the urban equivalent of Jefferson's nation of small yeoman farmers.

POWER AND THE PROBLEM OF SCALE

Some of the gap between democratic practice and democratic ideal is a matter of organization and scale. To some, the problem is that no one is in charge. They see a hyperpluralist world in which groups scrap with one another in an uncivil manner, so that immobility results. As they see it, veto groups are rampant, and no stable governing coalition can be formed.

This is a view not without merit. In a complex society, no one is in charge. There is no overall power of command. Still, it is a view that misunderstands in a fundamental way the character of power in a complex society. It imposes old notions on new social conditions. It is based on an antiquated viewpoint.

Conventionally, we have thought of power as a relationship in which one actor commands and another actor or set of actors obeys. Power is thus thought of as a demonstrated capacity to achieve intended results. With this notion in mind, we look around and see that much of what happens is unintended. No one holds a strong command position over very many others. We conclude, therefore, that power is dispersed (if we like that result) or fragmented (if we don't like that result).

In a complex society, it is indeed the case that no one enjoys an overall power of command. But that does not mean that all actors are relatively powerless. Power thus takes a different form. While much of what happens is unintended, that does not mean that everyone is helpless.

We need to learn to think in terms of compositional effects.[1] Business has no power to command obedience from public officials, but the mobility of investments serves to enhance business bargaining power enormously. Slum property holders cannot veto the enactment of housing codes, but they can threaten to abandon their properties if the codes are strictly enforced. White parents cannot prevent public school desegrega-

[1] Cf. Thomas C. Schelling, "On the Ecology of Micromotives," *Public Interest*, #25 (Fall 1971), 59-98.

tion, but, if very many of them remove their children from the system, it resegregates.

Fred Hirsch cautions us about "the tyranny of small decisions."[2] The failure to act with foresight and coordination can cause problems that might have been avoided or at least minimized—overcrowded freeways, inadequate open space, air pollution, barren streams and lakes, exhausted acquifers, and many more. A public without organization and some system of discipline becomes rapacious and spoils its common resources.[3] This is as true of its social resources as of its physical resources. Consider downtown areas deserted after 6:00 p.m. or school systems unable to achieve integration across racial, class, and nationality lines. Ours is a society rich in cultural diversity, but ill-positioned to use and celebrate that diversity.

Under conditions of complexity, those who are unorganized have little ability to restructure the conditions they face or upgrade their capacity to cope with contemporary life. They are not even informed about the choices they might make or the causes and consequences of the conditions they face.

Power in a complex society belongs to those who understand compositional effects and who have the capacity to modify conditions in line with this understanding. That is why more power belongs to those who are organized than to those who are unorganized. They know more and have more ability to act. That is why big organizations with broad scopes of action, much information, and a durable capacity to act are able to pursue their aims. Their power is not a power over others in the sense of a power of command. Rather, it is an ability to figure out what is going on and to apply resources which guide change in a preferred direction. In other words, it is a capacity to alter and take advantage of compositional effects. In this sense, it is indirect power.

The practice of democracy under conditions of complexity requires that the indirect power of big organizations be more widely dispersed. Whether this is to be done by increasing the organizational capacity of the weakly organized, by reducing the scale of interdependence in some activities, or by some combination of strategies remains to be seen. But that is the democratic challenge of the future.

SUGGESTED READINGS

BARBER, BENJAMIN, R. *Strong Democracy: Participatory Politics for a New Age*. Berkley: University of California Press, 1984.

[2] Fred Hirsch, *Social Limits to Growth* (Cambridge, MA: Harvard University Press, 1976), p. 40.

[3] Garrett Hardin, "The Tragedy of the Commons," *Science*, Vol. 162, December 13, 1968, 1243-8.

BENDER, THOMAS. "The End of the City?" *Democracy*, Vol. 3 (Winter 1983), 8-20.
DAHL, ROBERT A. *Dilemmas of Pluralist Democracy*. New Haven: Yale University Press, 1982.
ELKIN, STEPHEN L. "Market and Politics in Liberal Democracy." *Ethics*, Vol. 92 (July 1982), 720-32.
HARDIN, GARRETT. "The Tragedy of the Commons." *Science*, Vol. 162 (December 13, 1968), 1243-8.
HARVEY, DAVID. *Social Justice and the City*. Baltimore: Johns Hopkins University Press, 1973.
HILL, RICHARD C. "Market, State, and Community: National Urban Policy in the 1980s." *Urban Affairs Quarterly*, Vol. 19 (September 1983), 5-20.
HIRSCH, FRED. *Social Limits to Growth*. Cambridge, MA: Harvard University Press, 1976.
MOLLENKOPF, JOHN H. *The Contested City*. Princeton, NJ: Princeton University Press, 1983.
POLSKY, ANDREW J. "Welfare Policy: Why the Past Has No Future." *Democracy*, Vol. 3 (Winter 1983), 21-33.
SCHELLING, THOMAS C. "On the Ecology of Micromotives." *Public Interest*, No. 25 (Fall 1971), 59-98.
STONE, CLARENCE N. "New Class or Convergence: Competing Interpretations of the Impact of Social Complexity on the Structure of Urban Power." *Power and Elites*, Vol. 1 (Fall 1984), 1-22.

Index

B

C

D

E

F

G

M

N

Q

R